BY THE WAND
OF SOME MAGICIAN

BY THE WAND
OF SOME MAGICIAN

*Embracing Modernity in
Mid-Nineteenth Century Vermont*

G ARY G. S HATTUCK

Center for Research on Vermont
University of Vermont

White River Press
Amherst, Massachusetts

By the Wand of Some Magician
Embracing Modernity in Mid-Nineteenth Century Vermont

© 2020 Gary G. Shattuck

All rights reserved.

First published by White River Press, PO Box 3561, Amherst, Massachusetts 01004 whiteriverpress.com

ISBN: 978-1-887043-77-9 paperback
978-1-887043-78-6 ebook

Designed by Eliza Giles

Cover image: Winooski River, Vt., c. 1847, Vermont Historical Society.

Library of Congress Cataloging-in-Publication Data

Names: Shattuck, Gary G. author. | University of Vermont. Center for Research on Vermont, sponsoring body.
Title: By the wand of some magician : embracing modernity in mid-nineteenth century Vermont / Gary G. Shattuck, Center for Research on Vermont, University of Vermont.
Description: Amherst, Massachusetts : White River Press, [2020] | Includes bibliographical references and index. | Summary: By the Wand of Some Magician addresses the severe impact of railroad technology upon its arrival into Vermont in the mid-nineteenth century that introduced an unprepared, rural population to the effects of modernity. It is conveyed through the debates that legislators had following the destruction of their statehouse in 1857 when they considered various factors able to influence their decision in whether to relocate the capital to someplace other than Montpelier. The story revolves around three important aspects of Vermonters' lives that the solons considered: how the railroad changed one particular community (Rutland); agriculture; and the health of the state's inhabitants. Each of these topics is covered, with an emphasis on health. That issue has never been touched on before and includes drug addiction, abortion, and infanticide that increased substantially after the technology arrived. Additionally, new forms of business (corporations), debtor-creditor relations (grab laws), and the influence of out-of-state financiers on the direction of Vermont government and policy are discussed. Finally, there are many images that will accompany the text to provide further context to the story. Provided by publisher.
Identifiers: LCCN 2020022802 (print) | LCCN 2020022803 (ebook) | ISBN 9781887043779 (paperback) | ISBN 9781887043786 (ebook)
Subjects: LCSH: Vermont--History--19th century. | Social change--Vermont. | Vermont--Social conditions. | Railroads--Vermont--History--19th century. | Public health--Vermont--History--19th century. | Vermont--Rural conditions. | Vermont--Politics and government--19th century.
Classification: LCC F53 .S545 2020 (print) | LCC F53 (ebook) | DDC 974.3/03--dc23
LC record available at https://lccn.loc.gov/2020022802
LC ebook record available at https://lccn.loc.gov/2020022803

DEDICATION

To Nick Muller,

a mensch and friend of the highest order

Contents

Foreword 11

Preface 15

Acknowledgments 35

Chapter I: *Improvement* 41

Chapter II: *Steaming into the Green Mountains* 73

Chapter III: *Embracing Modernity* 101

Chapter IV: *The Grass Interest* 155

Chapter V: *Distorting Reality* 179

Chapter VI: *Criminal Abortions and Infanticide* 229

Chapter VII: *Prisoner 1641: The Scientific English Surgeon* 273

Chapter VIII: *Consequences* 311

Epilogue 347

Appendix 357

Bibliography 371

Notes 391

Index 435

About the Author 441

With lungs of fire, and ribs of steel,
With sighing valve, and groaning wheel,
With startling scream, and giant stroke;
With showers of sparks, and clouds of smoke;
The iron steed, the train is bringing —
So "look out" while the bell is ringing.

VERMONT PHOENIX (BRATTLEBORO), 5 JANUARY 1849

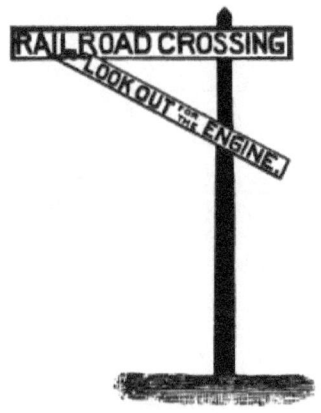

New crossing signage pursuant to *Acts and Resolves Passed by the Legislature of the State of Vermont, 1849*

"What's the railroad to me?"

HENRY DAVID THOREAU,
WALDEN, OR, LIFE IN THE WOODS (1854)

Foreword

Gary Shattuck's engaging history of Vermont in the mid-nineteenth century is a masterful account of a pivotal period often overlooked by Vermonters and Vermont historians. The Revolution, the Era of Reform, and the Civil War have been given their due. But the 1850s, in particular, have always appeared out of joint with what came before and after in Vermont's history. On the one hand, the period wasn't optimistic enough to spawn the passionate spiritual or reform movements of the 1830s and 1840s; on the other, it wasn't dark enough to enable people to foresee the cataclysm that would come in April 1861.

Shattuck's *By the Wand of Some Magician* makes a wonderful case for the singular importance of the 1850s. For him, the decade marks the dawn of modernity in Vermont: the moment when Vermonters first came to feel that their connections to the past and their longstanding traditions had been irrevocably broken, for better or worse. Vermonters were overwhelmed, in Shattuck's words, by a "daunting sense of presentism," as they tried to come to grips with the novelty of the here and now.

Modernity was an "intrusive," inescapable process. It was spearheaded by technological change, especially the coming of the railroads, which transformed not only the state's factory towns and quarry towns, but also its farms and villages. Modernity was also "a double-edged sword": it brought new opportunities to Vermont, but at the same time it brought new challenges and hardships. And rural people, who protested the loss of their land and their peace and quiet were not the only ones affected. Thanks to the urban growth spawned by the railroads, the residents of bustling small cities like Burlington and Rutland suddenly had to confront unprecedented social divisions and threats to public health.

Meeting these challenges tried the individualistic ethos of Vermonters. Confronting modernity was hard for them, and many insisted that they just wanted to be left alone. They resisted the implementation of regulatory measures and state boards and commissions that would have been necessary to rein in the power of the railroads, improve public health, place agriculture and forestry on a more scientific, sustainable footing, and professionalize education so it could better prepare their children for the novel world they would inhabit.

Each chapter of *By the Wand* tells a fully rounded story of a particular incident or development that challenged Vermonters' traditional way of life. None was more significant than the loss of the State Capitol Building in Montpelier to a disastrous fire in 1857. It unleashed an acrimonious debate between defenders of Montpelier and those who believed the capital should be moved to the state's most progressive, modern, and economically robust community, Burlington. Yet the debate overlooked the degree to which modernity had already transformed Vermont. Shattuck rejects the notion that Vermont was a society in decline, despite the slow growth of its population, the aging of its rural inhabitants, and its failure to attract as many immigrants from Ireland and French Canada as neighboring states did. Vermonters prospered like never before, not only because of their time-honored frugality and hard work, but because of the new markets opened by the railroads and the new techniques they were using to produce high-quality manufactured goods and agricultural commodities.

Modernity brought problems, however—severe problems. The temperance movement triumphed in 1852 when the state prohibited the manufacture or sale of alcoholic beverages. But it passed by a bare majority and met such massive resistance that alcohol dependency and abuse were as widespread as ever. And the focus of reformers on alcohol masked an even more serious problem of substance abuse that had begun to grip the state: opiate addiction. Opiate-laced patented medicines and sedatives like laudanum were affordable and widely available in Vermont's burgeoning consumer economy.

The increasing population meant problems with sewage, with drinking water, with diseases like tuberculosis and cholera, and with control of a warring medical profession. Public officials prided themselves in their minimalist approach to legislation and withheld efforts to stop quacks and charlatans from practicing medicine or impose laws to force railroads to enact safety measures able to reduce the appalling number of casualties the trains caused. Currying the favor of capitalists with money to invest and refusing to tarnish the state's image with unfavorable descriptions, they chose, instead, to let the population live as unregulated as possible, but with predicable results.

Modernity also brought with it rising ambitions, and those ambitions were often stymied by the increasing cost of opening a shop or buying a farm and starting a family. New forms of family planning appeared that meant a dramatic increase in abortions and infanticides, as women tried to control their fertility both before marriage and after. Demand increased for physicians, midwives, and druggists who were skilled at performing abortions and inducing miscarriages, but con artists also moved in to take advantage of women's desperation. William Henry Mansfield Howard, an English "doctor" with questionable credentials, set himself up as an abortionist in Orange County. Before he was caught, the deaths of several women and their fetuses were attributed to him because of his terrifying incompetence and indifference. Shattuck's descriptions of Vermont's experiences with abortion and infanticide and the creation of its registry system in 1857 are first rate and place each of these important developments into a proper perspective.

Vermont's encounter with modernity in the decade before the Civil War was thus both exhilarating and troubling. *By the Wand* reminds us powerfully that Vermonters had far more on their minds in the 1850s than the sectional crisis—a crisis few thought would ever lead to war. On the issues of slavery and free soil, Vermonters were united throughout the decade. By 1850, only six percent of Vermont voters supported the national Democratic Party. They were overwhelmingly committed to the exclusion of slavery from all territories under federal jurisdiction, present and future.

Vermonters still looked to the frontier, as their forebears had to northern New England, for a new start. They still believed they could preserve their traditional way of life as self-employed farmers and shopkeepers in small town and rural America, even if it meant pulling up stakes and heading West. Yet as *By the Wand* shows, the futures of most Vermonters lay in new directions—directions that had already been determined by a changing America.

Randolph A. Roth
Professor of History and Sociology
Ohio State University

Fellow, American Association for the Advancement of Science
Co-founder, Historical Violence Database, Criminal Justice Research Center, Ohio State University

Author:
The Democratic Dilemma: Religion, Reform, and the Social Order in the Connecticut River Valley of Vermont, 1791–1850 (Cambridge University Press, 1987)

American Homicide (Harvard University Press, 2012)

Preface

Trial By Fire

On the cold, wintery evening of January 6, 1857, around 7:00 p.m., fire destroyed Vermont's iconic Capitol building.[1] Heated by two large, wood-burning basement furnaces, stoked with logs four feet long to warm the large space in advance of a constitutional convention, their fires grew so hot they ignited floor joists above.[2] A distressing cacophony of noise greeted those rushing to the scene as the flames grew, embers crackled in the air, structural timbers crashed down and shouts issued directing the removal of what state treasures could be saved as books flew out the library's windows and into the snow. The devastation spread quickly and consumed all the building's wooden interior, leaving behind only its damaged granite walls standing before a shaken Montpelier community. Verse sorrowfully recalled the shocking loss:

> That lofty pile, one hour ago,
> The State's just pride, the Nation's show,
> Capp'd with its bright and virgin snow,
> In beauty shone:
> The next, a mass of ruined walls,
> Of columns broke, and burning halls,
> Its beauty flown.[3]

Destroyed Vermont statehouse, 1857. Vermont Historical Society.

The revered second Capitol (built between 1833 and 1836) where the state accomplished so much of its work for the past two decades replaced a first one erected in the town in 1808, a marked improvement from earlier years. It successfully ended difficulties dating to before statehood in 1791 when "the capital was placed on wheels, and trundled all over the State."[4] Warding off the prospect of future sectionalism, before finally deciding to make centrally located Montpelier the capital and end their onerous peregrinations, the state's leaders had met forty-seven times in various locations alternating from one side of the Green Mountains to the other, twenty-four on the east and twenty-three on the west. They convened in Windsor (fourteen times); Bennington (eight); Rutland (seven); Westminster (four); Manchester (three); Newbury (two); Middlebury (two); and once each in Charlestown, New Hampshire, Norwich, Castleton, Vergennes, Burlington, Danville, and Woodstock. With the capital place decided, many of the arduous difficulties accompanying travel ended and allowed the representatives to engage their work in a more predictable manner, less hindered by geography, in comfortable facilities and safe from the elements. Now, fire destroyed that convenience.

Nationally, the fire ranked tenth among the top twenty in the first half of 1857, with losses estimated at $130,000.[5] While the others consumed commercial facilities, factories, warehouses and stores, Vermont's struck at the core identity of a people. The conflagration ravaged not only an important element of the state's material culture, but also violently upended the sense of comfort that its population (315,098 in 1860) had become accustomed to. Government officials experienced great consternation as they sought to address this profound, unexpected disturbance that took place with legislators out of session and scattered across the state at their homes. To assess the damage and how to respond, on January 26 Governor Ryland Fletcher issued a proclamation ordering the solons to return and convene in Montpelier in a special session, the first in the state's history, to chart their future course. Between February 18 – 27, 1857, 230 members of the House of Representatives met at the town's brick Congregational Church, while twenty-eight senators convened at the nearby Washington County courthouse. The entire state closely followed their work and over the course of these few days many flocked to Montpelier to witness the proceedings. One representative described the notoriety of their special session and claimed that "On no question. . . of State Legislation, had there been more excitement than on this. This large House, in which we are convened, and these compactly filled galleries, of ladies and gentlemen, with anxious faces, bespeak the feeling on this engrossing subject. Never have our sessions been attended by such audiences."[6]

The loss of their State House deeply touched every Vermonter. Recent debates surrounding the imposition of a law prohibiting the manufacture and sale of alcohol in 1852 that made the state the second to do so after Maine had taken longer to resolve, but their intensity paled in comparison to the proceedings in February 1857. One newspaper predicted the emerging differences shortly after the fire recalling their forefathers' sectionalist concerns and wrote that the loss would "open a pretty war between the East and West side of the [Green Mountains] on the locality of the next

State House."⁷ The destruction caused great stress among the legislators themselves who soon unleashed their heartfelt, often raw emotions directly or by casting subtle derision against opponents. At times, the debates they engaged in emerged as congenial banter when the men laughed at their own violations of the prohibition law and drinking the banned substances. But, at others, it became mean and vindictive as one legislator reviled another and declared that "I don't like this gentleman. . . I don't wish to have him killed. . . but I desire that he should have a fair chance to die *sometime*."⁸ The debates, with their jousting and invective, underscored the huge challenge the fire presented. It forced all Vermonters to engage in a deeper perspective than they had in the past and to consider exactly what the building meant in their lives. They had to confront not only the symbolism that it represented, but also their own sense of place and identity that years of familiarity with the Montpelier community instilled and whether or not to even allow the capital to remain there as other towns scrambled to take advantage of the confusion and secure the seat of government. The sudden loss of their iconic building marked a defining moment in the state's development that forced its residents to grapple existentially with what the future might demand of them as they sought to preserve the comfort and security that the familiar past offered.

Vermonters also had to confront the stark, vertiginous realities that recent advances in technology presented, particularly the harnessing of steam power and its use by railroads to drive their engines and loaded cars over its imposing infrastructure that so recently spread across the state. When the legislators met, Vermont had already witnessed an impressive 557 miles of track laid down within its borders costing over $23,000,000, with more in the offering, and the presence of many investors seeking the opportunities that new forms of capitalism presented.⁹ But the history of Vermont's acceptance of the full benefits that such significant technology and investment promised clashed with the distinct hesitation, almost reluctance, expressed by many others. Certainly, those who resided in the growing cities and towns where the railroad conveniently passed along low-lying rivers and productive fields could experience the most direct benefits it offered. But, in its more isolated mountainous regions, where many others lived and industrious farmers worked the rocky slopes bringing them into production, the prospect brought something else. There, a more intense, visceral belief in the confidence of their own abilities instilled in them a heightened sense of independence that differed from their counterparts in the valleys. If they could conquer the elements that Nature presented and provide for their families despite those hardships, then, as Thoreau believed, "what's the railroad to me?"

Idealized image of Vermont, Jacob Abbott, Marco Paul's Voyages & Travels (1852).

History repeatedly teaches that the arrival of the railroad into the nation's communities largely won acceptance with open and eager arms. It had proved a powerful phenomenon elsewhere, but in Vermont its imposing aspects tested the change in subtle ways. Technology proved a two-edged sword in the Green Mountains as it promised future benefits while it also challenged the validity, and ongoing relevancy, of the state's strong traditions, ones that its population could experience daily, confirmed to them by accounts of their parents and grandparents. In 1848, a Rutland settler who had lived in the town since 1788 longingly recalled to a friend the halcyon days when children ran barefoot and hatless, women passed down primitive paths through dark woods following blazed trees to guide them, when looms worked in every abode, and "every house was a tavern." As the friend concluded in recording the man's account, "What a change has come over the spirit of the old man's dream. He amid a new generation; and the transformation of the wilderness into thriving villages, and rich farms, and splendid dwellings, and telegraphic wires, and railroads; the whole seems like a change produced in a night by the wand of some magician." "But he is faithful to the memory of the past," the friend ended, "and if the rude pioneer age of man has its trials, it is also free from much vice, and feebleness of an age of luxury and refinement.[10] The old man's fond and romanticized recollection of the past as he gazed at the wonders of newly arrived technology and its impact on his neighbors, envisioning a Ghost in the Machine twentieth-century perspective, defines precisely the underlying conflict that many Vermonters experienced.[11]

"An emblematic picture of the Green Mountain State," showing three Indians catching and preparing fish and "a snow scene, with school children wading through the drifts." Ballou's Pictorial, Boston. March 1, 1856.

The railroad that slammed into Vermont in the mid-nineteenth century unquestionably created the most powerful physical manifestation of change promising future benefits from afar in its relatively short history. It immediately collapsed all perception of time enabling rapid communications in ways radically different from any that mankind had ever experienced. In the process, the new technology became the defining object around which three aspects of Vermont culture concentrated that deserve attention beyond what historians of the state have provided it in the past. These concerns, ones foremost in the legislators' minds when they engaged in their debates, provide guidance to understand how they prioritized them in their lives in the face of the dual challenges posed by jolting devastation and the effects of modernity.

Foremost, the effects wrought by the railroad in the rapid development of the state's cities and towns became a topic of discussion. The strong tug of tradition made Montpelier on the Winooski River and Burlington on the shore of Lake Champlain the most obvious candidates to accommodate the capital, but Rutland now presented a severe challenge because of its astounding growth. That town's story rested most directly on the benefits

Preface

Montpelier, 1854. Vermont Historical Society.

derived from the railroad and the new sophisticated forms of capitalism becoming more common that makes the most direct connection to the new technology greater than either of those other two towns. A second concern of the legislators arose when they began to distance themselves from such a direct effect and focused on aspects of life more attributable to the unique independence that Vermonters insisted on in running their lives. Whereas capitalism presented immediate tangible benefits to communities such as Rutland, in an agricultural environment those living on distant farms with decades of experience taming Nature, resisted them in favor of their comfortable past routines. Steam driven technology made transporting their goods to market easier but they did not deem it of sufficient importance to adopt it directly into their everyday lives, a phenomenon that lasted for decades until the twentieth century when petroleum-based mechanical tools became more common. While removed

View of Burlington from Lake Champlain, 1858. New York Public Library.

from the urbanizing towns like Rutland, this so-called "Grass Interest" of the mid-nineteenth century demanded that the legislators, many of them farmers themselves, pay attention to its contributions to the state when considering where to relocate the capital.

A third issue presented by the railroad's presence required that the legislators also consider the physical health of Vermonters, a constituency that lived an average life span of only thirty-five years. In the time immediately following the imposition of the prohibition of alcohol in 1852, precisely as the new technology firmly established itself in Rutland, the unrestricted manufacture, sale, and use of drugs, particularly opium-based products, became so commonplace, and instances of addiction so evident, that it alarmed observant members of the medical profession. Alert to the negative impressions that the presence of ill-health could reflect on a state in need of external financial support to advance the railroad's interests, politicians carefully engaged in a public relations campaign that largely ignored the problem and allowed it to develop into a devastating epidemic of abuse by the end of the century.[12]

Rutland Main Street, 1840. Rutland Historical Society.

Additionally, as medical reports of the times repeatedly described in astonishment, the state's female population also suffered severely from tuberculosis, or consumption (a convenient euphemism that covered a variety of ailments including addiction), that carried many of them off at levels exceeding the experiences of other states. Doctors and church officials further decried the pre-meditated forms of "family planning," called "criminal abortions," engaged in by the state's independent, intelligent, educated, white, Protestant middle-class females, as well as the marked increase in infanticide they used when those other efforts failed. As one newspaper editor noted, the presence of "infanticide as practiced in a great many of the intelligent, enlightened, and even professedly Christian families of Vermont" should not be tolerated; but it was.[13]

Preface

The absence of effective forms of contraception other than abortions and infanticide, and the attending burdens placed on females enduring embarrassing bastardy proceedings, challenged them to find alternatives that allowed them to maintain control over their bodies apart from the wishes of lovers and spouses. The mid-century free-for-all atmosphere within the medical profession itself, exacerbated by the freedom of movement that the railroad allowed, was profoundly exemplified by, arguably, the state's first serial killer. William Henry Mansfield Howard, an English-born Orange County quack who operated freely in the state between 1857 and 1859, killed many women decades before the notorious Vermont-trained doctor Herman Webster Mudgett wrought his murderous havoc in the 1890s at the World's Fair in Chicago. Perhaps inspired by his Vermont counterpart, Mudgett even adopted the pseudonym Henry Mansfield Howard during his own rampage.[14] Despite the actions of Howard and others like him in the 1850s, the barbarous aspects of abortions that Vermont women engaged in continued into the following decades and deserve further attention to appreciate the state's slow embrace of modernity.

Modernity

Historian Kenneth Clark attributes the great advances in civilization to those times "when people, ideas and artistic creations circulated freely between nations."[15] In the 1850s, the most effective way to accomplish that goal came with the railroad, a tool that European historian Orlando Figes most recently emphasized as *"the* symbol of industrial progress and modernity" at the time.[16] North American historian Richard White agrees and believes that in the eyes of its contemporaries, the railroads of the nineteenth century constituted "the epitome of modernity."[17] Historian, politician, and diplomat Charles Francis Adams expressed the view earlier and in 1871 succinctly identified what the railroad wrought to American society: "Here, is an enormous, an incalculable force practically let loose suddenly on mankind; exercising all sorts of influences, social, moral, and political; precipitating upon us novel problems which demand immediate solution; banishing the old before the new is half matured to replace it; bringing the nations into close contact before yet the antipathies of race have begun to be eradicated; giving us history full of changing fortunes and rich in dramatic episodes."[18] The effects of the railroad in both America and Europe in the mid-nineteenth century proved immediate and profound forcing a "revolution in the cultural marketplace."[19] However, despite these easily penned, enthusiastic summaries of the radical phenomenon that the railroad presented, close examination reveals that it was not uniformly accepted at all levels of society, including in Vermont where distinct evidence of class differences and regional sectionalism also occurred.

Modernity, such as that exemplified by the railroad that historians refer to, is defined by sociologist Anthony Giddens as, "at its simplest. . . a shorthand term for modern society or industrial civilization," a situation "vastly more dynamic than any previous type of social order" which "unlike any preceding culture, lives in the future rather than in the past."[20] "In other words," it "has broken with tradition, the sense that the present is continuous with the past, that the present in some way repeats the forms, behavior, and events of the past."[21] A sense of optimism infuses modernity's separation from bygone years and makes it "a series of practices, ideas, and experiences that led Americans to see their world, first and foremost, as exceptional."[22] The effects wrought by sudden change crippled the present's connection to the past in many ways, manifested primarily by the physical aspects of technology that severely impacted the way the population experienced and viewed life, wrenched from its comfortable ways because of its radical effect on "aural, olfactory and tactile experiences."[23] Modernity in Vermont in the 1850s inflicted a form of turbulence on its society unlike that experienced in preceding decades or in other locations outside of the state. Underlying it, modernity introduced into a removed geographical location, challenged to develop at the speed of other states, new forms of capitalism sponsored by those seeking opportunity from the new technological advances. At the same time, it also posed a problem for the traditionalists among them, tied to the past and fearful of change, forced to grapple with and alter their own views "if only to halt or reverse the ongoing changes."[24]

Preface

New England traditionalist Henry David Thoreau expressed a similar conflicted view in 1854 when he sought to escape the effects of intrusive modernity at Walden Pond. There he wrote *Walden* and, in a chapter entitled "Sounds," decried the daily intrusions of the Fitchburg railroad that passed him nearby blasting its whistles, belching steam, screeching steel on steel, and pulling long lines of cars filled with people and goods heading from Boston to, among other places, Lake Champlain and Cuttingsville, Vermont. The endeavor, Thoreau wrote, forced many to alter their lives to accommodate themselves to this new "railroad fashion." Their habits and ways of speech changed overnight, he thought, because of the railroad ("Do they not talk and think faster in the depot than they did in the stage-office?") as they bent to the dictates of the train's whistle, a sound, Thoreau wrote, that "can be heard so far, that the farmers set their clocks by them" and allowed "one well-conducted institution [to regulate] a whole country." Refusing to succumb to the outside forces, he resignedly asked "What's the railroad to me?" and succinctly denied modernity's ability to impact him physically, concluding that "I will not have my eyes put out and my ears spoiled by its smoke and steam and hissing."[25]

After the January 6, 1857 statehouse fire, the tugs of modernity with its daunting sense of presentism demanded that Vermont's leaders, including those reluctant and sympathetic with Thoreau's mindset, to adopt a Janus-like perspective to face change as they moderated the prospect of a radical break with their past. They simply did not have the luxury of indulging those days of yore any longer as the Rutland settler might have wanted or ignoring the technological realities that Thoreau sought to dismiss. In Europe, people celebrated the incredible change and opportunities that technology offered, exemplified by the magnificent display presented during Britain's "Great Exhibition of the Works of Industry of All Nations" in 1851 and then copied by the French in 1855 at its Exposition Universelle des Beaux-Arts. Vermont would have to reflect, imagine, and create the conditions needed to allow the benefits of modernity that these others experienced to assume a place in it. Vermont in mid-century presents a vibrant kaleidoscope of rapid change unlike any time in its history. The events of those antebellum years present a fascinating period when tradition, technology, and imposing forces intruding from beyond the Green Mountains intersected and penetrated into the lives of a population composed largely of poorly educated rural farmers living in distant, difficult-to-reach towns.

CHALLENGING A SHIBBOLETH

A *sine quo non* of Vermont history insists that during the 1850s the population witnessed significant stagnant growth due principally to emigration of many of its young to the west. The 1860 U. S. Census for the state seems to confirm that fact and reports an increase over the course of the preceding decade of a mere 962 individuals, only 0.3 percent, compared to the 7.59 percent increase between 1840 and 1850. But further examination of this time reveals much more nuance than the standard accounts relate. The elevation of a single factor, such as emigration, to characterize the 1850s as a period of decline in Vermont's past allows other important factors to escape notice and obscures the impact of modernity. As history professor Hal S. Barron observes in his study of the Chelsea, Vermont region in the mid-nineteenth century, a focus solely on population levels is "subject to question," leading him to conclude that reports of the region's decline are "greatly exaggerated."[26] Similarly, another student opines that drawing gross conclusions concerning the reasons behind migration from Vermont presents a subject where the evidence is "sorely lacking."[27]

Simply assigning the tiny growth in Vermont's population to emigration abetted by other factors such as low wages or soil exhaustion does not explore the dynamic of the state at mid-century. Ascribing low pay as a reason for some to leave the state because the average income of workers in manufacturing jobs in Massachusetts and Rhode Island in 1850 paid "nearly twice as great as that of the agricultural State of Vermont" does not present a valid comparison.[28] A deeper analysis would also recognize the value that nominal wages played in the location where the worker resided. As another contemporary explained, "a carpenter who could obtain but $1.25 [a day] in Vermont, might by going to New York city get $2, or to New Orleans, $2.50," but "if the expenses of maintaining himself and family in health and comfort

[are] considered, the wages obtained in Vermont might be greater than in New York or New Orleans."[29] A Vermont physician similarly observed in 1857 after he viewed statistics from Massachusetts that appeared consistent with Vermont's experience that "The difference in the wages between the agriculturalist and mechanic is more apparent than real."[30] An 1861 report by the Vermont Board of Education reiterated the point and rejected the prospect that agricultural workers suffered for want of wages.[31]

The vigorous enforcement of Vermont's colloquially labelled "grab laws" in mid-century also deserve attention. Those draconian measures severely hampered the economic environment by unreasonably favoring creditors to the disadvantage of the state's hardworking, entrepreneurial-debtor class threatened with jail if they appeared unable to repay loans causing them to question why they should engage in trade in the first place. This oppressive practice caused observers to fear the state's ability to attract needed business and manufacturers because it scared away their young to other states to avoid suffering under such threats. Other arguments that the "exhausted" or "depleted" soil forced many to leave appears repeatedly in the accounts and may have had some validity in some locales, but agricultural experts of the time rejected those complaints and pointed out that Vermont ranked among the highest states in terms of agricultural production. Where the complaint of depleted soil had validity, it occurred because of a "thriftless system of husbandry" correctible by instituting different practices including the use of fertilizer to improve its condition.[32] Blaming the quality of the soil without acknowledging the abundant produce the state generated or addressing the seeming lack of initiative in those able to correct deficiencies adds to the inadequate analysis surrounding population levels. Any assessment of the quality of life of mid-century Vermonters requires that it include, among others, accurate descriptions of wages, the impact of grab laws and soil quality that past descriptions have overlooked.

Quantifying the situation in Vermont in the 1850s presents a challenge. Looking beyond the anecdotes of period Vermonters decrying the loss of their young to other states, relying simply on census schedules to substantiate the contributory effects of migration on stagnant population levels does not provide adequate answers.[33] To use any of the statistics accumulated by contemporary officials requires caution before reaching definitive conclusions. The United States Census for 1850 noted the challenge when it cautioned that "an enumeration of the living, or of the deaths only, is insufficient for the purpose, unless the population is stationary [and that] the assumption of a stationary population, however, can scarcely be entertained of even the oldest settled parts of the Union."[34]

When Vermont officials noted the small increase of population in the decade ending in 1860, they also recognized its fluid, dynamic aspects and wrote with emphasis that "the actual *change* of population in the different sections of the State has been considerable" in apparent reference to the rapid increase in the number of arriving immigrants.[35] Notwithstanding, between 1850 and 1860 federal and Vermont state officials decried the inadequacy and unreliability of figures cited in their reports and cautioned users to remain wary of making facile conclusions, with one federal official characterizing the earlier census as prepared by "entirely incompetent" people.[36] Such neglect contributed to an assessment that in mid-century between five and twenty-five percent of the nation's population escaped official notice.[37] In Vermont, a speaker before the Vermont Medical Society (VMS) in 1858 also warned about drawing conclusions from statistics describing the health of the state's inhabitants. For if "figures cannot lie," he related, "it is equally true that 'facts themselves are false when interpreted by false theories,' and of all things, figures are the most fallacious if incorrectly used."[38] In 1861, officials further explained the deficiency of their figures, noting that "Unlike some of the States of the Union, Vermont is obliged to rely entirely upon the returns made by the Deputy Marshals, and tabulated in the United States Census. These are obviously imperfect, and in particular, the returns from many of the towns are. . . proved to be incorrect."[39]

Attempting to derive a deeper meaning from census figures without considering the effects of such a transient population has the same limitation as trying to assess the health of Lake Champlain by observing its surface. That large body of water, fed by numerous rivers and streams, empties into the Richelieu River at the border with Quebec, but maintains a relatively stable elevation at some ninety feet above sea level. The dynamic lake, not static by any means with much water flowing in and out, provides a rich environment for life below the surface and at its edges. The quality of those waters that drain into it and which may contain any number of contaminants more accurately describe its condition. Looking at only its elevation level and surface will not provide a valid assessment of its true physical health. Vermont in the 1850s did not stand alone in witnessing the arrival and departure of transient populations that impacted calculating the state's number of inhabitants because other New England states experienced the same phenomenon. The validity of any conclusion of a stagnant population level without exploring the many factors that caused it to remain constant in number, such as the arrival and contributions of the Irish and French Canadians, requires further analysis. As historian J. Kevin Graffagnino notes, "Vermont was not necessarily losing its best and most energetic young people in the exodus, but that was the perception of many of those who stayed home, and that gloomy feeling would become even more widespread in the years ahead."[40] Accordingly, the often shallow impressions of the contemporaries have affected modern assessments of the quality of life that Vermonter's experienced in the 1850s and skews the actual situation in the same way that a tainted river could impact an accurate assessment of the quality of Lake Champlain's waters.

Historians Assess Vermont at Mid-century

Before the Civil War, Vermont remained somewhat an outlier among the thirty-three states in 1860. It had attained statehood sixty-nine years earlier as the fourteenth when it abandoned thoughts of its own independence and began incorporating its growing, vigorous population into the folds of a federal system. States along the Atlantic coast already had a vibrant centuries-long experience that tied them together socially and economically, including distant European markets, that they continued to develop in the early national era. In contrast, Vermont tended to remain on the sidelines in obtaining similar success, hampered by its relative isolation from the seaboard, considered in much the same way as in the last century when mocked from outside her borders as "lost in the woods; crying, *I can't get out!*"[41] Modernity would remedy that complaint in full measure.

Historian-scholar Thomas Day Seymour Basssett, propelled by what the state's dean of historians Samuel B. Hand characterized as a "powerful intellect powered by an unquenchable curiosity," identified many of the challenges that Vermonters faced in the mid-nineteenth century.[42] Notwithstanding the seeming consensus of historians that Bassett "suffered from a commitment to inclusion" when he wrote his 1952 Harvard Ph. D. dissertation "Urban Penetration of Rural Vermont, 1840-1880," it unquestionably constitutes the most comprehensive effort undertaken by any historian to date. The result of sixteen years of research, the two-volume, approximately 700-page type written work exhaustively identifies a wide spectrum of events caused by urbanization that crept into the state fostered by the arrival of the railroad. Overall, Bassett deemed it a positive effect and wrote that by the end of the 1840s Vermonters had become optimistic about their future as "their voices joined in the chorus of praise for the railroad."[43] Historian Graffagnino echoes that assessment and has provided a compelling portrait of the state at the time in his lavishly illustrated *Vermont in the Victorian Age*. After noting that the second half of the nineteenth century "has failed to receive its share of study and analysis," he determined the era worthy of further study because "Far from being a period of failure to keep up with the main currents of American innovation and vitality," it, instead, had developed "a complex interplay of old and new in Vermont."[44] Similarly, in its comprehensive survey of the state's history, the Vermont Historical Society's *Freedom and Unity: A History of Vermont* (2004) identifies the 1850-1870 period in a chapter entitled "Links to the Nation" with an emphasis on the impact of the railroad that made it possible. It characterized 1850 as the year when Vermonters "faced the future with ambivalence," accompanied by a sense of anxiousness.[45]

The work of other historians took a markedly different view from Bassett and Graffagnino that largely passes over this period to reach what they consider more interesting aspects of the state's history during the Civil

War, the Gilded Age and on into the twentieth century. In his important *Social Ferment in Vermont,* historian David Ludlum chose to "take leave" and halt his study of state society in 1850 in the belief it had matured to such a point it made answering the reasons for further change in the next decades "difficult."[46] Randolph Roth chose 1850 in his *The Democratic Dilemma* as the moment when the Age of the Democratic Revolution ended, heavily represented in Vermont's burnt-over district where a profound revolutionary spirit existed and submitted to the changing times.[47] Fixated on the fact that Vermont experienced a decade of stagnant population growth in the 1850s, others' stories repeatedly attribute its cause to soil depletion and a stalled economy that led young farmers and women to emigrate westward and to other New England states where higher wages for teaching or opportunities to work in growing textile mills beckoned.[48] One effort acknowledges the decade as a time of change, but concludes that in 1850 Vermont "existed in a twilight state," neither "sheep nor cow country, neither cow nor manufacturing country, neither frontier nor wholly domesticated."[49] Another adopts a seasonal representation of those years and identifies them as an "Autumn" period in Vermont's development, emerging from "Summer," on its way to "Winter" in late century.[50] In the 1930s the nation's Works Progress Administration conducted a survey of Vermont's attributes and prepared a summary of its past that identified the 1850s as "pivotal" in its history, and again assigned the reason for its downward turn to the population leaving its hill towns for the west.[51] A more recent effort similarly summarizes the period when "Vermont in the 1850s was a state and society in transition" and refers to the out migration story as the main reason.[52] Whereas Bassett and Graffagnino present a picture of optimism and opportunity in the 1850s, others chose to either halt their efforts at 1850 or to dampen positive assessments without engaging in deep reflection of the many different kinds of demands made on the population during that admittedly "pivotal" decade with its consequences for the future.

Conclusion

Too much evidence exists beyond the stark numbers that demonstrates the presence of vibrant action and interaction on many levels of Vermont society in mid-century upon the arrival of the railroad. This includes technology, agriculture, health, medicine, migration, and their impact on the psyche of the population and their elected representatives to deal with their challenges. It also presented the specter of rising sectionalism and division because of varied interests in different parts of the state possessive of their individual sense of security they believed threatened by aspects of modernity. The mid-nineteenth century was not a time of recession and decline so easily attributable to a single cause or data point. Instead, it presented an important transition period when the population pivoted and faced the challenges of modernity that in turn created the conditions conducive to, among other circumstances, out-migration that persisted into the future.

The consideration of this period requires adopting a perspective that eschews labels identifying it in a conventional manner. It presents a larger story than simply a series of events compressed into a neat ten-year timeframe. Instead, it encompassed "things," physical creations made possible by advancing technology with roots in preceding decades that intersected each other at this particular moment in time's spectrum and, in turn, affected the course of the future.[53] The story of these individual manifestations, such as the arrival of the railroad, the drastic change it brought to the Rutland community, its effects on agriculture and the health of Vermonters, together with the rebuilding of the state's Capitol before the Civil War, and their collective consequences in later years provides a more nuanced appreciation of the complexities and challenges that modernity presented without being compressed by the limitations that a classification such as "decade" imposes. Further, by advocating a view that descends from the large, or macro, level which many of the past accounts of this period utilize, and instead engaging in a micro-level study of the participants and the challenges they faced, reveals a rich tapestry of change and causation.[54] In the interstices between these notorious events lay some of the most telling facts of Vermont society. Engaging in such an effort also seeks to answer the lament of Norwich University professor of Ancient Languages and English Literature James Davie Butler in 1846 when he addressed the Vermont Historical Society about the woeful state of Vermont history at the time that failed to provide the details necessary to understand past events. "In all our Histories," he said, "there is a lack of characteristic minutiæ. We ask for face-to-face details, [but instead] we receive far off generalities."[55]

Detail, the very foundation of history, and the debates of the special session of the Vermont legislature in Montpelier in February 1857, demonstrates the importance of acquiring the perspective Butler advocated to fully appreciate this important period in the state's past.

Acknowledgments

This project originated while researching two prior books that bracketed the nineteenth century concerning, respectively, the violent impact that Thomas Jefferson's embargo of 1807 had on Vermont and the population's increasing use, and abuse, of addictive substances in the following decades.[56] As the research for these events revealed, those one hundred years opened with the murders of the first law enforcement officers working on the behalf of the United States Department of the Treasury in an alcohol-infused ambush (the so-called "Black Snake Affair") and ended with so many of the population consuming opium-related products that it resulted in the state's first drug epidemic in 1900. An intriguing, intervening moment occurred mid-century in 1852 when Vermont passed its divisive prohibition law that made it illegal to manufacture or sell alcohol that remained in effect for the next half-century. While little attention was paid to the increasing use of unregulated drugs after prohibition began, the prospect that they served as a convenient alternative to a population that refused to limit its consumption of mood-altering substances signaled that particular decade as deserving of further study than it had received in the past. Other fascinating aspects of the 1850s concerned the sudden arrival of modernity in Vermont in the form of technological advances forced on it by, notwithstanding Thoreau's reserved reticence, the railroad and an accompanying, strange lack of any appreciable increase in population for the entire decade. While examining these phenomena, other questions arose about the state of Vermonters' health traceable to modernity's effects that included the surprising widespread use of abortion and infanticide which, together with the research accumulated from these other investigations, has resulted in this account.

Vermont historian Dr. H. Nicholas Muller III has become a good friend these past years and has provided me, a post-retirement government attorney and now avid historian, with much guidance in interpreting the state's past. Our association has resulted in a rewarding relationship that has recently afforded us with the opportunity to work together to write a book with another historian, Dr. John J. Duffy, that involved one of their favorite subjects, and for which they are nationally recognized experts on, Ethan Allen. Ethan did not enter into considerations of the effects of modernity in Vermont in the 1850s, but Nick's many other talents did as he frequently discussed and answered my questions about this interesting time in the state's history through many emails and telephone calls, as well as his agreeing to serve as an editor for the initial drafts. One of Nick's greatest strengths is to recognize the overall picture of a time period that has assisted me in putting a mass of facts into a proper perspective. His constant probing and suggestions often directed me down other paths that provided new insights that might have otherwise escaped notice.

Nick has been an important mentor to many other Vermont historians, including J. Kevin Graffagnino, recently retired director of the William L. Clements Library at the University of Michigan. Kevin's involvement with Vermont's history is similarly extensive as Nick's and he has researched, written and curated his way to deserved national recognition for his contributions to the state's historiography. Fortunately, he has also examined conditions in the state in the nineteenth century and enthusiastically expressed his opinion that mid-century Vermont deserved further study. His confirmation that such a project would be worthwhile and email exchanges with suggestions on where to look for information has also been of great value to this effort.

Acknowledgments

Former Vermont state archivist Gregory Sanford and legal historian Paul S. Gillies have also become friends I have reached out to over the years to gain their perspective on various aspects of Vermont's history. Gregory's work on the state's early corporations and Paul's legal expertise of the time period have been a great help in delving deep into the state's past. Both have been generous on many occasions in answering my questions and providing guidance for which I am most grateful for their indulgence.

Research for this time period focused on three themes and how modernity affected each: the railroad and the development of its important railyard in Rutland, the farming population, and the health of Vermonters. Many have already written about Vermont's early railroads, but few have looked closely at the primary sources that involved its managers, surveyors and workers. One exception is Vic Rolando, an industrial archaeologist of great talents, who forged the way early on when others did not recognize or appreciate the worth of inquiring into the state's formative technological advances. We communicated often about his favorite subject and I found it of great value in understanding aspects of the early railroad in Vermont. For other information on that topic, I am thankful for the resources that Joseph Watson, Preservation Manager at Middlebury College's Davis Library, made available from the Rutland Railroad Archives that provided such rich detail on the town's railyard in the early 1850s. Rutland Historical Society's Jim Davidson also contributed by allowing me access to the early engineering logs, corporate records and company stores' accounts that documented the work of rail workers in Rutland and providing permission to use several of the images herein. The diary of Ambrose Lincoln Brown in the Society's possession provided many other obscure facts that explained the difficulties engineers and surveyors faced in establishing the Rutland rail yard that few have consulted. Additionally, the rich primary resources available at the Vermont State Archives and Records Administration, in Middlesex, under the charge of state archivist Tanya Marshall, provided many other overlooked details about railroad corporate activities, surveying and engineering in the mid-nineteenth century. For information concerning the direct impact of the railroad on the towns it passed through, I am grateful for the access to the land records in the custody of city and town clerks, including Henry Heck in Rutland, Gloria Menard in Clarendon, Susan Covalla in Mt. Holly, and Mark Goodwin in Shrewsbury. Finally, Manchester architect Bill Badger, an officer of the Rutland Railroad Historical Society, was very helpful in conveying interesting information that only amateur railroad enthusiasts could possess about the Rutland experience. Bill also graciously allowed the publication of a period stereoscopic image of the important Rutland Depot, the earliest I have been able to locate.

Searching for information that directly concerned the health of Vermonters in the nineteenth century has been a challenge. Past work on the state's first opium epidemic already familiarized me with the challenges that opium-infused patent drugs posed, but finding information about the dramatic use of abortion and infanticide for family planning purposes and its effects on population growth posed more of a problem. I returned to those institutions used in that last effort to re-examine familiar documents and found others that provided important circumstantial information to explain the phenomena. These included the very unique nineteenth-century medical theses prepared by aspiring doctors housed at Dartmouth College's Rauner Library in Hanover, New Hampshire that archivist Peter Carini made available. Important information about the early Vermont Medical Society and the challenges that it and Burlington town officials faced at the time is located at the University of Vermont's Silver Special Collections Library and librarian Prudence Doherty was very helpful in tracking them down. The records of the Addison County Medical Society are also of great interest and archivist Eva Garcelon-Hart at the Stewart-Swift Research Center in the Henry Sheldon Museum of Vermont History in Middlebury made those available. As usual, librarian Paul Carnahan at the Vermont Historical Society in Barre was helpful in providing access to many medical and temperance related materials, and photographs, that added further context to the story. Once again, the rich resources of the Vermont State Archives provided much detail that has never been published that came from the original registration reports beginning in 1857 that recorded the births, deaths and marriages of the state's inhabitants. Thanks to its many court files, I was also able to track down and trace the actions of what was perhaps the state's first serial killer, a notorious abortionist who brought great heartache to many Vermonters in the 1850s. Ohio State University history professor Randolph A. Roth, who authored the accompanying foreword, provided important insights based upon his extensive work on homicide in nineteenth-century Vermont and New Hampshire. His efforts confirmed the devilish inferences provided by the archival records that Vermont did indeed experience a burst of deaths attributed to abortion and infanticide in mid-century. Dr. Bryn Geffert, Dean of Libraries at the University of Vermont, and Alan Berolzheimer at the Vermont Historical Society also contributed to the final product with their helpful insights and suggestions. Lastly, I am most appreciative of the great interest and support that Richard Watts, Director of UVM's Center for Research on Vermont, has provided in bringing this project to publication, assisted by the able efforts of Eliza Giles.

The overall story of Vermont's accommodation of the sudden effects that technology imposed on it are not necessarily unique in the nation's overall experiences. But, in its geographical isolation removed from the Atlantic seaboard and the rich economic advantages that access to it allowed other states, its finer aspects meant that the effects of modernity in this rural state were not a commonly shared phenomena among its quickly separating classes. To penetrate into the reasons for Vermont's unique experience in the mid-nineteenth century, the resources available at these various institutions were of critical importance and to each of them I am most thankful for their assistance.

CHAPTER I

Improvement

"Our fathers felt that Montpelier was the proper place in their day... but this is a day of improvement. We do not use wooden plows because our fathers did, neither should we follow exactly their steps in legislation." [57]

REPRESENTATIVE WILLIAM F. BARNES OF RUTLAND, February 25, 1857

Gary G. Shattuck

The New Corporate Era

The thunderclap of the destruction of Vermont's Capitol building triggered the state's first meaningful introspection of the effects of modernity. On other occasions in their past the Green Mountain inhabitants experienced its vague tugs, but none with the force that the 1857 devastation wrought. From the times of earlier settler generations to the more recent times they faced the practical, pragmatic challenges of wresting a competency from an often described "howling wilderness" to assure the security of themselves and their families. The thought of suddenly transitioning from traditional, comfortable practices to confront and embrace the future simply did not have sufficient importance until mid-century when the railroad laid its intrusive tracks through their challenging geography and into their lives.

Decades before, national policy after the Revolutionary War sought the vigorous creation of internal improvements around the country to advance the common good through a variety of state-sponsored public works that included a network of canals, highways and other infrastructure to bind them together.[58] A local example of those important efforts involved the completion of the Champlain-Hudson Canal in 1823 that allowed the Green and Adirondack Mountain regions to ship lumber, iron ore, and other commodities to southern markets or west via the Erie Canal when it opened in 1825. However, growing Jacksonian libertarian policy of the 1830s and the Panic of 1837 stymied that enthusiasm and forced abandonment of such an ambitious, government-sponsored infrastructure. By 1840 creative entrepreneurs replaced those efforts and gladly stepped into the resulting laissez-faire environment without government interference to promote the construction of improved canals, roads and the new railroad technology. For Vermonters, that shift of responsibility from government to the private sector seeking to exploit the impressive strength provided by consolidating compressed, heated steam housed in massive creations of iron and steel that spewed up plumes of smoke and cinders able to convey the produce of remote farmers desperate for access to outside markets became an attractive way to solve their mountain isolation.

In the presence of such a phenomenon, the entire focus and tone of the voices of Vermont's legislators debating whether their new Capitol should remain in Montpelier or move elsewhere changed from their debates in previous years. They had no choice but to factor the never-before-seen railroad technology into their discussions. In their initial enthusiasm, the decisions they made soon resulted in consequences that resounded and impacted their constituency in disparate ways and with no thought whatsoever of their impact on the environment. Vermont government's attitude in the 1840s-1850s was one of "passive encouragement" advocating for the inhabitants to "exploit rather than preserve" the land in the same manner they had traditionally done "consistent with their frontier ethic."[59] It only dealt with those consequences reactively after witnessing the actual devastation it wrought. At the beginning of this period, Vermonters treaded cautiously to impose only such laws and regulations necessary to accommodate the creeping forms of capitalism the technology demanded. In 1847, eighteen banks operated in the state, followed by the formation an additional four the next year that permitted them to participate in and profit from the changes rapidly taking place.[60] The authority to create these corporate entities rested with the legislature and dated to the state's first constitution in 1777 (Chapter 2, section 8 permitting it to "grant charters of incorporation") and renewed in the 1793 version (Chapter 2, section 9) following statehood. Between 1793 and 1850 Vermont authorized over seventy charters for bridge building companies, mining ventures and various activities engaged in manufacturing (iron, glass, guns, cotton, wool, sandpaper, leather, nails, and bolts). Only a few of them concerned the formation of canal companies to facilitate transportation internally on the state's rivers and lakes. Between 1850 and 1861 the legislature allowed another twenty corporations that included several to companies directly supporting the physical demands of the new technology such as Brandon Iron and Car Wheel Company (1851), Rutland Car Company (1852), and the Island Pond Machine Shop Company (1852).[61]

Of particular interest to the railroad magnates at the time was a new, accompanying form of authority of critical importance that allowed them to exercise the devastating power of eminent domain, or condemnation, to take the land they wanted to build their roads. Assuming a marked degree of disinterest and blind unwillingness to intervene in the railroad's demands than what other states allowed, Vermont's legislators delegated wholesale this previously unique power of government to its managers. This allowed them to wield a devastating sword that saw them, without restriction, march over and seize large amounts of land of their own choosing (and payment of purportedly fair compensation in return), without explanation or justification, from Vermonters unwilling to accede to their encroachments. That authority also emboldened the railroad corporations in following years to take additional license with their charters and argue against proposed legislation seeking to rein them in. This early neglect by the legislature on a seemingly inconsequential matter had huge consequences in the future.

In his multi-volume documentation of the state's past, *Records of the Governor and Council of the State of Vermont,* Montpelier publisher, and former U.S. congressman, Eliakim Persons Walton, characterized the years when the first discussions of the railroad took place as "Internal Improvements in Vermont – 1823-1845."[62] He identified January 1830 as the moment when the state expressed interest in introducing that technology inside its borders to facilitate the transportation of goods following heavily-attended public meetings in Brattleboro, Windsor, Chelsea and Montpelier. The attendees' enthusiasm followed the experiences of others elsewhere when, in 1826, the Pennsylvania Society for the Promotion of Internal Improvements forged the way and favorably assessed the development of the railroad in England.[63] The impetus for the gatherings in Vermont four years later concerned the recent adverse assessment by national authorities in 1828 that, notwithstanding the cost and engineering challenges it posed, the construction of a canal connecting Lake Champlain with the Connecticut River was not feasible because "the supply of water was too doubtful." The *Rutland Herald* noted that steam already proved a much more reliable form of power able to propel a car on rails at eighteen miles an hour compared to a canal boat moving, at most, fifteen miles an hour, but usually much slower.[64] The additional challenge that Vermont's winters and freezing waters posed further doomed any canal proposal. In their place, residents enthusiastically endorsed the prospect of railroads to allow them access to outside markets via a connection along a route between Boston and "the waters of Lake Ontario, at Ogdensburgh, New-York." They understood and agreed that "the public good requires vigorous and persevering efforts on the part of all intelligent and public-spirited individuals, all friends of their country and of internal improvements" to assure it took place.[65]

In 1831, residents from several towns on the west side of the Green Mountains met to discuss their own internal improvement needs, envious of the successes they witnessed in nearby New York. A Whitehall, New York newspaper reported their meeting and welcomed the initiative stating that "Vermont is far behind New York in the spirit of entrerprize. We cannot therefore but watch with deep interest every movement calculated to inspire the belief that she, too, will soon march forward in the spirit of the age – that her vallies will soon evince the hand of improvement – and that her 'heaven-kissing hills' will soon pour forth their treasures, to reward the enterprize of thriving population."[66] While that particular effort did result in the grant of a charter for the Rutland and Whitehall Railroad Company, it proved a hollow victory when, following the failure to raise the necessary financing, it "gathered dust for a decade."[67] In 1835, Rutland residents also addressed the issue when they sought permission from the legislature to construct "a single or double Rail Road" from their town eastward to the

Connecticut River. The flexible venture proposed "to transport, take, and carry property and persons... by the power and force of steam, of animals, or of other mechanical, or other power, or any combination of them."[68] On the east side of the Green Mountains, a large convention of enthusiasts gathered in Windsor on January 20, 1836. Those attendees sought to exploit their geographical location and advance the building of a railroad northward to connect the seacoast with Montreal through the Connecticut Valley allowing them access and to secure "the present friendly relations between the two countries." An infectious spirit of goodwill to see the project completed to avoid any continued isolation led their committee of correspondence to forcibly state that "we are bold to... say, IN THIS THERE IS NO MISTAKE – THERE CAN BE NONE. A rail road can be built, at a small expense, with inestimable advantage to the country, and without which, the wealth and energy of these valleys must sleep, while other more enterprising sections [of Vermont] reap the harvest which our apathy would forego." "IT SHALL BE DONE," it ended emphatically.[69]

While some communities faced east and north, ambitious Bennington businessmen envious of the "wonderful growth and prosperity of the western States" looked much further in that direction. They too petitioned the legislature to allow them to construct a railroad to permit Vermont's "various and valuable minerals, immense quantities of marble and other building stones, lumber, timber, &c. &c." to gain access to large markets. By making such "public improvements," the Bennington men expressed the hope that both the value of the land and the population would increase. They also lamented the current state of the population and complained that "large numbers of our intelligent youth, and others, for want of sufficient inducements to retain them here, are expatriating themselves, and abandoning our salubrious climate for scenes of more attractive enterprize abroad."[70]

At the same time, dozens of Brattleboro area residents along the Connecticut River assembled for a similar purpose and submitted an extraordinary petition to the legislature seeking permission to construct a rail line eastward to allow them access to the coast. They related that "in their opinion nothing is wanted in addition to our water power & advantages from the prosecution of some branches of agriculture to render this state one of the most populous & prosperous in the Union but a cheap ready communication with the great Atlantic cities." "We must always labor," they wrote, "under a disadvantage in competition with the inhabitants of other sections of our land & our manufacturing privileges which might otherwise be great sources of wealth must remain to a great extent unimproved & our population comparatively sparse." The answer, they believed, lay with the railroads which "seem to offer precisely such a communication as is needed & are far better in many aspects than navigable streams."[71]

Their petition went further than the others and addressed the manner of funding the ambitious enterprise required that signaled a prescient concern with concentrating so much authority and money into the hands of a select few individuals overseeing the effort. They suggested that rather than loans coming directly from the state, that the sale of stock to the public would dilute that power because they viewed "with alarm the plan advocated by some of leaving in the hands of the state government a large amount of money to be loaned from year to year." Such a situation would, they argued, "tend to create a system of favoritism & a scramble by parties for the control of the power over it." By placing the effort into the hands of stockholding investors, the enterprise could avoid the prospect of sectionalism and necessity of paying commissions for loans to thereby permit the development of "a system of internal improvement." Ultimately unsuccessful in their noble attempt, they could only bide their time and read of the great improvements that New York continued to experience where one of its courts teased in 1837 about great value of the railroads. The improvements it provided to those with access to them, the court recognized, "tend to annihilate distance, bringing in effect places that are distant near to each other; tending in their magic influence to the extension of personal acquaintance, the enlargement of business relations, and cementing more firmly the bond of fellowship and union between the inhabitants of the States." "Next to the moral lever power of the press," it continued, "should be ranked the beneficial influence of railroads in their effects upon the vast and increasing business relations of the nation, and promoting, sustaining and perpetuating the happiness, prosperity and liberty of the people."[72]

Notwithstanding their admirable efforts in the 1830s, Vermont remained one of four states (in addition to Arkansas, Missouri, and Tennessee) without a single mile of track by 1840.[73] That began to change in the next decade when the successes of other states pulled it out of its lethargy to seriously consider adopting the technology. New Hampshire faced a similar challenge in deciding if the time was ripe to extend the railroad west across the state from Concord to the Connecticut River. If Vermont failed to do likewise and build from the river to Lake Champlain then the planned grand route connecting Boston to the St. Lawrence River would be significantly impaired. Railroad advocate and Dartmouth College Professor of Intellectual Philosophy and Political Economy Charles B. Haddock strongly argued for its construction across both states. Described as "among the most accomplished scholars" in the country, he appeared in Lebanon in October 1843 and Montpelier three months later in January 1844.[74] On each occasion, he provided well-attended conventions with lucid reasons to support the railroad capitalists.[75]

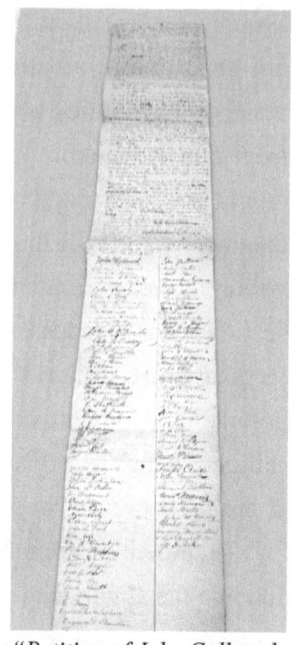

"Petition of John Colbrook and others" for a railroad, several feet long bearing dozens of names, October 19, 1836. Vermont State Archives. Photo by author.

IMPROVEMENT

In Montpelier, calling the new technology "a miracle of Art," Haddock both advocated on the entrepreneurs' behalf and addressed several objections that questioned if the state should embrace the coming changes. To the argument equating capitalists with monopolists that made them anti-republican, Haddock pointed out that in their rural condition, even farmers engaged in selling their products were capitalists at heart and could not separate themselves from those living in metropolitan centers seeking to fund railroads. Traditionalists who objected to the introduction of goods from far off because they threatened to "divert industry from the primitive, healthful and moral pursuits of agriculture" and thereby introduce "the vices and miseries of manufacturing and commercial places" into the Green Mountains were also refuted. Those products arriving from outside Vermont, such as clothing and tools, Haddock said, allowed the farmer time to address other needs that making them on his farm would have required. When opponents objected to the purported ill effects of manufacturing, deemed "immoral" by some, able to alter small towns, Haddock pointed out that already "our towns and villages. . . present more disgusting forms of vice and misery than the country around" them. Villages could not escape the effects of those who came into them from the farming community looking for adventure he described as "the unprincipled and dissolute flock. . . in quest of facilities of indulgence." There, they sought "the concealment, and the opportunities of plunder" that a concentrated number of people allowed them. However, Haddock also held out hope and argued that small villages embracing technology and welcoming manufacturing would, in turn, cultivate "elements of intelligence, virtue, and piety" able to counter the possibility of any degradation.

These various meetings and petitions in the 1830s and 1840s that repeatedly called for "improvements" to obtain the benefits of the railroad that the New York court glowingly described represent the restless state of mind of a rural mountainous population envious of those who did not have to overcome the challenges that geography presented, but which also threatened their traditional ways. Early references to their obtaining a better way of life in their difficult frontier condition dated back to their 1777 Constitution proclaiming that generation's hopes to "promote the general happiness of the people of this State, and their posterity, and provide for future improvements."[76] In 1794, Vermont's first historian Rev. Samuel Williams adopted the concept of improvement as a persistent theme throughout his *The Natural and Civil History of Vermont*. At the book's optimistic conclusion, he observed that the state experienced "the most rapid state of improvement, and population; with perfect freedom to make further improvements." "In this state of society," he continued, "every thing is adapted to promote the prosperity, the importance, and the improvement of the body of the people." Coaxing them on, he predicted that if they persisted, their "freedom will be perpetual!"[77]

Vermonters directed their efforts three decades later to advance aspects of improvement in their lives not in copying the consumption practices of those outside the state by importing their goods to inside their borders, but in exporting the surplus they had to offer. The voices of the farming, laboring and entrepreneurial members of the population forcefully convey their frustrations at the status quo in their isolation that inhibited that ability and believed the railroad would secure their economic well-being. Their expressions also anticipated awareness of the dangers that the untested, new technology presented. Large amounts of money made available by new methods of financing an imposing monopolistic industry and the concentration of power into the hands of a few able to direct its flow required close oversight. Concurrently, equal access to outside markets could alleviate the prospect of one part of the state experiencing growth and prosperity at the expense of others that could foster an environment of sectionalism. Internal discord arose when rural communities believed their interests in connecting to the railroad were slighted by others located in more geographically advantageous locations and who sought to dictate to them. "We farmers start slow," a Derby correspondent admitted when others tried to impose their will, "but we are sure to keep moving" as he called for them to recognize their common interests because "We belong to the same community. We are brethren, and best of all we are Christians, not Mahommedan or Greek."[78]

IMPROVEMENTS

Tracing the stop and go progress of improvement in Vermont, such as the railroad, explains why modernity attained such inconsistent, reluctant acceptance in the decades after its arrival in mid-century. While the many efforts to bring the new technology to Vermont lingered throughout the 1830s and into the 1840s, in 1836 the second Capitol building, destined for a fiery destruction in 1857, opened in time to welcome the first sitting of the newly created Senate that replaced the governor's council. Recently elected lieutenant-governor David M. Camp presided and continued in that role for the next five years.[79] He also oversaw the formation of the state's first concerted, aggressive effort to pursue a means to exploit the state's natural resources and to organize and solicit the contributions of its creative inhabitants to accomplish the goal. The creation of the Vermont Internal Improvement Society, and its nine-article constitution authorized on October 27-28, 1836, occurred at a meeting in the same Montpelier courthouse where the Senate convened following the 1857 fire. The large gathering of the state's notables came from all fourteen of its counties and included former governor Samuel C. Crafts, congressmen and future governors Hiland Hall and William Slade Jr., and St. Johnsbury scale magnate Erastus Fairbanks. Slade succinctly stated the reason for their efforts and told the gathering that "the internal improvement of a country by roads and canals, is among the most important means for the development of its resources, and its advancement in wealth, population and general prosperity." Next, he identified the principle cause for their concern, challenged by "the mild climate and productive soil of the western States, aided by their extensive internal improvements," that held "out inducements which are rapidly drawing off the population and wealth of Vermont to new and more promising fields of enterprise." To stem the problem, Slade called for the creation of the Internal Improvement Society "for the purpose of concentrating effort – exciting a spirit of inquiry, and embodying such facts in regard to the agricultural, commercial, manufactures, water power, and mineral resources of this State, as shall enable its people to determine upon the expediency of entering on such a system of Internal Improvement as may tend to advance the value of its staple productions – retain its population – give fresh impulse to its enterprise, and disclose new objects for the employment and industry of its citizens."[80]

The gathering went beyond just stating the problem and established a three-member Board of Managers to oversee committees in each of the counties directing them to search out local information to guide their future course that addressed their transportation needs and to elicit "such information in regard to the Agriculture, Commerce, Manufactures, Water power, and Mineral, and other resources in Vermont." The meeting also directed the committees to ascertain "the effect upon these interests in other states, of improvements by railroads and canals" to allow them to determine "whether it will be for the interest of the people of this State to undertake such improvements." Action quickly followed and on November 7, 1836 Governor Silas Jenison ordered that estimates be obtained to determine the cost of creating geological and topographical surveys of the state.[81] He took the action both because of the Society's request and to halt the haphazard way that the state's unregulated geological resources were being discovered and exploited. He advocated employing a different process in "a spirit of scientific research" to "take the place of pretended knowledge" of others and to bring about order. For the topographical survey, Jenison noted further that while the "superficial observer" might not appreciate its need, when looking toward the future "the state of science calls for it" in order to aid in locating railroads and canals and that it "would be productive of great public utility."[82]

The following year, the requested report estimated the costs of the geological survey at $10,800 and $12,500 for the topographical, and outlined the importance of the work for engineering purposes to construct the proposed canals and railroads. As the Internal Improvement Society noted earlier, the report also deemed it necessary to educate the public about the value of Vermont's mineral resources in order to lessen emigration. "Multitudes of our citizens are leaving this state," it related, "to settle themselves in what they suppose to be more favored parts of the union." To counter that attraction, it argued for a public relations effort to educate the populace and convince them to stay. "There can be no doubt," it wrote, "in the mind of any competent judge, that a correct exhibition of the true state of the case will do much to dispel this delusion, and show our community that when they are led by one or two inducements standing in a strong and deceitful light, to forsake the green hills of their forefathers for the prairie soils of the west." It asserted further that when they departed, they left "behind ten-fold greater and more numerous advantages, calculated to make themselves and their posterity, prosperous, virtuous and happy."[83] Despite their good intentions, a multitude of "calamities" befell officials in the next years, attributed to their inability to appropriate the necessary funds, that ultimately delayed completion of the ambitious geological survey until 1861 and rendered moot any possible contributions it could have made in the interim.[84] For a portion of the survey completed before the 1857 fire, the many rock samples collected from around the state to accomplish it and stored in the building succumbed to the conflagration.[85] The first portions of the topographical study did not appear until 1893.

Other attempts at improving Vermont continued a decade later when the same principal players, Slade, Fairbanks and others attending that first meeting, came together in Montpelier to form the Vermont Society of the Improvement of Common Schools.[86] Now governor in 1845, Slade acknowledged the continuing attraction that improvement had on the state's policies and declared that "Improvement is the great law of our individual and social existence."[87] Facing a similar public relations challenge as they did years earlier, on this occasion that sought to correct deficiencies within the educational system so that the overall message of improvement could advance, the attendees created a constitution as they had a decade earlier. They also identified how they would pursue their goal "by diffusing through the State information respecting the defect and deficiencies of our School System, and the best methods of removing the one and supplying the other." They intended to achieve it by keeping the subject "continually before the people by short, pithy, and pointed articles in the County papers." That effort, they hoped, would "arouse the people from their apathy on the subject of Education." Their concerns repeated those expressed years earlier about the state's educational deficiencies that included the marked disinterest of parents in the conduct of their schools.[88] Busy, rural adults involved with agriculture focused on maintaining their critical farms with the assistance of children providing necessary labor saw little need for education beyond what farming demanded. In 1846, Vermont instituted "An Act Relating to Common Schools" in an attempt to alter and improve the system and installed a superintendent who decried its persistent, dismal condition.[89] Unsurprisingly, the daunting challenge that sought to address the needs of 79,757 students in 2,276 separate school districts (that increased to 2,594 in 1850) in many rural locations frustrated improvement. "A change in the character of a people for intelligence, morality, or any other great and distinguishing characteristic," he presciently noted, "is not the work of a year, but of at least a generation. Indeed, progress of improvement of this character, from year to year, is ever so slow as to escape the observation of any but the closest observer; and the improvement may ordinarily be inferred with greater certainty from a knowledge of the fact that active means are in operation to effect it, than it can be from any actual observation."[90] Elsewhere, with the rapid pace of modernity on their doorstep in the form of the railroad, former Vermont educator Emma Willard noted with urgency in 1849 that "We have great need to quicken the process of education, to meet the demands of a new age of steam and electricity."[91]

The creation of the Vermont Internal and Common School improvement societies identified shared issues hindering the state's overall improvement and suggested an orderly process to assess the impact of the railroad elsewhere to determine if it was an appropriate technology for the state to adopt, as well as overcoming its educational deficiencies.[92] These large-scale statewide improvement efforts may have had an unquantifiable impact at the time, but they did prove infectious to some on the local level when residents on the north border formed the Derby Line Mutual Improvement Society and in St. Johnsbury the Farmers and Mechanics Mutual Improvement Society met that religious societies also replicated.[93] A speaker before a Burlington audience noted approvingly of the changes taking place despite interruptions: "there have been causes of retardation and delay in human improvement which can never happen again" and held out hope for the future because "there are causes of acceleration and progress now at work which are comparatively new, and the full power of which is even yet imagined."[94] Additional efforts had also begun within the farming community with the formation of agricultural societies aimed at improving practices.[95] A Randolph observer wrote in 1846 that "Although Vermont has been behind some of the States in the application of science to agriculture, yet she stands at the head of the other States in her agricultural production." "This is the result of her industry," he related, which, when combined with science, would allow the state to "become very eminent."[96] However, he lamented the lack of interest in his fellow Orange County farmers to create their own society to advance their interests. "It seems strange that a county almost exclusively agricultural should be so backward in this movement," he continued, before asking "Are the people all asleep to their own interest? There seems to be a lack of enterprise somewhere."

THE MARSH SYNTHESIS

At 11:00 a.m., on September 30, 1847, Vermont Congressman George Perkins Marsh (1801-1882) appeared before the Agricultural Society of Rutland County during its annual fair to provide the most profound discourse made to that time connecting the interests of the agricultural community to those involved with the quickly approaching new technology, the railroad mechanics.[97] Rutland was a particularly appropriate location for his address because the technology and its aggressive backers were on its doorstep at that very moment. His hardened audience was composed of well-experienced farmers familiar with all that nature could throw at them as they fought to sustain their rural existence in the hills and valleys neighboring Rutland in this time of unprecedented change. A newspaper article that reported Marsh's appearance preceded it with a poem of several stanzas they understood well, entitled "The Tiller of the Soil," that opened:

> A hardy sun burnt man is he,
> A hardy sun burnt man;
> No studier men you'll ever see,
> Though all the world you scan.
> In summer's heats, in winter's cold,
> You'll find him at his toil;
> Oh, far above the Knights of old
> Is the Tiller of the soil.[98]

Described afterwards as "an eloquent and instructive Agricultural Address" and "able and interesting," Marsh presented a much deeper and reflective discourse that few probably appreciated at the time. Born only thirty miles distant from Rutland in Woodstock, Marsh achieved a remarkable career after his graduation from Dartmouth College with honors. He served as a noted lawyer in Burlington, a member of the state's twelve-man governor's council, a Scandinavian scholar who spoke a reported twenty languages, a founder of the Smithsonian Institution, and as the United States minister to Turkey and Italy. He also provided important public service in Vermont where he served as one of three commissioners that oversaw the rebuilding of the Capitol after the 1857 fire and as a railroad commissioner the next two years when he made unwelcomed, scathing assessments of the corrupting influences of that industry. Marsh commanded attention and what he said on this occasion the thoughtful among his Rutland audience could not dismiss lightly.

In a wide-ranging discourse that took place in the midst of showing, judging and awarding noteworthy vegetables, animals, household manufactures, marble, "mechanic's work," and farming implements, Marsh made a number of astute observations that sought to engage the intellectual side of his farming audience. In the process, he also made what are regarded as the first statements concerning the impact of man's activity on the land that later singled him out as the nation's first environmentalist. The validity of the observations Marsh made that day became evident shortly afterwards when the railroad cut its intrusive path across Rutland County. His recommendations touching on agricultural practices first addressed several aspects of farmers' concerns: the current state of scientific work allowing for the understanding of the chemical composition of plants and their connection to nutrients in the soil; the acclimatization of plants from southern states into the harsh northern climate; accelerating the growth of vegetables; husbandry and improving the quality of different breeds of animals; monitoring the health of forests; and comments on horticulture and improving architecture. Marsh also referred to those in his audience involved with the mechanical trades who made "the greatest progress in these and other modern improvements [that] should have been made by persons not bred to agricultural pursuits." He endorsed their efforts and strongly advocated for additional improvements because of the positive effects the new technology provided and gently prodded his audience to abandon their biases and prejudices hesitant to acknowledge their value. "The farmer," he told them, "should esteem the mechanic arts in an eminent degree worthy of patronage and encouragement, especially in a country whose yet undeveloped natural resources are so boundless and diversified. It is by these arts alone, that those internal improvements can be effected." He contended that "The mechanic arts are worthy of patronage from their progressive character, and the promise they hold out to us of acquiring a complete mastery over inanimate nature. The progress of agriculture, within the last half century though great in itself and full of future promise, has been but a tardy movement, in comparison with the swift advancement of the mechanic arts." Vermont must have the mechanics and their railroads and Marsh urged the creative farmers, who also engaged in mechanical-related activities, to recognize and embrace their common goals as he warned them to consider the alternative should they not do so. "Suppose we were at once to be deprived of these great gifts of mechanic art," he asked, "and suddenly cut off. . . and what efforts and sacrifices should we not be ready to encounter to regain them?"

Cognizant of the impending arrival of a form of modernity the state had never experienced in the past, Marsh then revealed further his deep, inquisitive mind as he pivoted and envisioned what this all meant for the coming years. "Yet we may well judge of the future from the past," he said, "and the progress of natural knowledge, upon which all mechanical art is founded, authorizes us to expect that the remaining half of the nineteenth century will be as fertile in improvements as the portion of it which has already elapsed." "The mechanic arts are eminently democratic in their tendency," he explained, because "They popularize knowledge, they cheapen and diffuse the comforts and elegancies as well as the necessaries of life, they demand and develop intelligence in those who pursue them, they are at once the most profitable customers of the agriculturist, and the most munificent patrons of the investigator of nature's laws."

IMPROVEMENT

Marsh's probing call for unity among the laboring and creative members of the farming community with those pursuing the new technology acknowledged the presence of an early rift becoming increasingly apparent in Vermont society because of the railroad technology. "The herdsman, the ploughman and the mechanic," he told them, "are fellow laborers, not indeed competitors, but co-workers in a common cause, and every measure that tends to elevate any one of them at the expense of another, must in the end infallibly prove detrimental to the best interests of them all." In arguing for the interdependency of the agricultural and mechanic interests, Marsh gave expression to a similar observation made decades earlier by one of the state's founders. In 1798, Ira Allen described the difficulty he had in distinguishing certain roles of Vermonters who worked within the agricultural community. "I am really at a loss in the classification of the inhabitants," he wrote, "they are all farmers, and again every farmer is a mechanic in some line or other, as inclination leads or necessity requires. The hand that guides the plow frequently constructs it."[99] Allen also took deep offense that anyone could believe that Vermonters, because of the primitive ways they established a civilization in their forested mountain environment, suffered from any creative deficiency. Vermont was not a "little sucking state" to be looked down on, he said proudly, because the "mechanic arts are not in their infancy" and have resulted in "new roads... every day extending, bridges erecting, population advancing, agriculture improving, towns multiplying, and rivers marked out as objects worthy of inland navigation." To the extent that the farming and mechanic arts evolved and separated, becoming more specialized in the next five decades, Marsh's more recent observations admonished the Rutland farmers that the combination of the efforts of the husbandman and his cows, the plowman and his oxen and horses, and the mechanic and his railroads combining together had more importance than any one working apart from the other. The entrepreneurial inventor-farmers among his audience certainly

George Perkins Marsh, c. 1850. Library of Congress.

welcomed his message which their resistant neighbors also needed to hear because the traditions of their forefathers they followed to this time had either forfeited relevance or needed significant revision to meet the approaching challenges and benefits that the railroad technology posed.[100] Marsh's comments, only a short time before the engines arrived in Rutland on tracks then being surveyed as they penetrated into Vermont's countryside, marks an important moment that acknowledges the impending presence of forward-looking modernity and the farming community's need to minimize its reliance on past practices in order to improve their circumstances.

British scholar and historical archaeologist Sarah Tarlow considers the period between the mid-eighteenth and mid-nineteenth centuries as a time when conscious efforts at improvement became obvious. She instructs not to confuse Improvement with modernity *per se*. Instead, Improvement is a "characteristic" of modernity that differs from Progress.[101] Whereas Progress, she writes, "is a historical current by which passive humans are swept along; Improvement is strategic, active and was seen as a moral and ethical obligation."[102] She regards Improvement as an affirmative, conscious, directed social effort sponsored mainly by crusading educated members of the middle-class aimed at bettering their lives and who recognized the importance of what they did at the time, not in retrospect. The introduction of another aspect of the phenomenon dependent on physical changes that those efforts sponsored evolved in the 1780s and became known as "internal improvements." American historian John Lauritz Larson regards that movement as one that involved programs designed "to encourage security, prosperity, and enlightenment among the people of the new United States." At first, it dealt with expanding a network of roads, canals, schools and technological innovations aimed at alleviating the most pressing needs of the time. Its focus gradually "narrowed" until it became "synonymous with public works" devoted to improving transportation, principally the railroad, in order to remedy the isolation of distant citizens.[103] The general process of Improvement has come to assume its own individual importance for historians who identified it in many arenas through its material aspects, most notably on the landscape and its resulting impact on the people who occupy it. This appeared in a variety of ways that included the layout of towns and cities, diverse agricultural practices with the ability to affect demographics and the creation of specialized institutions to accommodate the population's needs, such as workhouses and prisons, architecture and the formation of utopian communities. These physical manifestations of improvement on the landscape also reveal deeper aspects of a society's ideology, morality, class structure, perceptions of beauty, and economic, moral and religious practices. In the Vermont of the 1840s and 1850s, no greater example of improvement exists from both the personal and public works perspectives defined by Tarlow and Larson than the titanic presence of the railroad. It alone unleashed a myriad of change that Marsh strongly trumpeted to the agricultural community when he admonished it to be flexible and accommodate it because the future would not allow them to do otherwise.

Aesthetics and Improvement: Where to Locate the Capital

An important, subjective aspect of improvement that entered into the Vermont legislators' debates in 1857 concerned the amorphous aspects of physical beauty and its effect in directing whether the capital should move from Montpelier. Vermont would certainly rebuild the statehouse itself, but as the solons debates ranged, and raged, with "insinuations and threats" over a variety of concerns, none was more contentious than whether or not the town should continue to host the new structure.[104] The jolt of the effects of the railroad among them propelled a new appreciation, a maturation of sorts, of things aside from technology and now offered them the opportunity to consider the prospect that aesthetics presented. The issue concerning the site of the capital remained a lingering one, raised repeatedly after 1805 during debates in 1816, 1826, 1832 and 1853 that saw Montpelier as the generally preferred, if only by compromise, site. The reasoning behind the initial decision of an earlier generation to make it the location was not because of its pleasing aspects, but, rather, in recognition of the base sectionalism they experienced. To diminish its impact, they agreed to locate the capital close to the state's geographic center, a place described as "on neither the east nor the west side of the Green Mountains' and where no one "could claim any great advantage over the other."[105] Montpelier represented, as one representative said, "a compromise, to preserve the peace of the people."[106] He believed that maintaining the capital in a central location had become such an important inalienable privilege of Vermonters that it must remain so. "The *rights* of the people are concerned in this matter," he said because "it is not *right* to force any portion of the people to go beyond the common centre in order to gratify or favor other sections." It worked for their fathers and grandfathers and fifty years of their traveling to the middle of the state instilled in the population a leveling belief that whatever physical hardships they encountered in going to Montpelier were ones that everyone shared equally. In turn, decades of that practice allowed them to become so deeply familiar with the Montpelier community that it instilled in them the belief that they owed an abiding "moral obligation" to remain and not abandon it for some other place because of the fire, a tragedy for which the town had no responsibility.[107]

But in a surprising revelation, before any debates commenced, senators conducted a non-binding straw poll to decide where they thought the best location for the capital should be. In a telling vote, Burlington (with 12 votes) topped the list, followed by Montpelier (11) and then one each for Rutland, Middlebury, White River Junction, Clarendon, Castleton and Bellows Falls.[108] While in the House some sought to move directly towards the rebuilding the statehouse in Montpelier, others refused until they could consider its relocation. Over the next several days, sixteen senators and twenty-eight representatives took to the floor, arguing in favor of moving to other towns because of the benefits that the railroad technology promised: Bellows Falls, Brattleboro, Burlington, Middlebury and Rutland. As one representative observed, "Whatever inconveniences ever attended the intercourse of the people on opposite sides of the State, the railroads have destroyed it entirely."[109] Montpelier's status had come under serious assault and its future as the state's capital not assured.

Those who favored a location other than Montpelier, derisively called "a hole in the mountains" and the damp location where the destroyed building stood "not a house on a mountain, but a house under a hill," argued that it had simply outlasted its usefulness. They found traveling there an inconvenience because the nearby Central Vermont Railroad did not service it directly and required a mile-long spur adding another step to complete the journey. The new technology's ability to collapse all perceptions of time and space had created such change in the minds of Vermonters in the short time since its arrival that everyone carefully measured how far, fast and long it took for them to complete their travels.[110] One legislator described their wonder at the new technology that announced its presence by "the shrill whistle of the Iron Horse" traveling at the "lightning speed" of "thirty or forty miles an hour" hauling wool, hay, iron, marble and slate to market as passengers comfortably lounged in "magnificent" cars.[111] Concepts of time and distance had already changed in the past two decades as other advances in transportation and communication improved and impacted the landscape itself. "Canals, steamboats, railroads, magnetic telegraphs, crowded together in the span of one man's life" had thoroughly disrupted people's comfort and familiarity with the past. Now, with the "breathless rapidity" that these newer inventions allowed, causing even disinterest in canals, "calculations of distance," a period observer described, "will be overland; they will no longer follow the lines of water communication" and "no more be disturbed by the seasons."[112]

The sounds and smells accompanying the new technology also transmitted a sense of immediacy and undeniable enthusiasm promising increased industry in ways that differed radically from the past. Whereas work and the speed of communications were dictated by the abilities of beasts of burden, accompanied by blasts of bugles that announced the arrival of stagecoaches, the air was now filled with new sensations. The traipsing of large numbers of unwashed workmen speaking their Irish brogue carrying picks and shovels marching through villages in the early morning hours on their way to work, lumbering and speeding trains belching steam and screeching on iron rails sending out their piercing whistles, the incessant clanging of warning bells in depot yards as switches shuttled cars about, and the grinding of new steam-driven machines in foundries and shops offered a variety of ways for the population to experience sounds, smells, and tactile sensations their forebears never imagined.[113]

Because of these impressive new changes in the challenging Green Mountain landscape and their effects on the population, the debate on the location of the capital focused on other geographical considerations to take it out of its "hole in the mountains." They faced a challenge because, of the six New England states, four of the ten highest mountain peaks rose up within its borders: Mount Mansfield (4,393 feet), Killington Peak (4,235 feet), Jay Peak (3,858 feet), and Equinox Mountain (3,850 feet). "Vermont topography," one Vermont historian has described, "is naturally rural, providing no vast watersheds to urban places, no mountain-flat land junctures at which people might cluster, and no seaports in which to mass the paraphernalia of urbanism."[114] Until they could overcome these limitations and the challenges presented by its north-south undulations between the peaks and valleys and down to Lake Champlain's ninety foot elevation, Vermonters faced the imposing difficulties and inconveniences that the stark physical forces of vertical gravity and horizontal friction played in their pursuit of speed and ease in order to accommodate the demands of the railroad.

The effects of the mountains on the dispersal of the state's population also played a role in the debates. In 1850, an estimated 136,000 people lived on the west side of the Green Mountains and 178,000 on the east where, one speaker stated, they possessed "a preponderance of the wealth."[115] These realities required that the legislators entertain, in their often political posturing, proposals from other locations of lesser renown seeking the capital that included Berkshire, Bolton, Bradford, Castleton, Clarendon, Groton, Island Pond, Northfield, Norwich, Randolph, White River Junction and Woodstock. For the others with smaller populations unable to sponsor such an ambitious undertaking it became imperative, one speaker in favor of Montpelier said, to acknowledge and address their interests so that the state would "be regulated by the interests of the whole people, not of a few large towns." Recognizing the presence of rising sectionalism among them, the proposals by the larger towns, he said, "are injurious to the small towns which cannot bid, and tend to monopolize and centralize the favors of the State in a few large towns." "No town, however humble," he warned, "should be depressed for the sake of favoring these large towns."[116]

Some in favor of maintaining the status quo on Montpelier's behalf advanced other creative arguments aimed at not abandoning their mountain location. "Most of our people live in the mountains," one said, "and they are satisfied to have their laws made in a like place. Where is the man that would be rid of the Green Mountains?"[117] For him, "the mountains tend to make the State perpetual." Another regarded Vermont as the Switzerland of America and proudly asserted that that country should call itself the "Vermont of Europe." "Let the mountains stand, in God's name" he argued, "for it is in His name that they *do* stand, and will stand. They have their functions to perform hereafter. Let us not defeat the objects of their creation."[118] The legislators frequently resorted to scripture as one recited John 4:20 in support of the capital remaining in the higher elevations. "Our fathers worshipped in this mountain," he said with emphasis, "not bowing themselves to the Adirondacks across the Lake, nor to the White Hills of St. Johnsbury; but THIS MOUNTAIN – the Green Mountain Range."[119] When Westford's representative John A. Woodward argued instead in favor of Burlington, Thomas E. Powers from Woodstock ridiculed him as a "Pelican in the Wilderness" and invoked Psalm 102:6 for the visage of a forlorn "bird in the midst of desolation" crying out.[120]

Not all agreed to their remaining in the mountains and one legislator, shrugging off tradition and embracing the new technology, provided perhaps the most compelling reasons for removal to Burlington. While he believed the capital should locate at a "*common centre,*" he redefined it as a "centre of *travel*" and not geography. "The mode of travel has changed entirely," he told his fellow solons, as "the steam-whistle is now heard instead of the driver's whip, and the people of nearly the whole State are accommodated by railroads." He viewed relocation as a pragmatic decision: "Give me the place where the tide of travel from the different portions of the State indicates that it is the centre of accommodation, both as it regards ingress and egress. This is such a centre as the people need." Neither did examples from other states and countries aid those arguing for the geographical center. Reciting the locations of the capitals of Massachusetts (Boston), New York (Albany), the United States (Washington, D.C.), England (London) and France (Paris), he stated that none of them sat at a geographical center. "Commerce, business, travel, *everything,* make these a practical common center, far more convenient than any geographical centre that could be found, in the interior, away from travel and business."[121]

Legislators repeatedly invoked subjective interpretations of beauty in favor of their particular location as one practically observed aesthetics as "a comparative term" that depended "upon the medium through which an object is viewed."[122] For proof, another referred his listeners to consider Woodstock native Hiram Power's acclaimed marble sculpture, the female nude "Greek Slave" (1844), and the different perceptions of beauty it instilled in its viewers. "Some men will talk about the figure... and not see anything to admire," he said, "while others will linger... hour after hour, seeing new beauties and fine touches of art that entrance and enrapture the whole soul with delight."[123] Montpelier possessed its own unique form of beauty some said and tried to divert attention from the noticeable amount of fog that accumulated in the town. "Here," one solon stated, "in the center of Vermont, are the variegated hues of our Autumn forests, the refreshing greenness of both sharp and undulating hills, the brilliancy of the purest running water, that quick succession of hill and vale that is peculiarly and largely Vermont."[124]

Others argued that beauty also resided in the lesser appreciated parts of the state, in places that most would regard as "quite inferior to that of Montpelier." "Wells River," one speaker suggested, "is a little cooped up place, nestled between a high bank and a river on one side, and a ridge close in the rear, covered with evergreens, on the other. Between the bluffs that surround the village, there is what would be regarded as scant elbow-room." Despite those disadvantages, he continued, "A landscape painter – a great lover of natural scenery – visited that place a few years ago; and from an elevation, which overlooks the whole landscape, took his survey of it. He stood there and feasted his eyes, and luxuriated upon the beauties of the village – declaring it to be the most beautiful of any thing of the kind he ever saw." "But another man," he observed, "might drive into Wells River, and discover nothing there but inducements to drive on and get out of the place as quick as possible. There is all this difference between men regarding the beauties of nature and art. One sees the greatest beauty, where another sees none at all."[125] Another listed additional attributes and argued that Castleton provided the ideal location because its "beauty, soil, water, grass, sun-light, and beautiful ladies especially" could not be exceeded by any other.[126] Other comparisons to the marital contract also entered into the debates when some who believed the capital should remain in Montpelier equated their relationship to a fifty-year marriage that could not be easily abandoned. But with the destruction of the Capitol another member observed that Burlington had suddenly appeared in the form of a "handsomer woman" enticing the solons to separate and move in with her.[127] While concepts of beauty provided moments of light entertainment for the legislators, one of them seriously inquired, in this atmosphere of national division on the issue of slavery, if it served as an appropriate basis on which to make their important decision. "Can beautiful scenery," he asked, "allay the bitterness of sectional jealousies? Has it the potent alchemy to transmute the deadly poison of sectionalism in legislation, into a healing balm?"[128] He did not think so and the Civil War began in four short years.

Despite their long debates, only two locations outside of Montpelier achieved serious consideration: Burlington on the east shore of Lake Champlain and Rutland sixty miles to the south. The physical attributes and ready availability of the railroad in each town brought support to both, but the extent of their respective development, and the reasons for it, underlay the legislators' arguments. The explosive growth and change in Rutland compared to Burlington in the years leading up to the fire propelled by the arrival of the railroad and its accompanying technology, drew their close attention. As one town historian described the situation in 1852, the financial impact of the railroad on Rutland's economy "was immense." "Land that had been sold at sixty dollars an acre [in 1847 when it became incorporated as a town] had risen to $2,500-$3,000 an acre. Even woodland several miles distant had quadrupled in price."[129] An assessment of the dramatic architectural changes that suddenly appeared on that land with the erection of "hundreds of new buildings" in the trendy Italianate and Second Empire styles reflected Rutland County's experiencing "a more positive economic impact. . . than anywhere else in Vermont" because of the railroad.[130]

Rutland's population also increased a remarkable amount far above the other two communities most directly affected by the railroad, growing one hundred per cent between 1850 and 1860 (3,715 to 7,577) compared to Burlington's 25% (6,110 to 7,713) and Bellows Falls' negligible increase (2,837 to 2,904).[131] The evidence of Rutland's undeniable economic success compared to other towns confirmed its high ranking when, between 1850 and 1856, the town's taxable base increased seventy-nine percent and the county's twenty-seven percent. Compared to Burlington's four percent increase (Chittenden County at six percent) and Montpelier's twenty-six percent (Washington County at thirty percent), Rutland became the most serious contender to host the capital.[132] In 1860 its marble quarries employed more than 600 men, four times more than in 1850.[133] At the 1870 celebration of Rutland's centennial, attorney Warren H. Smith boasted of the town's recent growth and called it "unequaled in Vermont, and unsurpassed in New England."[134] The promise of further development continued in the next years and by 1880 the town had become the largest in Vermont (12,149) and as late as 1937 its effects continued to display "the vigor which her railroad gave. Rutland, more typically than either of her rivals [Burlington and Barre at the time] is the small American city."[135] Rutland consistently earned admirable approval and deserved attention because of what the new technology delivered in its favor. A period tract acknowledged that fact and glowingly labeled the settlement as "an old and wealthy town, ranking as the second in agricultural produce, and the first in mineral productions in the State. . . . Large manufactures of iron, leather, cabinet furniture, marble, slate and slate-pencils, are in operation and getting under way here, and the town is doubling in population, at the rate of once in three years."[136]

Burlington unquestionably had a beautiful location in its favor, looking west across its impressive breakwater onto Lake Champlain, where steamers plied the waters between it and New York canals, and to the Adirondacks beyond, accompanied by its notable development with the University of Vermont occupying the prominent overlooking hill, the state's customs house, marine hospital, and nunnery.[137] But the remarkable growth taking place in Rutland is what drew the legislators attention instead. "Why sir," one speaker asked when considering Burlington as the capital's location, "If Rutland continues to increase in wealth and population for twenty-five years to come as she has for the last ten years, and Burlington decreases as she has for the last five years, what a contrast there will be between the two places." The situation would be entirely reversed, he predicted, and "Rutland will say to Burlington, as Burlington says to Montpelier, 'Come down here among us where the people live,' and bring down the State House, for we are more deserving of it – are nearer the center of the State, and are in fact the Young America of Vermont. And Rutland would have as good a claim upon Burlington, as Burlington now professes to have upon Montpelier."[138] No other location in Vermont drew the attention that Rutland did and sixty-two petitions from members of the public, many with dozens of signatures accompanying them, endorsed that choice; excepting one for Montpelier and two for Northfield. Modernity had unquestionably arrived in robust fashion in Rutland and it presented a serious consideration by the state's representatives.

Explosive population growth and a markedly increased tax base, both attributed to the new technology of the railroad, did not present the only evidence of Rutland's escalating stature. The physical landscape itself had changed in radical ways that reflected the progressive, forward-thinking of railroad and local officials. Other towns also experienced enforced adaptation in their layout to accommodate the railroad technology, but

Rutland's presents perhaps the most notable example and is a microcosm of the challenges they all faced. No other location had the kinds of mineral resources that Rutland possessed, located so close to the new form of transportation, in demand by a worldwide market. Other towns may have acted as convenient nodes for goods to pass through, but only Rutland made them so readily available at their source.

CONCLUSION

To assess the importance of these rapidly converging aspects of an increasingly complex capitalist economy, the Vermont landscape provides a rich resource to understand both the course of the railroad and its impact on the population. Landscapes provide multiple opportunities to examine the interactions brought about by human activity and they display "the richest historical record we possess."[139] Because they do not stand in isolation from each other, settlement patterns conform to the geography they encounter. This in turn creates unique aspects of the developing culture that occupies it and reveals the continuing change affecting it over the course of time.[140] Railroads, in particular, provide a unique means in understanding the values and cultural aspects of a society. They have a "profound impact" on "national destinies, the growth of cities, and the texture of everyday life."[141] Because of their specialized engineering needs, railroads physically impose exacting demands on the landscape that allow them to function effectively but which restrict them to certain routes because of the particular terrain they encountered.[142] Those areas that spatially permit the development of large accompanying infrastructure, such as railyards, increased the need to make deliberate and conscious decisions that concern their layout and to then manipulate the landscape accordingly.[143] These dynamic efforts significantly affect the surrounding area to include that needed by workers for living space and who become employees of the railroad dependent upon its success for their own wellbeing. This in turn creates the need for supporting infrastructure of civic structures, churches, schools, hospitals and more.

Evidenced by the many legislators' arguments, the improving aspects that the railroad presented caused a substantial impact on the Vermont population. While not acknowledged by them, it also imposed a hardship on the landscape itself wherever it penetrated; a fact that George Perkins Marsh soon attacked in the coming years. Beyond contributing to the stripping of its forested hillsides (compounding that attributed to the declining sheep industry) for ties to support its steel rails and to fuel its engines, the blasting of its mountain sides, grading, digging and filling in of its low spots and bridging its waters to accommodate its needs, its effects extended deeper down to the local level. It profoundly affected the formation of towns, the distribution of their inhabitants and the way they conducted their lives, as well as into the surrounding farming community. Students have exhaustively investigated the larger story of the complex merging and diverging of various railroads, corporate structuring, and restructuring, and convoluted financing, and refinancing, of Vermont's railroads beginning in the 1840s and lasting into the twentieth-century. But the finer experiences of the Rutland community that brought together the dynamic aspects of improvement caused by the railroad are the ones that command further attention. They are also the ones that had the full attention of the Vermont legislature in 1857 as it grappled with whether to upend its traditional reliance on Montpelier as the state's capital or to take it elsewhere.

CHAPTER II

Steaming into the Green Mountains

"The entire change in modes of conveyance have taken away what ground there originally was for building in Montpelier as a geographical center. Rutland [is] eminently easy of access by rail road from all parts of the state – the country [is] open and beautiful, none in Vermont more so."[144]

REPRESENTATIVE JUDGE ROBERT PIERPOINT OF RUTLAND, **February 20, 1857**

STRATEGY AND LOCATION: RUTLAND AS A RAILROAD CENTER

"Rail and rock" laid the foundation for Rutland's explosive population growth as it expanded in response to the demands of a burgeoning New England railroad system and reconfigured itself to accommodate the arrival of six lines running into the community in the 1850s.[145] One historian flippantly characterized the early days of the Rutland Railroad as "originally going from nowhere to nowhere, desperately trying to get somewhere," but a closer examination suggests much more nuance.[146] Instead, Rutland's contributions to the state's developing rail network became a critical aspect of several efforts to connect the Atlantic coast economy with the country's interior. Rutland became an important hub as part of a "four hundred mile pathway to siphon the riches of the [Great] lakes to the greatest seaport in New England" transporting cargo across Vermont to Boston via Ogdensburg on the St. Lawrence River in northern New York.[147] In 1852, Vermont became an integral part of the country's overall strategy to allow the entire Great Lakes basin to "communicate directly" with Atlantic ports by "avoiding the obstructions, the delays, and the winter embargo of the St. Lawrence."[148]

The railroad also served as the great equalizer among all the New England states as the emphasis in railroad building shifted westward in the 1840s. In 1849 an observer described the flow of populations for the past ten years and predicted that while "the greatest increase has been in Maine, and the least in Vermont," future increases would occur in the west and that New England would become "relatively more uniform [because] the same causes which will promote the prosperity of one will operate upon all. Maine and Vermont will no longer have the advantage, as before, of being new States." Settlement patterns began to stabilize in New England and he explained that new "manufactories in Massachusetts, Rhode Island, and Connecticut [have] had a tendency to change the tide of emigration, and its present tendency is rather *to*, than *from*, the old States. The more intimate connection now made between them, by means of railroads, will tend to give them a more uniform prosperity, and to develop more equally their resources."[149]

Main St., Rutland, looking south showing the courthouse with large cupola and Franklin Hotel immediately beyond, 1852. Rutland Historical Society.

Whatever stability other New England towns might experience in the 1840s waited to arrive in Rutland for several years. In 1848, a traveler passing through the village before the railroad established itself described it as "pleasantly situated on elevated ground" with "a court-house and jail, a bank, 3 churches, 15 stores, and about 150 dwelling-houses and is a place of considerable trade, being surrounded by a rich section of country."[150] Shortly after the statehouse fire, and years after the town embraced the new technology, the accolades on Rutland's behalf were repeated to a tourist audience as "a pleasant town. . . situated in the midst of some of the finest of the Vermont hill and valley scenery, at the foot of the western slope of [the Green Mountains]" and touted it for the many railroads that converged and connected from there "to all points of the compass." Other forms of communication also centered in Rutland as the New York City-based

American Telegraph Company established its lone Vermont office at the "R. R. Depot."[151] In only a few short years, Rutland had firmly established itself as a center of activity in the state that connected state-of-the-art technology with far-off locations and allowed it to gain considerable attention as it also incorporated a growing, diverse population into its midst.

Rutland unabashedly incorporated everything that the railroad could provide. In the process, as occurred in some other Vermont towns, it became necessary to accommodate its demands by physically uprooting virtually every important aspect of its past life to relocate them from one traditional, long-established location to another, out onto a nearby, low-lying twenty-five-acre tract of land.[152] While other towns also experienced some benefit from their adaptive changes, none had the dramatic impact of what occurred in Rutland. The town's first meaningful settlement took place immediately after the Revolutionary War on terraced land overlooking the Otter Creek floodplain to its west. The first road built in 1779 followed the elevated land in a north-south direction that passed in front of the wooden stockade Fort Rutland. Here, officials "laid out a highway. . . six rods wide in the easterly part of said town on and nigh the road that leads from Pittsford [Fort Vengeance] to Clarendon."[153] It also intersected with the east-west Crown Point Road (1759) that connected Charlestown, New Hampshire on the Connecticut River with the east shore of Lake Champlain at Chimney Point opposite Crown Point. In the next decades, various businesses, a church, post office, and courthouse rose up on the east side of Main Street where a developing transportation network converged connecting southern towns to the northern frontier. The Great Road that ran from Boston to Montreal, the West Road leading from the town to Castleton and then Troy, New York and a turnpike that headed east to Woodstock intersected at the village where heavy stage traffic concentrated at the Franklin Hotel adjacent to the courthouse. The early traveling legislature also met in Rutland on occasion at the nearby "State House" on West Street and it became one of the most important towns in the state attracting many notables to take up residency and build their new homes along Main Street. Rev. Samuel Williams, the state's first historian, lived there and contributed funds that allowed for the creation of a village green on the west side of the street in 1790. He went on to found the *Rutland Herald* and write and publish the first edition of *The Natural and Political History of Vermont* in 1794.[154]

The residents of Rutland's shiretown village and county occupied a region blessed with an abundance of easily accessible geological resources that determined their future course because of the railroad. The ambitious entrepreneurs among them, unafraid of hard work, exploited the opportunities that marble, slate, copperas, iron ore, asbestos, gold, limestone, quartz, and a variety of other minerals presented as they erected many manufacturing establishments to process it. Quarries and mills that serviced and added value to their products opened in many county towns that had a significant impact on the decisions of railroad managers selecting their routes in order to facilitate loading and transporting the heavy, cumbersome products. Pittsford (two quarries opened in 1795 and 1799), Rutland (1804), West Rutland and Middletown Springs (1807), Tinmouth (1821), Clarendon (1825), Castleton (1830), Brandon (1831 and 1840), Center Rutland (1839 and 1844), Sudbury (1847), and Wallingford (1848) represent a portion of the many quarries that attracted attention before the railroad arrived.[155] The *Rutland Herald* newspaper made certain that the world knew of these advantages and touted the region's mineral wealth as a reason to bring the railroad to the community. "Marble, Iron, and manganese are found in abundance on the Rutland route. . . . Five marble mills are now in process of erection in the county of Rutland, three of which are to be furnished from quarries in the town of Rutland, capable of cutting 650 tons each annually," it described. Nearby towns also had "slate of an unequalled quality for pencils. . . in the town of Castleton, and now manufactured to a considerable extent, at Rutland. A superior article of graphic slate is found in any quantity in Fairhaven, and the manufacture of slates is about being entered upon extensively. Roofing slate is also found in abundance at the same place, and a quality equal to any other." The newspaper also extolled that "Soapstone is found upon the route, and serpentine of a most beautiful quality. We have copperas too.... More than one third of all wool produced in Vermont is grown in the counties of Rutland and Addison. Rutland county ... has the largest Grand List in the State ... and the largest dairy products."[156] The Rutland route was the best, it continued in another article describing its existing infrastructure, "with greater resources for production of business and freight than any and every other part of Vermont, with 16 cotton and woolen factories, with ten Bloomeries which this year will make some 6500 tons of bar and block iron, and capable of a greatly increased production, with 8 blast and pot furnaces, pouring out almost a continuous stream of melted iron, (those of Brandon and Pittsford producing the last year 2600 tons) and with fifteen marble mills capable of cutting at least 6000 tons annually. . . and with the capacity to multiply this kind of freight and to extend our business to any amount which the market will warrant." "Let us work then," it ended, "for the time has come."[157]

Sheldons, Morgan and Mason Marble Company, West Rutland, one of Rutland County's largest quarries, 1851. Rutland Historical Society.

Similarly, to the north of Rutland, members of the recently-formed Brandon Railroad Association demanded their own access to outside markets to get these materials transported out of the state via the railroad and expressed their impatience at its delayed arrival in emphatic terms.

Speaking to its members, President John A. Conant urgently called for "the immediate necessity of *action,* deliberate, but vigorous and untiring action in order to [ensure] its success." Another speaker endorsed those sentiments and described the effects that the railroad would have "upon our business and our products, both of which would start into new life and be greatly increased." "It was," he said, "as certain as any law of trade, that such increase would follow any improvement in the means, or reduction of the cost of transportation."[158]

VERMONT'S LAISSEZ-FAIRE ATTITUDE

If Vermont state government did not have sufficient financial resources, or interest, to assist in conducting the necessary geological survey to aid its constituents in exploiting their natural resources to the fullest extent possible, then business interests quickly filled the vacuum. The entrepreneurs welcomed the notable lack of government oversight they found uniquely infused into Vermont's way of life. "Free from the debts (and voters) that hobbled state authorities, men with money to invest took over internal improvements" in the 1840s and vigorously pursued the steam-driven railroad technology.[159] Vermont government, unhesitant to proclaim to the world, took great pride in its singular caution to limit intervention in its citizens' lives. As Governor Horace Eaton confidently stated in 1846, "Perhaps no state in the confederacy has been characterized by greater simplicity in its legislation and government than has the state of Vermont. The line of policy. . . has been to govern as little as might be consistent with the protection of her citizens and the advancement of their substantial interests." He explained that while the state had "extended her favoring smiles and fostering care to all useful enterprises calculated to promote the general good. . . she has never yet sought to assume the special and exclusive guardianship even of public and common interests when they could be adequately sustained and promoted in any other way."[160] Three years later, Governor

Carlos Coolidge acknowledged that, despite the persistent changes taking place, the "spirit of the age," in apparent reference to temperance efforts to curb the state's consumption of alcohol, required caution when passing new laws. He admonished the legislature to remain watchful when it considered intervening in people's lives. "I submit," he said, "that prudence demands a steadfast opposition to every legal change which is radical, until its necessity shall be made manifest."[161] Vermont government's cautious, self-satisfied, extremist policy that abhorred proactive measures to protect the public and refused to intrude into its inhabitants' lives created an environment that invited much of the discord that enveloped the railroad industry and other aspects of life in the coming decades.

In this uninhibited atmosphere, two railroads sought authority to traverse Vermont's landscape as they competed vigorously with each other, one headed by Burlington's Timothy Follett and the other by Charles Paine of Northfield. Huge battles raged between the two for sole authority, but, unwilling to hazard alienating the many followers of each interest, the legislature took the middle road and chartered both in 1843. According to Ambrose Lincoln Brown, the man who took the lead in transforming Rutland's landscape in the next years and a future railroad commissioner, "perfect apathy pervaded the Legislature" when it made this pivotal decision. He reported that many of the representatives and senators deciding between the two factions simply remained uninterested in advocating on the behalf of "any such chimerical projects as building railroads along and *over* our mountains." He recalled that a senator "who had been persuaded to introduce one of the bills. . . confessed that he never read the bill, as he had no confidence in the project. And this gentleman was by no means alone or singular in this opinion."[162]

Unlike other states giving serious consideration to the future effects in accommodating the new forms of corporate enterprise that the railroad industry represented, "perfect apathy" accurately describes only a part of the Vermont lawmakers' indifference for its potential impact. A future legislator, and Civil War veteran who led Vermont troops in defense of Union barricades during Pickett's charge at Gettysburg, Senator Albert Clarke recalled in 1874 this earlier period with great distress because of the unforeseen consequences that their disinterest caused.[163] He identified October 23, 1843 as the moment when "Vermont ceased to be a free and independent state" because on that day it effectively surrendered its oversight responsibilities to the railroad corporations when it chose not to interpose its authority statutorily and thereby diminish generous provisions under consideration for their charters.[164] Significant opposition to any state intervention in railroad operations arose as some legislators vigorously contended that the threat of creating statutes allowing such oversight constituted both an intrusive violation of constitutionally protected contracts (U. S. Constitution, Art. 1, sec. 10) and could potentially harm future investments. If charters were impinged by the passage of such laws, the opponents argued strongly, they would "unquestionably deter capitalists of other states from [purchasing] stock, and thus this great enterprise for the public good would be defeated."[165]

Proponents of such laws, insistent in looking towards the future impact of the railroads and preserving the legislature's prerogative to exercise oversight of these new forms of corporations it created, thought the issue too obvious for debate. "If members were not prepared to act definitely now," one argued, he "hoped they would go home and consult their mothers." Another seconded his thought and believed that "the mothers of Vermont were too wise to saddle the state with such corporations." While the opponents to legislative intervention of the railroads' charters ultimately claimed victory, Clarke noted they only accomplished it "by a strict party vote." "Thus," he said, "the most important questions relating to our internal police that have ever come before the legislature were settled. . . not upon a pure and unalloyed consideration of their merits, but by the bare preponderance of one organization over another, banded together with reference to national issues alone."[166]

New Hampshire railroad advocate Charles Haddock explained to his Montpelier audience in 1844 why this legislative surrender of authority to corporations occurred and laid the fault at the inability of solons to fully anticipate, and their unwillingness to take responsibility for, the effects of their laws. Addressing official oversight of the railroads, he stated that "Scarcely an act of legislation, of any importance, can be said to be fully understood, in all its bearings and consequences, by the wisest politicians. Nothing is more common in history, than to find both the hopes and fears of sagacious and honest men disappointed; nothing more instructive, than to see how systems of public policy, which have been pursued with enthusiastic confidence, are, at last, disavowed and condemned by their advocates."[167] Though the legislature did eventually capitulate and establish a commissioner of railroads in 1856, but constricted with minimal authority to examine its operations, its otherwise pervasive hands-off policy meant it did nothing more to institute means to protect other aspects of Vermonters' lives. Those decisions placing the interests of capitalists and others outside of Vermont above those of its inhabitants soon affected the state's culture in many ways following the engines' arrival that involved their public safety, increasing evidence of drug abuse, exacerbated growing class distinctions, and harm to the environment.[168]

Days after "Vermont ceased to be a free and independent state" as Senator Clarke lamented, Follett obtained a charter for the Champlain and Connecticut River Rail Road Company and Paine received one for the Vermont Central Railway. While the Vermont Central's authority allowed it to extend north along the Connecticut River from Bellows Falls to White River Junction and northwest through Paine's hometown (allowing him to reap huge benefits) to reach the Winooski River and follow it to Burlington, the Champlain and Connecticut cut immediately diagonally northwest from Bellows Falls to Rutland and then north to Burlington.[169] For the latter route, following surveying expeditions in 1843 of corps of engineers accompanied by interested participants from Massachusetts, officials determined it possible to breach the challenging spine of the Green Mountains at Mount Holly (1511 feet) and then extend to Rutland.[170] From there to Burlington, the *Rutland Herald* touted, "for 80 miles, northerly the route is through an open, fertile, and highly cultivated territory, and with a surface very favorable to the construction of a railway. This route. . . passes through or near 24 villages some small, and many of them large and flourishing, and the immediate territory rather thickly settled."[171] The proposed path included passing through Brandon, Middlebury and other villages in Addison County along the route inhabited by many citizens clamoring for access to the new technology.

Other voices and the business interests in Rutland County made themselves heard to advance construction of the road. On January 12, 1846 the stockholders of the Fitchburg Railroad Company held their annual meeting in Boston to discuss ongoing efforts to connect their line with one in Vermont. Keen to gain access to northern markets, they deemed access to Rutland a critical part of their business plan. The stockholders agreed that the connection between Rutland and Burlington was "one of the most favorable lines in Vermont" and forecast, with emphasis, that "*Rutland* is to become – *if its citizens are alive to their own interest* – the *central* point in the 'Evergreen State.'" "Let the people of Rutland be awake and active," they warned, for "If they do not move in their *own* favor, others will not be very likely to act for them." In a second shareholders meeting conducted immediately afterwards at the request of "Nathan Rice, of Boston," they took an additional step to demonstrate their strong intention to establish a connection at Rutland. They resolved that, "We, as stockholders in the Fitchburg railroad company, many of us being also stockholders in the Cheshire railroad company, do greet with great pleasure and satisfaction the enterprize and public spirit now prevailing in western Vermont. . . . [and] hereby pledge ourselves to use our individual exertions to promote its success."[172]

Two days later, a huge meeting convened at Rutland's Main Street courthouse, led by Follett and the directors of the Champlain and Connecticut River Rail Road Company, that drew an estimated 2,000 residents, including Nathan Rice from Boston. The gathering drew so much public attention that "large numbers were unable to obtain admission" and the meeting was adjourned to the nearby North Church.[173] Upon reconvening, the attendees listened to William B. Gilbert, the principal surveyor retained in July 1845 to survey the line between Rutland and Burlington, provide his audience with "some very interesting and satisfactory statements" about his work. Nathan Rice ("whose presence was most cordially greeted") spoke next for one and one-half hours. "In an eloquent and most interesting and acceptable manner," he described the work of the Fitchburg railroad and conveyed the support of its shareholders' recent resolution favoring a connection with Rutland. At the conclusion of the meeting, enthusiastic directors unequivocally determined, and formally entered a resolution, that "we will have a rail road."[174] While he reported little of the substance of the meetings, the editor of the *American Railroad Journal* that published their brief accounts indicated that financing the project through stock offerings was also discussed. The future would bring much economic trouble for Vermont's railroads, but the excitement experienced by many during their formative years led them to purchase shares. For the *Journal's* editor, the prospect carried the potential for heavy loss and he warned purchasers to avoid doing so because of unbridled enthusiasm. "We say emphatically to the people of western Vermont," he cautioned, "*take* the stock yourselves, *as far as possible,* that you may have a controlling influence in its management, and thus be always able to avail yourselves of the advantages *and a choice* of the two great markets, Boston and New York without being under the control of *either.* Let it be a *Vermont* road, open to the use, and for the convenience of all, but *made* and *managed* by *Vermonters.*"[175] Well-intended at the time, his advice failed to predict the divisive effects within Vermont society when the interests of those able to purchase stock exercised their authority to the disadvantage of a less well-heeled rural farming community.

The attractive aspects of modernity, on Rutland's doorstep in 1846, encouraged its political and business leadership to turn volte face to position themselves favorably to exploit it fully.[176] They had only to look west from their high-terraced Main Street location down West Street, improved by the presence of only a few homes and businesses, that crossed over the north-flowing Otter Creek and connected them to Castleton and New York and where an intervening 150 acres of floodplain pastureland beckoned. The local leaders directed their immediate attention to this tract that the railroad did not own and thereby radically altered the community's way of life that had unfolded for the past several decades. The magician's wand began its sweep.

Preparing for Construction

In 1856, Charles Linsley, Vermont's first railroad commissioner (chosen from a field of over seventy applicants), issued a report briefly describing his impressions of the state's railroads. His legislative mandate required him to look into concerns over public safety because of the many injuries and deaths that occurred on the railroads, and their overall financial condition. A past member of the Rutland Railroad board of directors, Linsley did not seriously challenge the status quo in his assessments of corporate colleagues and exhibited great deference to their efforts while applauding the hands-off actions of the legislature towards the railroads, calling them "kindly and cherishing." His report instead focused largely on the physical condition of the roads themselves where noticeable deterioration had occurred, while expressing little interest in providing any meaningful analysis or guidance concerning public safety or their financial situation.

Even in the face of ample evidence of injuries and deaths inflicted by the railroad, Linsley made it clear that he did not foresee the necessity of any state intervention to correct the mayhem. Instead, he expressed an implicit policy should apply that embraced the concept of *caveat emptor* ("let the buyer beware") as he blamed travelers and the public for their own mishaps. His attitude reiterated a policy set in 1849 that placed responsibility on the traveling public when near any railroad crossing to obey signs posted pursuant to law warning it, in capital letters not less than twelve inches high, to *"Look out for the Engine."*[177] Even then, he lamented that "It is to be regretted that no warning is sufficient, to prevent passengers from attempting to get on and off from the trains, when in motion, from which so many fatal accidents occur." He further discounted any effort to either hold the railroads accountable for the public's injuries or insist that they work to minimize the problem. "No repairs or improvements ought to be required," he said, "which public safety does not clearly demand; for the state of their finances does not warrant the expenditure of money to please the eye; or for mere symmetry and finish." Many of the problems that people faced with the new technology could be attributed simply to a learning curve that everyone had to adapt to. "The introduction of any art," he wrote, "into a part of the country where it was not known and understood, has usually, in the outset been attended with disappointment and loss. . . . Railroads are not exempt from this law."[178]

Two years later, the intrepid George Perkins Marsh replaced Linsley as commissioner and issued a scathing assessment of the railroads that far exceeded any of his predecessor's mild expressions. "The Report will probably bring a hornet's nest about my ears," he wrote to his wife, "but I shall tell the truth at whatever cost."[179] Marsh agreed with a brief, deferential observation of Linsley's that the industry had insufficient oversight, but he went further and traced its reason to the distinctive way that Vermont viewed its role in caring for the affairs of its citizens. "The position of the government and people of this State," he wrote, "in relation to the railroads chartered by their authority is peculiar, and perhaps unique."[180] Because of the lack of accountability that the absence of laws allowed railroad managers, Marsh alleged that the money raised from the public to construct the roads "was partly squandered and wasted, if not pilfered." In the same unabashed, outspoken spirit he used when he appeared before the Agricultural Society of Rutland in 1847, Marsh unhesitatingly stated his unwavering opinion that, despite whatever reservations others might have in holding the railroads accountable, he had "no doubt of the legal power of the Legislature to subject railroad corporations. . . to such general regulations as the public, moral and material interests may demand." Marsh reassured his readers that while he did not intend to impugn the integrity of any particular company, "the railroads in Vermont are all imperfect in construction." Concerning the unrestricted way that the railroad had been built on the Vermont countryside, he held that "the lines have often been selected with little judgment, if indeed good faith." Marsh continued in this belief in following years when he gave full expression to his frustrations with the nation's railroads and their effects on the environment in his highly influential *Man and Nature; or, Physical Geography as Modified by Human Action*. "Railroad surveys," he wrote then, "must be received with great caution where any motive exists for *cooking* them." Railroad companies found it difficult to obtain financing when lenders faced the prospect of funding construction that crossed challenging landscapes and Marsh believed that their falsification of surveys to show obstruction-free routes would remove investors' concerns. He also remained deeply suspicious of any goodwill coming from railroad corporations and argued for their close supervision by state and national legislatures passing appropriate laws, measures that would not take place in Vermont for decades.[181]

Marsh did not identify any particular instance of questionable surveying in Vermont during the early 1850s that drew his ire and, in light of the care that the Champlain and Connecticut Rail Road board of directors exercised in their work between Bellows Falls and Burlington through Rutland, it does not seem possible. Notwithstanding the historical accounts written in hindsight that described the various railroads' ineptness, the extant minutes of the company's board of directors after 1846 provide an entirely opposite perspective. They reveal a sophisticated series of meetings where many issues attending the construction of the road were addressed with precision demonstrating great awareness, however overly optimistic, of the titanic difficulties before them. They also reflect a concern that members of the board not receive excessive compensation because they worked on the behalf of, as secretary Charles Linsley recorded, "a people to whom large salaries are unknown."[182] His recognition of the role that compensation played in the minds of the public were prescient as the railroad served as a defining force creating further class differences that crept into Vermont culture.[183] The board appointed Follett as the full-time superintendent and named Gilbert, who spoke before the Rutland crowd, "chief engineer to take charge of the construction of the road." They also employed agents "to procure title to lands" they needed to cross and assigned their military-experienced brethren to handle the delicate negotiations with landowners resistant to sell.

During the construction phase, the pragmatic board identified the geographical challenges the road faced between Burlington and Bellows Falls and broke it down into distinct sections entrusting each to contractors able to assure rapid progress. They entered into contracts with many construction firms that submitted bids for work on particular sections of the road. Time was critical as they needed to complete their assignments in order to join two other lines merging at the Rutland facility, the Western Vermont Railroad that connected the community with Bennington to the south that allowed access into western Massachusetts and the Rutland and Washington Rail Road that extended westward into New York. The work attracted a wide variety of individuals, including future railroad magnate Jay Gould who eventually took over the Rutland and Washington line in 1863 when he lived and worked out of Rutland's Bardwell Hotel.[184] Overall, this was not the slipshod enterprise that some historians have claimed, but one that the directors dealt with creatively and expansively in the face of the huge challenges that the railroad technology presented, while hampered by an expanding and contracting budget that made predicting their course into the future difficult.

In November 1847, the company changed its name to the Rutland & Burlington Railroad Company and became better known in the next decades as the Rutland Railroad.[185] Its chief engineer, William Bradford Gilbert, a Rome, New York native, graduated from Norwich University in 1828 and oversaw the road's surveying and construction. The timely arrival of the railroad technology allowed Gilbert and many of his engineering classmates to pursue important roles in developing the nation's railroad infrastructure in the coming decades.[186] The challenging work first required a survey that took into account the varying topographical elevations, the presence of obstacles such as waterways, wetlands and rock formations, and the physics that attended the actions of large amounts of heavy steam-driven steel rolling on slender rails that required calculating the radius of curves and banking needs of the rail bed. The contributions that Vermonters made in constructing the state's southern lines earned the glowing assessment of one national publication devoted to describing the progress of the country's railroads. That effort "has relied mainly," it recorded, "for its success upon the rich agricultural and manufacturing population of southern and western Vermont. There is scarcely any private enterprise within our knowledge that more fairly illustrates the tenacity of purpose and the unconquerable energy of the New England character."[187] Not everyone working for Gilbert had similar training and some initially came from the agricultural countryside attracted by the prospect of working in new endeavors.[188] These included the skilled and unskilled construction laborers, trackmen, section hands, watchmen, yardmen and shop hands required to service the many needs of locomotives and cars. For the most capable among them, opportunities might also allow them to work on the trains themselves as brakeman, conductor, fireman and engineer. With the exception of the valued engineer position, young men mainly filled the remaining jobs, with only a few staying beyond the age of fifty. Between the 1840s and 1860s "only half of all workers stayed on the job longer than six months, with yard and track laborers most transient," reflecting the region's "high rate of labor mobility." Irish and French-Canadian immigrants provided much of the backbreaking labor, and fewer than fifteen percent of them ever attained sufficient expertise to allow them to rise above their menial level.[189]

Gilbert's critical surveying work established the road's centerline on the landscape that defined a right of way of varying rod widths measured perpendicular on either side. It marked the course the roadbed would follow, alongside rivers whenever possible, where laborers leveled high spots, filled in the low ones, built culverts to divert water, and constructed bridges. The staked centerline became such an important reference point on the landscape that immediately after surveyors passed through land transactions adjacent to it recited its location in their own surveys and which included references to physical improvements later made in the Rutland rail yard such as the depot and service buildings near it. Documentation of Gilbert's work over the course of the 125-mile track north and south of Rutland and through the community have not survived, "said to have been destroyed when the Company's offices in Burlington were burned about 1850 or 1851."[190] Without the aid of those records, in 1893 the Rutland Railroad conducted an exhaustive effort to verify the work overseen by Gilbert and his engineers and assistants and concluded that there were significant reasons to question the quality of their effort. Because of the lack of corporate information available to him, the investigating chief engineer, Thomas Chappell of Rutland, made his assessment based on descriptions of the routes filed with the various clerks of the towns the railroad passed through and to previously unknown, hidden, dusty papers that survived conflagration and those discovered, squirreled away, at depots in Burlington, Middlebury and Rutland. From these sparse records, Chappell learned to his surprise that his predecessors had adopted "no uniform system" for their work over the entire line, using instead a variety of methods. While a survey with its stakes driven into the ground indicated the road's route, practical considerations arose when construction teams under the supervision of independent contractors conducted the work. Rushed laborers and their employers pressured by the railroads' managers to finish the work quickly inevitably led to those sweating under the demands to literally "cut corners" to meet the needs of the geography and work outside of the staked lines. In one instance of slow work on a section of the road in Rutland, the resident engineer wrote to the contacting company and demanded that the problem be addressed or it would be fired and a replacement substituted. Citing a popular 1843 minstrel song, he told them to speed up their work, "So 'get out of the way old Dan Tucker' the cars are coming."[191] Rutland town clerk Ambrose Lincoln Brown identified this aspect of the railroads' birth as a major factor that tarnished their collective reputation in later years. The problem, he described, did not rest with the boards of directors personally, but in their delegation of authority for particular sections of track, "including engineering, to the control. . . of the contractor." The neglect of the railroads' managers, consumed in their exuberance to finish the roads, Brown attributed more to a "want of knowledge and experience" than to a "want of integrity," a fault that also contributed to the "incompetency of the engineering department."[192]

Thomas Chappell's 1893 report also identified many instances where the road was "built outside" (and sometimes "far outside") of its described location filed with the town clerks. He found many of the filings "inaccurate, incomplete and inconsistent," which he attributed to "the many irregularities in the original numbers and errors in the original chaining [surveying]." Much of Chappell's accompanying work appears to have fallen victim to a 1909 fire in the upper floor and attic of the Rutland depot when "all the records of the Rutland railroad for a half century back was burned out."[193] In 1921, city officials faced the challenge of sorting out the accumulating damage caused by inaccurate property lines that dated back decades. They found many homes and businesses built on land that did not belong to their current occupants and attributed it to "faulty engineering and the destruction of reference points taken when various parts of the city were laid out."[194] How much of this trouble can be assigned to the earlier work conducted by Gilbert and his engineers remains unknown, but it probably played a role.

Condemnations: Seizing the Land

With a survey completed, no work could commence until the railroad managers received actual ownership of the land it crossed. Taking land from owners unwilling to relinquish it to the imposing technology presented a new phenomenon in the Vermont experience and violently awakened the state's inhabitants to modernity's demands. It also exemplified the legislature's hands-off policy ("perfect apathy" Railroad Commissioner Ambrose Lincoln Brown called it) of not intruding into decisions made by entrepreneurs pouring money into an infrastructure able to eliminate the isolation so many in the Green Mountains experienced. Eminent domain, or condemnation, until then a privilege conferred on governments, was one not available to private enterprise.[195] Vermont's 1793 Constitution held that the right of an inhabitant to maintain possession of his personal property was not subject to surrender except for compelling reasons and declared that it only "ought to be subservient to public uses when necessity requires it." It further directed that "when any person's property is taken for the use of the public, the owner ought to receive an equivalent in money."[196] This draconian authority allowed to town governments up to this time to lay out roadways had never before been delegated to a private legal entity such as a railroad corporation.

The important case of *William Gold, Jr. v. Vermont Central Rail Road Company* in 1847 presented the Vermont Supreme Court with the first serious challenge to the railroad's use of the condemnation process. Gold did not contest the actual taking of his land, but argued the Constitution entitled him to an amount of compensation determined by a jury. In reaching a decision that held otherwise, Associate Justice Charles Davis observed that "Rail road corporations are new bodies with us and the taking and holding another's land *in invitum* [against his wishes], for the purpose of constructing such roads, is a novel proceeding, now for the first time authorized by our

January 1, 1848 Map & profile of the Rutland & Burlington Railroad, Wm. B. Gilbert, Chief Engineer, facing west. Library of Congress.

laws."[197] In this moment of legal uncertainty caused by the technology and without clear statutory direction, the court looked to analogous situations to rationalize its ruling.[198] It had no trouble in finding that authority to take land already existed when towns laid out roads. Further, the railroad's generous charter authorized by the legislature in 1843 had conferred on its board of directors the authority to impose their enterprise on the landscape as they deemed necessary. "All lands thus entered upon and used" the charter specified, "which are not gifts or donations, shall be purchased." In instances where "the parties disagree upon the price" of the land taken, the charter further allowed the county court to name three commissioners to mediate a reasonable price. If either party disagreed with their decision, it authorized an appeal only to that court (which decision "shall be final"), thereby removing any prospect of further review by the Supreme Court.[199] In reaching its conclusion in *Gold,* the court determined that when the legislature created the process it did not provide a right to a jury trial thereby undercutting the plaintiff's claim and ruled in the railroad's favor. In actual practice, it appears that Vermont railroads never failed to obtain title to the land they wanted and, in every instance that resulted in an aggrieved landowner, the process only allowed him to contest the amount of compensation without further recourse.

Gilbert and his surveyors staked out the Rutland Railroad line in 1847 and filed the description of their work in Rutland with its clerk, Ambrose Lincoln Brown, on February 8, 1848.[200] Signed by the eleven members of the railroad's board of directors headed by Follett, the document detailed more than 130 surveying points established over an exact 46,667 feet (8.8 miles) with varying distances in feet marked out perpendicular to the centerline that identified the right of way they took. The preceding month, the board explained to its shareholders the troubles it faced in this work and that "much effort has been made, and a deep anxiety felt to secure the land for our road bed by private negotiations" with landowners. While the effort to that time was deemed "successful to a considerable extent," it did "not entirely" succeed.[201] The problem continued and the next year the board repeated its frustrations and explained that "In Railroad construction there is no subject. . . more prolific of dispute, controversy, and bitter feeling, than that which relates to the right and power of a Corporation to occupy the lands of private individuals for their road-bed and other accommodations." The managers met with much trouble from landowners and reported to shareholders that they encountered resistance and "exorbitant demands" for payment of the land "which were not infrequent."[202] By 1851, the board's solicitude towards the public evolved noticeably when it addressed the objections of a local marble dealer on the road's path just west of Rutland that he thought did not meet his business needs. "It is needless to remark," a special company committee wrote in brazen justification of its actions, "that an enterprise like ours must know no respect of places. Its province is not to make the centers of business, but it must be central to find them where natural wealth, or accidental circumstances, or the enterprise of man shall fix their localities."[203] The board's willingness to accommodate the public's needs were further tested when it testily ordered some of its members "to take measures to obtain" whatever land they thought was necessary in Rutland.[204]

Other examples of resistance to the intruding railroad's uninhibited authority that caused the managers' displeasure as they coursed through the Rutland community without regard to the needs of its inhabitants are present in the town's land records. They demonstrate that over this portion of the road a considerable number of people refused to sell their land or were dissatisfied with the compensation offered to them. No sooner had Gilbert's surveyors passed over an owner's land did they express displeasure and demand the county court to appoint commissioners to decide their complaints. Over thirty landowners filed objections in Rutland (an average of 3.5 for each mile of road, while only three landowners accepted their offers), set for hearing at 9:00 a.m. on December 11, 1847 at the Franklin Hotel on Main Street.[205] South of Rutland in Mt. Holly, where railroad managers wanted to blast their way through the Green Mountain's height of land, more opposition arose. Not one landowner agreed to sell and twelve objections were filed with the court, predictably decided in the railroad's favor on November 17, 1847. Incongruous results occurred in the two towns separating Rutland and Mt. Holly that the railroad passed through. In Shrewsbury only three aggrieved landowners received sums for their land (two others agreed to sell) and in Clarendon, there is, inexplicably, no record of any transaction occurring with the railroad until 1848 when a single voluntary sale took place.[206]

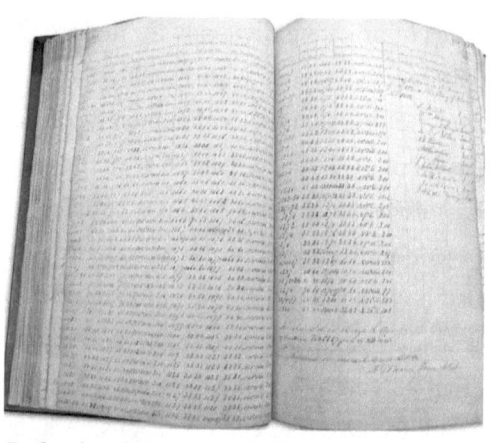

Rutland and Burlington Railroad centerline survey through Rutland, Feb. 8, 1848. Clerk, City of Rutland, Vermont. Photo by author.

An eclectic cross-section of the aggrieved Rutland community attended the December proceedings that included some of its most notable residents. Farmers, mechanics, and businessmen all appeared demonstrating the power of the railroad to create a leveling event that did not distinguish between them. They included the son of Vermont historian Rev. Samuel Williams, the Hon. Charles K. Williams, who had served in many public capacities including major-general of militia, representative in the assembly (he served again in 1849), state's attorney, collector of customs, chief justice of the Supreme Court (retiring in 1846), president of the 1848 Council of Censors, and future governor between 1850 and 1852.[207] His immediate neighbor, Lieutenant Governor Robert Pierpoint, also appeared in opposition to the railroad's efforts.[208] Similarly acclaimed, Pierpoint served previously as tax collector, county clerk, a member of the assembly, senate and governor's council, probate judge, circuit court judge between 1850 and 1856, and as Rutland's representative participating in the 1857 debates concerning the relocation of the capital and rebuilding the destroyed statehouse.[209]

Four individuals of lesser distinction also filed objections and who had a direct impact on the course of local development in accommodating the Rutland Railroad. These included: Mrs. Harriet Strong, the widow of large land owner, advocate of the Champlain Canal, and early railroad supporter, former county court chief judge Moses Strong; Jonathan C. Thrall, an attorney and perpetual democratic candidate for state office; and businessmen Gershom Cheney Ruggles and James Barrett Jr., neighbors of Pierpoint.[210] Harriet Strong's presence at these proceedings was particularly important when in 1851 she assumed a role in the newly formed Rutland Land Company that further impacted the development and configuration of the community. In this time of the rapidly arriving railroad technology, she, together with Williams and Pierpoint, made a vital connection to the past that gave their contemporaries a sense of stability as they sought to adapt to the changing times. When Harriet died in 1870, at age 80, a local newspaper recalled her contributions in glowing terms as "one of the oldest and most esteemed ladies of Rutland":

> She made her home known for its genial hospitality in olden time, by the graceful manner with which it was dispensed. She had been for many years a connecting link between a former and the present generation, and was one of several highly esteemed elderly matrons who enjoy the high regard of our community. She was proverbial for her benevolence in times past, and her eminent kindly sympathy and generosity. Thus, has another landmark of the first families, whose prominence made Rutland society among the most genial and cultivated in Vermont, passed away.[211]

Other merchants, tavern keepers, tradesmen, farmers and entrepreneurs alike, regardless of social or economic standing, all rubbed shoulders with Strong and joined together in their opposition to the way the railroad treated them in taking their land.[212] As various appeals were instituted in the county court by those further aggrieved by commissioners' awards, many other suits and countersuits were brought by the railroad against investors who refused to continue paying promised amounts owed for shares in the corporation they purchased. The success of the railroad in these cases varied but often to its disadvantage when it was awarded damages of only one cent on occasion. When successful, it vigorously pursued debtors and instituted attachments on their property.[213] While those contesting the railroad's voracious appetite did not succeed in halting the work, they provide an example of coalescing interests from within the Rutland community forced to accommodate and adapt to the new technology on their doorstep.

CONCLUSION

Only weeks separated George Perkins Marsh's September 1847 memorable oration to the Agricultural Society of Rutland County on the importance of the herdsman, ploughman and mechanic working together, at the very moment railroad surveyors staked out their land, and the court proceedings in December that put a real face on the stresses the work imposed on the community. While the railroad investors, managers and clamoring businessmen in its favor saw only advantage, the burdens that modernity imposed on others less well-off and uninterested in abandoning their comfortable way of life and traditions was palpable and not warmly received. Vermont, on the cusp of change, struggled to accommodate these opposing interests while it faced the siren call of foreign markets to allow it to finally find a way to transport its rich mineral and agricultural products beyond its borders and bring in the luxuries that so many other Americans already enjoyed.

The experiences of the Rutland community in the middle of the nineteenth-century starkly presented the effects of modernity and its increasingly complex challenges, representative of those that other Vermont communities faced. Because of the railroad, the town exploded with development and opportunities in the next few years in ways that nobody envisioned in the past. The changes were so new, so positive, so inviting that they simply overwhelmed any thought of returning to their old way of life. It also attracted the attention of foreigners looking for opportunity and a means to alter how they had lived their lives to this time. Vigilant capitalists enabled by legislators unwilling to stand in their way recognized and exploited the newfound opportunities that the rush of modernity offered. As a result, Vermonters experienced its positive and negative influences simultaneously as their culture and very lives were profoundly changed, both mentally and physically.

The admiration that many held for Harriet Strong, one of those early land speculating entrepreneurs, at the time of her death in 1870 recalling her ability to bridge the past with the present constituted both a respectful and superficial assessment of her worth to her Rutland neighbors and friends. As brief as their statement was, it also expressed a sense of forlorn loss they could only appreciate in retrospect in later years when they recognized more fully the true impact that intrusive modernity had on them. Only then could they begin to understand that their complaints in mid-century of a stagnating population attributable to their young leaving for the west or to New England mills might have been too simplistic an explanation after all. Other uncomfortable factors attributable to the changes they experienced also existed and were about to make themselves widely known.

CHAPTER III

Embracing Modernity

"The genius of improvement, of progress."[214]

REPRESENTATIVE RODNEY V. MARSH OF BRANDON, February 18, 1857

Booming Rutland: The Irish Arrive

The progress made in embracing the mid-century pull of modernity and eager acceptance of technology that underlay it depended on the convergence of a wide range of factors. These included a cadre of entrepreneurs seizing the opportunity with the capacity to raise capital and the willingness to accept risk, recruiting able professionals and securing labor. It also required a government that would enable it. In Vermont the railroad depended on the state's location between the Great Lakes basin, Canada, New York, Boston and coastal New England. In Rutland, it took further advantage of its geographical location to encourage the steam technology that passed through it to better its prospects for the future.

THE LAST "DON QUIXOTE."

"The snort of the dreaded monster is already heard – the 'bell is ringing,' and if you won't do anything else, in all conscience, for your own safety, clear the track!" A warning to readers of the "folly – to say nothing of the danger – of any further opposition to the 'Rutland Road.'" Rutland County Herald, 3 Dec. 1846.

The rapid growth that the Rutland community experienced and later drew the legislature's attention in 1857 began at this time as the railroad managers solidified their iron grip seizing land. From then on, all eyes pivoted from their comfortable, traditional Main Street plateau location and focused downhill on a twenty-five-acre tract that quickly turned into a bustling economic center replacing the role that Main Street performed in the past. The development of this area, and an adjacent one hundred acres west of it extending to the east bank of the Otter Creek, took place in stages and involved a number of participants whose varied interests intersected in different ways. These included the railroad managers, civil authorities, businessmen, lawyers, land entrepreneurs, religious leaders, and native and immigrant laborers. Each grasped the opportunities presented to them by the changing landscape and they progressed in a distinct order dictated by the dominate needs of their new master, the railroad.

The steam-driven technology demanded that it have access to a pliable environment to allow it to function in the most efficient way possible. It made no practical or economic sense to consider building the important structures that supported its infrastructure in locations other than near each other.[215] As various lines converged on this tract of land it became necessary to forecast the placement of tracks, the different types of buildings needed to service engines and cars, warehousing large quantities of goods, containment for livestock, accommodation of the traveling public, and space for railroad managers. Beyond creating roads to service these functions, the planners had little appreciation for the immediate, huge impact their work would inflict on the site, the surrounding landscape, the housing of laborers who made it all possible, the business interests attracted to newfound opportunities, and the potential harm it posed to those living adjacent to it. Wherever the railroad managers dictated the location of the line and its supporting structures, the community followed in lockstep without question. That subservience continued for the next three decades until the 1890s when second-generation immigrant workers, tired of their exclusion from Rutland's mainstream, asserted their interests that resulted in concessions from the railroad managers allowing for needed physical changes (a pedestrian bridge was built over the rail yard in 1895) and saw their increased participation in local politics.

With the favorable results from the condemnation process completed, the managers turned their energy to making their dream a reality. Unhindered by the prospect of any state or local interference, they imposed the most significant, rapid transformation on the landscape in the state's history as Rutland became the site of "the largest railroad junction in Vermont."[216] It altered the community's traditional way of life centered on the overlooking plateau so quickly that "it soon became a matter for wonder why the business part of the place was ever placed on the hill."[217] Despite the rapidity and enormity of their undertaking, a close reading of Rutland's land records shows that the frugal railroad managers proceeded in a cautious manner and only expanded their operations in response to the amount of investments made in their endeavor.[218] Except for the twelve costly engines ordered from the Taunton Locomotive Manufacturing Company in Massachusetts in 1849 and specialized tools needed for their maintenance, necessity dictated that frugality rule in all other expenditures for goods and services that resulted in the introduction of those of inferior quality. Rutland's experience generally duplicated that of other communities around the country coping with the railroad where the dominate philosophy was to "get the track laid and the locomotives built, and start running trains as quickly as possible to generate income, even if that means cutting corners that push up operating costs. Improvements could be made later, once the line started generating a profit."[219]

The enforced parsimony and pragmatic attitude of the Rutland Railroad managers had a significant impact on the financial life of the company in the next years as those first improvements that included ties, rails, cars, buildings and bridges began to deteriorate and affect the safety of the traveling and local public. Notwithstanding, the increasing momentum of unrestrained, optimistic enthusiasm that propelled the managers to progress at a breakneck pace, they looked to the experiences in surrounding states for examples to follow. They prioritized the construction of the road and its servicing facilities in a way that recognized the primacy of conveying large quantities of goods and only later addressed the needs of the traveling public. It proceeded from survey, to leveling the land, laying the track and building inexpensive, temporary sheds ("cheap" according to their records) to protect the valuable engines and store the large quantities of goods that became their cargo. In the Rutland rail yard, they dug out the high spots and filled in the low, identified in recent times archaeologically as utilizing "white marble (some displaying evidence of machine processing), brick debris, and significant amounts of gravels, sands and soils" detected below the surface.[220] Careful in spending money, between 1848 and 1850, the only buildings the managers erected in the Rutland yard consisted of a wooden station house measuring 150 x 50 feet and a freight depot of 150 x 30 feet.[221] The diverse kinds of additional work projected to take place in this confined area would require more money and a substantial amount of labor to accomplish.

Construction on Rutland's rail yard could not begin until the grounds were staked out, leveled and drained. Ambrose Lincoln Brown, one of the railroad company's most capable men, organized the work. He served as Rutland's town clerk at the time (re-elected in 1848 to a twenty-second term), had studied law in the office of aggrieved landowner Charles K. Williams and was admitted to the bar in 1819, spent time manufacturing paper and selling books, edited the *Rutland Herald*, acted as a probate and county court judge between 1844 and 1847, served in the legislature, and had a keen interest in civil engineering.[222] His devotion to the new technology and implementing its needs on the landscape in these years earned him such wide recognition and respect that in 1860 he received appointment to succeed George Perkins Marsh as the state's third, and sole, railroad commissioner. Eminently qualified to assume oversight of much of the work taking place throughout the Rutland area, including the yard, Brown documented his activities in a diary he maintained throughout 1848.[223] The entries reveal the deeply religious Brown's strenuous efforts as he worked virtually every day throughout the year on the railroad's behalf, staying in constant contact with Chief Engineer Gilbert and laboring in his office until eleven at night. He also attended church sermons and temperance meetings and admitted to falling asleep during one. His responsibilities concerned many of the grueling aspects of railroad construction from overseeing the quality of the first surveying efforts by verifying its calculations and placement of centerline stakes, adjusting them when necessary, and repairing damaged equipment. He also worked to assure that contractors performed according to their agreements in grading, leveling and draining the land, and installing culverts, fencing and cattle guards, all conducted regardless of the inclement weather that he routinely encountered and recorded. The work was grueling and, together with the work Brown oversaw, the entire 125-mile project connecting Burlington with Bellows Falls ultimately required the removal of "approximately 6,000,000 cubic yards of earth and gravel, 325,000 yards of solid rock and 25,000 yards of loose rock" and an additional 80,000 yards for culvert, bridges and supporting walls.[224]

Ambrose Lincoln Brown. Rutland Historical Society.

After the county court commissioners awarded the various sums of money to landowners contesting the seizure of their land and a month after the results were filed with him in the town's records, Brown went to work on the yard. He began on Monday afternoon, March 13, 1848, as the snow fell and recorded "Began to stake out Depot ground" before the weather forced the work to stop. While Brown did not identify who assisted him that day, issues with laborers constantly presented problems. A week earlier, he noted that a "general strike among hands for better wages" had taken place and that on town meeting day, March 7, he found it "more disorderly than last year." There was "very loud singing in the streets," he wrote, and that "Hughes (colored) enraged the neighborhood by profanity & noise" because of the "effects of liquor" and, with alarm, the presence of "too many indifferent intemperance men!" On May 19 problems continued when he noted that "Laborers quit at noon." Brown also had to deal with local residents unhappy with the decisions of the commissioners as they continued their opposition to the railroad crossing their land by verbally accosting and forbidding him permission to enter, accompanied by demands he could not satisfy.[225] Despite the opposition, he continued with the work and noted at the end of the season that on November 8 the depot ground had frozen. Stress was evident elsewhere and on December 14 he recorded that "evidence is multiplying that drinking is on the increase." He ended the year's entries by expressing his frustrations with the work of contractors who interfered with the staked out survey lines and wrote that he had become "impatient at [a] foreman for his carelessness and others for disturbing [staked] references by which we were much hindered."

While Brown did not specifically identify who engaged in the excessive drinking, singing in the street and altering the survey's centerline, he made a brief reference on October 7, 1848 to "an Irish Ball at Mason Hall." The Irish presence in the Rutland community had slowly accelerated since 1840 and gained such momentum with the region's railroad construction that it attracted further migration inland from the Atlantic seacoast and south from Canada. Many of the young, illiterate Irishmen and women and their families fleeing the devastating potato famine at home first landed on the North American Atlantic and St. Lawrence seaboards before relocating to the interior cities and towns to seek work as menial labors, servants, farmhands, and in textile mills. In 1835, Nathaniel Hawthorne voiced his Brahmin displeasure when he passed through Burlington "struck" by the numbers of Irish immigrants present, living "in huts and mean dwellings" near the Lake Champlain waterfront. He saw their large numbers and mean manners (they "lounge about the wharves, and elbow the native citizens") as doing little to instill confidence in their future employment and predicted an absence of demand for "these wandering hordes."[226] In June 1847 "a vast influx" of sick Irish appeared in Burlington, stricken with ship fever, that a compassionate local population took into their homes to care for them.[227] Employment for those returning to health looked promising as the discovery and extraction of Vermont's mineral resources attracted small numbers of Irish to travel south to Rutland County in the 1840s. There, they found employment in the newly opened marble and slate quarries that paid them fifty cents a day during the winter and seventy-five cents in summer.[228] With the arrival of the railroad, by 1850 an estimated 852 Irish lived in Rutland, almost twenty-five percent of its population of 3,715, compared to thirty-one percent in Burlington.[229] By 1860 they had become an "overwhelming presence" in both communities.[230]

At first, the Irish found work in the mineral producing towns of Poultney, Castleton and West Rutland (the town's west parish) where companies provided them with poor quality housing. They lived in crowded conditions with as many as ten families sharing a common living space. Starvation was not uncommon when the produce from their crude gardens could not provide enough to tide them over during the lean times unless neighbors helped out. Sanitation became a concern as bouts of consumption, pneumonia and diphtheria took their toll and cut lifespans short.[231] An outbreak of cholera in New York City in 1849 was closely associated with the filthy living conditions of the poor, of whom forty percent of all deaths associated with the disease fell upon the immigrant Irish.[232] Vice, poverty and the belief that cholera (the "poor man's plague") inflicted its ravages only on sinners tainted New Englanders' views of the Irish and hindered their integration into communities where they wandered. The Irish lived and worked hard, and they played hard. Their legendary bouts of heavy drinking, with many accounts of drunkenness escalating into violence, took a heavy toll on both their families and the communities where they lived. An autopsy of an Irishman conducted in Middlebury in 1840 revealed that the deceased "determined to have a spree" and had procured a quart of rum that he quickly consumed. Unsurprisingly, it rendered him "unconscious and apoplectic," and dead thirty hours later, leaving behind his wife and their seven children "dependent on him for support" and who then became the community's burden.[233] In 1850, Vermont temperance workers described the difficulty they encountered when they sought to identify the amount of alcohol consumption in the state because of their experiences with the transient Irish. "This is specially true," they wrote, "along the lines of railroads, where liquor is kept in shanties and sold exclusively to Irish laborers." The temperance workers recognized the impossibility of stemming the problem at the imbiber's level and directed their efforts towards the vendors of spirits hoping to have an effect on "a numerous class of foreigners who are daily increasing in our State." They believed they had to do so because "These men will surely drink and be drunken; and we must take care of them, till mother earth receives the trust."[234] The Vermont State Prison in Windsor reported a marked upsurge in its population at the time "owing to the increase of Irish on the Railroads."[235] In Burlington, Chittenden County Sheriff Nathan P. Bowman's inventory of prisoners locked up for intoxication identifies many bearing Irish names, including "Irishman forgot his name."[236] The same occurred in Rutland where an extensive list of prisoners includes many intoxicated Irish names.[237] In 1854, Michael Ryan was murdered in Hydeville, west of Rutland, on St. Patrick's Day by Matthew Halloran ("two friends from Ireland") during a huge drunken brawl that included their womenfolk who tried to separate them. Halloran ended the fight when he struck Ryan in the head and killed him with a "stick of wood from a pile of railroad wood," described as being "about five feet in length."[238]

Ambrose Lincoln Brown's reference to an "Irish Ball," excessive drinking, and workers walking off the job in 1848 indicates that the Irish had become a large and notable, if not particularly wanted, presence in the Rutland community by this time. An extant account book maintained by the Strong & Chamberlain construction firm working north of Rutland village at Sutherland Falls that summer reveals a large presence of men working on the railroad. It lists dozens of Irish names (111 of them in July), earning between thirty and ninety cents a day reduced by amounts they spent at the company store for personal needs. It identified several as "Quit" and "Discharged," while Michael O. Daniel's employment ended on August 14, marked as "Killed."[239] South of Rutland, a witness recorded in 1851 seeing as "many as 700 hands" working on the twenty-mile stretch of rail connecting Danby and Manchester. He also observed laborers in the Salem, New York area digging ditches and grading the ground to connect Rutland with Troy and reported that "the Irish who work on this as well as all other Rail Roads are treated as bad as slaves."[240] The presence of so many Irish in the region had an immediate, direct impact on the development of the Rutland community as its residents sought to accommodate their increasing numbers while they dealt with demands in developing the new depot grounds. Concerns over

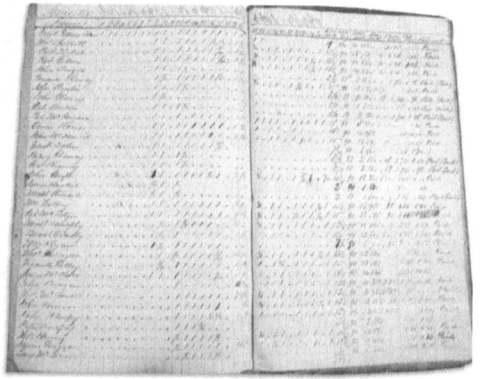

Rutland and Burlington Railroad contractor Strong and Chamberlain's roster of laborers, June 1848. Vermont State Archives. Photo by author.

the tendency of unhappy Irish workers to resort to violence also appear as an unspoken factor in locating them. The incidents of violence involving Irish railroad laborers, most notably in Bolton in 1846 that required a large armed response by the Chittenden County sheriff (a "Light Infantry Co. and the Company of Firemen. . . to maintain the supremacy of the law") to quell certainly did not escape the attention of Rutland's railroad and community officials.[241]

Notwithstanding the potential for violence, many appreciated the hard work of Chief Engineer Gilbert and his "efficient and capable corps of Assistants" working north of town where he pushed forward a "steady, rapid and noiseless progress. . . [that] attracted almost universal notice and admiration."[242] There is little evidence of meaningful numbers of the Irish laborers working in the Rutland area living with their families in the established residential area on the plateau above the yard. Instead, the nascent immigrant community began to settle immediately north of the twenty-five-acre tract where only an "old tin shop. . . and a bakery next to it" operated nearby.[243] Descriptions of their living conditions at the time do not exist, but probably did not differ much from those they fled in Ireland. In 1843, one-half of that country's population lived in so-called Class 4 housing, the worst grade possible according to its 1841 census: "This type of housing comprised a mud cabin consisting of only one room or. . . a larger overcrowded house inhabited by up to five families."[244] Another contemporary description provided that it was "impossible not to mourn over the general aspect of the cottages. The tent of the Red Indian and the hut of the Esquimaux, are constructed with a greater degree of care and more attention to their rude notions of comfort, than the cabin an Irish peasant erects on the side of the road, or mountain."[245] When Rutland entrepreneurs recognized more space was needed for the growing numbers of Irish, and no doubt seeking to avoid the repetition of such dire living conditions in their midst, they gazed at the large undeveloped floodplain (the "neglected flats") immediately downhill and west of the yard.[246] They thought that the value of Rutland land would explode and that speculating in it promised "the most important" opportunity available to them to make a profit.[247]

The Rutland Land Company

Although it existed for only three years between 1851 and 1854, the Rutland Land Company (RLC) had a significant impact on the arriving Irish population and the community at large that continues to the present time. The identity of its members, inaccurately described in the past and their involvement in developing the low-lying tract of land have been largely overlooked, reported simply as "a syndicate of six men... who cut it up and sold it in lots."[248] However, the Rutland town land records reveal a much more complex story that specifically identifies the RLC members and the significant impact they had on a community that gained such notoriety by 1857 it was deemed a worthy candidate to become Vermont's capital. The records also demonstrate the unintended consequences that occurred as it split this section of the town in half and fostered division between the old settler tradition living on the hill and their new, foreign-born neighbors opposite them to the west, below and out beyond the emerging yard separating them.

The RLC was not a six-man syndicate, but an unincorporated association composed of five local men and a single woman, sixty-five-year-old Harriet Strong who had opposed the railroads taking her land in 1847. Her associates included: former state representative and Rutland County State's Attorney Caleb B. Harrington of Middletown; local attorney Evelyn Pierpoint (the son of Circuit Court Judge Robert Pierpoint who also contested the seizure of his land), an active member of the Know Nothing Party and who became a member of the Council of Censors for the Revision of the Constitution in 1855; local architect and builder John Cain, an ardent Jacksonian who served as selectman, grand juror and justice of the peace, described as a "warm friend and bitter opponent";[249] former Clarendon constable, farmer, lister, merchant and agent for the company, Henry Olin Perkins; and, local merchant Orrick L. Robbins.[250] The six associates completed purchase of the 125-acre parcel of floodplain land on May 30, 1851 when they paid $11,000 to local businessman, farmer and tavern keeper Jonathan C. Thrall, who had purchased it in 1839 from Strong's late husband, Moses.[251] All of the RLC members knew each other well as Thrall and Harrington ran as democratic nominees for Rutland County senate seats in 1845 and Cain had served with Thrall as officers of the "Free Democracy of Rutland."[252] The contentious Cain, a strong backer of the railroad, enthusiastically sold subscriptions to support its financing. However, his actions on its behalf were not universally appreciated, notably demonstrated when he was ignobly snubbed by a Rutland member of the railroad board who refused to allow him to attend the opening of the road at the December 18, 1849 ceremonies in Mount Holly. It was an event likened to a marriage when samples of Lake Champlain water were mixed with some from Massachusetts Bay brought by Boston representatives and cannons fired. Expressing his disappointment with the director's choice of whom to invite to the proceedings, Cain complained to the *Rutland Herald* that "the parties said to have been united in the holy house of matrimony must be older than the 'oldest inhabitant' who in their primitive simplicity and original habits could not sanction or recognize the modern fashions of the class which the discriminating taste of the Rutland Director selected."[253]

Before he sold his land to the RLC, in 1849 Thrall gained local notoriety when he harvested a remarkable "88 ½ bushels of good quality" Indian corn from a single acre of the alluvial, low-lying land that he prepared that spring using a plow loaned to him by a man identified only as "Ruggles."[254] Thrall's land abutted the twenty-five acre plot where all of the rail yard construction took place, owned by local furniture manufacturer Gershom Cheney Ruggles before the railroad exercised its condemnation authority and took several acres of it from him the preceding year.[255] Ruggles had inherited 165 acres at the time of his father's death in 1831 and appears to have sold portions of it to Moses Strong in the following years and which became the subject of probate proceedings that involved Harriet when the railroad arrived to take it.[256] Thrall also had land taken by the railroad at the same time that she and Ruggles did.[257] Only a few individuals who owned adjoining land avoided the condemnation process, including merchant James Barrett Jr. who owned a parcel that gained notoriety with the construction of the important depot building in 1852. Barrett has received acclaim over the years for reportedly "donating" the land to the railroad, but the land records reveal it was a financial transaction that allowed him to reap $325 for relinquishing his interests.[258] Reflecting the railroad management's intentions to take land incrementally as needed based upon the amount of investments made by stockholders, and perhaps unwilling to hazard further court proceedings, in 1850 and 1852 Ruggles sold additional land adjacent to what it had seized in 1848.[259] Together with other parcels the railroad condemned, including another of Harriet Strong's in 1857, it gained full control over the twenty-five acre parcel and plunged into developing it without any further interference from anyone.

The RLC, intent on making an immediate profit, vigorously sold portions of the 125 acres in over forty transactions by 1854.[260] While no evidence supports an inference of the participation of any of Vermont's early railroad executives in the layout of this area located beyond the yard itself, the land records suggest that the improvement of this space for housing involved Irish workers who negotiated to purchase it from speculators prescient enough to recognize its increasing value. No Irish names appear among the initial purchasers from the RLC, but others that seems to have been of modest means who, in turn, sold their interests to their newfound foreign neighbors do. Only a couple of local businessmen (one involved with marble and iron manufacturing and the other a mill owner) made purchases, as well as School District No. 18 located near the depot and the Rutland Marble Company, accompanied by interested individuals from other southern Vermont communities. In 1853 Harriet Strong liquidated all of her interests and sold them to her five associates for $2,000.[261] The railroad's heavy-handed efforts to take her land and that of her elite friends that included Robert and Evelyn Pierpoint, Perkins, Ruggles and Robbins resulted in a strong association among them as they engaged in these various transactions and went on to assume powerful positions as trustees in control of the town between 1850 and 1854.[262]

The land that the RLC sold to entrepreneurs became known as "Nebraska" and gained such common recognition that in 1893 its residents called it the "Nebraska District."[263] The reason for the name is not certain, but is perhaps attributable to the current notoriety that distant part of the country had gained when the United States obtained it in 1848 after the Mexican-American War and before it became a territory in 1854 with the Kansas-Nebraska Act.[264] As the RLC made its sales and heavy construction continued in the rail yard, the itinerant Irish began to settle in Nebraska. Their experiences varied little from those arriving in the larger metropolitan centers, such as New York City or South Bend, Indiana, where they lived together in neighborhoods near their places of employment that allowed them to provide each other with "religious, social, and financial support."[265] The Nebraska neighborhood where they gathered duplicated the settlement pattern of Irish arrivals elsewhere who, in their poor condition, "built themselves rude, temporary cabins or shanties and ate at a common table."[266] Those crude structures appeared immediately adjacent to the rail yard near the loud, busy machine shops located away from the local population who had settled the higher ground on the east side. By 1855, modest one and one-half story houses began to appear in Nebraska that replaced those first rudimentary abodes.[267] Immediately to their south along the tracks, Irish workers continued their shanty-town existence for the next two decades and paid rent of "$15.00 a year for a half or quarter acre patch" before further development forced them to relocate.[268]

Many Vermonters in the mid-nineteenth century viewed poverty as a personal failing, but not in every community, including Rutland, where the "deserving poor" that included the Irish received some form of public assistance, albeit minimal and infrequent.[269] The presence of the Irish did not spark overt opposition from the native Rutland community that it did elsewhere, but a degree of resentment at having to accept a Catholic population, deemed throughout New England as inferior, resulted in some alienation from the population at large.[270] Between 1843 and 1853, Vermont's Catholic population exploded, increasing from 4,940 to 20,000 statewide, with an estimated 500 in Rutland.[271] The Irish and their religion went hand-in-hand throughout New England as workers spread out over the region to build the railroads. This forced their employers and the communities they lived in to allow their churches to rise up or they would leave and go elsewhere.[272] In the 1840s Rutland had a minimal Catholic presence, but the more numerous recent arrivals required a church of their own to avoid sharing the Main Street courthouse above the rail yard with local Methodists. In 1855, RLC member John Cain sold Nebraska land on Meadow Street to Father Zephyrin Druon for $125 where his congregation erected a modest brick building. While the Irish found it difficult to establish and nurture a church so close to the native population, circumstances in nearby West Rutland allowed 1,300 members to attend Mass in 1857.[273]

Nebraska did not easily identify in a physical or social sense with the rest of Rutland. Isolated to the west, separated from others by the growing yard, it did not experience the kinds of improvements being made on the hillside between Main Street on the plateau and its bustling base. Nebraska residents had to walk or ride on two streets, one on either end of the yard that required their crossing the busy rails that only added to their sense of separation from the rest of the town. Crossing directly over the twenty-five-acre yard itself was fraught with danger and led to many deaths and serious injuries inflicted on those who attempted to negotiate the many tracks and trains that ran between Nebraska and the hill. With the development of the yard, businesses on the nearby east side scrambled to locate as near as possible to it creating dramatic change. Before 1846 only West Street descended the hill, but between 1852 and 1853 twelve new, major streets and thoroughfares were created near the yard that connected up the hillside to Main Street.[274] A "deep swamp" and stream where trout once swam at the base of the hill succumbed to the development with so much stone and debris from building construction filled in that in 1923 city workers uncovered it seven feet below the existing road surface. As the work continued to alter the terrain, local residents used a creative form of "sidewalk" with an iron railing elevated eight to ten feet above the ground that descended by a steep flight of stairs in order to enter a home or business.[275]

The Rutland Yard

Railroad managers and community officials in Rutland received reminders daily of the importance of their work, deemed by a Middlebury newspaper as "a crowning event in the history of western Vermont."[276] It drew the constant attention of outsiders who admired the "steady, rapid, and noiseless progress [that] has attracted almost universal notice and admiration" and heaped praise on "the board of Directors, the Chief Engineer, Mr. Gilbert, and the efficient and capable corps of assistants."[277] Governor Carlos Coolidge singled out their work because of its "large influence over our internal trade which these modern improvements are destined to exert." Because of their efforts, "the spirit of enterprise in our inhabitants will be quickened," he said, and "the agricultural power of the State enlarged, its general resources developed, and its aggregate wealth enhanced." Railroads, he proudly proclaimed "are already among the wants of a civilized world. They will become features of its glory."[278]

Among the structures built along any of the nation's railroads, aside from those needed to service the rolling stock, the depot building had paramount importance. This structure put the face on a community as it sought to make the best possible first impression on arriving passengers. A huge banner with the words "WELCOME TO RUTLAND" stretched across Center Street in 1870 facing the depot during the town's centennial celebration and warmly invited arrivals to partake of all it had to offer. The depot, also used for religious services, quickly became the pivotal location in Rutland and gained such importance that at the time of the centennial forty-eight trains used its services over a twenty-four-hour period. That would increase to 102 daily trains in 1900.[279]

As the railroads displaced the stage coach lines (eighteen crossed Vermont in 1850), their personnel either took over those vacated offices or set up business in nearby homes or hotels.[280] Rutland followed a different path and abandoned any thought of relying on the Franklin Hotel on Main Street as railroad personnel occupied rough accommodations at the base of the hill that were "invariably not places of charm or distinction."[281] In June 1849, the Rutland Railroad board of directors authorized a committee "to recommend plans for Depot buildings and way stations," but postponed a final decision for several days. The ongoing negotiations with the Washington and Rutland Rail Road board to arrange for its junction at the depot grounds was deemed of more importance and convinced the cautious directors to delay further building of "permanent depot buildings. . . until the road is completed and running over its entire line."[282]

As the road managers rushed to complete the line before January 1, 1850 (accomplished in December at the Mount Holly summit) they ordered that a telegraph line be established between Rutland and Boston and declared it "a desirable public improvement."[283] They also retained the services of one of the country's most important architects who had a significant impact on both the Rutland rail yard and the Capitol building in Montpelier. A native of Lebanon, New Hampshire, Ammi Burnham Young designed Vermont's second Capitol in 1831 and was consulted about its replacement after the fire that destroyed it in 1857.[284] His reputation grew immensely over these two decades as he designed other prominent buildings in Burlington that included the Marine Hospital, Custom House, and Post Office. Similarly, he designed the courthouse and post offices in Windsor and Rutland, the Woodstock courthouse, Boston's impressive customhouse and the Bangor, Maine customhouse. Young also designed and erected the Greek Revival residence of Rutland Railroad's president Timothy Follett in Burlington, identified as the "focal point for the city's high society."[285] In 1852 he became the nation's first Supervising Architect of the Treasury charged with overseeing the construction of all federal buildings.[286]

West Street looking west from Main Street when businesses moved downhill towards the new rail yard below, January 1857. Rutland Historical Society.

View from Rutland's new downtown looking east uphill to Ammi Young's Courthouse and Post Office (center, built in1858) showing the filled in and noticeably elevated Center Street that required steps down in order to access adjacent buildings, 1861. Rutland Historical Society.

In early 1849, Young traveled from Boston to Burlington where the Rutland Railroad board of directors selected him to design depots there, as well as in Rutland and Bellows Falls, along with other structures across the line. The *Burlington Free Press* described the occasion in glowing terms and provided important insights into the kinds of challenges that Vermont architects faced in erecting buildings of substance and meaning. "The public has always a right to demand," it wrote, "that the *exterior* of all buildings, public or private, and the *exterior and interior* of public edifices shall be in good taste." By adhering to this example, "the people have, constantly before their vision, lasting memorials of architectural beauty" to induce them to imitate their "various excellencies and conveniences." After noting that "throughout New England, a very great improvement in the style of private residences and public buildings" had taken place in the past fifteen years, the article articulated a deeper perspective. "The influence, the moral influence, of such monuments of good taste is more powerful and lasting than can be imagined," and ended optimistically that it took "pleasure in chronicling the truth that Vermont is making great advancement in this particular."²⁸⁷ By 1854, the Rutland community would deliver on those promises and provide rich examples of Vermont's elevated sense of taste exemplified by its beautiful depot, impressive structures occupying its rail yard, and sophisticated forms of architecture on the hillside above.

While Young was responsible for the overall construction of various depots, Vermonter Gurdon P. Randall, a native of Braintree, designed and executed the Rutland depot. Randall proudly described himself as a mechanic who learned his trade working alongside his builder-millwright father before he moved to Boston at age twenty-one to begin architectural studies. After he returned to Vermont, and following his employment in the engineering departments of various railroads designing many of their buildings, he moved to Chicago. There, he pursued a remarkable career designing many so-called "heavy buildings" for public and religious use throughout the Midwest.²⁸⁸ Randall became a beloved presence in the growing region and a biographer described that "there lived not in the State of Vermont a man of greater moral rectitude than old Squire Randall."²⁸⁹ He wrote extensively on the design of public buildings, courthouses, schools and private dwellings and in 1883 obtained patent no. 273,151 for a "heating-furnace."²⁹⁰ Between 1849 and 1851, the capable Randall assisted the Rutland Railroad engineering department in the design and construction of wooden depots in Vergennes, Middlebury, Ludlow and Chester, as well as overseeing the erection of a paint shop in the Rutland yard. He

Architect Ammi Young. Vermont Historical Society.

also oversaw complicated arrangements to bring water to the depot grounds to serve the locomotives of the several converging lines and to fill troughs for livestock. The nearest source, uphill from the yard over a mile to the east, required that the land of five individuals undergo the condemnation process to allow the railroad access to a recently built reservoir to install "an aqueduct of iron pipes" across their land.²⁹¹

Architect Gurdon P. Randall. Book of Designs for School Houses (1884).

More by happenstance than design, the Irish neighborhood in Nebraska became isolated on the west side of the yard. Gershom Cheney Ruggles sold off his remaining land to the railroad to allow the yard's expansion and to businessmen who put up machine and foundry shops next to it, serviced by rough roads that wove between them and connected to the main thoroughfares. In 1850, the railroad managers attended to the needs of their valuable engines and decided to replace the "temporary shanties" used to house them for the past two years. Modernity and technology demanded that the new structure be state-of-the-art and they decided that the "engine house at Rutland be built on the plan of [the] Boston and Maine engine-house at Lawrence [Massachusetts, completed in 1848]."²⁹² This huge structure promised to affect the landscape radically as it dictated that whatever accompanying facilities it required to support its operations also be located nearby. Since it was large, busy and noisy, the only logical place for it was away from the commercial side of the yard on the east. That resulted in its placement immediately next to the Irish community.

As Randall worked on depot construction projects elsewhere along the Rutland line in 1851, Pittsford's Nicholas Powers went to work to design the first structure to service the engines. The thirty-four-year-old followed Randall's example as a mechanic and directed his talents in erecting bridges.[293] The railroad technology created a growing need for such specialization and many able Vermonters like Powers turned away from their agricultural heritage to explore its advantages and develop their building skills. Both before and after his involvement with Rutland's engine house, Powers earned a reputation that put him in great demand because of his creative ability to address the complicated needs of bridges spanning challenging waterways. In 1855 he was consulted in the design and construction of the 210-foot long Blenheim bridge, arguably the longest single span wooden bridge in the world, that crossed the Schoharie Creek in North Blenheim, New York (destroyed in 2011 by Tropical Storm Irene). Together with Syracuse, New York master mason J. W. Hickox, the two men erected a remarkable structure in Rutland unlike any that the community had ever witnessed.

The engine house, or roundhouse, that Powers designed and Hickox built served the critical need to allow the railroad to operate year-round as a place to work on and store its valuable engines out of inclement weather. Twelve state-of-the-art engines came from the Taunton Locomotive Company in Massachusetts, eight weighing eighteen tons each for passenger service and four at twenty tons apiece for hauling freight. Named for towns the line passed through (*Rutland, Middlebury, Burlington, Bellows Falls,* etc.) and costing $7,000 each, the steel behemoths provided the most convincing manifestation of modernity's presence in the community. The highly sophisticated structures designed in a circular fashion to house them allowed the heavy engines access to sixteen bays via a sturdy rotating turntable that supported and directed their path into and out of them. The turntable was fifty feet long and the bays they directed the engines into of similar length. Sixteen supports and brick masonry made up the exterior walls holding up a large conical roof pierced by ventilation stacks to carry off the smoke and noxious gases from within. That same year, Hickox and his assistants also erected the nearby machine shop, the Bardwell Hotel across the street, and the Rutland Academy up the hill from the yard.[294] While the board of directors reported the completion of the roundhouse on April 15, 1851, it waited until 1853 before receiving its final distinctive addition. "I notice a beautiful vane on the Engine House of the Rutland and Burlington Railroad Co," an observer wrote, "It is the representation of a Locomotive, made from sheet copper, and gilded. Beneath the vane are four arms, supported by two finely ornamented circles. Upon the ends of each are letters, designating the points of the compass. The whole rests upon the new electrical conductor, producing a pleasing and unique effect." Appreciating its fine detail, he praised the work of Rutland's mechanics stating that "any one of whom is competent to combine the fine and fanciful with work of utility."[295]

Inside, mechanics worked on the many aspects of the new technology that included using specialized tools, including a stationary "first-rate" steam-driven, thirty-horse power "Engine Lathe" that cost $2,000 and a "Plaining [sic] Machine" housed in the nearby machine shop.[296] Its operations appear to have encountered early problems as the board of directors ordered the hiring of a "master mechanic and other help" with "the responsibility of thoroughly reforming the expenses of the Shop and running of the machines."[297] They had much at stake, revealed by an 1854 inventory of its contents that valued the shop's machinery at more than $41,000, the tools at over $3,000, and twelve "snow ploughs" at $1,200.[298]

Detail, Rutland machine shop inventory listing state-of-the-art equipment, 1851. Middlebury College. Photo by author.

The railroad managers built three roundhouses in the Rutland yard in the next fifty years. Powers and Hickox's first effort stood until the afternoon of January 8, 1864 when it met a spectacular and fiery end witnessed by a throng of people. Because engines that operated in confined spaces generated much soot and many noxious gases, they had to be constructed with fireproof materials. Early railroad buildings used wood shingles, but they deteriorated and could easily catch fire. Until the late 1800s, when the use of slate became more commonplace, sheet metal (iron) roofing, coated to prevent rusting, was used. In 1857 Ammi Young's Rutland post office carried a roof of "galvanized iron," probably the same kind of material that Powers and Hickox used in the construction of the first roundhouse.[299] Despite their caution, its loss was attributed to sparks thrown up by an engine that ignited accumulated soot in the rafters. The *Rutland Herald* described the conflagration: "Although in the middle of the day, the fire presented a magnificent spectacle – the large conical roof of the building one sheet of fire, and a steady stream of smoke and flame rushing from the top where the cupola stood, reminded one of the picture of a burning mountain. . . . At last the roof, with a tremendous crash, fell in, taking with it part of the circular wall, and the fire then gradually went out."[300] As the weight of engines began to increase in the next years in order to haul heavier loads, they required stronger rails and bridges and more sophisticated facilities to service them. Rutland's second roundhouse, covered by a huge

Rutland rail yard (center) dividing traditional uphill Main Street business district (right) from developing Irish Nebraska district (left), 1854. Scotts Map of Rutland County. Library of Congress.

eighty-foot wide, fifty-foot tall, cathedral-like dome with four 10,000-gallon water tanks on top, lasted until 1899 when it had outlived its usefulness and two engines attached to long cables affixed to its supports pulled it apart.[301] Its replacement, built to the southwest of the original location, remained in service until the 1960s before the railroad also pulled it down.

On January 21, 1852, the Rutland Railroad board of directors decided the time ripe to build their important depot building and limited its cost to no more than $15,000.[302] Months later, as they rushed to accommodate the connection of the Washington and Rutland Railroad in the yard, the board amended its decision and ordered that a committee considering "a passenger station at Rutland be authorized to erect there a building of wood or brick, as they may determine best, after examining the character of the foundation. The building to be about three hundred feet long by eighty feet wide, and if of brick, the cost not to exceed ten thousand dollars."[303] Gurdon Randall now turned his creative talents to comply with the directors' resolution in their efforts to impress arriving passengers and make the Rutland community proud. Sensitive to not only their wishes, Randall also appreciated the benefits its environment could offer to further their goal. When he created a list of architectural concerns in the design of a building, Randall wanted more information than just the client's desire for one with specific dimensions. He took into consideration "the general direction of the portion of the town from which the building will be most seen, and the principal approaches." He also assembled information that involved "the nature of the soil, and whether dry or wet, and whether the ground or site is high or low as compared with the street or streets and other surroundings... and from which direction the prevailing winds blow."[304] Only by knowing the perspectives the public would view the building from and the character of the area around it he could then provide the most appropriate design.

Randall's original plans for the Rutland depot do not exist, but many photographs, the beautiful colored drawings rendered by Chief Engineer

Thomas Chappell in 1893 and extensive measurements taken of the building demonstrate its substantial nature.[305] This included both a depot building for the public to access from the increasingly busy street where they could buy tickets (indoor plumbing with restrooms awaited the future) and a large, attached shed that trains pulled into to allow passengers access out of the weather. Surviving details of the depot's construction were obtained in 1917 because of a directive from the Interstate Commerce Commission that the physical assets of all of the nation's railroads undergo valuation down to the smallest detail. Despite renovations of the building between 1902 and 1905, the records reveal much about the original design and construction techniques. By the time of the 1917 valuation report, the railroad had removed the shed, but the depot building itself remained, described as a two-story, brick faced, forty-six by sixty-seven foot structure that rested on a foundation of "stone in mortar."[306] In its design, Randall also included unique, undefined openings in both gable ends of the building that never appeared in any other Vermont railroad structure. It

Rutland railyard and the first, conically-shaped roof roundhouse (left) destroyed 1864, with depot (far right), 1854. Detail, Scott's Map of Rutland County. Library of Congress.

Contemporary roundhouse (center) in Salem, New York that may have been duplicated from Rutland. Courtesy of William A. Cormier, Salem, New York, Town Historian.

consisted of a six-foot circle with flanking triangles that defied understanding, even when incorporated into modern day buildings erected after the rail yard was abandoned in the 1960s.[307] However, the 1917 report reveals that an assessor described them as a "clock space," filled in by "T & G Spr. [tongue and groove spruce]." Whether Randall intended to include clocks on both ends of a building devoted to assessing the timely arrival and departure of trains, passengers and goods remains unknown, and no renderings or pictures suggest that he completed it as the spaces remained unfilled for the duration of the building's century-long life. Notwithstanding, the community deemed the building's overall design a proud, much appreciated accomplishment that led the *Rutland Herald* to proclaim at its opening in February 1853, "If the inhabitants of Rutland are not proud of their new Depot when finished, we shall believe 'there is no virtue extant.' It will be a splendid edifice, worthy of any locality; and reflects an enviable degree of credit not only upon those who first projected, and have thus far carried out, the idea of its erection, but also upon those whose energy and enterprise have thus far carried forward the material of the idea with so much promptness and skill. It will not only be the best building of the kind in Vermont, but unequaled, in point of looks and convenience, in New England."[308] Food was also available to the public when, soon after its opening, on April 12, 1853, Rutland's town clerk and railroad civil engineer Ambrose Lincoln Brown recorded in his personal day book "Depot for dinner" that cost him twenty-five cents.[309]

Engine Pittsford, built at Taunton, Massachusetts, June 25, 1849, one of eight passenger locomotives ordered by the Rutland and Burlington Railroad. Rutland Newsliner: The Rutland Railway Magazine (Dec. 1955–Jan. 1956).

While a state-of-the-art facility at the time of its construction, by 1894 railroad commissioners characterized Vermont's depots generally as "decaying relic[s]" that had "supplied the wants of their day and generation... and the less exacting and urgent demands of the travelling public."[310] After four decades of service, they described Rutland's depot as "old and dingy, dark and dirty, and the closets [bathrooms]... damp and filthy."[311] In 1898 when the board of directors debated the fate of the second roundhouse, the commissioners recognized that Rutland required "a modern union depot, corresponding to its commercial importance and size." In 1901 Shelburne's William Seward Webb, husband of railroad heiress Eliza Osgood Vanderbilt, sought to advance that goal and proposed to the railroad board his purchase of thousands of shares of its stock if it agreed to "remodeling the yard and in erecting a new depot and office building at Rutland."[312] The directors consented and for the next two years they monitored extensive work and renovations removing the imposing two-hundred-foot-long train shed, described as having "been afire more times than any building" in Rutland. Solidly built, it required the use of dynamite and a thirty-man crew to tear it down revealing the surprising presence of "about 100 rats of all sizes" scurrying away.[313] They also renovated the depot building, making many modern upgrades that cost an estimated $100,000 to allow Rutland to maintain its decades-long reputation of having "the most perfect building of its kind in any New England provincial city."[314]

Within only a few years after Brown first laid out the Rutland yard, it experienced explosive growth in addition to the construction of the roundhouse and depot. In 1852, a New Hampshire newspaper man who attended the nearby Vermont State Agricultural Society exhibition reported that "like many other towns similarly situated, [Rutland] has until recently been enjoying a Rip Van Winkle sleep, but the sound of the steam whistle and the heavy roll of the car, have awakened the slumbering energies of the people and the past two years have shown wonderful changes, and now on every street and all about town new houses are going up and improvements making their appearance."[315] A speaker at the exhibition described the new technology he witnessed with further awe. "But hark!," he inquired of his audience, "What is it, that hauls over the mountain side, and rushes, irresistible, through the valley?" With hyperbola and a bit of mid-century rhetorical flourish he answered, "This fearful creation of Science! Its eyes are flaming fire, its breath is black smoke, and it rushes along its iron road with the roar and the strength of a cataract. It is a terrible [wonderful] evidence of the human mind." The railroad "wildly flying, as it were in mid-air, you see it now upon the mountainside, now shrieking it springs across a yawning gulf, spanned by an arch of heavy masonry; and now it scours with its long train, through the valley. Over rivers, at a dizzy height, runs its track, and through the heart of the mountains."[316] Another traveler described what he saw when he departed the yard on a journey to Bennington. "At about half-past ten," he wrote, "we got under way from the Depot at Rutland, and after passing an infinite number of freight cars, switches, &c., which the largely increased business of this place renders necessary, we reached the open fields." There, he caught "a glimpse of husbandmen, as the men lean upon their scythes and the boys upon their forks, gazing with astonishment upon the frightful speed of the 'iron horse.'"[317] Twenty regular and two express trains ran through Rutland each day. They included "New passenger cars of an improved style, beautifully finished. . . some of them capable of seating eighty persons each, with comfort" another observer noted and exclaimed

Rutland's rebuilt, domed second roundhouse and rail yard (depot on left), with the growing Nebraska neighborhood in the background, c. 1869. Historical Rutland (1911).

that the railroad's "business is increasing with a degree of rapidity unprecedented in the history of any road in Vermont." "Let the toast be, *Success to enterprise.*"[318]

Land on both sides of the yard saw further development with roads built for wagons and carriages to accommodate the needs of freight and passengers, machine shops blossomed in Nebraska on the west side and merchants' shops and the Bardwell Hotel sprang into existence immediately opposite the depot. After its completion, the depot gained such renown that advertisements for businesses frequently identified their location in relation to it. It also became a place of civic utility after Methodists were not allowed to assemble in the Main Street courthouse because, the judges argued, it could only be used for county business. Undissuaded, one member who worked for the railroad arranged for the use of "the spacious depot," where its members swept the floors clean, put in seating and closed the gates for service leading one to observe that in resistant Rutland *"Methodism came in by the railroad !"*[319] For those riding the trains on Sundays and unable to attend formal services, a conductor passed down the aisles and read aloud passages from the Bible as required by law.[320] At the long-established Rutland Congregational church, the railroad meant it also had to adapt to accommodate its demands. On the occasion of its 125th anniversary in 1913 one observer looked back on its history and recalled that when "the railroad entered the town. . . an era of progression opened which resulted in the agitation for a larger church edifice."[321] Between the depot and Main Street on the hill new styles of architecture became more common. Thirty-four-year-old George W. Strong, son of Moses and RLC matriarch Harriet Strong, a forceful advocate of the railroad who served on the board of the Rutland and Burlington line and as a contractor, built portions of it.[322] In 1852, while his mother attended to the activities of the RLC, he subdivided the family's land between the yard and Main Street and laid out several streets. He also joined with James Barrett and Bardwell

Period view of Rutland Depot and attached train shed. Courtesy of William Badger.

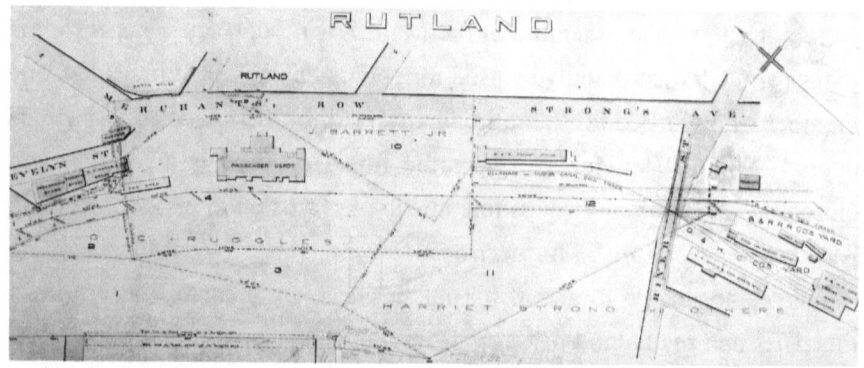

Rutland Railroad Chief Engineer Thomas Chappell's drawing of Rutland's depot (center left) with railroad centerline extending from south (right) to north (left) immediately below, 1893. Vermont State Archives.

Hotel owners Otis Bardwell and E. Foster Cook to pay to improve Washington Street.[323] At the corner of Washington and Pleasant streets Strong built "a brick Italianate palazzo house, a style beginning to appear in. . . builders' guides," while a short distance away across from the Bardwell and within close proximity to the depot the first town hall was erected in 1853.[324] Other opportunities also arose that saw Strong join with Rutland's U. S. Senator Solomon Foot, RLC member John Cain, and other notables to mimic the rage underway in Europe and other large American cities to form the short-lived Vermont Art Union in the town.[325]

Moving Downhill

The early 1850s also marked the time when the federal government transitioned from using rented buildings to conduct its operations to ones it owned outright. Architect Ammi Young was now the Treasury Department's supervising architect and experienced heavy demands on his time, working "at least 12 hours [and] sometimes 14 hours out of 24" as he sought to create a uniform style of architecture throughout the country inspired by his experiences in Vermont.[326] Because of his increased responsibilities that probably prevented him from providing little more than cursory supervision over Randall's design work for the Rutland Railroad, the board of directors' minutes in June 1853 indicate his departure (perhaps dismissal) from their employ. In a dismissive tone that omitted the routine references of gratitude for contributions made by others on their behalf, their clerk recorded simply that "Mr. A. B. Young, architect presented his account to the board for services rendered. Whereupon it was Resolved, that the Treasurer be authorized to issue to Mr. Young two shares of the common stock of the Corporation, which shall be in full payment of his claim."[327] Two shares of Rutland and Burlington Railroad stock at the time was a trivial amount for someone of Young's ability and reputation, valued at around $100 each, indicating they considered his contributions minimal.[328]

As Young ended his association with the Rutland Railroad, he began work with Captain Alexander H. Bowman, U. S. Army Corps of Engineers, recently assigned to create an Office of Construction within the Treasury Department. Responsible for identifying the criteria ("as far as practicable") to guide the government's decision-making process, Bowman played a central role in locating its buildings in the next years of frantic federally-funded construction in many communities around the country. His guidelines required him to consider a variety of concerns: placement of buildings near the "present and prospective" center of a city's population; the assurance of a quiet atmosphere for courtroom proceedings; to protect women and children from harm on adjacent streets; cost, choosing less expensive locations over the more expensive, centrally located ones; and, sites "best calculated to show the building to advantage."[329] The placement of government buildings in communities became a point of constant debate as local authorities sought to situate them in the center of activity to propel growth that often conflicted with the national criteria. In 1854 Burlington businessmen failed to convince Treasury officials to place its new federal building adjacent to the public square. The *"principle reason"* for their request did not seek to gain the benefits that such as structure could provide to the community as a whole, but rather, their petition stated, "to get rid of the *old shell* [an unidentified decrepit wooden structure] that encumbers that corner." Unable to make a convincing argument, the federal government chose a less expensive location away from the public square.[330]

In May 1855, Rutland attorney and avid railroad advocate, Senator Solomon Foot introduced a series of bills in the United States Senate. One of them sought appropriations "for the erection of a suitable building for the accommodation of the circuit and district courts of the United States... and of the post office at Rutland, Vermont."[331] Federal cases had been heard in Rutland for decades beforehand, but the times called for more modern facilities to enhance the reputation and prestige of the judiciary and to resolve the new types of litigation coming before the courts in mid-century. These involved many tariff-related matters and cases instituted by far off inventors alleging patent infringements committed by Vermonters of the developing technology springing into existence. Extant federal court records describe their many suits contesting a wide-range of interests over the unauthorized sale of various types of machinery. These included those used for "planning [sic], tongueing [sic] and grooving boards," "working and pulverizing potatoes," "for cutting irregular forms out of wood, iron, brass or other materials," "improved sewing machines," "improvements in the Portable Circular Saw Mill," the "new and useful improvement of railroad frogs" (devices used to secure rails to ties), casting car wheels, "means of supporting the bodies of Rail Road cars and carriages," improvements in "the hot air furnace," lamps, coal stoves, horse rakes, harvesters, Seraphines (a keyed wind instrument), methods to improve "the making of cotton bunting and wadding," "threshing and cleaning grain," "the enamel composition of bricks," "metal tips applied to the toes of boots and shoes," and the manufacture of India rubber.[332]

Senator Foot's bill for the construction of the courthouse and post office was approved in 1856, accompanied by an appropriation of $25,000.[333] Young and Bowman each became involved with the project and, although no specific information describes their participation in deciding the building's site, the evidence indicates that they did and applied the national criteria that Bowman oversaw. The increasing presence of intrusive railroads into communities elsewhere in the country engendered great concern that the two wanted to avoid. In Cleveland, the commercial district objected to its "noise & dirt," a situation replicated in Rutland. The committee responsible for identifying an appropriate location for the facility had to consider the benefits and pitfalls of being near either the existing, established "uptown" side of the community on Main Street or the emerging "downtown" burdened with "its attendant noise and confusion" from the railroad yard.[334] Contemporary and detailed maps of Rutland prepared by civil engineers and surveyors from Jersey City (Presdee & Edwards in 1852) and Philadelphia (James D. Scott & Co. in 1854) make readily apparent the phenomenal growth that the downtown area already experienced at the expense of Main Street businesses in such a short time. The road in front of the proposed depot had already assumed the name of "Merchants Row" and the maps identified the many tracts of land owned by local residents (Ruggles, Barrett and Strong) who played a role in establishing the yard.[335] A team of six arsonists may have also given the committee concern when, on May 9, 1857, the American House hotel and Barrett's store on Main Street "burned to the ground" while the nearby Franklin Hotel survived an unsuccessful attempt. The arsonists also targeted the Bardwell Hotel located further away nearer the depot, but it did not suffer any damage as authorities took all of the suspects into custody.[336] Adding to the confusion, and with a touch of humor, two Irishmen lugged "a ten gallon keg down the hill" headed towards Nebraska, apparently unaware that it contained vinegar.[337]

The twenty-four-hour-a-day, incessant "noise and confusion" from the Rutland yard and dangers presented to women and children who passed near and through it precluded any thought of placing the courthouse close by. A Brattleboro correspondent described the impact the railroad imposed on his community just a month after the line opened connecting the town with Rutland. "The engine came up," he wrote, "in grand style and when opposite our village the Monster gave one of its most savage yells, frightening men, women and children considerably and bringing forth deafening howls from all the dogs in the neighborhood."[338] Others in Rutland entered their resentment at these kinds of intrusions and the rapid, unregulated development of its rail yard and the Nebraska neighborhood as they sought to maintain the status quo.[339] But events accelerated and made any thought of keeping the community's business on the plateau above untenable. The loss of the important commercial buildings on Main Street may have also played a role in the committee's decision as remaining businesses considered what the railroad meant for their own futures and whether it served any purpose to locate a courthouse and post office intended to serve the entire

Pencil drawing of the view from the Rutland depot uphill to the Trinity Episcopal Church tower on Main Street, 1853. Rutland Historical Society.

community away from the new commercial district. Additionally, the ability to show off the architectural attributes of Young's creation (that also included the timely use of modern fireproof materials) may have influenced the ultimate site selection located only a short distance west of Main Street at Center and Court streets overlooking the yard that allowed viewers to see it to its best advantage. Cost was also one of Young's concerns and just two months after the Main Street fires, the government purchased the site on July 4, 1857 for $1,900. A contract for the courthouse's construction, awarded to a Lynn, Massachusetts company, Colby & Bird, for $52,827, inevitably ballooned by some forty percent to $70,324.43.[340] Former RLC member, local businessman, architect and builder John Cain also had involvement and probably associated himself with the out-of-state construction company in the work. The building soon served as the community's important pivotal point marking the transition between the old and new, its "nucleus of the mid-century building boom," that attracted the construction of other important civic buildings nearby: the county courthouse, a bank, and congregational and Baptist churches.[341]

Young's design for the courthouse and post office, a variation of others he worked on, had an immediate impact on the Rutland community as local residents adopted the increasingly popular Renaissance Revival forms of architecture, specifically the square palazzo and more elaborate Italianate for their own homes and businesses.[342] At a time when bouts of consumption killed Vermont's females, a disease attributed, in part, to breathing noxious air caused by the new technology, situating a building to obtain maximum light and ventilation was of great importance. To obtain the best access to untainted air, Young found that by placing a palazzo-style building close to a lot's front lines along a street permitted the space left behind to allow additional light and air to enter.[343] Young and Bowman, pragmatic designers and builders, also found that iron could easily replace the costly stone used for structural and ornamental features and employed it as a common feature. They expressed each of these aspects in Rutland's courthouse from its location close to the street's corner, to the palazzo design and use of iron wherever possible.[344] While acceptable for a public building, other homes built nearby chose to locate further back on their lots, but adopted many of its architectural features.

Ammi Young's United States Courthouse and Post Office, Rutland, located midway between traditional Main Street and the developing rail yard below, 1858. Rutland Historical Society.

With the courtroom on the building's second floor, Young's post office at street level provided the public with ready access to 1,500 letter boxes, as well as a separate, private area devoted to serving only women.[345] Each of Young's designs in the 1850s for the Rutland, Windsor and Burlington post offices set off these distinct areas in recognition of the difficulties that women experienced when they visited urban post offices. Historian Richard John describes why as these environments were identified as "a bastion of white male solidity and an adjunct to the racially and sexually stratified world of politics and commerce."[346] In order to avoid the scrutiny of lingering, leering males and having to mingle with the rougher sorts of the community, the special ladies delivery windows allowed women to drop off and pick up mail in a place of safety with a degree of privacy. Not all of the nation's post offices had these segregated areas, but the fact that some of Vermont's did reveals an aspect of the kinds of obstacles that women in the mid-nineteenth century had to negotiate on a daily basis in performing simple tasks.[347]

United States Senator Hon. Solomon Foot of Vermont. Library of Congress.

When Senator Foot died in Washington in 1866, following funeral services in the Senate chamber, his body came to Rutland by a special train. On April 2, his casket, attended by a large crowd on a rainy, muddy day, was brought from the Rutland depot up the hill to the courthouse. Once inside, it was carried up Ammi Young's iron stairway to the courtroom and placed in front on a "catafalque, with its evergreen pillars, significant of the old Green Mountain State, with its canopy beautifully festooned and draped, with its raised base." The courtroom was similarly decorated and "under a fine painting of the deceased Senator. . . was suspended the following beautiful and expressive motto: 'We honor him dead, who honored us while living.'"[348] When Foot's casket eventually reached the town's Evergreen Cemetery and interred, his grave was marked by "a monument of granite. . . taken from the same quarry from which the granite of the Vermont State-House is built."[349] Together with RLC member Harriet Strong who died four years later, their deaths marked the passing of a venerated generation that had lived through and experienced the railroad's impact on the community in the 1850s. Foot vigorously responded to its challenges and played an integral role in accommodating the sacrifices it demanded, arranging for the creation of its important courthouse and post office that allowed the inhabitants to obtain the benefits that other communities around the country experienced. In the end, it was only fitting that his gravestone should be cut from the same stone used to rebuild the third Capitol building after fired destroyed its predecessor in 1857.

OFFICIAL OVERSIGHT AND CLASS DIVISION

The 1850s brought innumerable, significant benefits to Vermont in general and to Rutland specifically. The speed of communications accelerated as never before when the telegraph linked Burlington and Rutland in 1848 and allowed Ambrose Lincoln Brown working on the depot grounds instant coordination with the road's distant managers. The telegraph connected to Boston saw increased usage, including the first time in the nation's railroad history when orders were transmitted over it for the movement of rail traffic between Rutland and Burlington in 1852.[350] The number of miles the mail moved in the state increased substantially between 1850 and 1853 from 188,604 miles to 393,588 because of the railroad.[351] Newspapers saw increased circulation despite the delay in getting timely news to the state's capital. "My constituents in Rutland county," one legislator in Montpelier complained during the 1857 debates, "receive their papers from New York and Boston the day of their date. From Montpelier, they receive them in from two to four days."[352] While some traditionalists continued to resent the intrusive technology, others did not that explains the solon's frustration at the delay in obtaining news from outside the state. As one Rutland commentator succinctly described its many benefits the community experienced:

> The introduction of railroads into this State has done vastly more than adding to our wealth. Whenever it has increased wealth, it has done it by rewarding labor, and creating productive industry. It has decreased idleness. It has virtually transported the whole State half-way to the seaboard. It has added value to every acre and to every rock even. Its benefits are on every farm, and at

every waterfall. Its good results are felt in every work-shop, and at every fireside. Hardly a man exists in the State, but wears a better coat, eats a better dinner, has a fuller pocket, and sleeps warmer at night, from the running of railway trains through this state. "Wish the Railroads were destroyed?" You might as well wish that July and August were stricken out of the year.[353]

The benefits far exceeded the pitfalls as opportunities presented from beyond the state's borders allowed for a dramatic increase in the number of Vermont trades and those employed in them to satisfy the populations growing demands and expectations. While quantifying the impact is difficult because of inconsistent accounts, it was huge.[354]

A variety of conflicting issues arose because of modernity's effects. Many people did well enough by 1854 that religious leaders lamented the lack of proportional monetary support they received from the public for their missionary work compared to the increased resources that workers accumulated for themselves. "Upon what ground can our thriving farmers and mechanics and merchants and lawyers justify themselves in withholding assistance?" they asked.[355] In 1856, Governor Fletcher also noted the changes Vermonters experienced because of the "great accumulation of business in some of the counties of the State" that had an adverse effect on the courts' ability, exemplified by Senator Foot's efforts to modernize the federal court in Rutland, to promptly resolve the increasing commercial case load brought before them.[356]

At the same time, discernable cracks in Vermont society became more evident because of the effects of the railroad. One industry historian conclusively states that in the eastern United States, while the railroad was both a "creator and enabler" of opportunities, it was also a "destroyer" because it "stimulated the growth of town and cities" but "at the expense of their rural hinterlands."[357] However, contemporary historian Daniel P. Thompson described in 1860 that Montpelier inhabitants experienced a refined alternative of that scenario that was not quite so dire. Instead, he reported that the farming community viewed the railroad as providing it with "few or no prospective benefits" causing it to withhold investing in it while those in the village believed otherwise and contributed "most liberally in the whole movement." The merchants' dreams were dashed when their subsequent retail experience, Thompson reported, did not follow ("unquestionably been diminished," he wrote) because of competition from other towns that also invested in the technology and cut into the profits they expected to gain to recoup their investments. Farmers unburdened by such losses reaped the benefits as they saw the value of their land increase greatly making them, "as a body, the most forehanded and independent class of community."[358]

The separation between rich and poor, whether in the villages or farms, was inconsistent in the rocky Vermont environment because of the various ways that residents transitioned from subsistence to the new forms of capitalism that the railroad sponsored.[359] In 1855, the Council of Censors responsible for proposing changes to the state constitution identified the presence of three distinguishable classes of people becoming increasingly apparent. Among them, they argued, the young needed the most support and encouragement to take on the opportunities and challenges that the new technology presented:

> The first, or rich class, having a competency, and generally being men somewhat advanced in life, are satisfied to manage their own personal affairs in the easiest and safest manner, without any very strong desire of improvements, or expending their means for public utility.
>
> The second, or poor class, are generally, from age or other incapacity, or misfortune, men who are unable or unqualified to take the lead in business transactions.
>
> And the third class constitutes the bone and muscle of the State. They have strong bodies and strong minds, but lack for capital to carry out their business designs, and are under the necessity of soliciting, and obtaining pecuniary aid from men of more capital and less enterprise.[360]

Many towns reported the loss of their young residents leaving because they lacked opportunities to advance themselves and in 1856 groups of them departed from Rutland bound for Kansas to establish a Vermont colony. They included, one newspaper reported, those "of the right stamp – being men in the prime of life" able to "carry with them a large share of New England enterprise and industry."[361] As some left, others remained and simply relocated elsewhere in the state, including Rutland. Reading attorney Josiah Hawkins recorded that he had "sold out of this town & have an idea of Rutland being a large business town & county seat.... I have two children & wish in locating the advantage of a good school."[362] Rutland, Burlington and St. Albans each gained resentful attention from envious communities around the state as immigrants flocked into them. "Some speak with contempt" of those towns fortunate to receive the newcomers, one observer wrote, "saying it is of an illiterate and transient character, and therefore of little value to the State." "But not so," he continued, "for at the head of these enterprises are men of intelligence, who by their planning and direction cause a thousand arms and hands to do their bidding, thus making them like their own hands increased a thousand fold in power."[363] Their numbers increased substantially and by 1880 the Census Enumeration of those living on streets in Rutland's Nebraska neighborhood revealed the strong presence of successful first and second generation Irish, many living together in the same household. Hundreds worked in trades related directly to the railroad itself, in the mechanical shops servicing its needs, and in catering to the public in stores and hotels run by natives on the east side of the yard.

The railroad technology slammed into Vermont and enveloped the unprepared population so quickly it was unable to respond in a timely way when problems began to appear. They telescoped outwards from the predictable kinds of trouble associated with becoming familiar with the imposing, sophisticated, steam-driven machinery to the more serious concerns that placed the public's safety, and the roads' financial backing, at risk. The managers first encountered difficulties in the way the engines and cars were operated under the control of overzealous engineers and conductors. It included their racing and negligence that resulted in not only collisions and derailments causing heavy damage to the equipment, but also injury and death.[364] Significant design and quality of materials problems emerged, ignored in their rush to build the road by managers who, despite the care they might have taken, failed to fully appreciate how quickly many aspects of their enterprise could deteriorate in the harsh Vermont environment. Their experiences differed little from others where, according to a British Royal Engineer assessing the railroad's development in North America in 1856 wrote that, "In a rapidly developing new country, capital is dear. Hence a rough and ready cheap railway although it entails increased cost for maintenance is preferable to a more finished and expensive line."[365] Hard-pressed to deal with the mounting problems, the financial situation forced the Rutland Railroad into receivership in 1854 and left trustees examining the health of the road with much work to repair its engines, cars, road bed, and buildings.[366] Assigning responsibility for "many of the state's agricultural, industrial, and commercial problems" that accompanied the defaults of the railroad industry, Vermont landscape historian Jan Albers concludes, was not because the railroad "system did not develop, but rather that it developed out of sync with the economy."[367] Failure to contain unbridled enthusiasm in the face of modernity extracted heavy costs.

Physical harm on the railroad became apparent in many ways. Brakemen on top of cars were killed by low bridge overheads, engineers, firemen and brakemen lost their balance and fell between moving cars resulting in their instant or lingering deaths, or dismemberment, as passengers walking between or alighting from cars stumbled and suffered similar fates. The trains ran down trespassers who walked drunk on rural rails or those taking short cuts through the Rutland yard. An impatient public caught up in an increasingly sped up way of life traveling on roadways in wagons and carriages tried to avoid long delays at crossings and raced their frightened horses to get across them that resulted in many thrown out and killed or seriously injured.

Just as the early railroad managers cautiously adapted through a learning process forced on them by their operational problems, Vermont legislators exhibited the same in their work. Foremost, they had no interest in hindering any of the railroad's operations that could delay their communicating beyond the state's borders. "The interruption of interstate commerce and interference with the transportation of the mails were not much if at all considered" the Vermont Supreme Court wrote of these times when it assessed the integrity of official oversight of the railroad on the public's behalf.[368] The legislature's laissez-faire attitude over the operations of railroad corporations that favored economics above safety repeated state policy that viewed a "less is more" attitude when it considered new legislation. That myopic process survived the impact of the new technology in the 1850s and manifested itself in other arenas soon afterwards that imposed serious consequences on the immediate and future physical health of Vermonters.

In mid-century, Vermont lawmakers hesitatingly considered legislation to implement protections for the railroad-traveling public. The process evolved and began with claims filed by farmers directly with the railroad seeking compensation for their loss of horses, cattle, and sheep run down by its engines and cars. When that did not bring satisfaction, they brought lawsuits, some of which, unlike the prohibitions imposed by the condemnation process, eventually reached the Supreme Court. The farmers made a variety of ultimately unsuccessful claims that inadequate fencing or absent cattle guards at crossings were at fault and that the railroad should pay for their resulting losses. They failed in their cases for various reasons: they could not prove the railroad had a pre-existing contractual relationship with them that obligated it to construct barriers; their inability to demonstrate they breached a legal duty that extended to distant claimants who lived away from the road; or, in one case, the plaintiff physically interfered with the railroad's efforts to install a cattle guard that could have prevented his loss.[369] Those claims notwithstanding, a case decided in 1854 involving farm animals broke through the prevailing perception that the legislature had no authority to intervene with the railroad's operations to ensure the public's safety.

In the case of *John S. Thorpe v. The Rutland Railroad Company* an aggrieved Charlotte farmer argued that the loss of several sheep run down by the defendant's locomotive and cars happened because the company failed to install a cattle guard.[370] Arguing for a restrictive interpretation of its 1843 charter, the railroad said it was only required to put up fencing in that particular area and did not specifically include cattle guards. It also contended that a later legislative act passed in 1849 imposing such an obligation on all railroads interfered with its pre-existing rights laid out in its charter thereby precluding any finding of liability on its part. In opposition, Thorpe argued that the state did have that right to impose such a requirement as one of its inherent police powers to protect the public. Chief Justice Isaac F. Redfield, described as "a well-known writer and editor of legal works. . . [and] the nation's leading authority on railroad law" and who became known internationally for his important *A Practical Treatise upon the Law of Railways* (1857), agreed and rendered the court's decision.[371] Redfield believed strongly in the legislature's right to exercise control over corporations it chartered and regarded Thorpe's claim as one of "vast importance, both to the [railroads] and the public." He had little trouble in finding that the 1849 law superseded the railroad's charter provisions and agreed with Thorpe that it was a proper exercise of the state's inherent police authority granted to it by Article 5 of the Constitution: "The people of this state by their legal representatives, have the sole, inherent, and exclusive right of governing and regulating the internal police of the same."[372] Redfield determined unequivocally that this power rested with the state and was "a responsibility which legislatures cannot divest themselves of, [even] if they would [wanted]" and directly countered contemporary belief that laws curtailing corporate activity should be limited. "This police power of the state," he wrote, "extends to the protection of the lives, limbs, health, comfort, and quiet of all persons, and the protection of all property within the state." The state's legislative imposition on the railroads, regardless of their pre-existing charter provisions, to install cattle guards was an issue of great importance to the public's safety and the protection of its property and Redfield saw no reason to concede the point. His views that railroad corporations required legislative oversight remained unchanged thereafter and in 1857 he succinctly wrote that, "Railways being a species of highway, and in practice, monopolizing the entire traffic, both of travel and transportation, in the country, it is just and necessary, and indispensable to the public security, that a strict legislative control over the subject be constantly exercised."[373] Redfield did not stand alone in arguing for such legislative oversight to advance the public's safety and was a point strongly endorsed by George Perkins Marsh.

In the wake of Redfield's important decision and just before the appointment of the state's first railroad commissioner in 1856, a resistant legislature entertaining the prospect of its creation prevailed upon three "profound constitutional jurists" (Jacob Collamer, Daniel Kellogg and Hiland Hall) in 1854 to recommend the scope of authority that such a position, if allowed, should exercise.[374] The next year, the three men drafted a proposed eleven-section act that allowed a commissioner to examine the financial viability of the railroads and to recommend infrastructure changes on the behalf of public safety. In reaching its conclusions, the commission acknowledged the unique challenges it faced with the new technology and sought to mollify the skeptics that viewed their work as intrusive. "The only practicable object of a revision we consider," they wrote with defensive emphasis, "is, not *indemnity for the past*, but a reasonable expectation of *security for the future,"* a profound issue for Vermont as it sought to determine whether legislatively-created corporations should operate unmonitored or subject to state-sponsored oversight.[375] The commission clearly held oversight of the railroad as the proper course to follow and recited their reasons why corporations could not police themselves. "The rivalry of competition amongst the roads," it wrote, "the cupidity of private interest in their officials and the recklessness of employees, rendered by use familiar with and regardless of, danger in the conduct of engines and trains, involving the destruction of lives and property, and even of the roads themselves, imperatively require that some efficient power of constant inspection and control should be provided for the public safety, in addition to the legal responsibility of the corporations to actions for private damages."[376]

The commission's reasonable proposal represented only a tentative, cautious attempt to wrest back some of the authority the legislature surrendered to the railroads in 1843 when it issued their generous charters and, according to the senator in 1874, "Vermont ceased to be a free and independent state." By 1855, the results of that failure instilled in the minds of some a continued belief that legislative interference was unnecessary leading them to question why the commission even existed. "The outcry against Railroads is not a popular one," one writer explained, because "it does not come from *the people*" who daily favorably viewed their presence and saw that "passenger trains grow longer from year to year, and the freight trains groan with continually increasing burdens." Rather, he alleged, some lodged inaccurate aspersions against the technology, primarily "stockholders who do not find the investment in Railroad stocks as good a speculation as they had hoped, and some bond holders who are disappointed because they do not receive their interest" and advocated on the behalf of commission's authority.[377]

The House committee reviewing the commission's report adopted a similar mindset and vehemently opposed its recommendations, dismissing outright any thought of allowing state employees to engage in oversight of corporations. If allowed, the proposed act, it argued, could be "executed with most summary despotism, to the detriment and even destruction" of the railroads and, dismissing the overwhelming evidence of clear harm taking place, was "uncalled for by any exigency." Most importantly, such an effort of *"absolute despotism"* would present the capitalists that invested their money in the railroads with "evidence of a deep seated and inverate [inveterate] hostility on the part of the people, to any further investments in Railroads within this State."[378] That sentiment repeated the first expression of opposition to intrusive legislative oversight of railroads lodged in 1843 and validated the observations of a New York newspaper that the construction of the Albany and Rutland Railroad occurred, in part, because of "the exertions of some of our capitalists."[379]

The committee's attitude opposed to the warnings and calls for change made by others that might inhibit Vermont's economic interests replicated the earlier concerns of New York officials who feared that premature claims by physicians of the presence of cholera in the city would adversely affect business.[380] The uninhibited flow of commerce and the perceptions of outsiders that might question Vermont's ability to protect their investments, as well as its reputation, were at stake and its legislators were not about to allow their denigration in any way. The committee also rejected any contention of the roads being operated in a manner that endangered the lives, health, or property of the people and demanded "conclusive evidence" of it before taking action. Of added importance, it saw no reason to allow state-paid employees (those dishonest and incompetent "couriers for executive favor," the members believed) access to the internal financial arrangements of a corporation. All the public had a right to, it wrote, was "the cheap and safe transit of persons and property" and "when that is attained, public interests ceases."[381] In their defensive posturing, the legislators engaged in a strong display of public relations that betrayed their true intention to avoid any manner of interference with capitalists' interests threatening the state's economic well-being as they sought to exploit all aspects that the new technology promised.

While the commission's proposed act was dead on arrival, the call for change continued when some recognized that doing something to protect the public from dangerous aspects of the railroads surmounted blind devotion to the capitalists' wishes. During his 1856 inaugural address to the legislature, Governor Fletcher added his voice to the debate and observed that the railroad industry was "an important item in the catalogue of our interests."[382] Notwithstanding, he argued that it required official oversight because "Vast amounts of property and the safety of great numbers of the people are committed to the charge of corporations, which exist by the authority of the Legislature and are to a great extent subject to your regulation and control." "While these agents of the public convenience should receive such favor as a wise Legislature would bestow," he reasonably stated, "they should also be subjected to rigid police regulations to guard against the melancholy and wholesale destruction of human life, which has too often marked the history and marred the utility of this great modern invention." Rejecting the exercise of expansive authority, the legislature did concede in a small, petty way and imposed a penalty on any conductor or engineer who allowed his stopped train to block a public highway. Failure to move or separate cars when demanded by travelers to allow the passage of carriages between them resulted in the imposition of fines of between ten and fifty dollars.[383] "Blind legislators," Franklin County station agent P. G. Stone ridiculed in response, passed such laws without consideration for the difficulties that the railroads faced in unloading goods in busy cities and towns. The law brought great consternation among railroad workers now subject to ridiculous suits brought against them by the very farmers they tried to assist, impatient at the prospect of any obstruction in their way. The feeling was so great that the bewildered Stone wrote "this is the feeling which many have towards the road, and this same feeling is a damage to the community, and a great damage to the road and its employees, whose exertions are for the benefit of the community." "I have no objections" to people insisting that the company do its duty, he ended, "but have charity and be reasonable."[384]

Accommodation of the new technology touched on all levels of Vermont society, from the mundane experiences of farmers delayed at railroad crossings to the life-threatening challenges that its workers faced. Continuing in its minimalist intervention in railroad affairs, the legislature finally authorized the appointment of Vermont's first railroad commissioner in 1856, former Rutland Railroad board member and rail sycophant Charles Linsley, but with constricted authority. When George Perkins Marsh replaced Linsley in 1858 he echoed the arguments of Chief Justice Redfield and Governor Fletcher that the legislature needed to become more involved on the public's behalf. But, despite the evidence of mayhem taking place throughout the state on its railroads, as the Supreme Court later noted in reference to Marsh's arguments, "Nothing for a long time" addressed them.[385] The problems continued beyond mid-century in robust fashion and between 1886 and 1900, when statistics were kept, over 700 accounts of death, injury and dismemberment on the state's railroads entered into the records.[386]

Conclusion

By 1850, the prospect of intrusive railroad tracks crossing Vermont's landscape bearing behemoth steel engines spewing steam, ash and smoke into the air, pulling their freight and passenger cars, had passed from giddy anticipation into a physical reality. It was no longer a hard-fought dream, but something the people could actually see, breathe a sigh of relief and begin to appreciate that their mountainous isolation was finally breached to allow them rapid connection to the outside world. The imaginations of unbridled entrepreneurs among them burst forward to seize the newfound opportunities suddenly made available. For many, the railroads could take their land and force them to accept the amounts they wanted to pay in a legal system that denied them any right to appeal those decisions to their highest court, but they could not corral their aspirations to exploit everything else beyond their tracks and railyards. In Rutland, the RLC sprang into existence, with a respected matriarch among its few members, to exploit the opportunities that nearby land offered for housing the arriving railroad workers, including the itinerant Irish. Buildings servicing railroad-related businesses and others tapping into the flood of new merchandise offered to the public suddenly rose up. The change meant that Rutland moved the focus of the town's decades-long center of activity from its original plateau location to the area immediately adjacent to the railroad yard. New public buildings devoted to servicing the community appeared with some, such as Ammi Young's federal courthouse and post office and its special ladies' delivery windows, offering services never seen before that provided a strong, silent testament to the treatment that the state's female population received. The architecture of the town's public and private buildings changed dramatically and introduced new designs thanks to Young's, Gurdon Randall's and Nicholas Powers' creativity. Their efforts captured the rapt attention of many in the community and beyond, drawn in by the particularly spectacular, tall and imposing engine roundhouse and glorious depot building.

The dramatic change because of the railroad and the immediate benefits it provided awed Vermont's leaders and challenged their resolve to not forget the past in their rush to embrace the future. Their excitement was palpable and enthusiastically expressed early on immediately after the road through Rutland opened in 1849 that allowed so many new products to reach Burlington with ease. "The Atlantic Market – the Boston Market," one newspaper exclaimed, "is therefore fully opened. . . independently of the obstructions of bad roads and frost. Boston and Burlington, New

Embracing Modernity

Altered Rutland landscape showing the rail yard and new businesses on the lower side and traditional Main Street above, with the Nebraska neighborhood in the foreground, 1859. Rutland Historical Society.

York and Burlington, are in ESTABLISHED business connection! A great avenue for the introduction of BREAD STUFFS, Iron in all its manufactured forms, WOOL, and other staples of our own State and the Great West, into Boston is OPENED! Let those who are incredulous about the alleged *importance* of this event 'wait a minute' and *see !*"387 Despite the evidence of increased instances of physical injury inflicted by the railroad on people, animals and property, the prospect of continued, uninterrupted interstate commerce proved so powerful that many refused to do anything that threatened to hinder its further development. There was too much at stake. The people would have to understand that priority and adapt their behavior to avoid becoming a victim of the new technology. Imposing government oversight of monopolistic corporations in the name of public safety that affected their capitalist investors who offered so many needed improvements to Vermonters was unacceptable and brought the ire of legislators when pushed to consider such intrusive measures. As some of the state's young departed for the west others arrived to take up their place and allowed communities like Rutland to rapidly increase in number. At the same time, economic divisions among the population became more apparent, identified as an older, traditional and comfortable class followed by the dependent poor and then the young and strong seeking ways to better their prospects in a challenging economic environment weighted against them. While those disparities that seemed to separate them on one level exploded into view, another factor strongly bound them together. Their decades-long agricultural traditions that permeated every level of society from laborer to legislator withstood the attack of modernity during mid-century and allowed the population some level of comfort that, at least, this part of their identity remained under their control.

CHAPTER IV

The Grass Interest

"From the grass. . . our three hundred thousand citizens are fed, and clothed, and housed, and educated, and governed, and made to abound in all good things; and the grass is to be the main source of accumulation in all coming time." [388]

HOUSE REPRESENTATIVE JOSEPH UNDERWOOD OF HARDWICK, February 26, 1857

Organizing Farmers

The legislature's debates in 1857 surrounding the relocation and rebuilding of Vermont's statehouse implicitly extended to a second matter affecting their lives beyond any of those imposed directly by the dramatic railroad technology. Agriculture was undeniably such an integral part of the state's cultural identity and economic wellbeing that its presence loomed above those considerations. Governor Fletcher noted only months earlier that "large portion of the members of the Legislature" engaged in agriculture when he called on them to consider its importance to support of the state's nascent manufacturing interests dependent on it.[389] Although they devoted relatively little time to agricultural concerns during the debates, of all the issues raised none had the implicit ability to transcend party interest and unify them in the way that matters relating to the earth did. It was the unspoken glue that healed their differences regardless of the effects that modernity had on any other aspect of society. Vermonters prided themselves in their ability to overcome the challenges that mountains, valleys and rivers posed that allowed them to produce a dizzying bounty from the soil well in excess of any other New England state and to reap the benefits that a unique Yankee persona created in the process. There was no activity mid-century more important than agriculture until 1860 as that tone gained a perceptible change when Governor Erastus Fairbanks began to qualify its importance and said that while, "Vermont is essentially an Agricultural State," the railroad opened up other opportunities in distant markets.[390] Increasingly, manufacturing interests and the development of marble, slate and soapstone interests provided additional opportunities for Vermonters and Fairbanks called on the legislature to begin advancing all of them jointly ("the industrial interest of the State"), beginning with an Agricultural Bureau to collect "statistical and other information." While he viewed it as an inexpensive, modest proposal that would employ only a single person, little was actually accomplished in the next decade until a more inclusive Board of Agriculture, Mining and Statistics was created in 1870.[391]

Fairbank's call for an organized effort to coordinate these various efforts was not new. In 1806 the legislature authorized dozens of individuals to form the Vermont Agricultural Society "to promote and encourage agriculture, economics in husbandry and useful domestic manufactures."[392] However, the ambitious effort soon failed because it "extended over the whole State, the members being so remote from each other, and the field for examination so extensive that it proved ineffectual."[393] Despite the setback, in 1809, Governor Jonas Galusha reminded the legislature to "never lose sight of the two most important interests of this state, the agricultural and manufacturing," but nothing more happened at the time.[394] During his second term, in 1818 Galusha returned to the subject and reiterated that "the main source of our wealth and the subsistence of every class of citizens, must depend on the cultivation of the soil."[395] He emphasized that maintaining soil quality required close attention to both assure future crops and convince the population to remain and "prevent the too frequent emigration of the laboring class of our citizens." He also suggested that the lawmakers authorize "patriotic and enterprising individuals to form into societies. . . for the beneficial purposes of advancing agricultural interests, encouraging manufacture, and improving our breed of domestic animals." In 1822, Methodist minister John Lindsey provided additional support when he admonished the legislature in his election sermon to remember "the growing interest of agriculture, manufactures and commerce."[396] These were important concerns and he identified the benefits they could provide to improve the health of Vermonters. "By the use of those mineral and vegetable substances," he said, "which the God of nature has so plentifully provided," they could alleviate the "enormous waste of life" attributed to disease. By joining together "the sciences of chemistry and mineralogy" he believed they could, in turn, not "fail by their influence on medicine, agriculture and the arts, to produce consequences of great national importance." To do otherwise would only result in the continued "enormous waste of life." In 1826, the legislature again incorporated the Vermont Agricultural Society with the same goals authorized two decades earlier, but only experienced the same ineffective result.[397]

The inability of officials to implement an organization with state-wide responsibility to advance the interests of rural agriculture working on a diverse landscape is attributed to the same concerns expressed in 1806: too large an area under the responsibility of people "being so remote from each other." Until the railroad technology arrived in 1848 able to overcome that obstacle, the focus was on local efforts to accomplish the work that saw the legislature authorize county societies in 1843 "to encourage and promote agriculture, domestic manufactures and the mechanic arts." To assure their economic viability, it also decided that a portion of $2,000 available for the entire state be provided to any society able to attract a sufficient number of dues paying members.[398] The farming community enthusiastically greeted the news and immediately called for the many societies springing into existence marking the beginning of their "golden age" to take advantage of the state's financial assistance.[399] These societies, one newspaper wrote, "create a laudable emulation among farmers, excite a spirit of improvement, and diffuse a knowledge of products and soils, and the best modes of cultivating them, together with the management of flocks and herds, and the dairy and implements of husbandry so essential to the development of the ample resources of our fertile soil, and the prosperous condition of nine-tenths of our population."[400] In 1849 the legislature increased its support when a senate committee advocated for the creation of a national Bureau of Agriculture within the U. S. Department of the Interior that could aid state and county societies and further research efforts. "It is right that our own State of Vermont should be a foremost, a zealous pioneer in this business," it said, because "Our people are an agricultural people" engaged in the "Art of Arts."[401]

The creation of local societies coincided with the sheep mania boom the state experienced for the past two decades. Hill farms once occupied by the settling generation and their children became home to large flocks that resulted in a marked decrease in the number of cows. That began to change in the 1830s with the loss of protective tariffs and cheap wool from developing western states that allowed the dairy industry to return to dominance in the 1840s.[402] In 1850, Vermont had 2,601,409 acres of improved and 1,524,413 in unimproved land overseen by a farming population of over 48,000 men tending more than 146,000 milch cows, 61,000 horses and a million sheep valued in excess of $12,000,000, more than any other New England state.[403] Despite the large numbers of individuals that arrived and left during the next decade, those identified as farmers and their laborers remained constant. While manufacturing interests began to establish themselves (over 8,500 workers in 1850), the population continued to focus largely on agricultural pursuits. Those efforts allowed Vermont to claim first place that year over any other New England state in the production of "livestock, butter, cheese, wood, wheat, oats, potatoes, hay and a variety of other crops."[404] Those numbers only increased during the 1850s, reflected by a thirty-one percent increase in butter production (15,900,359 pounds in 1860), cheese (8,215,030 pounds) and number of cows (162,356).[405] During an eight-month period in 1856, Franklin County alone shipped 1,888,793 pounds of butter and 1,208,614 pounds of cheese.[406] Whereas Vermont experienced a ratio of five to one working in agriculture compared to those in manufacturing in 1850, the numbers were starkly different in neighboring Massachusetts where three engaged in manufacturing for every one on the land.[407] Agriculture was "not merely the leading, but the commanding, even the absorbing occupation," one committee noted, "Agriculture is the mistress, and every other vocation is her servant... 'We are all farmers in Vermont.'" [408]

Gary G. Shattuck

*Daguerreotype of Vermont barns and stonewalls, 1847.
Vermont Historical Society.*

While the technology that modernity offered during this time greatly affected other New England states and allowed their manufacturing capabilities to expand, Vermont's farmers remained little touched by it in their daily lives. Instead, dependent on the fortunes of geography, they experienced its effects indirectly as developing communities located in the valleys and along lower lying waterways where the railroad passed served as laboratories for change that attracted industry and, in turn, drew off their young. Scholar Christopher Harris notes that this forced farmers to adapt and choose whether to pursue a subsistence-based existence or seek to participate in the larger markets made possible by the railroad.[409] Those that chose the latter then faced the consequent economic reality of whether to maintain the status quo of their farms or to expand or reduce their size. Those with sufficient means grew and specialized their operations as each sought to employ more intensive practices made possible by the new mechanical and scientific technology to maximize returns. Farm layout, building architecture and even methods of plowing were affected as farmers sought to adapt and balance what worked in their particular locale. Between 1850 and 1870 the number of Vermont farms remained the same, but the way that the work was conducted on them made a marked turn away from earlier diversified efforts towards specialization and intensification seeking efficiencies not previously available, or understood. The transition took place statewide and created distinguishable regions that concentrated in particular commodities.[410]

Harris has further determined that the average age of farmers increased during this time and their household numbers shrank "as rural industry dried up" and "the transient population that fed it moved on, and birth rates plummeted." The out-migration that many historians have attributed to an amorphous portion of the population did not come from the established, long-resident farming families, Harris writes, but from the transient "working classes who had spent a limited time in the state" propelled to move on because of their inability to set down "deep, stable economic roots." The various organizations that formed in distant cities to honor their connections to the state, such as the Vermont Association of Boston and the Brooklyn Society of Vermonters, were not made up of the immediate members of these families, but largely of the children from these mobile groups. Marriage practices were also affected in these years that may have been because Vermonters unwittingly copied some aspects of the experiences of other cultures. Increased instances of abortion and infanticide were committed in stressed Japanese communities in response to changing farming practices in 1870 and may explain, in part, why Vermonters also did so at mid-century. In toto, modernity inflicted a corrosive effect on Vermont farmers and proved "an acidity" that ate away at "a diversified lifestyle, forcing people to become specialists in the industrialized mainstream or relegating them to the cultural and economic margins of society."[411]

The farms forced to accommodate these changes because of the demands of modernity are typified by the experiences of some in Addison

County in the 1850s. Harris describes the typical lowland New Haven farm of 155 acres, with three-quarters of it improved, occupied by 100 sheep and fifteen to twenty other animals. Only a few acres were devoted to raising wheat, corn and potatoes, while at least thirty were needed to provide an average harvest of forty-six tons of hay for livestock, with the remaining used as meadow and pasture lands. To the east in hilly Lincoln, the differences were more apparent where farmers located because of the unavailability of such favorable land. A change in elevation, types of flora and a shortened growing season dictated that wood lots became their focus. While they were able to extract a degree of sufficiency from them, the value of their products increased a minimal 15% between 1850 and 1870 compared to the 75% experienced by their lowland neighbors.[412]

PRODUCTIONS OF AGRICULTURE IN RUTLAND COUNTY IN 1850.				
Acres of Land { Improved	263595	Barley, bushels of	333
{ Unimproved	144509	Buckwheat, bushels of	4452
Cash value of Farm	7866230	Value of Orchard Products in dollars	35452
Value of farming Implements and Machinery	246644	Wine, gallons of	11
Horses	6392	Value of Produce of Market Gardens	536
Milch Cows	16081	Butter, lbs. of	937241
Working Oxen	3322	Cheese, lbs. of	2133250
Other Cattle	13446	Hay, tons of	109016
Sheep	202649	Other Grass Seeds, bushels of	762
Swine	20707	Hops, lbs. of	103
Value of Live Stock	1622673	Flax, lbs. of	967
Wheat, bushels of	28274	Maple Sugar, lbs. of	1332148
Rye, bushels of	23494	Molasses, gallons of	75
Indian Corn, bushels of	248052	Beeswax and Honey, lbs. of	36459
Oats, bushels of	181409	Value of Home-made Manufactures	10020
Peas & Beans, bush of	2892	Value of Animals slaughtered	162130
Irish Potatoes, bush. of	383331		

Productions of Agriculture in Rutland County in 1850.
Detail, Scott's Map of Rutland County (1854).

"Grass is the heart of a diversified farm," Harris writes, and "hay represented some 40% of the total value raised on the New Haven farms." It was also a defining factor that differentiated those low-lying farms from ones on hilltops. In 1852, Maine children's book author Jacob Abbott penned a fictional tale that unfolded in accurately described locales ("strict and exact truth and fidelity of all the descriptions," he attested) that included Vermont's grass farms.[413] "The great agricultural production of the northern states," Abbott wrote, "is grass, and these farms among the mountains in Vermont are grass farms." Because hay was so prevalent and cheap to grow, it made no sense to transport it elsewhere as those costs would exceed its value. Instead, cattle, horses and sheep consumed it on the farm before they were in turn slaughtered or sold to drovers who shuttled them off to Boston markets for sale. The way that Vermont's hill farms utilized their grass lands allowed them the prospect of a distinct economic advantage over those at lower elevations and an 1861 Senate report related that the farming community understood this difference well. "And yet what Vermont farmer does not know, and has not known," it wrote, "that the very valley lands that stretch out so smilingly before the eye, are not in truth as valuable for agricultural purposes, do not return as many dollars for the same amount of labor, as the rugged and rough hill farms that seem to hang over and frown down upon them."[414] Whereas an acre of low-lying intervale grass sold for an average of $5.25, or $52.50 for ten acres, the same number of acres of upland grass could sustain at least three milch cows that allowed the farmer to pocket an increased $75 when sold off. Cutting hay was also a laborious task that hilltop farmers could avoid when they allowed grazing to replace it. The burdensome task was described by one contemporary as "a thirty or forty days' war, in which the farmer and his [helpers] are pitted against the heat and the rain and the legions of timothy and clover" and that "Everything about it has the urge, the hurry, the excitement of a battle."[415] Whether they came from Vermont's hills or the valleys, hay consumed the attention of its farmers in mid-century, a persistent fact stressed in 1872 when two papers devoted to the subject were read before the State Board of Agriculture, entitled "The Production of Grass for Hay. Importance and Value of the Crop" and "Grass Culture."[416]

Vermont State Fair

Hay was the predominate crop to support the livestock that produced the essential manure needed to enrich the soil and grow crops. As scientific methods became increasingly available, balancing the requirements that grass required meant that farmers had to closely monitor a number of factors. It was so important that it headed the presentations made during the gathering of the Vermont State Agricultural Society in Rutland in September 1852. Located in the center of the state's rapidly increasing railroad industry, over the course of three days an estimated 50,000 people (possibly as high as 75,000) from Vermont, other states and Canada arrived in what one newspaper described as "dense masses which not only thronged the show ground, but literally swarmed every street and avenue of that beautiful village." It was "unquestionably" the largest gathering of people "ever before assembled, for any purpose, within the limits of this State."[417] "Every hotel, private dwelling, barn, and shed is overflowing with strangers," another account described, "while thousands are compelled to leave the town nightly to seek lodgings at the various villages and hamlets in the neighborhood."[418] The gathering was so noteworthy it also attracted pickpockets from Boston and New York who faced arrest, conviction and sentences to the state prison to serve five years of hard labor.[419]

On thirty, ten-foot-high-fenced acres, three large pavilion buildings, grand stands and a huge stage rose up overlooking a half-mile track where the largest gathering of horses ever assembled in the country for judging. Creative, and allegedly fraudulent, means to finance the construction meant that contractors received exorbitant payments for their work in exchange for the minimal bids they paid to obtain their contracts. A parsimonious legislature unable to appreciate the importance of the efforts of fair organizers refused to provide any financial support to the Society. As a result, it earned their derision, critical of the solons' "laudable zeal to protect the morals of the State" in instituting prohibition, but lamenting its loss of "sight of its great industrial and business interests."[420]

Many exhibits displayed the strong influence that modernity delivered upon the railroads' recent arrival. In the concourse a "musical machine called a Seraphine" and Whitcomb's Brass Band from Middlebury ("thirteen fine looking fellows, clad in neat and appropriate uniform") played as large numbers of cattle, sheep and swine went on display. The importance of hay to make this possible was evident because of the large numbers of creatively designed implements used to process it appeared for judging by the Committee on the Mechanics' and Manufactures' Department. Fourteen different styles of plows and four hay cutters were presented by Rutland's Barrett & Son; four plows from D. Taft & Son of Taftsville ("the plows were most handsomely finished, of good forms and would 'pass muster' anywhere"); three straw cutters from R. Daniels of Woodstock; Hodges & Owen of Rutland presented eight plows and two straw cutters; a riding horse rake came from C. Carlisle of Hartford, Vermont; and J. H. Manny of Freeport, Illinois introduced Manny's Patent Adjustable Northern Illinois Reaper and Mower, among many similar others available for purchase. Dozens more were also on display: threshing machines, cutters, horse rakes and the ubiquitous manure fork with the two forks shown by H. Partridge & Son of Medfield, Massachusetts described as "of the most beautiful workmanship" that made them "almost a pleasure to pitch manure."[421]

As impressive as the various displays were, one New Hampshire reporter had a different impression when he left before the event ended, matter-of-factly concluding that "the show is *great* in sheep and horses, respectable in neat cattle," but "very ordinary in everything else."[422] In a second article he reiterated that while "our Vermont friends stand high" in raising livestock, "in all other departments of the exhibition they are sadly deficient." He suggested that they "awaken an interest in the departments of fancy work, domestic manufactures, implements, machinery, and the productions of the soil" if they hoped to succeed in the future and invited them to attend the New Hampshire State Fair the following month "when our ladies, our mechanics, our merchants, not less than our farmers" to view their goods on display.[423] Friendly competition between the two neighboring states may have been the basis for his comments or constituted a pointed reference to Vermonters' lack of inventiveness and failure to rise to meet the opportunities that modernity presented.

Despite their purported differences, Vermont and New Hampshire farmers shared a common interest to improve their practices on the land and presented a ready audience to consider suggestions for change. William S. King of Rhode Island, the editor of the Boston-based *Journal of Agriculture*, attended both states' fairs that fall and spoke before large, interested crowds from the farming community.[424] His message was the same in each location as he confronted, and gently suggested, the traditionalists among them to acknowledge and adapt to the changes that modernity presented in the same way that George Perkins Marsh did in 1847. They now lived in a new world where transportation allowed them rapid access to distant markets and he prodded them to change their ways to take full advantage of it. "The butter that is churned in the morning," he said, "is eaten hundreds of miles off at night; and the egg laid in Vermont, is on the table of the Tremont House, in Boston, before the cackle is fairly out of the hen's throat."

This was also the time to employ "Scientific Agriculture," King said, and defined it for them simply as "the cultivation of the earth by rule, and not by guess-work." There was no reason why agriculture should not take advantage of what science had to offer, he reasoned, as other pursuits already did so such as examining the galaxies, improving all manner of mechanical instruments, and the administration of justice where forensics "confronts the murderer with his murdered victim." He told them to ignore the narrow-minded, "loud-mouthed" voices among them who rejected and ridiculed science and called it nonsense. Too many Vermont farms suffered because they failed to take advantage of the science already available to them. Innovative ways to plow and drain fields, breeding methods, and horticulture all offered ways to better their practices. King also questioned whether those that struggled understood the need to reduce the size of the fields they cultivated in proportion to the amount of manure they had available to fertilize it instead of trying to spread too little of it too far. He also told them to improve the ways they handled the valuable substance and to construct barns to keep it out of the weather and not allow it to deteriorate before spreading.

King further identified the prejudices that farmers held among themselves, calling them "too-matter-of-fact people," where the "practical farmer" viewed "book farmers" with suspicion because the latter worked only in the comfort of his home or office while they toiled in the field. He admonished them to remove this distinction from their minds. "Is it true," he asked, "that this is, and this alone – *labor with the hands* – HARD WORK – that makes the practical man? Then is your hired help, who follows the plow, day in and day out; who shivers in the wintry stable, and sweats at the harvest, many an hour when you are occupied about other affairs, a better practical farmer than you; for he often works more. Then is the ox, that he drives, the most practical, for he wears rougher and tougher garments, has harder hands, and does more hard work, than either of you. Farmers! You greatly mistake the meaning of the word *practical!*" King's solution to overcome the strong traditional mindset many farmers had against the learned and scientific men was to create and invigorate local societies in order to shatter their "strong inbred prejudices" that esteemed an independent, separate existence apart from their neighbors. By comparing their respective experiences in these associations, their "friction of opinion with opinion" he called it, could "bring smooth surfaces harmoniously together" and both sides reap the benefits. In conclusion, he further recommended that while their town societies were "valuable" and the county societies "more valuable," an overarching State Organization "is most valuable."

The Vermont farmers also heard former New York governor, and future United States Secretary of State under Abraham Lincoln, William H. Seward speak to them for over an hour on their need to adapt in the face of "the quickly-coming and forever-growing future."[425] He recalled that for the past twenty years Americans "flattered ourselves with a belief that we equaled, if, indeed, we did not excel other nations in invention" only to experience embarrassment at Britain's recent Great Exhibition when European inventors revealed products far superior. Seward admitted that their foreign competitors had already taken advantage of international markets because of their sophisticated mechanical inventions and warned that it should not be allowed to happen with America's agricultural efforts. He called for the creation of schools and seminaries to educate the farming communities' young men in the new Agricultural Science. Seward also acknowledged the prejudice that existed among farmers against learning new methods and in the way that young men rejected the laborious work it all entailed. He called on them to embrace the importance of their work in supplying the means that allowed the rest of society to function. He further coaxed them to increase their participation in government and inquired "Have you considered that in practice [farmers] widely renounce the functions of representation in the conduct of the Government in favor of other classes, no more privileged that their own!" "This is unnecessary," he warned, "unwise, unsafe; indeed it is not republican, it is not American." However, to take on those responsibilities required education and he urged them advance its prospects.

Hay continued to draw the attention of farmers and while an 1869 publication noted that great progress had been made in its production "within the last half century than ever before," references to the benefits that modern technology might provide were absent.[426] Despite the power and conveniences that the steam-driven technology delivered to rural communities that made transport of farmers' products easier, it did not transition into practical use in their fields until the twentieth century. Many reasons might explain why it was not accepted that includes a general inertia among the farming community, "the ideological climate," and the extent of farmers' "desire for innovation."[427] Practical changes did occur as specially bred horses able to haul harrows, plows and cutters replaced cumbersome oxen and did less damage to crops. Mowers and rakes to cut and arrange the hay pulled by horses became the norm and while balers were available after 1850, their cost drove the average farmer away and forced him to continue to rely on manual labor to accomplish those tasks.[428] By 1870 farming machinery, such as "swivel plows, improved cultivators and harrows, mowing machines and horse rakes" saw increased usage and one appreciative observer wrote that they "tended to improve the system of culture, besides alleviating the manual labors on the farm."[429] As the century progressed two styles of farming assumed distinct identities as the low-lying farms took advantage of the technology and the benefits that easier access to railroads provided while the distant hill top "plugger" retreated hermit-like and did what he had to in order to survive. These more removed farmers were characterized as being "undereducated, undercapitalized. . . [who] avoided risk whenever possible and saw agricultural research and progressive farmers. . . often as destroyers of economic equilibrium."[430] They were cautious in their work and viewed government's efforts to educate them on current practices with suspicion. Constantly risk averse, they were also frugal with their money and only made purchases that could provide them with the best value.

Grab Laws

The unique economic environment that entrepreneurs faced in mid-century Vermont was not attractive to some risk-takers and offers an explanation of why aspects of technology were not fully exploited that could have benefited the farming community. Those conditions also reportedly contributed to the emigration of the state's younger members who left in pursuit of more favorable financial situations that did not threaten them with either ruin or the prospect of jail for their missteps. In 1861, John Sullivan Adams, the state's first secretary of the Board of Education (appointed in 1856), forcibly argued in a noteworthy report that an economy based mainly on agriculture that did not take advantage of modern financial practices would suffer because of its neglect.[431] Among the New England states that also exhibited a degree of backwardness in this regard, but to lesser extent, Adams singled out Vermont for its more derelict ways and advocated for change. He had great credibility behind him and whenever he spoke, together with his ability to "argue, flatter, scold [and] ridicule" others, he "rarely failed to make his hearers see as he saw, feel as he felt." When Adams died of consumption in 1876 his obituary described him in glowing terms and claimed that "The State owes to few of the public men who have devoted themselves to her highest interests a greater debt of gratitude."[432]

Adams's comprehensive report unequivocally demonstrated the strength of Vermont's agricultural base. His recitation of reasons why it stood statistically in first place among its neighbors in the production of goods from the land was unimpeachable. At the same time, the developing western states and their ability to easily transport similar goods rapidly to eastern markets posed such serious competition that he believed Vermont had to alter the way it treated monetarily those engaged in agriculture and nascent manufacturing efforts to assure their efforts flourished. Ample capital was already available to do so, he said, demonstrated by the many investments that Vermonters made in banks, the railroad and in real estate. At the same time, much of it left the state because investors did not believe its laws could provide them with adequate protection. Those with money required a sense of safety to preserve it and when Adams compared the state's laws with those in Massachusetts it was clear why Vermont remained a backwater. While its agricultural pursuits exceeded those in the Bay State, its manufacturing abilities were woefully deficient. "The iron horses often hurt manufacturing," historian Albers explains, "for the high expenses incurred in making things in the north country and getting them to market were often not competitive."[433] Whereas Massachusetts invested over $83,300,000 in manufacturing facilities, Vermont's efforts stood at $5,000,000. The products of those efforts provided Massachusetts with over $151,00,000 while Vermont could claim a much smaller sum of $8,500,000. Manufacturing wages paid by Massachusetts stood at $39,000,000 compared to $2,200,000 in Vermont. Whereas Vermont had lost an estimated forty-six percent of its population to emigration in the 1850s, Massachusetts calculated its at six percent.[434]

Adams's comparison of the laws of the two states relating to creditors and debtors revealed that Massachusetts utilized a more modern, compassionate approach than Vermont that did not result in draconian outcomes if their circumstances soured. Both creditors and debtors in Massachusetts appreciated that the law clearly set out their respective rights and obligations that permitted them to resolve their differences in an ordered fashion in a court of law if the need arose. This, in turn, allowed each interest to concentrate their respective efforts elsewhere without the worry that one could place the other at a disadvantage. The situation in Vermont was so decidedly different, and inconducive to investment, that Adams derided its efforts as "the grab laws of Vermont." While a few other states also employed a version of grab laws, his singular attribution of them directly to Vermont indicates that its practices stood out markedly and desperately called for change. His forceful statements extended into public appearances where he spoke against the laws before three large, appreciative audiences in Chester in June 1861. A newspaper reported on his presentations and wrote that Adams "deprecates what he aptly styles the *grab laws* of our State, which drive away our young men and capitalists to seek more lenient regions for enterprise and investment." His straight talk was understood by everyone, "he treated plain evils in a plain way, and made an impression on the minds of this community that will not soon fade."[435]

Vermont's generous attachment statutes, or grab laws, that allowed creditors to easily seize defaulting debtors' property were blamed for hindering the state's economic interests. Governor Fletcher forcibly decried them because, he said, they "seriously cramp the enterprise and industry of our people, by impairing that feeling of confidence and security which must characterize all healthy business relations."[436] The Council of Censors also recognized the problem and called the attachment laws "existing evils."[437] They favored creditors to such an extent they inhibited the younger generation from taking risks in creating businesses, posing a problem, it said, "in every part of the State." The grab laws that Vermont enforced, described in 1873 by *The Commercial Law Register* devoted to assisting business interests around the country as "a system peculiar to a few States," was the result of decades of legislation that sought to balance the interests of creditors and debtors.[438] Vermont struggled ever since its creation in 1791 to establish a pathway to protect and encourage investment and, while the laws were a nuisance issue beforehand, the business climate created by the modernity introduced in the 1850s by the railroad forced its deficiencies into view.[439] The peculiarity of the grab laws concerned the ability of a creditor to intervene into the business of someone he loaned money to by suddenly attaching ("grabbing") his property and forcing the liquidation of assets without considering fully the legitimate interests of the surprised debtor or other, similarly surprised, creditors. While Vermont previously abolished aspects of debt-related laws in 1839 that allowed for imprisonment of those in default, that possibility remained in other ways.[440] If a creditor alleged, with or without evidence, that his debtor "intentionally converted" or "diverted or misapplied" funds, he was subject to immediate confinement that required him to post a bond to obtain release. Additionally, a more onerous prospect allowed for claims against a defaulting debtor years after a court determined the underlying case, without providing him with a full discharge of his debts, that meant he could be hounded for payment for the rest of his life.

The "first-in-time, first-in-right" environment that allowed a creditor suspicious of a debtor's default to obtain an attachment from a court before other creditors learned of the situation caused great concern in Vermont's business community. It made little sense for the law to allow a single, frightened creditor to obtain a full return on his investment before others simply because he was the first to the courthouse. In 1857, Middlebury correspondent John M. Stearns described these unfavorable conditions in an article entitled "Attachment Laws; Their Effects on Commercial Credit and Industrial Enterprise."[441] He questioned why such laws existed that allowed "the local shylock" to obtain an advantage over other creditors and lamented such a system "tending to diminish or annihilate mercantile confidence or creating artificial jeopardies" that were "suicidal to the state adopting or perpetuating such a policy." Merchants and those providing vitally needed credit were living in a state of "perpetual panic" he said, and referred to the huge loss in population departing for New York. The situation warranted an inquiry into "whether the want found in Vermont of mercantile confidence or of that generous good faith between men and men which fosters enterprise induced by the grab game attachment laws of the state, has not fairly driven away a majority of these emigrants." "Enterprise everywhere needs *confidence*," he continued, "more than capital. But, if a young man at the onset of life can secure neither, the cold bleak hills of a Vermont winter become desolate indeed; and he must seek a new home and other more genial associations." Laws that treated such men "as rogues" and allowed creditors "to intimidate or to punish him as if he were a thief" required change. Stearns also faulted "the wool growing nabobs who have added farm to farm and converted the late nicely cultivated fields of their late neighbors to sheep pastures" that in turn drove "the practical, industrial enterprise from Vermont by the distrust inculcated in the minds of her people by the laws in question." "Vermont may boast" of the changes created by the sheep interest, he said, "but they represent the poverty, while the practical and active agencies of a new life are driven from her borders."

The thoughts of a young man pursuing a career in business and subjecting himself to such a hazard appeared unlikely in Montpelier in 1860 where the tables were turned to the farmers' advantage because they did not monetarily extend themselves and invest in the railroads. Whereas, "once the farmer came into the village with his old work horse, plain harness and plainer sleigh or wagon," local historian Thompson described, "now he comes with his two hundred dollar horse, the best plated harness and the gayest and most costly sleigh or wagon, with corresponding equipments." The times had changed he said and explained that "Once the farmer's son's highest aspirations were to be a merchant, his daughter's to be the wife of a villager; now the son 'don't know about going into the small business of measuring out tape,' and the daughter looks clear over the head of the counter-jumper. In short, the villagers have had their day, and the farmers are now having theirs."[442] Similarly, a national publication warned young men against abandoning a farming way of life to engage in selling "silks and laces, toys and tobacco, rat-traps, grindstones, and ribbons for a living." Bankruptcy was their fate it said and counseled them to "Stick to your farms; your lands will never desert you, nor cease to supply your wants, unless you first desert them."[443]

Calls for change in the onerous grab laws clamored after the warnings of the Council of Censors and from governors Fletcher and Hiland Hall in 1856, 1858 and 1859.[444] The public demanded they be abolished and one writer claimed that "nine-tenths of the people *ought*" to support the effort because "it is only the tenth and sharpest and hardest man who succeeded in the game of grab. . . at the expense of the other nine."[445] Despite the repeated demands, nothing was done in the next decade. The delay became so concerning that in 1870 Governor John W. Stewart forcibly demanded the legislature to address "the evils of our law of summary attachment," calling it "a positive hindrance to business enterprise" that deserved to be "stripped of its harsh and unjust features."[446] In 1872, the *Rutland Daily*

Herald described the ongoing situation, "In Vermont, where we have no insolvent laws, or any laws at all in reference to insolvency, we go back at one to the 'grab law.' First come, first served, and the rest kept out in the cold. This is all well enough for those who are lucky enough to be first in, but it is decidedly unjust to the mass of the creditors, and many times to the debtor."[447] Finally, in 1876, the same year it instituted crying change within the medical profession, the legislature created the Court of Insolvency. While needed order was instituted that removed the existing rushed, inequitable atmosphere caused by the grab laws, it occurred only after decades of troubles that, as in other fields, could have been avoided had Vermont not resisted and instead duplicated the methods utilized in neighboring states.

Conclusion

The legislators' debates in 1857 never addressed the looming impact that emigration or the grab laws had on Vermonters when it considered the location of the capital. Their brief discussion on the importance of grass, initiated by Hardwick representative Joseph Underwood in favor of Montpelier's geographic position, was more in a light-hearted manner than in seriousness. He asked his audience to consider what was *"the principal source* of wealth to the State?" *"From the grass,"* he answered with emphasis, "which grows on all the surface of the State – on the east side, and on the west side – on all the hills, and in the valleys. From *the grass, mainly,* our three hundred thousand citizens are fed, and clothed, and housed, and educated, and governed, and made to abound in all good things." Montpelier should remain the state's capital, he said, because it was "fortunately central to the grass interest." Brattleboro's J. Dorr Bradley, also in favor of Montpelier, immediately endorsed Underwood's suggestion and invoked a biblical quotation that since "'all flesh is grass' and all grass destined to be flesh," he invited a Burlington representative advocating for his town to "cheerfully come into the grass interest."[448] While nothing more was said during the debates that concerned agriculture, it is not surprising because of the unspoken power it held over all of the attendees. Vermonters in mid-century did not need to be reminded of agriculture's importance because it was at the core of their identity. It constituted such a powerful presence that it resisted the kinds of wholesale change taking place in other aspects of Vermont society because of modernity's effects.

Nonetheless, the new times imposed a grinding evolution in other aspects of the state's inhabitants' lives in ways never before experienced when the very health of Vermonters responsible for maintaining the important agriculture industry received marked emphasis beginning in the 1850s. The laissez-faire, caveat emptor attitude that allowed the railroads free reign to operate in a virtually unregulated environment during the decade, interrupted only by the vociferous calls of moralistic temperance societies opposed to the presence of alcohol, persisted. The strident efforts of the teetotaling community proved so effective that they commanded the attention of officials away from attending to other unregulated practices also having a direct effect on Vermonters' well-being: the squabbling medical profession and increased usage of addictive drugs. The prevailing attitude that government should minimize passing intrusive laws beyond prohibition in 1852 without overriding evidence of a dire need, and its demonstrated subservience to prevailing corporate interests, presents a failed example of its ability to rise and meet these new challenges posed to Vermonter's health. It also introduced the harsh reality that their political leaders refused to lose any public relations contest that could damage the state's image and threaten their ability to attract and exploit distant opportunities promised by the capitalists. In their myopic blindness that suppressed the warnings of medical professionals, the accelerating effects of modernity took the matter out of their hands and passed from their easily recognized physical aspects exhibited by the railroad on to something much more personal and sinister.

But how much of this information actually became known outside of Vermont is questionable because of a condition that a Rutland correspondent complained of in a letter to the *New York Times* in 1857. He confided that because instances of crime in Vermont (he facetiously called "a virgin State, unpolluted by [its] stain") generally escaped outside scrutiny, he wanted to report the seduction of a young girl by a railroad worker who arranged for her to have an abortion performed "by a physician of previous good standing in our community." He explained his reason for making the report known in this manner was because such crimes were "too often hushed up and only known to the town and but seldom out of the county."[449] His complaint was timely because Vermont officials of this period had much other information relating to the state's health, including many other instances of abortion and rising instances of infanticide, that it did not care for the outside world to know about.

CHAPTER V

Distorting Reality

"All Vermont is healthy." [450]

SENATOR REUBEN C. BENTON OF ESSEX COUNTY, February 24, 1857

Consumption

The legislators' debates concerning the relocation of their capital from Montpelier considered not only the economic benefits other towns might offer, but also the healthfulness of the local population. It made no sense to move the symbolic, physical manifestation of a government from one place to another unless assured the new location did not pose harm from disease or unhygienic conditions. The changes pressing in on them as they accommodated the demands of the railroad technology, the new economic realities it delivered, and explosive growth in cities inhabited by a diverse and mobile population threatened by the arrival of disease from far off metropolitan centers meant that the physical and mental health of everyone within their borders was touched in one way or another. This third scenario that followed the impact it all wrought directly on the landscape and indirectly on the farming community affected a broad spectrum of other concerns. They ranged from the physical and mental travails that individuals experienced personally, to their families, and out into the communities they lived in to such an extent it posed significant challenges to the traditional values that Vermont society clung to.

Issues related to health became a contentious point among the legislators arguing strongly on the behalf of either Burlington or Montpelier, the two most compelling candidates. Their differences exposed more than an individual's favoritism of one place over another and, instead, put on a woeful display of ignorance, or premeditated misrepresentation, about existing medical issues that exposed the degree of trust, or distrust and dislike, they had for that profession. The legislators expressed their ill-informed, dismissive opinions about things of which they had little understanding, even in the presence of incontrovertible evidence that the state's female population experienced a remarkable rate of death attributed to tuberculosis, also called consumption. That persistent condition continued to grow and became so widespread and obvious that by 1864 the VMS labeled it "the unequaled destroyer of our population."[451] Mounting evidence also demonstrated that many women uninterested in the burdens of motherhood participated in criminal abortions and that the population in general experienced such increased use of opium-related products that it raised significant concern within the medical profession. In the same manner that they hesitated to address the physical harm that railroads inflicted on the population, Vermont's legislative leaders myopic and parochial attitudes also opposed and discounted the legitimate concerns of knowledgeable physicians when modernity demanded creative solutions that directly affected their constituents' well-being. Their inaction offers the prospect that it stemmed from a palpable fear at this critical juncture in the state's development that if they acknowledged the true condition of Vermonters' health it could frighten investors from providing the critical capital needed to bring the railroad and other improvements into the Green Mountains.

The diagnosis that one suffered from the communicable disease, one so prevalent in Vermont, commonly called "tuberculosis" entered into the vernacular through the work of German bacteriologist Robert Koch in 1882. His use of powerful microscopes allowed scientists to see for the first time the dreaded bacillus and to understand it as a transmittable infection. Previously, the medical profession called it consumption because it manifested itself by depleting, or consuming, a body's vitality that made the victim appear in a wasted condition. Widely known in the ancient and medieval worlds as phthisis and scrofula, the disease's symptoms included a swollen neck, sore throat, hoarseness, cough, empyema, asthma, pleurisy, pneumonia, heart tremor, fainting, and spitting up blood. In the early nineteenth-century, stethoscope inventor Frenchman Rene Laennec identified its first telling presence when he found gross, putrid swellings, or tubercles, (mycobacterium tuberculosis) in the lungs of cadavers.[452] Students attending the Dartmouth Medical College in Hanover, New Hampshire throughout the nineteenth-century, and where many Vermont physicians studied, received instruction on current medical practices that included treating consumption and identifying the presence of tubercles in the lungs. Their degree required that they prepare a thesis to demonstrate their competency and, of the more than 1,100 papers that exist, only a few chose to write about consumption. These papers make it possible to recreate the kind of instruction they received and to understand why medical practitioners of the time took the actions, or inactions, they did in treating the disease. Their words reveal the prevailing hopelessness many felt as they confronted a widespread condition in the population that seemed to defy a cure. They further demonstrate that even their professors had no common understanding of the disease as they struggled to identify its various stages and how to treat each one, calling it variously pulmonary consumption, dyspeptic phthisis, tubercated lungs or, the truly descriptive, "melancholy disease." The students' papers repeatedly describe treatments provided to patients to make them comfortable as they helplessly watched them descend into a breathless death, drowned by the tubercles in their lungs.

Four of the students' papers prepared between 1831 and 1851 reveal the profound frustration within the medical profession during these two decades when it failed to find a cure.[453] They focused on trying to understand the causes for consumption and attributed it to those they believed affected the quality and flow of blood on the functioning of the victims' lungs. In their ignorance, they identified virtually every aspect of life as causes, including those attributed to: climate; atmospheric conditions; dampness; ventilation; the common cold; pregnancy; predisposition (heredity); diet; fashion ("the dress of our females and with a few of the more effeminate of our own sex is too coquettish & dandyfied"); posture from leaning over desks and work benches; too little and too much exercise; "mental labor;" "depressing passions;" "excessive venereal indulgence;" intemperance (overuse of mercury and ardent spirits); singing; raised voices (the "Clergyman's Sore Throat"); playing wind instruments; and uncleanliness that struck the rich and poor, the city-dweller, farmer and "the merchant, the mechanic and scholar."[454] One student noted consumption's contagious effects and warned that "it would be well to avoid sleeping with persons far advanced in this disease or being constantly about the bedside of consumptive patients." Another described a "family in the northern part of the State of Vt." that the malady wiped out over the course of six months. Frustrated in not having corralled the disease, one student wrote that while "the march of consumption should be stayed," instead "for a full half century back, it has been one steady increase, keeping even handed with caprice, fashion and dissipation." They also acknowledged the effects of modernity as a cause when another noted that "Our modes of living, customs, and occupations differ much from what they were formerly." They further blamed the new technology and described the "surcharged noxious gases" in the air of developing cities and towns, the inhalation of fine particles thrown up during milling operations that involved metal, minerals and foodstuffs, methods of "modern cookery," and the repeated observation that many women used excessive tight-lacing of their bodices that constricted and irritated their chests.

While the students lamented the absence of a cure, occasionally a lucky practitioner might see his consumption-diagnosed patients get well despite whatever outlandish treatment he provided. "Dr. Biddons," one of them wrote, "has successfully treated many he says with the Cow-house; the warmth of which was constantly kept at 65 or 70° F. [However] impractical it at first might appear, yet Dr. Biddons asserts, that by confining his patients for months to a room in which were kept a number of cows, with inhalation of digitalis and opium, he succeeded in curing a variety of consumptive patients committed to his charge."[455] Other creative treatments that sought to relieve a patient's discomfort included a variety of substances ranging from the benign effects provided by tea and honey to the more serious relief afforded by opium and calomel (mercury). "Opium, one of the students reported, "is a valuable palliative, and should be given freely, increasing the dose regularly, so as to ensure to the patient the full benefits of the medicine." Other treatments dot their accounts that continued to refer to the strong drug in the form of "Calomel combined with opium" and "Tincture of digitalis with opium." But one skeptical, sober student lamented the futility of what they tried. "We do not seem to have any very general plan to follow," he wrote, "but the process of treatment must be varied, according to circumstances and when we fail in performing a cure, as we often shall, we should still endeavor as much as possible, to mitigate the patient's suffering, so as to prolong his existence, or sooth his passage to the tomb." The undefined labeling of the disease that allowed many other unrelated ills to fall under consumption's rubric and escape the separate attention that they deserved complicated the public's choices in its pursuit of remedies. A diagnosis of consumption did not differentiate between illnesses and covered a wide range of complaints that the use of opium could disguise and quickly calm, even if it could not heal. In each of the many accounts of men, women and children described in the records of Vermont experiences complaining of consumptive symptoms over the course of the second half of the nineteenth century, regardless of whether or not their lungs suffered from the dreaded tubercles, they used opium as a convenient treatment for their ills.

Among the medical challenges that Vermonters faced in the contentious 1830s, confronting the perceived "monopoly" that physicians had over their lives caused more unnecessary harm than any other.[456] Andrew Jackson's admonition that the "common man" possessed the innate ability to care for himself and his family greatly impressed the public where the "artisans, mechanics, and farmers among the Green Mountain communities" agitated their newfound appreciation of their intrinsic worth and created Working Men's societies.[457] Jackson's views resonated strongly throughout a rural society opposed to the intrusions of others into their lives; a factor abundantly evident in the way that their legislature conducted its work. Heads of families repeatedly heard admonishment to stand up against a medical profession viewed as monopolistic and favored by a law that allowed it to sue for their services in the courts. Following a relentless petition drive and many instances of vociferous public protest against the medical establishment, in 1838 the state legislature repealed an 1820 law that required doctors to obtain a license to practice from the supreme court.[458] Until 1876, when the legislature returned to the subject to finally invoke a licensing requirement, the laissez-faire attitude that Vermont society had towards its virtually unrestricted businesses allowed the environment for medical services to also remain unregulated. The attention that the legislature paid to prohibition in mid-century remained foremost in its mind for over fifty years, starkly demonstrated by the laws it passed and itemized in 1894 where concerns over alcohol occupied an expansive 111 sections of the statute book, spread out over twenty-two pages, while those concerning drugs amounted to a mere four provisions contained on less than a single page.[459] Their neglect allowed the outlandish claims of physicians, apothecaries and pharmacists and the drugs they dispensed, those supplied by an increasingly large and sophisticated drug manufacturing industry, and the average farmer concocting his own potent creations in a roughshod shed to flood across the pages of daily newspapers or be plastered on the sides of buildings. During these decades, each of these varied interests dispensing drugs sought a financial advantage over the other and engaged in a titanic struggle to convince the public that their methods and treatments offered benefits unavailable elsewhere. Fierce competition from outside of the state also threatened the interests of Green Mountain drug producers because of similar products brought in by the railroad.

Abetting the mayhem, two schools of medical theory prevailed and fought against each other for much of the nineteenth-century. These included the "regulars" (also called allopaths or rationalists), academically-trained, degree-holding practitioners and the untrained "empiricists" (homeopaths), or derisively referred to "quacks," composed of those pursuing the holistic-benefits they believed nature's plants and waters offered to treat disease. How much attention the public paid to the medical men varied significantly. It remained an individual choice consistent with Jacksonian teachings in deciding whether to follow, refuse their recommendations or simply employ them as advisors, described by one "as a sort of necessary evil. . . needed occasionally, as pilots are at sea or at the entrance of difficult harbors" to guide them.[460] Identifying the numbers of those who pursued trades related to Vermont health care presents challenges. While the 1850 Census describes 663 physicians in the state, that same number was erroneously repeated by Vermont officials in 1860 when that year's national Census placed them at 594. A privately prepared summary in 1849 provided a markedly different estimate and identified 390 physicians and thirty-four "botanic physicians" in the state, a category that does not appear in the U. S. Census. The number of apothecaries varied between fourteen in 1849 (together with sixteen "Drug and Medicine Dealers") to nineteen in the national census in 1850 that increased to forty-five in 1860 bearing the more commonly called name of "Druggists."[461]

In 1857 the VMS met in Burlington to hear Dr. H. H. Niles discuss the current state of the profession. His address concerned the relationship of its educated members with the public and the competing quacks, and the lackluster support it received from its own membership. "The Doctor referred to the relation between the Physician and the people," the Society's secretary recorded, "the duties and obligations of each to the other, the want of frankness on the part of the Physician and of confidence and trust on the part of his employers and justly complained that so small a number of the medical men in Vermont attended the meetings of the Society and took part in its transactions." Niles lamented further their sparse membership numbers that compared unfavorably to the advances made by other professions. Envious of them, he noted that the "merchants, tradesmen, mechanics, manufacturers and agriculturalists hold their conventions, councils, associations and meetings for the improvement of each other – the advancement of science art and the improvement of man in his every relation." He also "referred to the various forms of Quackery and the extent in which nostrum [bogus medicine] vending is practiced and patronized by the masses," finding it "discouraging to many Physicians, irritating to some and disgusting to others." Despite the problems, Niles sought to end his presentation on a bright note and said that "notwithstanding the many <u>isms</u> and nostrums we can congratulate ourselves in the fact that the Medical Profession has always been, is now, and ever will be appreciated and sustained by the most intelligent and best educated members in [the] community."[462] Niles' optimism aside, by 1862 the continued presence and deleterious effects wrought on Vermonters by unregulated practitioners became so frustrating to the VMS that it took drastic action to marginalize the "large class of men in our State who are practicing medicine as Quacks, calling themselves Homeopaths, Thompsonians, Eclectics, or Botanical Doctors" and forbid any of its members from associating with them or suffer the forfeiture of their membership as a consequence.[463]

One of those physicians that practiced in Vermont's unregulated environment after the repeal of the licensing law in 1838 was Philadelphia doctor Samuel Sheldon Fitch. Fitch attended the University of Vermont (UVM) between 1822 and 1823 before he received his medical degree from an unidentified institution; UVM later awarded him an honorary A. M. degree in 1837.[464] In 1827 he began to specialize in treating consumption and between 1841 and 1847 published two books claiming he

Dr. Samuel S. Fitch, Six Lectures on the Uses of the Lungs (1856).

discovered how to alleviate the suffering of those afflicted by the disease.[465] His work gained such notoriety that by the time of the Vermont legislature's 1857 debates his second book, *Six Lectures on the Uses of the Lungs,* had gone into twenty-four editions. That year he also authored a "Guide to Health" where he touted himself as "The first physician in this country who had taught and demonstrated the curability of consumption."[466]

Fitch carefully crafted his proof to avoid claiming he could actually cure the disease and focused, instead, on his purported ability to lessen the symptoms of sufferers. He pursued a course of treatment that differed from that described by the Dartmouth Medical College students and argued that patients should never use opium. He explained that because of its "very injurious" effect on the lungs functions, as well as unhelpful to treat other maladies, "I never give any of it in any form, not even in the smallest doses."[467] He went further and made "a solemn declaration and in the most emphatic manner" condemned many of the treatments doctors provided that he believed caused consumption to occur in the first place. "The usual routine of practice laid down in nearly all the medical authorities, adopting the use of emetic tartar, blisters, setons, tartar sores, caustics, housing up the patients, confining them to their rooms, using opium and its preparations, drastic emetics and purgatives, much bleeding, iodine, low diet" could all cause consumption, he said, and not cure it.[468] Instead, he applied a concoction that blistered a sufferer's skin. He also employed mechanical means that included a system of external supports attached to the front and back of a sufferer's abdomen and counseled them to breath periodically through a specially-designed breathing tube he created. Notwithstanding his unique, and questionably effective, approaches others in the medical profession persisted in the traditional methods that included "opium and lies" to quiet their patients' complaints.[469]

To expand his busy New York City practice, Fitch included many testimonials in his publications from patients and fellow physicians (some of them sufferers) attesting to his remedies' effectiveness that also drew the attention of resentful detractors.[470] In 1847, one medical reviewer dismissed with emphasis the accolades he published as "a *quack* advertisement."[471] When the Vermont legislature met in 1857, Fitch was already well-known throughout the state because of his past relationship with UVM and newspaper advertisements he placed that described his many products ("Celebrated Preparations and Mechanical Remedies") offered at numerous locations accompanied by their claims of success. Legislators also recalled his earlier presence in the state when he traveled through it in 1842 to treat patients and lecture on his work in several towns, later publishing his experiences that angered many of them. The account of his meeting "Miss Hawley" in Vergennes that December typified the kinds of patients he encountered. "I can hardly describe the agony of her countenance," he wrote upon first seeing her. "I found her very much emaciated, and ulcers in the tops of both lungs. She had a bad cough, and raised [expelled] blood occasionally. She raised ulcerated matter, pus, every day. The day I was there, she raised blood, and had all the general symptoms of consumption in a rather aggravated form." Two years later, Hawley wrote to Fitch to thank him for his attention and advised that "I am now quite well, and am able to be about the house; can walk and ride without inconvenience. In fact, my health is full as comfortable as it has been for the last ten years." Another of Fitch's patients living in St. Albans also wrote to him with thanks. "I have used up your prescription," W. R. Ames wrote, "and am much better; but yet I am not well. My chest is yet very weak; and my lungs also. I

Comparison of consumptive patient to healthy individual. Fitch, Six Lectures (1856).

use the tube yet; but, perhaps I need something else. . . . I am very thankful I have received so much benefit; but, still, I hope to receive more."[472]

Ignoring the obvious concern and care that Fitch exercised in dealing with the conditions he saw in Vermont and uninterested in his timely warnings about the use of dangerous drugs that included opium, the legislature dismissed him out of hand. They derided him as "the traveling Consumption doctor" and labeled his report of disease in the state as "ridiculous and absurdly false."[473] His description of Burlington particularly angered some, especially those who touted the town as the site for the capital. "Burlington," Fitch wrote of his trip in 1842, "contains about 4,000 inhabitants, and is one of the richest villages in New England, or in the United States." He admired the "beautiful and well-built" homes and believed that "most of the best ones have double windows." But, he said, "Some physicians of Burlington have, for many years, taught the necessity of shutting" the windows "in winter, and keeping very warm." Because of that, "the houses are closed in November" when "the double windows are put up and kept up without being once opened until April following" as the "well defended vestibules to the outside doors shut out the possibility of cold air entering their houses." This resulted in "luxurious living, with much clothing, and almost a total want of exercise, [to] complete the picture. A female is rarely seen in the street." Fitch concluded that having "visited one hundred and fifty cities in Europe and this country, yet my impression is, I never saw so much Consumption anywhere as in Burlington, in proportion to its population, in the same classes of people. A great many cases were there when I was there. The disease was principally with the best classes."[474] When this extract from his book was read aloud to the debating legislators, the clerk recorded that it "provoked much merriment," and no doubt angst in the Burlington advocates.[475]

While Fitch had a few supporters among the representatives and senators, others of them and the press continued to express indignation against these perceived attacks from events that took place years earlier. They vehemently argued that no state in the Union could compare more favorably with it when it came to health and that Fitch only tried to "kill off" Burlington. To counter his unwelcomed allegations they introduced affidavits from two doctors who wrote that "after a long experience as physicians, in various parts of the State, they had found no place more healthy than Burlington, and few or none equal to it."[476] One of them, Dr. Samuel W. Thayer, provided another theory to explain why any consumption may have been noted and opined that a sufferer experienced the disease because of trauma associated with their move to the community. In somewhat seeming disjointed reasoning, he wrote that "Consumption has seldom occurred in any native home citizen of the town, and those whom have come to Burlington with a native as [sic] acquired predisposition to that disease have in my opinion never suffered by the change, and in many instances have... benefited by the change."[477] Fitch's views were "ridiculously false" another legislator said and singled out a meaningless detail from his account to correct his description of people shut up in their homes because "it was well known that the latch-string was always on the out-side."[478] Another, shooting the messenger, derided his medical credentials. "Dr. Fitch," he asserted, "might be an A. M. and an M. D., and it might be added, A. double S."[479] Trying to put a light touch on the inflammatory allegation lodged against Burlington, another representative suggested that rural Barnard might serve as a more appropriate location for the capital. There, he said, the people "seldom *think* of dying and the children don't believe there is any such thing as death, and when the subject is mentioned they say, *they will never die.*" He continued and described that "Some old men have lived until they were tired all out of life, and have *died on purpose...* and got up a contrivance for quitting the world, and got off *somehow.*"[480] The legislator's attempt at levity implicitly acknowledged occasions when some of the state's elderly chose to end their lives and "got up a contrivance" that allowed for it to happen. His slip infers the presence of other important aspects of Vermonter's health ignored by the state's leaders.

Ardent Spirits

The legislators' debates in 1857 also addressed the attitudes of the Montpelier and Burlington communities towards their consumption of alcohol. Five years earlier, Vermont passed a version of what the public called the "Maine Law" (1851), "An Act to Prevent Traffic in Intoxicating Liquors for the Purpose of Drinking," that made it illegal for anyone to manufacture or sell alcohol unless for medicinal, chemical or mechanical purposes or involved "the fruit of the vine for the commemoration of the Lord's Supper."[481] Its far-reaching, thirty-one provisions included several written in the spirit of eighteenth-century laws adopted by Revolutionary War-era Vermonters who imposed draconian penalties for various offenses. Searches without warrants were authorized, intoxicated persons compelled to disclose where they obtained their liquor, witnesses could be jailed until they provided evidence, limited appeals were allowed, violators were disqualified from serving on juries and officials threatened with large fines if they failed to investigate or prosecute reported violations. It constituted a significant change from just a short time before when ineffective laws were unable to dissuade even government officials from public displays that condoned the consumption of alcohol. In 1850 a Burlington newspaper reported that an unnamed "State's Attorney likes a social glass," and had "lately ran a foot race *for a quantity of liquor!*" The article also referred to the extensive use of alcohol in the community and alleged that a few individuals acting as vendors "are allowed to monopolize the whole TRADE and its profits" that it reported as "*immense!*"[482]

Despite its five-decade existence, Vermont's prohibition law was not overwhelmingly popular and a referendum conducted in 1853 to determine the date it became effective after its passage revealed a statewide majority of only 1,171 votes in favor (22,215 to 21,044), and twenty towns in opposition.[483] Chittenden County Sheriff Nathan Bowman recalled that upon his election in the fall of 1852 he overheard "two gentlemen, strangers, talk rather disparagingly" of his ability to enforce the law and which convinced him to take an aggressive stance.[484] Although on paper Burlington voters supported the effort (477 in favor and 144 against), Bowman understood that overall the community was in opposition. Regardless, when the law went into effect on March 8, 1853 and with his "pockets full of warrants," he proceeded to Pat Murphy's grocery store, where the reported "king of the traffic" held court. In the presence of an interested crowd, he found the armed proprietor arguing that he "had a right to defend his property," but who backed down when Bowman produced an ax and threatened to use it on a locked storeroom. Upon gaining entry, he discovered 200 gallons of liquor in eleven barrels, took them into custody and destroyed them on the street the following week before another large gathering. According to Bowman, recalling the event five decades later, it was "but one of hundreds of cases" he handled in the next years.

State's Attorney Levi Underwood (future chairman of Vermont's first Republican convention in 1856 and Chittenden County senator during the 1857 debates) also portrayed Burlington's law enforcement efforts at the time in a positive manner to national temperance officials. "The law has put an end to drunkenness and crime *almost entirely*," he reported and advised that prior to its implementation he received daily reports of crimes he believed were "nine-tenths. . . caused by drunkenness." But with the law, Underwood emphasized that "*two complaints only have been made for such offenses*, and only one was caused by drunkenness."[485] Extant records appear to confirm his account and show that in April and June immediately following the law's implementation, only nine individuals were arrested in Burlington. However, they also demonstrate the law's temporary effects when, later in 1853 after his election, Underwood's successor Torrey E.

Wales experienced a marked increase and a return of these types of nuisance offenses. Rather than a drop in drunkenness, his records reveal the names of dozens of the community's less fortunate men and women incarcerated and prosecuted for alcohol-related offenses.[486]

The records also demonstrate that the prohibition law had little impact on those able to negotiate its loopholes that permitted town liquor agent A. S. Dewey to dispense alcohol to anyone claiming they needed it for medicinal purposes. While he reportedly turned away the destitute seeking alcohol, his files indicate the presence of a careful, wary clientele able to obtain it without suffering any consequences.[487] They disclose the impact that the railroad had with his receipt of dozens of barrels full of spirits and payments made to out-of-state suppliers and freight haulers for brandy, gin, rum, wine, ale, and cider. Between March 1853 and February 1854, Dewey sold over $3,900 worth of rum, brandy, gin and wine in half-pint, pint and gallon quantities that cost his customers between a few and fifty cents each. Consistent with the pleasant time of the year and celebration of the Declaration of Independence, the highest sales occurred in the months of July ($511.72) and August ($446.71), indicating a dubious connection to maintaining a purchaser's physical health.[488] That situation repeated elsewhere as large amounts of various kinds of spirits were sold by Hyde Park town agent Edward B. Sawyer to his many customers.[489] There was no absence of suppliers of alcohol from outside of Vermont able to make the many town agents' work possible as Boston-based dealers I. D. Richards and Dudley and Company aggressively advertised their products for sale.[490] By 1865, Burlington town agent P. H. Catlin's records reveal an marked increase and robust level of consumption with a huge inventory of many different kinds of alcohol on hand supplied by New York City vendors. That year over $13,000 in sales took place as Catlin repeatedly clamored for town officials to authorize his purchase of additional barrels of many types of liquors to meet the demand. "I have a sample of Blackberry wine,"

Catlin wrote, "that I think would be a good thing to have, also Catawba Brandy." The thirsty Burlington community clearly had easy access to alcohol, despite whatever constraints the prohibition law threatened.

In southern Vermont, traveling out-of-state liquor agents unafraid of apprehension hawked "cheaply made up liquors" across the countryside, adulterated with "drugs and poisonous mixtures" to unsuspecting customers. When the Brattleboro town agent was offered fifty dollars by a supplier if he purchased ten dollars of his product, he asked why? The dealer told him that "I could then go through the county, and by telling others that I supplied you with liquors sell great quantities to them."[491] Other agents became embroiled in town controversies with accusations lodged against them alleging their mishandling of funds. The Randolph and Braintree agents each faced allegations of purchasing liquor "on the credit of the towns" and then appropriating it for "their own use and behoof."[492] In Reading, town agent Joseph A. Davis struggled to explain the inconsistent quantities of spirits in his possession recorded in his inventories. He professed that the prior agent falsified records before he took office and that "leakings, evaporations, tappings and *stealings*" explained the discrepancies.[493]

Unless those visiting the town agent for their alcohol became involved in unlikely public displays of disorderly conduct, they had nothing to fear from the prying eyes of law enforcement if they enjoyed their alcohol and medicinal purchases quietly in the privacy of their homes. Ambrose Lincoln Brown, Rutland's respected town clerk and civil engineer responsible for altering its landscape with its new rail yard exemplified the discrete actions of many. His detailed account book for the 1850s reveals his periodic purchases of brandy, principally for his wife, costing forty cents a pint and on other occasions gin at twenty-five cents for each.[494] For the poor, transients and hapless without the necessary connections and unable to escape attention from authorities, the newspapers reported dozens of their arrests and seizures of alcohol taking place throughout Vermont. However, official records do not uniformly confirm those accounts. In Caledonia County the grand jury conducted its annual visit of the local jail in 1854 and determined it sufficient for its current use and that no upgrades were necessary "while the Maine Law is in force." Their opinion ran contrary to the assessment they made the prior year, reporting now that the sheriff had told them "for the past Two years & the present year" the number of prisoners had decreased to the point where "for the first time for several years past the Jail has been entirely free from prisoners."[495] Perhaps indicating a shift in the way that offenders were penalized by fines instead of incarceration, the same thing happened in Burlington in 1855 when the grand jury happily reported "We feel highly gratified to find *the jail destitute of inmates* – a circumstance attributable, in a very great measure we believe, to the suppression of the sale of intoxicating liquors." An official at the University of Vermont stated further that "There is a very great diminution in the use of liquors by students. We have not had, for a year past, any rowdyism."[496] The state prison also reported a marked reduction in the number of prisoners, down to sixty-five from a high of ninety-two in 1851, as other counties reported similar results.[497]

Vigorous enforcement efforts continued and during the four-day State Fair in 1856 Sheriff C. W. Reynolds and nine deputies, wearing their newly created badges, patrolled the grounds to keep the peace and watch for those illegally selling alcohol.[498] "A Report of the Fines Imposed" between December 1, 1857 and December 1, 1858 prepared by Burlington Justice of the Peace F. G. Hill reveals further the prosecutions and fines imposed on thirty-three men and women for selling liquor, twenty-seven men for intoxication (many with Irish surnames) and the destruction of many barrels, kegs and jugs of liquor.[499] Despite their work and seeming absence of occupants in the jails, violations continued, and in 1860 Governor Fairbanks suggested tightening the laws to deal further with the persistent vendors of alcohol to alleviate "the deep injury of many families, and the demoralizing of many of our youth."[500] Notwithstanding the belief of some Vermont officials that the prohibition law reduced the levels of disorderly conduct, evidence from elsewhere in the country renders that conclusion problematic. Studies reveal that between mid-nineteenth century and 1920 over half of all urban arrests occurred because of drunkenness and disorderly conduct. By 1860 the country already experienced a noticeable downward trend for these kinds of offenses that continued into the next century.[501] This occurred in jurisdictions that did not have the kind of prohibition laws that Maine and Vermont passed and indicates other factors may have had an impact. These included the effects that public arrests had on the future conduct of those who witnessed them and the public's increasing intolerance for this kind of behavior. In the latter half of the 1850s, Vermont's efforts to curb public displays of disorderly conduct, whether caused by alcohol, drug use or other reasons, were not necessarily connected to the prohibition law.

Despite the arrests and prosecutions for alcohol abuse in the 1850s, excessive drinking appeared in other instances, including the state's railroads. While reports of drunkards run down on tracks in urban and rural locations were a common occurrence, in 1852 the Vermont Supreme Court decided a unique case that concerned alcohol, insanity, and the railroad. In the matter of *Ellis Bliss v. Connecticut & Passumpsic Rivers Railroad Company* the court addressed the rights of a railroad corporation to condemn and take the land of someone who claimed they were insane. Ellis Bliss owned the Bliss Hotel in Bradford and a parcel of local land that drew the attention of the railroad's surveyors when they crossed and staked out its centerline. Consistent with other railroad charters of the time, the Connecticut and Passumpsic's allowed aggrieved landowners to appeal the amounts of money that the corporations wanted to pay in order to gain ownership. Relatives acting on Bliss's behalf disagreed with the amount the company offered and appealed that decision to the county court. In response, the railroad's attorneys argued that they filed their appeal too late which precluded the court from hearing the case. Bliss's representatives managed to avoid dismissal when they presented evidence from two doctors and a relative that he was a raging alcoholic whose condition allowed them to take advantage of an exception to the railroad's charter that allowed late-filed appeals caused by a petitioner's insanity. The undeniable evidence of Bliss's disability allowed the Supreme Court to hold that the effects of intoxication caused it. Bliss "was out of his mind," the court determined, "so crazy as to require close attention to prevent his doing mischief, threatening to commit personal violence upon others, to burn his buildings, and was necessarily held in restraint by force, that he was rapidly verging towards delirium tremens.... Members of his family often tried to talk with him about it, but could never communicate anything to him, or make him understand anything on the subject." In summing up the evidence warranting their decision in Bliss's representatives favor, the court wrote that "It is difficult to conceive of a case, not merely of excessive inebriation, but of insanity and legal incapacity arising therefrom, if this is not one."[502]

Bliss represented the kind of person that drew the continued attention of the moralistic members of society seeking to curb alcohol abuse in the 1850s. The powerful Vermont Temperance Society (formed in 1828) in response to increased displays of disorderly conduct had gained such a loyal following that it had a significant impact on both the behavior of Vermonters in the consumption of highly potent distilled alcohol (ardent spirits) and in affecting the course of legislation. The movement's restrained initial focus sought to limit only the amount of spirits available in the state by attacking its production capability. The tactic succeeded so well that by 1850 only a single, unidentified distillery remained, employing two people who produced 500 "Barrels of ale, &c." a year.[503] The absence of such a capability explains why town agents acting pursuant to the 1852 prohibition law looked for bulk quantities of alcohol in the metropolitan centers beyond the state's borders and their dependency on the railroad for its transportation.

In the next years, the temperance movement slowly turned its attention to other forms of intoxicating beverages in its efforts to limit the production and consumption of fermented drinks such as beer and wine. However, its leaders never sought to intercede into the increasing presence and use of strong drugs, such as opium, that coincided with the use of alcohol. If people consumed them quietly to feed their growing addictions, neither its leaders or the legislature deemed it necessary to pass legislation that curbed their availability. The movement in mid-century reacted more to public displays of distasteful behavior than to conduct engaged in the privacy of one's home. Not until after the founding of the Woman's Temperance Union in 1874, and its creation of committees that specifically addressed the effects of stimulants and narcotics, did Vermonters begin to appreciate more fully the dire effects that drugs had on them, regardless of the location where they were consumed.

The tortured course of legislation that finally resulted in the prohibition of manufacturing and sale of intoxicating beverages in 1852 invoked aspects of moralistic behavior also reflected during the 1857 debates concerning the relocation of the state's capital. In 1853 Governor John S. Robinson related that the law had "engaged the attention and excited the feelings of the community perhaps more than any other legislation since the organization of the Government."[504] The archives substantiate his claim with the large collection of temperance petitions from around the state bearing hundreds of names on long lists demanding prohibition. They employed vitriolic language that belittled both those who sold and consumed the substances, calling the vendors, as others did of the medical profession, a monopolistic, "privileged class," and their drinking customers as devoid of morals. Many argued, with the troubles that railroad laborers caused in mind, that they did not want "to become like Ireland" and that if the legislature passed laws dealing with horseracing, lotteries, and whorehouses, it had no excuse not to institute prohibition on the basis of morals.[505] The enormous pressure on their representatives eventually resulted in, arguably, the most contentious piece of state legislation of the nineteenth century when they instituted prohibition. The law may have satisfied some, but it did not extinguish the thirsty inclinations of many others, quenched by the never-ceasing arrival of barrels of spirits flooding into Vermont via the railroad contrary to it, and those feelings became clear once again during the 1857 debates.

The morals of both the Burlington and Montpelier communities received extensive attention and debate concerning their suitability to host the capital. Representatives from around the state aired ugly aspersions against each other and the two communities revealing the continuing raw effects that the recent prohibition debates exposed. The firestorm arose when Representative John A. Woodward (a minister and admired future Civil War commander), from Westford in Chittenden County, compared the efforts of the two towns in enforcing prohibition. He alleged that Montpelier's resistance to the law was well-known throughout the state, that "one of the clergymen of Montpelier had been unfaithful to the cause of law and order" and contended that "legislators ought not to be subjected to [the] temptations" by continuing to meet there. He argued further in support of Burlington and stated that the community stood on "high moral ground" because "the court records showed that the people were in earnest" in support of the law.[506] Representative Thomas E. Powers of Woodstock echoed Woodward's concerns, noting the Montpelier community's failures, and refused "to cover up the enormity of their multiform sins in this matter."[507] He called those in the town who opposed the law "wicked above all men" and that "many of them. . . were now writhing under the goadings of their own guilty consciences for their shameful indifference to the work of death that has so long been going on in their midst." "Poisoned streams had been issuing from here," he said, "deluging the whole county for years, and they had either exulted in their triumphs over temperance men, as the tide of desolation rolled over the hopes and prospects of wives and children, or folded their arms in listless indifference to the mischievous results of their cowardice and their fears." He went further and singled out the minister that Woodward referred to and who preached in the church where they now met. The Rev. William H. Lord, vociferous in his opposition to temperance efforts, became the recipient of Powers' strong condemnation who relished the opportunity to do so "in the very sanctuary where the heresies of which he is charged dropped from his sacrilegious lips."

Other legislators took an opposite position and gleefully admitted that they did indeed consume alcohol and belittled Woodward in his efforts to cast aspersions on entire communities because they also did so. Brattleboro's Representative Bradley conceded that he joined with Burlington senators at one time and shared gin, an event that would have included the former Chittenden County state's attorney and chairman of the Republican Party Levi Underwood. The clerk recorded the interruptions of Bradley's discourse on several occasions with "Laughter," "Much Laughter" and "Merriment" expressed by many in his audience unwilling to openly admit their own transgressions. Bradley described the encounter, but related that he could not remember if he had consumed the gin bottle's "last drop" or whether "the Burlington delegation had drank it nearly all up before I got there." Directing his ire at minister Woodward, Bradley asked "Does the reverend gentleman really regret that so great a crime was brought to light? Does he wish *all* breaches of law concealed? Or only the *peccadilloes of his Burlington friends?*"[508] Ridiculing any attempt to cast him as a law breaker, Bradley reminded Woodward that "There is no law against *drinking* gin" because it only punished *"furnishing* or *giving it away,"* an act committed by the Burlington senator and not himself.

These hypocritical exchanges of lawmakers and the flippant way they openly admitted to engaging in conduct contrary to the spirit of the prohibition law they passed, while ignoring the example they set for the public and called for its restraint, are telling. For half a century the penalties of the notorious 1852 prohibition law affected those members of Vermont society least able to conceal the circumstances of their drinking. Still, in 1855, Governor Stephen Royce's brief inaugural address expressed the need for less legal protections for those who fell within this class. He reasoned that "Among the causes leading to idleness, poverty, immorality and crime, the unrestricted use of intoxicating drinks is, beyond question, the most effective in its disastrous results."[509] To assure timely action against those charged with offenses, Royce recommended reducing and streamlining legal protections to allow punishments to be "rendered more summary." On the other hand, as the 1857 debates clearly demonstrated in exposing the presence of increasing class differences in the state, its well-to-do members had little to fear from such a threat. Their elevated position permitted them to witness the law's punishments meted out selectively on the less fortunate and those who engaged in public acts of disorderly conduct, or upon the hapless establishments accused of permitting that behavior because they sold alcohol to them. Little evidence suggests that any Vermonter of means, and certainly not any legislator, ever faced the prospect of prosecution.

Moral Obligation or Official Responsibility?

Before and through much of the nineteenth-century, Vermont had no effective means to assure compliance with the laws the legislature passed. Each county had an elected state's attorney and constable, but in its rural condition and enforcement left to their individual discretion, dictated by the particular whims of their constituency, the law saw inconsistent application, despite what the legislature intended. Much was left to the goodwill that Vermonters chose to extend to particular provisions. They continued to adhere to the Jacksonian admonition that each knew best how to conduct their lives and continually resisted efforts that threatened to impinge on their freedom. Absent an ability to enforce legislative dictates, officials sought to instill a sense of guilt in the minds of those who thought about breaking the law and reminded them of their "moral obligations" to society. The literature of Vermont's early years repeatedly appealed to the public's consciousness and goodwill to abide by the law or to lend its backing of movements, such as temperance after the 1820s, that sought to advance their collective wellbeing. The legislature recognized early on the futility of enforcing prohibition and in 1856 indicated that it understood it needed to appeal to the "moral sentiment" of the people to convince them to support and abide by its provisions. "In a republican government," it recognized that importance "to the successful operation of such a law, and to its permanence, that it should have the public sentiment on its side."[510]

The concept of a moral obligation entered strongly into the 1857 debates when the legislators considered the devotion that many extended to the Montpelier community. To move the capital from Montpelier represented, according to many, a violation of their moral obligation to the town. Hardwick representative Joseph Underwood spoke earnestly on Montpelier's behalf and described why the town deserved to remain the capital because of the moral obligations the state owed to it. While he discussed a physical location, his points also pertained to the relationship of Vermonters to their laws. "Moral obligation," he stated, "is founded on the nature of things, and grows out of the relation, which individuals and communities sustain to God, and to one another." He continued, "Moral obligation binds individuals and communities without promises or contract. . . . Moral obligation is that which the government of God enforces upon moral agents – upon communities, states and nations, which are composed of moral agents. Moral obligation underlies all civil obligation, and gives it all its force and effect; it is the bond which binds human society together in families, churches and states. Without it, statute law would be ineffectual." One's moral obligation lay at the very foundation of human society he claimed and that if it were banished it would leave behind "nothing better than distrust, treachery, terror, confusion, and death. A pervading sense of moral obligation is infinitely more important to the State, than legislation and all the apparatus of civil government. We had better annihilate the civil constitution and all the provisions for enforcing it, than to trample down moral obligation."[511] Underwood's eloquent appeal to Vermonters to listen to their inner voices on this momentous occasion and the importance of obeying the law without requiring authorities to compel compliance was clearly understood. Months later, Governor Fletcher reiterated the seriousness of the subject when he asked the legislature to require that prisoners at the state prison receive "a greater amount of moral instruction" in order "to advance the great ends of all human punishment, the reformation of offenders and the prevention of crime."[512]

The effects of modernity severely tested Vermonter's willingness to answer the call to abide by the dictates of their amorphous moral obligation to others. Technology and newfound opportunities tempted them psychologically and diverted their attention and inclination to follow the law in an environment where enforcement was inconsistent and unreliable. When they failed to do so in the 1850s, the legislature initiated its first tentative, albeit incremental, efforts to assure the wellbeing of the community's larger interests and inquired into the methods used to enforce the law. The transition to responsible oversight only became apparent in retrospect because it occurred in such a slow fashion. In 1851, legislators first noted the effects of modernity with alarm when they discovered that fully one-third of the state's expenses went to the administration of justice. They determined that the expenditure of these sums "was to be expected from the increase in population and business" and attributed it to the challenges that each, inferring the railroad and Irish immigrants, presented because of "the nature of the business and character of the population."[513] To curb those particular expenses, they suggested that salaries replace the fees paid to county sheriffs and state's attorneys for matters they pursued at their discretion in order to eliminate the whims of "the temperament of those to whom these offices are entrusted." Little was accomplished at the time and by the end of the decade they still complained of the "great abuses" in the way that court officials imposed fees on litigants and continued to argue that salaries could alleviate the problem.[514] In an almost apologetic manner, the lawmakers also began to institute other provisions that required officials to consider, in part, the physical health of the state's inhabitants beyond the prohibition law. Their creation of a railroad commissioner in 1856 and his authorization to inquire into the condition of the state's roads for the purpose of managing public safety failed to provide for any enforcement authority and rendered the effort largely symbolic and meaningless. Hesitating, conflicted and splintered in creating uniform laws to protect the public and instituting a centralized method apart from county state's attorney and sheriffs to assure compliance (the creation of the office of the attorney general waited until 1904), the legislature continued throughout mid-century to witness the mayhem their inaction permitted.

At the same time, officials allowed the ongoing, heated infighting between the medical regulars and quack empiricists to continue and refused to intervene and impose an effective licensing requirement on any of them. On many occasions during the nineteenth century Massachusetts served as a convenient example for Vermont officials to consider when prickly issues surrounding governance arose. When they compared Vermonter's health to those in other locations, they closely examined the experiences of Massachusetts and England to determine if the state was progressing or declining in any way.[515] While Massachusetts witnessed the same kinds of discord within its medical community as Vermont, beginning in 1818 with the creation of that state's medical society responsible for overseeing the competency of its medical profession, it did not fail to continue to monitor its effects on the population and mandate the licensing of diverse kinds of practitioners.[516] There, the alternative practitioners composed of the Thomsonians and homeopaths each found a way to establish their credentials and obtain a degree of legitimacy, though persistently disputed by the regulars. Despite the displeasure of its own regulars, the Vermont legislature finally took action and in 1858 authorized the incorporation of the Vermont Homeopathic Medical Society and two years later allowed its members to use the representatives' chamber for a meeting.[517] Emboldened by their official recognition, the homeopaths elevated the discord between them and ridiculed the regulars as "men who arrogate to themselves the right of umpire, and say our practice is a system of 'do nothing.'"[518] With no prospect of a licensing law, the VMS regulars could only watch helplessly and bide their time.[519]

Vermont trailed Massachusetts in other respects that affected the state's health. Whereas the Bay State established a department of health in 1869, Vermont delayed the effort until 1886. It only came at that late date because Burlington physicians sponsored the enabling legislation to create it out of a fear that the state could not handle an impending epidemic. However, and in an example of the continuing differences that existed between the communities after the 1857 debates, Montpelier farmers objected to the effort. "We are well enough as we are," one of them testified to a committee considering the legislation, "Vermont is an agricultural state and does not need a State Board of Health. It is an experiment that is not wanted."[520] Officials ultimately overrode that objection and acknowledged the undeniable widespread problems that sanitary conditions around the state posed, dating back decades, forcing them to take action. They gave the board the specific mandate to address particularly "the location, drainage, water supply, heating and ventilation of public buildings and the drainage and sewerage of towns and cities."[521] This represented a noticeable change from the 1850s and 1860s when Vermont made no effort to participate in any of the proceedings of the National Quarantine and Sanitary Association active in many states that met on a yearly basis to identify and discuss remedies for current health-related problems. The lack of a seaboard threatened by arriving ships carrying cholera that required quarantine before landing made it less imperative for Vermonters to become involved in such efforts and resulted in their missing an early opportunity to consider proposals to regulate the distribution of dangerous drugs.[522] Had Vermont representatives attended, listened and acted on the increased warnings of others, the growing opium problem in the next few years might have been reduced.

By 1865, Vermont's surgeon general Samuel W. Thayer of Burlington (who strongly objected to any insinuation of consumption in his town during the 1857 debates) began to express great concern at the state's ability to withstand the arrival of cholera. His observations constitute the first objective assessment of the challenges that Vermonters faced in sustaining their health as their past neglect allowed conditions to deteriorate so noticeably to this moment. Thayer understood that while the state's laws conferred authority on cities and town officials to enforce sanitary requirements, they had never before faced such "incursions of pestilence" that required a more comprehensive response. He asked the legislature to become involved and act as a "stimulant" to goad local officials to take action and clean up "places in this State, particularly in our large towns and along the principal public thoroughfares." Thayer further warned about the lack of fresh water and good sewerage, "deficient in all our large towns," prompting him to recommend that "All decomposing animal and vegetable matter should be removed from cellars and the vicinity of dwellings – cellars and crowded apartments thoroughly cleaned and whitewashed – drains and sewers covered – cess pools and sinks frequently emptied and supplied with fresh lime – streets and alleys kept clean and free from accumulations of all kinds, and a free circulation of air and temperance 'in all things' encouraged in all places and among all classes of people."[523] His warnings were repeated a decade later when another physician decried Vermont's refusal to acknowledge and institute measures to alleviate the consequences of epidemics made possible by unsanitary conditions. England had already done so for the past twenty-five years, as well as Massachusetts, Rhode Island, New York, Michigan, Minnesota, and California by creating boards of health, but not Vermont. "Let us awaken from the stupor begotten of the ignorance and habits of the past," he said, "to a full sense of the fact that millions perish annually from preventable diseases."[524]

The inconsistent attention given by town and city officials to health problems until the creation of a Board of Health in 1886 after other states had already done so provides another example of local hesitancy to intrude into the lives of resistant residents who persisted in their pursuit of Jacksonian independence. As further demonstrated later in the century with the presence of an opium epidemic, it was only when circumstances reached a level that threatened the health of the larger community before the legislature finally intervened, but then only in its traditional, reactionary manner. Despite the examples of other states that took proactive measures on the behalf of their citizens, Vermont refused to intervene in ways that could have lessened the impact of these same kinds of threats to their health. Lobbying by special economic interests threatened by the intervention of authority that could inhibit them, such as the railroad corporations and the increasing presence of drug manufacturers, together with the state's ever-present parsimonious philosophy, may well have contributed to these delays.

REGISTRATION

Before the alarming descriptions of the state's sanitary conditions in 1865, in the 1850s the legislators did begin to listen to the requests of the regular physicians to adopt a way to at least assess and quantify the health of Vermonters, albeit in stumbling fashion. The glowing, but misdirected, reports they made of the state's health during the 1857 debates ("all Vermont is healthy"), aside from their clear bias in favor of one location for the capital over another, remained largely anecdotal because they lacked specific information about their constituents' actual physical and sanitary situation. Many other states already had procedures copied from centuries-old European practices that made reliable statistics available to officials concerning births, marriages and deaths that helped them to more effectively chart their future. Decades earlier, George Washington recognized the importance in accumulating this kind of information when he wrote to a Scottish researcher "I am fully persuaded that when enlightened men will take the trouble to examine so minutely into the state of society. . . it must result in greatly ameliorating the condition of the people, promoting the interest of civil society, and the happiness of mankind at large." He applauded such an effort and observed that "These are objects truly worthy the attention of a great mind; and every friend to the human race must readily lend his aid towards their accomplishment."[525] In Europe, Napoleon Bonaparte instituted a comprehensive registration system in France in the early nineteenth century, followed by Spain and Austria and then England in 1836 that drew the attention of American authorities. Massachusetts already had a long history of recording the dates of marriages, births and deaths back to 1639 and in 1842 authorities codified a more comprehensive system similar to the British.[526] Notwithstanding their good intentions, officials recognized the deficiencies in the statistics they accumulated in the first several years because of the inconsistent levels of cooperation and poor practices of towns gathering the information requested, but they deemed it important enough to begin to understand the state of health of their residents. Some entries in the early Massachusetts reports referred to the effects that Vermont had on its population concerning marriages in towns near their shared border. There, local officials complained they could not gather accurate information because the betrothed crossed into the Green Mountain state to perform the ceremony. As the Bernardston records for 1846 reported, "every year some go there, where the laws and practices are more lax, to be 'united with the silken cords of Hymen.'"[527]

Vermont officials could have had access to the same kinds of information years earlier, but their tight-fisted fiscal policies rejected such processes because they do not appear to have fully understood their intrinsic worth. The towns already reported the numbers of the most obviously needy individuals within their borders that included the paupers and insane, but they collected no specific information about the overall health of their inhabitants. In 1850, Governor Charles K. Williams cautioned the legislature on its persistent restrained fiscal policy to take care with how it dispersed the people's tax money and admonished that "no reform should be attempted unless called for by the public good, nor until the whole subject is fully and thoroughly considered."[528] That view only began to change in the 1850s as the effects of modernity intruded into their lives when, in 1851, the VMS recognized that gathering health-related statistics ("age, sex, time and cause of death") concerning the state's inhabitants as "highly important" and formed a committee "to present this subject before the Legislature."[529] However, their stumbling attempt stalled and minutes of their 1855 meeting disclose that while they had chosen three of their members the preceding year to pursue the proposal, they "had never been notified of their appointment."[530] The Society reappointed the men and after another year of delay an impatient public began to consider the effort abandoned and lamented its deficient condition in comparison to the fifteen years of progress made in neighboring Massachusetts.[531]

The VMS's struggling efforts coincided precisely with the new changes that modernity imposed throughout the state when a speaker at one of its meetings in 1856 made it clear residents could no longer depend on their physical isolation to protect them from the health problems experienced in distant metropolitan environments. "Although the state of Vermont is at present, in a great degree, exempt from the attendant circumstances which so often impart a fatal character to disease among a dense population," he said, "we cannot look forward with security from our mountain fastness; these fatal causes are already within our limits, and gradually infesting our villages and manufactories. . . . Our mountains and valleys are not inaccessible to the legion of epidemics; they still invade us, and leave sections of our state in mourning."[532] Understanding their causes required the accumulation of statistics and which would also be of value to prove an individual's lineage in legal proceedings during the distribution of estates. As the speaker further related, "Many instances are known in the history of New England, of great and often fruitless expenditures of money, time and mental labor, in tracing out family relations. . . in order to establish a claim to property. And it must be well known to the legal profession, that in the state of Vermont, nothing is so meagre and uncertain as the recorded data necessary for these injuries."[533] Nationally, the American Medical Association deemed the collection of health related information so important that it sought the cooperation of all states to participate in gathering it. "The great duty then devolving. . . on the medical profession of Vermont," the VMS speaker described in support of the effort "is to endeavor, through the intervention of our state government, to obtain the ability, by means of a suitable law of registration. . . in a manner which shall do justice at least, if not honor to ourselves and the state."[534]

In November 1856 an act was finally passed that required the accumulation of statistics of the state's inhabitants on a yearly basis to record births, marriages and deaths.[535] Despite whatever guidance Massachusetts could have provided to aid with compliance, Vermont's experience came up decidedly deficient. While the law ordered town clerks to record the information, the means of their obtaining it relied on the goodwill, or moral obligation, of a diverse community with huge differences in interest and competency to report. Secretary of State Charles W. Willard tried to allay the concerns of those opposed to the effort and recognized that forcing compliance would prove difficult. He appealed to Vermonters sense of furthering the common good and pointed to the same kind of work conducted elsewhere: "the people of Vermont are only following a few years behind the best regulated governments in Europe, and in many States of our Union" that had "been constantly stimulated to increased efforts for the improvement and faithful execution of Registration Laws."[536]

The burden in gathering the information fell on the many district school clerks around the state, "especially in populous towns" that experienced a constantly "changing population," indicating the transitory effects that the railroad allowed in its moving about. Willard directed the clerks to exercise "much vigilance. . . to ascertain all the births and deaths and requisite circumstances, occurring in their precincts" and, for the deceased, to describe "the apparent cause of death" based on information provided by any "physician who may have attended" the event. The specific instructions provided to the clerks to guide them for each of the three categories were complicated, particularly for anyone not familiar with medical issues and when subjective interpretations, or societal pressures to suppress the facts surrounding their deaths, were recorded in a way that differed from what actually happened. "Give the causes of death the right names," one instruction stated and provided an example: "For instance the term 'Consumption' should be applied only to that disease of the lungs. . . and not any other disease which may be accompanied with a general wasting and decay. This rule is most frequently violated in giving the causes of death among young children and aged, hence more particular enquiries should be made." Another instruction explained that "Such names should be used as will give a clear definition of the cause of death." It became even more complicated when the clerks had to record "by numbers, the duration of the disease, or diseases if more than one have concurred in producing the death, in years, months, or days." In the event "poison has been the cause of death," the instructions required them to enter "the time which elapses between its administration and the death."[537] Unable to compel the assistance of doctors and clergymen to travel to the clerks' offices to provide this information, Willard solicited their participation for "the advancement of the moral and sanitary improvements" of everyone. For clerks seeking guidance in working through the complicated directions, Willard suggested that they "ask some competent physician to look over his record and correct any errors he may discover." Practically, in the absence of any mandatory method to assure the quality of the records, the clerks had little to fear if they failed to provide the requested information because of lax enforcement measures.

After additional delay, because of confusion over the distribution of blank forms to the town clerks, the initial accounting of the state's vital statistics appeared in 1859 as the *First Report to the Legislature of Vermont, relating to the Registry and Returns of Births Marriages and Deaths in this State for the Year ending December 31, 1857*. Prepared under the auspices of Middlebury physician Dr. Charles L. Allen, he admitted that while generally pleased with the first attempt, it had flaws and called it "imperfect and incomplete."[538] While Allen and his fellow VMS members set lofty goals in modernizing this aspect of their profession, the general practitioner saw little reason to participate and make the required reports of deaths and their causes to town clerks. The weak attempt to force their compliance with a minimal three-dollar fine appears to have had little effect. "It is very much to be regretted," the report for 1859 related, "that the members of the medical profession should so generally neglect the duties imposed upon them by the Registration Law. Although the statute expressly requires the attending physician to furnish the town clerk with a certificate of the cause of death in every case attended by him, yet it is undoubtedly very rare that any such certificate is given." It explained further that, "This neglect is due in some measure to the indifference of the profession upon this subject. Some physicians refuse to perform this duty, claiming that it is neither just nor constitutional to demand of a medical man professional services without remuneration. The government expects to pay lawyers, architects, or mechanics for their labor, but compels physicians under penalty, to work for nothing."[539] Officials, hamstrung in enforcing the law's provisions, also caused noncompliance. "It is true," the report continued, "that, under municipal law, the State has a right to call upon its citizens for such assistance as may be necessary to its safety and welfare, but in a rural region, like Vermont, municipal laws are not readily borne or easily enforced." Without any ability to assure compliance in this unregulated, unlicensed climate, the problem could be avoided and the assistance of physicians obtained, the report related, if they received official recognition by the state as members of an honored profession they believed was due to them. Without that cooperation, the statistics in the reports describing the causes of death "must be very defective." In their persistent refusal to accede to the calls of regular physicians to impose a licensing law that would elevate the status of their profession and separate them from the untrained quacks, the legislature had directly undercut the integrity of the registration law.

Without the help of physicians most knowledgeable about Vermonter's health, exacerbated by inept but well intended school and town clerks, the potentially important annual reports remained deficient. In 1858 the president of the VMS lamented the continued "indifference on the part of the great mass of the people, and [the] disregard of its provisions by a small proportion of the officials concerned in fulfilling them." He called again on the VMS members to help with the registry, "May I not appeal to you, gentlemen, for your aid. . . by enlightening the public mind and awakening an interest in its success – a success attainable only by prompt and accurate performance of all its requirements, sustained by an intelligent, educated public sentiment." The effort promised additional benefits beyond gathering statistics, he said, that could also educate the medical profession about "the laws of health and disease" they encountered and thereby assist in elevating their standing in the community. In ending, he appealed to their egos and reminded them that as "peculiarly representative men. . . committed [to] the honor and fair fame of the profession of our State, as well as the welfare and happiness of its citizens," they had a serious responsibility to "seek earnestly for individual, personal improvement" to advance the recognition of their worth.[540] Despite that lack of cooperation given to the registration process and claims of inaccuracies, two weeks later the Society expressed its thanks to Allen. "We regard with the highest satisfaction," their minutes disclose, "the report, as evincing both a great amount of labor, and great intelligence and accuracy in the manner of its accomplishment."[541] Following its publication in 1859, the Society held its annual meeting at the recently rebuilt State House where Allen proudly "presented to each member. . . a copy of his first Report." Fifteen new members gained admission into the Society's rolls that day and a pleased recording secretary ended his entries with marked emphasis: "This meeting was one of more than usual interest & pleasantness; & gave promise of greater usefulness & increase for the future; & has tended largely to establish the Vermont Medical Society as a valuable institution of the State."[542] In the minds of its members, the VMS believed it had made a serious contribution in understanding the state of Vermonter's health with the first report and would further their efforts to gain the recognition it deserved.

The enthusiasm and hopes the VMS had for the registry did not resonate with some during these first years of change wrought by the effects of modernity. In 1860, for an unstated reason, the House of Representatives unsuccessfully sought to repeal the gathering of health data.[543] By 1864 registry officials had become increasingly concerned about the continued lack of attention paid to the registration law when twenty-four towns, including the larger ones of Burlington, Barnet and Berlin, failed to make their required yearly reports; a notable increase from the five that did not do so in 1857.[544] Again, the VMS expressed its dismay, and resentment, at the way Vermont officials administered the program compared to other states that placed the onus on doctors. "In this country," it related, "nearly all that is valuable of statistics of disease and mortality, has been done voluntarily and gratuitously" and not assigned as a duty, except "in our own

State" where it was required "without remuneration or reward." Adding to its chagrin, the Society noted that among those who administered it were "unqualified persons [to whom] a paltry sum is paid for the service, sufficient to induce them to perform it in a careless manner."[545] The absence of cooperation, particularly with the effects of the Civil War present in the state, caused many to question the intrinsic value of the reports. The tabulation of soldiers' deaths who returned home to convalesce and then died posed a problem in assigning them causes specific to Vermont. The concern over the reports' accuracy remained when, as late as 1888, the State Board of Health complained that despite the system being in place for thirty years, its statistics remained "very incomplete and imperfect, particularly in regard to deaths and their causes."[546] Because accurately identifying the number of deaths and the reasons behind them remained such a persistent problem, the Board called for "a radical change in the system." The reliance on school clerks unfamiliar with the law's dictates continued to present a major problem. "Of course many deaths are forgotten," the Board wrote, "particularly those of children, unless the death was caused by accident which became town talk. Many families have changed residence and thus births and deaths fail to be recorded." Other problems existed in ascertaining the causes of death because "neither the householders nor the school district clerks are conversant with medical terms or diseases or their names. They conclude that because a person was sick a long time or was much emaciated the cause of death was 'consumption.' Or if there was trouble with the urinary functions they decide the disease to have been 'Bright's disease.' If the death was sudden they infer it was from 'heart disease.' And so on, thus supplementing their lack of knowledge or memory by guesses."[547]

For the Vermont legislators in 1857 who ignored the examples of other states that could have guided them, these were precisely the kinds of problems they set into motion with a registration law that lacked easy application, an effective enforcement mechanism beyond the threat of a fine that nobody feared, or understanding of the discomfort within a profession at the lack of a licensing law that recognized the importance of their calling. Still, the deficient oversight by Vermont government of such an important responsibility in mid-century continued to fall on that profession as it refused to abandon its obligation to attend to the population's health.

ALL-INCLUSIVE "CONSUMPTION"

Accurately assessing the effects of modernity on the physical health of Vermonters in mid-century presents challenges. The legislature's uninformed acclamations of good health that so forcibly dismissed both the glaring presence and prevalence of consumption throughout the state were reinforced by the carefully crafted assessments of governors in their addresses to the public throughout the 1850s. In their unwavering pronouncements of good health they effectively concealed its actual condition and allowed an inaccurate perception to exist at a time when capital was needed from outside investors to further the state's development. In 1849, Governor Carlos Coolidge issued a Proclamation calling for a day of "Humiliation, Fasting and Prayer" when cholera threatened to arrive to allow Vermonters to stop and reflect on their many bounties, inferring the benefits bestowed on them by the railroad, and asked God to "overrule the tendencies of hastily increased wealth and dominion" they had received and not allow it to "corrupt us." "The grim Scourge which has recently touched our border" had appeared and Coolidge prayed for divine intervention to grant them "the invaluable blessing of health."[548] While Vermont experienced relatively less effects from the disease (two died in Burlington in August 1849), elsewhere in New England it struck with a vengeance killing many, including "the filthy, gluttonous, drunken portion of the Irish" in New York City.[549] Others found comfort in Vermont's isolation and its geological formations that seemed to inhibit cholera's presence, but it was of little solace because of the railroad's ability to transmit disease.[550] After Coolidge's acknowledgment of the undeniable threat of pestilence that other nearby states experienced, in the next years Vermont's governors deviated little in their messages presenting a picture of wholesomeness among the inhabitants: "the almost universal prevalence of health" (1852); "the general good health of the citizens of this State" (1853); "the general health which the people have been permitted to enjoy" (1854); "general health has prevailed" (1856); "continued material prosperity and general health of our people" (1857); "our people have been blessed with an ordinary degree of health" (1858); "our people have been blessed with a common measure of health" (1859); and, "we have been exempt from pestilence or the ravages of wasting sickness" (1861). No further official reference to Vermonters health graced the governors' assessments in the 1860s until 1872 when Governor Julius Converse had confidence enough to assert that "An unusual measure of health has prevailed."[551]

Until Converse's statement the evidence ran to the contrary to any notion of universal good health and demonstrated instead that in the preceding two decades Vermonters experienced a significant number of deaths attributed most notably to consumption. Notwithstanding the state's admittedly inaccurate registry, it did identify a consistent, combined life span of males and females between 1857 and 1870 that held at approximately thirty-five to thirty-six years.[552] Stark assessments by the VMS in 1858 that large numbers of females died because of consumptive symptoms and the 1864 registry report reiterating that doctors still faced "the unequaled destroyer of our population" strongly indicate that the disease had remained a killer for a long period of time. Some medical practitioners argued that "female diseases," those exhibited by their menses, the types of coughs women experienced, and questionable health of the uterus was a strong predictor of whether one would get consumption.[553] Many advertisements appearing in the state's newspapers for remedies to treat consumption, regardless of their effectiveness, demonstrated that the public understood well and feared its widespread presence. Searching for some form of relief for women, many, including physicians, argued that pregnancy could prolong the life of a consumptive patient and advocated that they marry and establish families. In 1864, the VMS recognized that some esteemed practitioners elsewhere agreed with that prospect, but it refused to endorse the practice or provide any definitive direction other than to recommend that "Physicians and parents should properly inform themselves upon this subject."[554] Suggestions that pregnancy could lessen the prospect of incurring consumption notwithstanding, when considered with the circumstantial evidence of illegal abortions and instances of infanticide taking place, exacerbated by the insidious effects of alcohol and drugs, the politicians' protestations in 1857 of widespread health had little factual basis.

While officials recognized the imperfection of the registry's annual figures prepared by school clerks, when carefully scrutinized they did provide interesting insights, considered by one newspaper as "exceedingly valuable."[555] However, they did require additional context before anyone could reach valid, albeit qualified, conclusions. Other reasons existed beyond deficient recordkeeping that explains why they must be examined with caution, including the way that diseases and causes of death were characterized. Protests by doctors required to report them without receiving compensation remained an important factor as was the failure of the law to define what a "physician" actually was. The ongoing rejection of a licensing requirement for practitioners provided no way to assess the credentials and competency of those who actually made the reports. Did it include both the regular and the empiricist, or only the former? Did the uneducated empiricist make reports about causes of death that he had little understanding of or may have actually contributed to? Did the entries made by questionably qualified clerks rest on fact or community rumor as the registry report for 1864 lamented?[556] Did the reports of consumption have a basis in fact or did it serve as an all-inclusive, convenient category to group unrelated causes of death? Massachusetts had reported a similar problem a decade earlier, but Vermont persisted and repeated the error in its reports. Did physicians seek to protect the reputations of their well-to-do patients by attributing their deaths to consumption when they actually died of a disease, such as cholera, that usually fell on the poor, filthy members of society, mainly the Irish? Additionally, instances of malpractice and the intentional concealment of crimes, such as physicians engaged in overdosing and/or performing death-inducing abortions on patients, may have allowed an alleged consumptive classification to serve as a more convenient, less-incriminating way to record an event that others knew about. For those that took place in remote locations or without bothersome witnesses that involved the voiceless members of society, such as helpless infants and children, invalids, the elderly and insane, the faceless poor and the transients, each could escape the notice of officials and allow for malefactors responsible for their deaths to avoid detection and punishment. Finally, what effect did geography have on the reports' credibility where those living in hilltop environments tenaciously maintained tight control over their health care decisions, including the consumption of drugs, and secreted their actions from the eyes of prying outsiders? Europeans recognized the reports' inadequacies and viewed America's "very loose style" in the way it conducted its registration efforts leading one Frenchman to attribute it to self-interest. "In America," he told the Anthropological Society of Paris, "the law does not enforce the registry of deaths. In many States it is only done when the relations have an interest in doing so; children, people without relations who take an interest in them, etc., are not registered."[557]

Despite their admitted inaccuracies, between 1857 and 1868, Vermont's registry reports consistently tell of the devastating toll that consumption inflicted, especially on the state's female population. So many women died from the disease that both the 1857 and 1858 reports identify their numbers as "wonderfully increased" beyond what males experienced. In 1863, the report described the difference between the sexes in those deaths as "remarkable" and noted in 1868 that "this disproportion is increasing from year to year." "*What causes*," the reports repeatedly asked with alarmed emphasis, "*are in operation in this State, to produce this comparatively large female mortality?*" While Massachusetts reported a similar phenomenon, in apparent shock at its increased presence in Vermont, the 1858 report admitted that "There is scarcely another State or country in the world where the male mortality" did not exceed the female. These females, the innocents of the population, deserved the attention of professionals compared to the ones who died because of their own personal failures such as those who did not receive vaccinations for small pox and then contracted the disease. The VMS expressed little sympathy for this group of sufferers and dismissed them in 1859: "It becomes the special duty of every person to protect himself against this disease. Anyone who permits himself to be sick with it, is as justly chargeable with ignorance, negligence or guilt as he who leaves his house open to be entered & pillaged by robbers known to be in the neighborhood." For any state or town that failed to "interpose its legal authority to exterminate the disease" and require vaccination "should rest the responsibility as must rest the consequences, of permitting the destruction of the health & lives of its citizens."[558]

Vermont's first registration report for 1857 identified the "wonderfully increased" numbers of female deaths because of consumption (that "sweeps off more than any other disease") at 526 individuals (or 67.33 percent) dying that year compared to 259 males (32.67 percent). "This fell destroyer seems to delight in striking down the weaker sex," the report related, particularly those "during the period of development, and of early adult life." Because the medical profession could not identify why the phenomenon occurred, the report offered no additional information to explain it.[559] As large as those numbers were, officials recognized that they underestimated what was actually taking place. "The annual abstracts show. . . that there has been great remissness in collecting and reporting the facts," Secretary of State Benjamin W. Dean decried in 1858. "No reason is obvious why our State should differ so widely from others similarly situated. Probably not over *one-half* of the births, *three-quarters* of the marriages, and *two-thirds* of the deaths, have been reported."[560] The reports through 1868 repeatedly noted with alarm the marked preponderance of female deaths. As late as 1879, the report identified the number of males dying that year because of consumption at 308 compared to the females at 540 and stated that "The disproportion of the sexes is noticeable." Whereas consumption was the reported cause of death of 24.11 percent of the population in 1857, which declined to 10.74 percent in 1879, it still had a devastating impact on females during these two decades that saw 6,125 of them fall to the disease compared to 3,589 males.[561]

The effects of deaths attributable to consumption and the depopulation of females during the 1850s was felt elsewhere in the overall impressions of the state's health. This included the loss of young people ("the productive part of community") that emigrated to the west between 1856 and 1861. As a result, Vermont turned its attention to the many residents left behind, expressing resentment that they did not contribute to the state's economy. The reports referred to them as "the aged and the infirm" (1858), "the more feeble and less active" (1859), "those that must be maintained by others" (1860) and "the aged, the non-producers, the consumers [that] remain in our midst" (1861). Their descriptions of Vermonters closely follow the language used by the Council of Censors in 1855 when it identified three classes of people impacting the state's business activity: "the first, or rich class, having a competency;" the "second, or poor class. . . unable or unqualified to take the lead in business transactions;" and "the third class [that] constitutes the bone and muscle [with] strong bodies and strong minds."

Dr. Carleton Pennington Frost

The Civil War reinforced the importance of gathering detailed personal information in order to understand the country's military capabilities and prepare for the future. In the process, state and national authorities accumulated a mass of statistics on soldiers and sailors that described their various physical characteristics. It constituted a marked improvement from previous efforts to understand the capabilities of the military when an 1840 assessment simply described Vermont soldiers as "firm, compact, hardy, have activity and enterprize, with the boldness of mind and valor, that constitute them natural soldiers."[562] At the outbreak of war in April 1861 over 34,000 Vermont men answered the call for volunteers, met by officials unprepared to fully assess their suitability for the hardships they would encounter. The initial rudimentary statistics accumulated by the loyal states' adjutants-general, who hastily gathered them in ways inconsistent from each other, became the basis for the first publication devoted to the subject, *Investigations in the Military and Anthropological Statistics of American Soldiers* (1869). The report differed little from the 1840 assessments and provided no information on the health of the men. Instead, it focused on their most obvious characteristics: nativity; age; height (noting that "the Green Mountains of Vermont furnish a race of men among the tallest in all the New England States"); color of hair and eyes; complexion; and, occupation.[563] Similarly, when the United States Sanitary Commission began to examine the condition of army and navy personnel more closely in the war's first years, it also limited its inquiry and focused on their "physique." The questionable value of these kinds of elementary facts and the

Surgeon Carleton Pennington Frost, 15th Vermont Infantry. Library of Congress.

problems that authorities encountered in recruiting and dealing with the unique challenges presented by enlistees and draftees forced national authorities to reconsider how to make the process more efficient, useful and credible. In 1863, the War Department's Provost-Marshal-General's Bureau, created to oversee those efforts, established a medical branch the following year and provided it with the authority to deal with "all matters pertaining to the medical examination of men for military service." In turn, trusted physicians from each of the states were enrolled to assist in a *"systematic* medical examination" of the men. Their exhaustive work later appeared in a two-volume publication in 1875, *Statistics, Medical and Anthropological of the Provost-Marshal-General's Bureau,* that described many physical characteristics of over a million of the country's military men in great detail.[564]

The Bureau's work in Vermont was conducted by three physicians from the Board of Enrollment in each of the congressional districts: past president of the VMS (1860) Dr. Benjamin F. Morgan on the west side of the Green Mountains (in the First District in Rutland); Dr. Carleton Pennington Frost on the east side (in the Second District in Windsor); and, Dr. John S. Chandler, VMS recording secretary, in the north (the Third District in Burlington). Most notably, Frost's important contributions to the Bureau and Vermont medicine in the middle of the nineteenth century mark him as one of the most influential physicians in the state. Born in Sullivan, New Hampshire in 1830, Frost graduated from Dartmouth Medical College in 1857 and achieved election as a member of the VMS shortly afterwards in 1859. That same year he testified as an expert witness in an Orange County court in arguably the most notorious prosecution of another doctor for criminal abortion that ever took place in Vermont. His reputation grew so rapidly in the next decade that in 1868 he became president of the VMS, charged to investigate and report on the increasing threat that Vermonters faced from opium abuse. The following year he was appointed dean of the Dartmouth Medical College and named professor of the science and practice of medicine. Between 1862 and 1869 Frost also served as a surgeon on the Board of Enrollment for the U. S. Army and went into the field with the Fifteenth Regiment of Vermont Volunteers between October 1862 and May 1863. At the time of his death in 1896 at age sixty-six of heart disease, he earned a solid reputation as progressive and possessed with an intense interest in improving the medical profession, including conditions within the Hanover community where he lived and worked. [565]

Frost strongly supported the VMS and served on many of its committees authoring various studies that included epidemics, consumption of the lungs, insanity, therapeutics, Bright's disease (inflammation of the kidneys) and puerperal convulsions (pregnancy disorders). A serious student of medical history, he made a presentation on "The Past and Present of Medical Science" and, as a member of the committee on the "Medical History of the Vermont Regiments," accumulated information from the state's doctors concerning interesting medical and surgical cases they encountered during the war. Together with Morgan and Chandler in their own districts, Frost also prepared an important summary of his work in the Second District that he provided to both the Provost-Marshal-General's Bureau and the VMS.[566]

Frost had extensive involvement in assessing the health of Vermont's soldiers and estimated that he examined a total of 8,974 men (2,700 drafted, 3,500 recruits and substitutes, and 2,774 enrolled) that included one-half of the Third Regiment of Vermont Volunteers and his own Fifteenth Regiment. He accomplished his arduous work by examining an average of ninety-five individuals each day over the course of seven hours. The men came from the east side of the Green Mountains and he provided a glowing, perhaps overly exuberant, summary of their overall condition. "The inhabitants are industrious, temperate in eating and drinking, law-abiding and justice-loving," Frost wrote. They were also "economical in their expenditures; thoroughly loyal to the General and State Governments; and as well-educated and generally intelligent as any people on the face of the earth. They are most thorough believers in universal freedom, and the equality of all before the law. Their dwellings are warm for winter, neat and tidy in appearance; their tables are provided with a plenty of well-cooked and substantial food; and in general they are comfortably and neatly clad." He reported that the diseases the population experienced from that part of the state were those "incident to the latitude" and "for the most part, atmospheric and accidental." In a population so heavily involved with agriculture that required strenuous physical labor (1,900 of the 2,600 Vermont men drafted in 1863 were farmers or farm laborers), he reported that the disqualifying conditions of "hernia, and varicose veins of the extremities. . . and loss of teeth" were "very frequently found." He also described their consumptive symptoms and reported that "Tubercular disease is often seen, although I think pulmonary phthisis is less frequently the cause of death than formerly." While he made no specific comparison to Vermont's female population in his assessments, when Frost addressed "diseases of the nervous system" he noted that it did "prevail considerably" among males, but occurred "more generally. . . among females." Many men attempted to conceal or misrepresent their actual physical condition as enlistees sought to hide ailments in order to profit from generous bounties unlike the draftees who accentuated them or made up illnesses to avoid service. All three district physicians described the many frauds that the draftees tried to pass off on them (Frost reported deafness as the most frequent complaint) and the ways that they had carefully examined each in order to substantiate or reject their claims. Only Morgan in the First District referred specifically to consumption and reported with emphasis that he had seen some men "come forward drawn down on one side, with short cough, and panting breath, declaring that he has consumption" because *"the doctor told him so."*[567] While none of them reported any instances involving the abuse of medicines, a Salem, Massachusetts surgeon described two instances when men presented themselves "under the influence of some drug," evidenced by their pulse being "small, feeble, and irregular."[568]

CONCLUSION

Frost's assessments of the physical characteristics of Vermont's volunteers served a specific purpose to fulfill the state's obligation to provide a quota of men in a time of war. Despite the overall favorable aspects of their reports, none of the Enrollment Board surgeons had the responsibility to assess the health of Vermont's female population or to examine the circumstances that surrounded their persistent rate of death above that of males because of symptoms attributable to consumption. Similarly, the state legislators' claims in 1857 that Vermonter's experienced widespread sound health is questionable because they also avoided the need to competently and fully examine the issue. The solons' myopic and uninformed statements sought to advance the interests of the state over others and they dismissed the assessments of knowledgeable medical men, as demonstrated by the VMS, with important information that could have countered those representations. Aspects of modernity such as the railroad, telegraph and the increased availability of newspapers allowed for the rapid transmission and sharing of valuable information both within and outside of the state could have informed and swayed their arguments had they chosen to be more fully engaged. However, they persistently displayed a willing blindness to such concerns and engaged in petty differences that detracted from the more important considerations. By the time of their debates, they had wearied of the battles that surrounded the recently passed prohibition law and turned, instead, to raise a tired aspect of the long-lasting alcohol question that concerned amorphous "moral obligations" and whether one town would prove more morally worthy than another to host the capital. In doing so, they ignored glaring truths before them: that Vermont women died in large numbers and that the very doctors they refused to allow the privilege of obtaining important licenses as their peers did in other states were being dismissed and ignored. As a result, the law makers failed to obtain the full assistance of Vermont's educated doctors to advance the state's overall health that allowed the unregulated harmful quacks and growing opium trade to remain and flourish among them. Any thought of interfering with Vermonters sense of Jacksonian independence by introducing state authority that meant acknowledging these distasteful facts of their constituents' lives and the actual state of their health and thereby scare off the economic benefits promised by capitalists was something to avoid. In their inaction, modernity moved ahead as other uncomfortable aspects of life already experienced in the large cities outside of Vermont arrived via the railroad to alter its traditions.

CHAPTER VI

Criminal Abortions and Infanticide

"Skill, caution and silence are the three important elements." [569]

DARTMOUTH MEDICAL COLLEGE STUDENT
ALBION K. STROUT, 1872

Before the Law

Negotiating the impact of modernity's effects on the legislature, the public and the medical profession required a careful hand when any consideration of intruding into individuals' right to make independent choices over their health was involved. The challenge it presented was immense because of concurrent forces demanding attention that intruded into Vermont's traditional notions of gentility. These included accommodating an increasing middle class, growing urbanization, a shift from agriculture to industry – transportation, extractive operations, textile mills, and forest-based activities among the changes – that came to so dramatically influence the shape of Vermont society. Single women now recognized and pursued the new opportunities these changes made possible as they left farms to work in factories and where they had little interest in being burdened by the demands of childrearing. At the same time, when they found themselves in a "family way" and needed to escape the accompanying social stigma, they increasingly engaged in secretive procedures allowing them to avoid that outcome. Those efforts were initially only frowned upon, but as the nineteenth century progressed it forced Vermont, as well as other states, to impose legislation, albeit ineffectively enforced, to curb their actions. Modernity and accompanying Improvement were difficult taskmasters whose tentacles reached far into the future with significant consequence for Vermont culture.

Three significant events bracketed the 1850s that affected the health of Vermonters and involved lawmakers and the VMS. Following examples set by Connecticut (1821), Missouri (1825), Illinois (1827), New York (1828), and Massachusetts (1845), in 1846 Vermont succumbed to "the sensational publicity of the period" and criminalized attempts to perform abortions.[570] Despite its salutary intent, the law received so little attention that by 1865 Woodstock doctor William McCollom (VMS secretary in 1860 and president in 1866) posited that the large number of criminal abortions taking place posed such a "growing evil" it made it difficult to estimate accurately the number of births and people living in the state.[571] Four years later, the VMS returned to McCollom's observations and officially acknowledged for the first time the presence of "professional abortionists" at large, calling them "men who for no more palpable reason than their love of gain, make criminal abortion an everyday affair."[572] The Society also acknowledged that Vermonters had another problem with their "too strong dependence on drugs" consuming so much opium that in 1868 it appointed respected Civil War veteran, surgeon and society president Dr. Carleton Pennington Frost to prepare a report to the membership on the "Uses and Abuses of Opium."[573] The accelerating number of threats made against Vermonters health make it clear that the technological and capitalist-driven modernity of the 1850s succeeded so completely it overwhelmed a complacent, farmer-oriented legislature hesitant to intrude into their private lives to curb those abuses.

Abortion and infanticide are unattractive phenomena that have received no attention in Vermont's nineteenth-century historiography. Because of their amoral and illegal features, accounts of their practice by women and doctors are understandably vague, if not absent. Among the hundreds of theses prepared by Dartmouth Medical College students throughout the century only a single one, simply entitled "Abortion," provides important insights into how it was conducted and the important need to maintain secrecy when it occurred. It was written in 1872 by twenty-four-year-old Albion K. Strout who, after making several observations concerning the practice, ended with a warning that any physician who performed abortions must proceed with "skill, caution and silence. . . both for his own benefit and the good of society."[574] His advice was already implicitly followed by those members of the medical profession who quietly engaged in a practice they did not want to be associated with, but remained unrepentant to extract any profit they could from it.

Vermont's inaccurate, understated registry reports provide little assistance in assessing the extent of the problem and record that: only eight women died because of abortions between 1857 and 1868; between one and five percent of babies were stillborn; and made no reference to infanticide. At a time when lobbyists clamored for more legislation to address the killing effects of alcohol, only twenty-nine individuals (including four females), or approximately three each year, reportedly died from intemperance; a demonstrably woeful basis on which to argue the presence of widespread death in the state. During the same period, some forty-six individuals died by accident or negligence from consuming the generically-referred to "poison." An acronym that applied to a variety of substances, poison included the increased presence of opium and medicines that pregnant females could have consumed in the hope of inducing convulsions leading to miscarriages and which death could also be misidentified to another suspect classification, consumption. Further investigation that might have connected their deaths to specific compounds did not exist because Vermont, together with other states, viewed these kinds of statistics, according to one critic in 1860, as a way to keep "tally of the evil done, and with no view of preventing the evil itself."[575] The dire situation the VMS described concerning abortions and drug usage for the same period make it clear that the numbers of women who died and the accompanying descriptions of their causes are deficient. The 1862 report reiterated the extent of the problem when it admitted that "over ten percent of the deaths occurring yearly in this State, escape record."[576] For that kind of information, aside from the incredible accounts in the late 1850s of an Orange County abortionist and possible serial killer William H. M. Howard, anecdotal reports from physicians, religious leaders, community members, and newspapers provide only brief glimpses of what actually took place.

Definitions for abortion and infanticide have varied over time. While Vermont's 1846 law generally criminalized the act of inducing abortion at any time during pregnancy, medical practitioners used the euphemistic terms "criminal abortions" to those taking place in the first six months and "premature labor" to those up to nine months. Intentional abortions occurred most frequently in those first months and not afterwards when movement (quickening) became noticeable.[577] The murder of a child after birth in the nineteenth-century, commonly called infanticide (charged as murder, but hardly ever successfully done), has assumed added distinction by modern day scholars that call the act within hours of birth "neonaticide" and when it occurred over the age of one, "filicide."[578] The complex motivations of women who participated in any of these practices at any particular time depended on a number of factors that can be attributed to modernity's increasing influence in their lives.

Notwithstanding the distasteful and illegal aspects of abortions and infanticides, the paucity of their recording in Vermont's registry reports rested, in part, on a medical profession that persisted in refusing to cooperate and provide the necessary information for the causes of all kinds of deaths. Their general disinterest stemmed in part from the continuing effects of the legislature's refusal to allow them the privilege of a license able to distinguish them from the competing quacks, midwives, folk herbalists and their own alienated members who undercut their charges and competed for paying patients.[579] Abortion scholar James Mohr writes that these kinds of concerns, or "medical regulations," were the principle reasons behind the formation of the nation's attitudes and policies on abortion.[580] The challenge that the regulation of doctors posed in Vermont without a licensing requirement throughout mid-century had the profound consequence of forcing many of the frustrated regulars to compromise and, out of economic necessity, act contrary to their medical oaths and traditions and secretly perform abortions. If they did not do so, the quacks would have profited while earning a degree of respect from their patients that allowed them to elevate their status. In the 1840s, the regulars opposed abortion for ideological, scientific, moral and practical reasons that allowed them to assume a role superior to the quacks and gain such credibility they could influence the course of legislation. While Mohr contends that the regulars' combined influence enabled them to prevail on lawmakers to codify measures restricting abortion that afforded them an advantage over the empiricists, others disagree. Villanova law professor Joseph W. Dellapenna strongly disputes Mohr's arguments and rejects the existence of "conspiracies" of regulars combining in opposition to the irregulars to pass these laws. Instead, he argues that they simply followed a natural progression of nineteenth-century enlightenment that espoused stances favoring the health of infants.[581] Others have taken a more vindictive, scolding interpretative approach and argue that the early abortion laws served as a means for the punishment of "lewd and dissolute women" who produced "bastard children" and lacked "natural affection" to keep them alive.[582]

Mohr's argument may better state the Vermont experience. No evidence suggests that the state's first law prohibiting abortion in 1846 attempted to advance the interests of the unborn or to punish a woman from engaging in the activity. As in other states, the legislature expected those kinds of laws to protect the health of females by penalizing harmful abortionists, doctors and apothecaries who administered their treatments that caused injury. A commission examining the situation in New York in 1828 when it considered that state's law described the motivation behind the effort. "The rashness of many young practitioners in performing the most important surgical operations," it reported, "for the mere purpose of distinguishing themselves, has been a subject of much complaint. . . and the loss of life occasioned by the practice, is alarming."[583] In seeking to outlaw practices performed by such irresponsible individuals, New York's law had the dual effect of validating the worth of the regulars while targeting the irregulars, and errant regulars, for prosecution. Nothing suggests a different situation in Vermont in 1846 than elsewhere which raises the question of why the state waited so long before implementing similar legislation. The answer may lie in the inordinate amount of discord that existed within the medical profession, caused in part by the absence of a licensing requirement, that minimized their credibility in the eyes of legislators delaying favorable circumstances for its passage. Additionally, while officials certainly understood the harm abortion caused in other states, sufficient evidence of its effects on the female population had not accumulated to such an extent that they deemed it necessary to intervene.

Before lawmakers created statutes to regulate abortions, throughout the eighteenth and early decades of the nineteenth centuries women had rights under the common law to engage in activities to preserve their health. This included virtually unrestricted use of any process to remove a fetus, pursuant to the common law, up to the time of quickening. Until the practice actually became illegal, "the acceptance of induced miscarriages before quickening tacitly assumed that women had a basic right to bodily integrity."[584] In that pursuit and their efforts to maintain an internal balance, women closely monitored the ebb and flow of menses that, when delayed for whatever reason, became of concern. To remove a suspected "blockage" and regain their desired internal balance, women employed a variety of methods that began with their own efforts and, when unsuccessful, required the assistance of others. The spectrum of activities undertaken to remove a suspected pregnancy involved mechanical and medicinal means intended to shock and agitate the uterus to induce contractions that led to expulsion of its contents.[585] One period treatise recommended "Blows upon the back and abdomen" and another instructed, "dancing, riding on horseback, lifting heavy weights, splitting wood, violent exercise."[586] When truly desperate, some women submitted to beatings or threw themselves from heights or down stairs to accomplish their goal.

Women also consumed a variety of substances they believed could induce contractions. Vermont's newspapers published a litany of advertisements between the 1840s and 1867, when they finally became illegal, offering women relief from their blockages, or obstructions. Editors exercised little restraint and unabashedly published the outlandish claims of advertisers as exemplified by the prevailing philosophy of Orleans County's principle paper, the *Caledonian,* in 1858. "Our paper is filled with accounts of revolting crimes and disgraceful affairs," it wrote, "which as private individuals we would gladly suppress, but as public journalists we feel bound to give to the public."[587] It was also an economic decision for newspapers that depended on the income these advertisements provided as they published outlandish claims that included: Dr. Relfe's Aromatic Pills for Females and Reynolds and Parmely's Celebrated Female Health Restorative;[588] Dr. Spenser's Vegetable Pills;[589] Dr. G. C. Vaughn's Vegetable Lithontriptic Mixture;[590] and Dr. Geissner's Celebrated Menstrual Pills ("not to be used by pregnant women").[591] Their phony efforts did not hide the true intention of these drugs to cause abortions and the chimera of legitimacy surrounding them is easily pierced as evidenced by the constant advertising for Dr. Duponco's French Periodical Golden Pills. "Ladies whose health will not permit an increase of family, will find these pills a successful preventative," it claimed, and that women "supposing themselves so, are cautioned against using these pills while in that condition, as the proprietor assumes no responsibility."[592] Sir James Clarke's "Celebrated Female Pills" similarly claimed that "This invaluable Medicine is unfailing in the cure of all those painful and dangerous diseases incident to the female constitution."[593] Purportedly able to remove "all obstructions," it disingenuously cautioned with emphasis that *"These Pills should not be taken by females during the FIRST THREE MONTHS of Pregnancy, as they are sure to bring on Miscarriage."* For those patients interested in personal attention for their problems, Dr. D. Carley established an office in Brattleboro to treat a variety of illnesses that included "female obstructions, seminal weaknesses, [and] Private Diseases."[594] When these efforts did not work, women then turned to the abortionists willing to take more aggressive action and actually penetrate into their bodies to achieve the end. Should those measures fail to stop the birthing process, and as repeatedly evidenced in the state's newspapers, the last resort included the actual murder, or infanticide, of the unwanted child.

As Vermont women sought to maintain control over their bodies before the state's abortion law in 1846, regular doctors in the unregulated times continued to engage in serious battle with the quacks to gain the public's trust and convince it of the efficacy of their treatments.[595] In June 1845, the highly respected Woodstock doctor Joseph A. Gallup wrote to the VMS recording secretary, Middlebury physician Jonathan A. Allen, and vividly described the challenges that the learned members of the profession faced from the increasing numbers of untrained individuals who flocked into the state's cities and towns.* He had great reason to fear what he saw as instances of the quacks' harmful concoctions adversely impacting an unsuspecting public became increasingly common. One tragic example of the kinds of harm the untrained inflicted occurred in July 1841 when botanical doctor Jehiel Smith killed Jon Sherburn in Randolph over the course of four days with his treatments. An autopsy of his body revealed the devastation that Smith inflicted on him:

> Head swelled to double size – black tongue out, eyes stand out of sockets, blood running from the nose, blistered in various places. One hand a complete blister, thighs blistered, one leg seemed par-boiled, no feature of the face or body that would be recognized, a number of blisters on the inside of the stomach and intestines, nothing in the stomach except vegetable powder, perhaps a quart of that kind of stuff in all the body. Inside the stomach appears to be ironed over as with a hot iron as likewise is the lower parts of the intestines, probably scorched with hot drops of Cagerin pepper.[596]

---

*Gallup's previously unpublished informative letter and the 1836 lecture notes of Castleton Medical School founder Theodore Woodward provide a telling exposé of medical practice in Vermont before the first abortion law. See, Appendix.

Gallup pleaded with Allen in a despondent tone about the broken medical system that allowed things like Sherburn's death to occur and pragmatically, and reasonably, asked, with all these various interests clamoring for Vermonters' attention, "what constitutes the profession?" How could a naïve public discern the legitimate from the illegitimate when faced with the outlandish treatments proclaimed by the homeopathics, hydropathics, steamers, Thomsonians and "botanical physicians," he asked. "We know that public opinion is fickle [and] is liable to be misled," he wrote as he lamented that even among the regular doctors "there has been great discordance of opinion" how to treat diseases. "Who shall decide when doctors disagree," he asked, for it was "notorious that the most ignorant gossip will undertake to decide for them." He further feared the result of those counsels that included the unregulated dispersal of drugs as demonstrated by the "general use of patent medicines so liberally bestowed or supplyed [sic] by selfish and interested individuals."

Beyond the discord within the medical profession and the harm that drugs inflicted in the years before Vermont passed its abortion law, ample evidence of its practice in the state exists. Books that described abortion were readily available, including Philadelphia doctor Alexander C. Draper's 1839 *On Abortion. With an account of the means both medicinal and mechanical employed to produce that effect*.[597] Despite Draper's contentions that he published his how-to abortion book as a service to females to warn them of its dangers, his descriptions left no doubt in how to accomplish it successfully. Years earlier, in 1808, the Brattleboro Bookstore offered *Burns on Abortion* for sale that provided a similar service.[598] John Burns's *Observations on Abortion: containing an account of the manner in which it takes place, the causes which produce it, and the method of preventing or treating it* unabashedly enlightened curious readers on all manner of the subject. The various ways it taught to induce contractions that led to displacing a fetus included "violent exercise" in the form of dancing and "much walking, or the fatiguing dissipations of fashionable life" to increase circulation to prematurely cause its demise. While Burns professed that he abhorred such an outcome, he did not hesitate to instruct that "emmenagogues [abortifacients able to terminate a pregnancy] or acrid substances, such as savin and other irritating drugs, more especially those which tend to excite a considerable degree of vascular action, may induce abortion."[599] One of the Dartmouth Medical School students reporting on consumption also cited agitating a woman's circulatory system by introducing substances into the blood able to alter it to an impure state as a way to cause an abortion.[600] An 1817 New York publication went further in a tract entitled *An Inaugural Dissertation on Infanticide* and explained that "criminal means," those occurring outside of natural processes, were used to induce abortions. These included: "repeated venesection [bloodletting]; drastic purges; powerful emetics; mercurial salivation; diuretics; emmenagogues; violent exercise; and electricity."[601]

Between 1811 and 1812 a serious outbreak occurred in New York and Vermont "when a great number of lives were lost from the consumption of spurred rye being used as food, and the liquor distilled from the rye."[602] The malformed grain bearing a spurred fungus, also called ergot and St. Anthony's Fire, contained high concentrations of alkaloids able to induce a variety of symptoms that included spasms, hallucinations and paralysis. The well-known abortifacient was so powerful that one doctor witnessing its effects recorded "It appears to be injurious to the child at all times; for in every case, in which I have seen it exhibited, the child has been still-born; and, in the greater part of them, it is not possible to restore it to life."[603] Another observer similarly noted the effects that only a small amount of ergot caused and found it "no uncommon thing to administer it to facilitate child-birth; this it will do in an hour after it is taken – sometimes to the serious injury of the child, but always contributing to the ease of a lazy and money-making accoucheur [male midwife]."[604] New York City obituaries in 1822 identified so many stillborn infants from the suspected overuse of ergot that the local medical society began an investigation.[605] While ergot was recognized as a dangerous nuisance when it appeared in Vermont fields, in 1830 and throughout the following decades many entrepreneurs acted as middlemen and advertised in the state's newspapers seeking to purchase many hundreds of pounds of the substance from farmers. Their reasons are not identified, but could only have been in order to resell to others that included: the regular and quack medical men; apothecaries who compounded substances they distributed to the public without any restrictions; women, or their representatives, seeking to terminate unwanted pregnancies; farmers that created their own concoctions seeking a substance able to deliver an effect to assure future purchases; a burgeoning patent medicine trade; or to ship to others outside of the state for similar purposes. The ergot trade, fraught with danger, led one to caution that "there should be some legal prohibition against its indiscriminate prescription by *Old Women* and *Quacks.*"[606] While Vermont did not penalize the distribution of such substances, including adulterated drugs and medicines to others without cost, in 1839 it did criminalize such actions when done for money; a regulation that does not appear to have halted the trade in any way.[607]

Vermont women could also obtain their abortions through the assistance of doctors who invaded directly into their bodies to remove their blockages. Doctors knew that piercing the embryonic sac and draining off the fluids that protected the fetus resulted in the expulsion of the womb's contents. Two notorious events involving those efforts took place in Vermont before it outlawed abortion that resulted in the deaths of two women. In 1819, Burlington doctor and VMS member John Lyman saw a "Mrs. Fay of Richmond" because she suffered from consumption. She also complained of excruciating headaches that led Lyman to conduct "twelve or fourteen bleedings" over the course of a few weeks that provided no relief. In her eighth month of pregnancy at the time, she appeared in such rapid decline from her symptoms that Lyman deemed it necessary to intervene and remove the fetus. In attempting to justify his actions, he said "he believed… that a severe periodical head ache was occasioned by advanced pregnancy" and could only be relieved, by what another doctor described as, "an act, at naming which, delicacy recoils, and humanity revolts," one resorted to by "villains and prostitutes." While Lyman removed the fetus with what he reported as "complete success," it did not stop Mrs. Fay's further decline and she died.[608] An outraged Chittenden County Medical Society conducted an investigation and, without specifically naming abortion as the cause, found that Lyman was "guilty of that kind of practice which is unprecedented and unsafe" and expelled him from their rolls.[609] He experienced no further sanctions.

In 1830 a second case of abortion in St. Johnsbury that utilized both abortifacients and mechanical means to accomplish affected the public's perceptions of the medical profession and directly involved the Vermont legislature. Following his conviction for murder and facing a death penalty, respected Irasburg doctor Norman Cleveland was glowingly described by 137 of his supporters seeking the legislature's intervention as a person with "a fair reputation for honesty, uprightness & correctness as a good citizen & an exemplary member of society."[610] Testimony from several witnesses months earlier at his April 1830 trial disclosed that the thirty-year-old Cleveland had become intimately involved with Mrs. Hannah Rose, a woman described as between "30 and 35 years old, of bad character." Hannah's husband, reportedly absent because he went "to parts unknown," left her living with her children at her mother's house, a woman also referred to as "of bad reputation in every respect."[611]

Cleveland became enamored with Hannah and soon impregnated her. After a few months when her condition became noticeable, the two panicked and Cleveland explained to her mother that "unless an abortion was procured both should be sent to the State Prison" for their adultery.

Hannah "took medicines for that purpose" and obtained "herbs, and made and took decoctions, of her own preparing" with the approval of her mother. When that did not succeed, she solicited Cleveland to penetrate into Hannah "with a wire" to cause the abortion, but which he was unable to affect. The next steps involved Cleveland using a "sharp-pointed instrument" in an attempt to puncture the embryonic sac that resulted in Hannah's death soon afterwards. An autopsy performed by three doctors concurred that, while there was no evidence of any external injury to Hannah or to the fetus, her uterus suffered "six thrusts" of a sharp instrument, each one-half to three quarters of an inch wide, that pierced her iliac vein and caused her abdomen to fill with blood and kill her.[612]

After a two-day trial and an hour of deliberation by a jury that predictably found Cleveland guilty of murder, he was sentenced to death by hanging. When the court refused to delay his execution to allow an appeal to the supreme court, concerned citizens took up Cleveland's cause and petitioned the legislature to intervene. A special committee was established and published 500 copies of its report recommending leniency. After a lengthy, spirited two-day debate of the solons, attended by Cleveland, the governor and council, a final vote of 120 to 72 agreed with the committee and reduced his sentence to five years in the state prison. The result did not rest well with many and one expressed outrage at the leniency meted out to one "who was guilty of *adultery* and *murder both*," and asked how that sentence could be reconciled to the five years a man received for passing a counterfeit five dollar bill and another a seven year sentence for stealing a yoke of oxen. The writer wondered if Cleveland's membership as a Mason had something to do with it and inferred that secretive things happened outside of public view.[613] One member of the legislature, representative Schuyler Murdock from Whitingham, became so agitated with Cleveland's situation that he committed suicide by cutting his throat with a razor.[614]

CRIMINAL ABORTIONS AND INFANTICIDE

The Irasburg petition, signed by so many members of the community in support of Cleveland, demonstrates both the solicitude they felt towards him and their collective attitude about abortion. They expressed no concerns over the fate of the fetus and called for leniency, claiming that Hannah's death "was involuntarily and accidentally occasioned by the unskillfulness and misdirection of the instrument" that Cleveland used. In an attempt to further distance him from guilt, they blamed Hannah's and Cleveland's unfamiliarity with the abortion process. The "operation was undertaken at the request of the deceased," they wrote and that had "Cleveland been aware of the dangers of said operation he would not have undertaken it." Cleveland's neighbors concluded that he committed his actions "rather through indiscretion and misjudgment than through malicious design to commit the crime of murder." Had he possessed the necessary skill and familiarity with the abortion process as he penetrated into Hannah's womb and extracted the fetus, the petition reveals that the result, if it became known, would not have met with condemnation. The only problem that the case presented was because the death was known and thereby exposed Cleveland to criminal liability.

By the 1830s Vermont women began to form associations to advance the well-being of families and children. The recognition of the strength that a unified effort allowed them evolved from a time when women wrote in relative obscurity about childrearing. In 1811, Mary Palmer Tyler, the wife of Vermont Supreme Court chief justice Royall Tyler, wrote a childrearing treatise, *The Maternal Physician*, that described her experiences.[615] By 1833, maternal associations began to form, described by one newspaper as "objects of deep and special interest, they are lifting high the standard of parental obligation and family government."[616] In 1835, the Barnet Maternal Association formed and quickly assembled forty members, with their 116 children, to meet and share in a common goal to nurture, educate and support families. They sincerely believed that their efforts met with success and proudly proclaimed "We are happy to say, that we think that mothers have been led to feel more of their responsibility as mothers, and the best method of discharging them, than ever they have done before. And we feel determined, more than ever, to press forward." "Mothers, combined," they continued, "can do more towards achieving the triumphs of our national glory, and renovating a lost and ruined world from the power and dominion of sin."[617] Their work was copied elsewhere in the state and in 1838 Chelsea members published *The Mother's Book* to provide maternal associations with essays on motherhood written by "several distinguished literary ladies."[618] These guides admonished women to choose carefully those they allowed to have access to their children. "As you value the souls of your children," one writer warned, "do not receive into your family any filthy girl or young man, or old man, that will tell falsehoods to your children, tell them vile stories, use vulgar language, or in any way corrupt their morals, or their manners."[619]

These admirable efforts to strengthen families to assure their wellbeing stood in stark contrast to the challenges facing their formation in the first place. In the 1840s, Vermont witnessed the dire effects of abortion that had become "an obvious social reality, constantly visible" when instances of its occurrence rose sharply. It continued at high levels until the 1870s as a popular method of family planning engaged in by "white, married, Protestant, native-born women of the middle and upper classes."[620] Vermonters were also frequently exposed to the dark side of abortion in other locales because of the many unsavory accounts in newspapers that detailed the work of professional abortionists in cities, the deaths of young women working in New England mill towns whose bodies were often discarded on roadsides and in rivers like trash, and the trials of physicians who ran afoul of the law and tried to cover up their deeds.

The most notorious case of abortion that Vermonters learned of involved Ann Lohman, alias Madam Restell. Described as a "persistent hag, [working] under the guise of female physician," Lohman was arrested in New York City in 1841 and charged with performing abortions. She managed to escape serious penalties and, with much publicity attached to her, moved her operations to Boston and Philadelphia. With no laws to stop her Lohman employed salesmen to peddle abortifacients to the public, and, when they did not work, they referred patients to her New York clinic.[621] The absence of laws to prohibit such activities had a similar effect in Vermont where Lucy Ainsworth of Reading, also known as "Sleeping Lucy," replicated Lohman's example. A purported clairvoyant, Lucy concocted many remedies to deal with a variety of ailments that included inducing abortions. Untrained in medicine and dismissive of the regulars, she established a lucrative trade in a variety of drugs that she compounded and sold for many decades.[622]

Eighteenth-century attitudes towards pregnant women had a profound effect on the course of nineteenth and twentieth-century abortion policy. Defective or malformed babies, called "monsters," posed a particular concern to earlier societies required to accommodate their presence as they threatened to disrupt orderly cultural practices that related to inheritance proceedings, social organization and political power.[623] In the belief that pregnant women's mental powers affected the development of their fetuses, they were held accountable for their children's conditions with the expectation to conduct themselves responsibly during pregnancy to avoid unacceptable results. A woman's refusal to abide by this societally-imposed duty was noted by a medical profession intent on gaining recognition as a legitimate scientific pursuit. As one Philadelphia physician disdainfully described women who refused to abide by their expected obligations, "They eat and drink, they walk and ride, they will practice no self-restrainment, but will indulge every caprice, every passion, utterly regardless of the unseen and unloved embryo."[624] Records do not specifically disclose whether Vermont doctors sought to exploit those wayward, indulgent pregnant females to advance their professional standing, but sufficient circumstantial evidence that they experienced harm convinced the legislature in 1846 to take action. The year before, Joseph Gallup warned the VMS of the great divisions within the medical profession and clamored for peace to advance the health-related interests of Vermonters. Additionally, the homegrown examples provided by abortion physicians John Lyman and Norman Cleveland, botanical doctor Jehiel Smith and free-spirited Lucy Ainsworth, the extensive trade in harmful drugs and raw compounds such as abortion-producing ergot that Vermont farmers grew and sold, the many advertisements in newspapers directed at women offering concoctions to remove their "obstructions," the influence of blatant conduct by people such as Madam Restell using intrusive instruments to penetrate pregnant women's bodies and the growing influence of maternal associations advancing family-oriented interests provided many incentives to intervene into the lives of the state's females and regulate the actions of profiteers seeking access to their vulnerable victims.

The Law and its Effects

Vermont's first abortion and drug labeling laws passed through the legislative process simultaneously in rapid fashion. On October 17, 1846, Cabot representative Allen Perry introduced House bill H. 68, "An Act to Punish Unlawful Attempts to Cause Abortion," that Governor Horace Eaton signed into law on October 30.[625] In the Senate, on October 21 former Washington County state's attorney Senator Oramel H. Smith sponsored S. 38, "An Act to Prevent Imposition and Accident in the Sale of Medicine," that Eaton made law on November 2.[626] On November 3 it also became unlawful for traveling peddlers to carry or offer for sale "any patent medicine, or any compound medicine, the composition of which is kept secret from the public."[627] Petitions to lawmakers in the 1830s demonstrate that Vermont merchants did not exhibit concern with the potential harmful effects of drugs they sold, but that they did not like the competition that hawkers and peddlers posed when they undercut their prices and sold foreign goods to their customers.[628] With the increasing availability of questionable patent medicines in the following years, unscrupulous peddlers began to offer them for sale which caused the legislature to pass the 1846 law that imposed liability on them unless they disclosed their contents. These provisions were the first health related efforts undertaken by Vermont officials to address the growing vacuum in the law following their 1838 abandonment of licensing requirements for doctors that had been in place for the preceding eighteen years.

Representative Perry's reasons for introducing a bill to criminalize attempts to cause abortions is unknown. He served as Cabot's representative for a single session between 1846 and 1847 and sponsored no other legislation. A thirty-one-year-old farmer at the time, Perry served as an active steward in the Methodist Church and later as town clerk, treasurer and selectman. Beginning in 1838, he made regular trips to Boston hauling freight with a six-horse team pulling a large covered wagon. Modernity quickly encroached on his livelihood with the approaching railroad in 1846 that led him to take up farming and become Cabot's elected representative.[629] What prompted Perry to sponsor the abortion bill remains obscure, but clearly someone connected with the medical profession approached him for assistance. At the time, legislatures in other states also experienced heavy pressure from regular doctors to pass laws that criminalized this behavior in order to drive off the quacks and abortionists, and Vermont likely experienced the same influence from its own regulars.[630]

In 1845, legislatures in Massachusetts and New York responded to the clamor calling for reform (an estimated 20% of all pregnancies in New York were aborted in the 1840s) and they passed laws that rejected quickening as a defining moment during pregnancy, making it illegal to abort at any point.[631] Both states directly attacked the abortion trade and criminalized the administration by anyone of "any poison, drug, medicine or noxious thing" or the use of "any instrument" on a woman with intent to cause her to miscarry.[632] Not certain this would dissuade the many abortionists practicing in New York, it took the added precaution to criminalize the participating woman with a misdemeanor conviction punishable by imprisonment of between three and twelve months and a fine up to $1,000. It also included a therapeutic provision that removed that liability if the conduct was "necessary to preserve the life of such mother." Whereas Massachusetts provided for penalties of between one and seven years imprisonment (and a $2,000 fine) for an attempt (misdemeanor) and five to twenty years if the woman died (felony), New York chose to impose the relatively lenient three to twelve month sentence for attempt and the possibility of a manslaughter charge if the patient died.

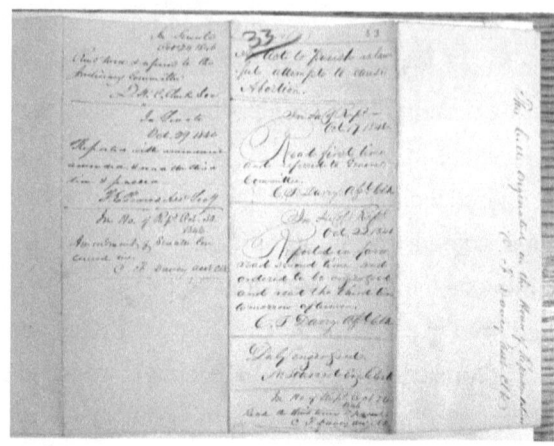

Act to Punish Abortion, October 1846. Vermont State Archives.

In Vermont, Perry's bill followed a middle path that penalized only the conduct of abortionists and declined to hold women accountable or include a therapeutic escape clause. His proposal copied the Massachusetts statute verbatim and differed only in the penalty imposed. If the woman died, the law provided for a sentence of between five and ten years for the perpetrator, but if she survived the guilty party faced a misdemeanor sentence of between one and three years and a $200 fine. The noticeable reduction in the amount of time a convicted person might serve and accompanying fine when compared to Massachusetts may reflect a recognition that a culpable, willing female participant, assuming she survived, should not face liability. Regardless, both the Massachusetts and Vermont penalties exceeded those in New York. Notwithstanding their laudatory aspects, the laws in each of the states had little effect when defendants' peers sat in judgment of them. In Massachusetts, between 1849 and 1858 only thirty-two trials for abortion took place and none ended in a conviction. That led disappointed doctors to estimate that "for every arrest for this crime, a thousand instances of its commission escape" prosecution.[633] Ultimately, public opinion stymied the laws' application in each state because, in the absence of effective alternative forms of contraception, people demanded access to abortions and feared that criminalizing the efforts of the necessary practitioners performing them would diminish its availability.

In response to public disgust at the presence of "immoral and corrupting advertisements" in Massachusetts' newspapers, and an early recognition that its recently passed law was "simply unenforceable," lawmakers boldly confronted issues of free speech and made it illegal for abortionists to advertise their services.[634] While Vermont experienced the same types of complaints, it waited until 1867 before adopting a similar effort that made it illegal to advertise "for the purpose of causing or procuring the miscarriage of any pregnant woman."[635] Despite other states imposing liability on women for their participation in abortions, Vermont continued to provide them with refuge and refused to do so. That inaction, together with the legislature's persistent refusal to provide regular physicians with the ability to obtain professional licenses, abetted the grave consequences of the flourishing abortion practice. It also had the effect of emboldening women to participate in other conduct outside of the law in order to limit the size of their families.

By mid-century ample evidence suggests modernity's effect on the composition of Vermont families. It significantly reduced the numbers of children in them, identified in 1850 as an average of 5.36 people in each of the state's 56,421 dwellings.[636] This differed substantially from conditions earlier in the century, described by Dr. Lucius Castle Butler in an 1867 address to the VMS that in years past "it was not uncommon to see families numbering 6, 8, 10, 12, and even 15 children" compared to the more recent times when "very many households" had "but one, two or three children."[637] During the state's early years between 1771 and 1791, the population increased at a robust rate of over twelve percent each year doubling every five and one-half years; a phenomenon attributed to the fecundity of women that averaged five to six births each.[638] In 1797, eight families living in Clarendon Springs had a total of 113 children with none "ever had more than one wife, and there was but one pair of twins in the lot."[639] Between 1850 and 1860, population growth stagnated and garnered national attention for its "nearly stationary" rate of increase, identified at one third of one percent, or 978 individuals.[640] While the last half of the decade saw the state's birth rate remain at a purported steady rate of just over two percent per year, officials noted the count's inaccuracy because "one fifth, perhaps one fourth, of the births, escape record."[641] Historians repeatedly ascribe emigration as the prevailing cause for the absence of overall growth, but those numbers command deeper attention because of the observations of Butler and other VMS doctors who interjected that the increased use of abortion by Vermont women could also have contributed to impeded population growth.

Whereas women in the 1830s sought to terminate pregnancies silently to avoid the embarrassment of their secret trysts, by the 1840s abortion, considered "one of the first medical specialties in American medical history," became openly discussed and allowed them a means to command control of their bodies.[642] This included candid conversations with their husbands and having a role in determining the number of children that would occupy their households.[643] "A valuable book," Vermont booksellers touted in 1858 in reference to Henry C. Wright's *The Unwelcome Child; or, the Crime of an Undesigned and Undesired Maternity,* is where women could read of others who had similarly seized control and used abortion to rid themselves of those burdens.[644] If they encountered resistance or disapproval, women still pursued abortions and counseled with others how to accomplish it. While no data allows a confident identification of the number of abortions in Vermont, national estimates by mid-century, identified that it occurred at least once for every five to six live births.[645] In Vermont, by 1862 the number of reported stillborn infants became so glaringly obvious that officials had "good reason to believe that less than one-half, perhaps not one-third" of them had been recorded. In an attempt to identify the reason, they looked to Massachusetts for guidance and recited the many instances of abortion its population experienced.[646] In 1863, alarmed that the practice also affected the health of the mother and at the continued "small proportion" of stillborns reported, they again expressed their concern. "It is a subject of great importance," a Vermont report related, "in connection with the health of women and their offspring, as well as the investigation of the causes of the loss of life which has become so common." Because of their inability to fully understand those causes, they again summoned the assistance of doctors, relating "It is very desirable that medical men attend to their duty in recording this class of cases."[647]

Motherhood, and marriage itself, was severely attacked by some in this new era of modernity during what was described as the most unusual gathering of people to have assembled in Vermont's history to that time. Between June 25-27, 1858, a "Free Convention of the Friends of Human Progress" convened in Rutland where some 3,000 people ("white, black, partially black, badly sun-burned and fair in face") suddenly intruded into the quiet community. After disgorging from special trains sent from New York and Boston, the attendees walked a short distance north from the rail yard to a field where they erected their tents adjacent to the town's first-generation Irish neighborhood. Sparse warning of the gathering appeared in the state's newspapers earlier that month and few in the state seem to have understood its intentions. Advertised as an occasion when devotees of "abolitionism, spiritualism, free-love, free-trade, and all other queer things" could gather to discuss common interests, angry local residents were left unimpressed at their proceedings.[648] While its sponsors argued that it was an important moment in the nation's history to put on display the vibrancy of freedom of speech, one newspaper called their meeting nothing more than "mingled nonsense, indecency, insanity and blasphemy" that it hoped would never be repeated.[649]

The *New York Times* devoted an entire front page to describe what happened in Rutland, including speeches given on the continued relevancy of marriage in these new times and the obligations of motherhood. Twenty-nine-year-old Julia Branch from New York, described as a rabid "Free-Lover" and proponent of women's equal rights, provided a scathing assessment of both institutions and attacked marriage at length as, the *Times* reporter wrote, a "prodigious nuisance, and husbands an article to be done away with."[650] Lamenting the absence of women's rights, she provided a telling example of her complaint and described a recent conversation she had with a married man. "My wife is a woman's rights woman," he told her. "She talks of her rights, and I allow it, but she really has none. I am her husband; she is my property, and if I do not like a thing I say so; and I do not consider she has any right to dispute it. I do not hold any argument, for I consider my will law." In such a hopeless condition that denigrated the role of a woman in marriage, what promise did she have when her husband decided she must bear children she did not want? "In her isolated household," forced to obey his wishes, Branch said, "she threw away her life, and added to the too many already children thrust into the world half made up – children of chance, children of lust, abortions who feel that they have no right to existence – children of disease, whose tainted flesh and running sores are a disgrace and an everlasting reproach to the morals and purity of any community." To combat that condition, a woman "must demand her freedom," she exclaimed, that included *"her right to bear children when she will, and by whom she will."* Her views were shared by others and closely tracked one of the convention's several resolutions that propounded motherhood as "the sacred and important right of woman [for] her to decide for herself how often, and under what circumstances, she shall assume the responsibility and be subjected to the sufferings and cares of maternity." "Man can commit no greater crime against a woman," it warned, "as wife and mother, against his child, against society, and against humanity, than to impose on her a maternity whose responsibility and suffering she is not willing to accept and endure."[651] Although Branch never raised an alternative for women trapped in loveless marriages bearing unwanted children, another outlet existed for their frustrations, one that suggested instances of premediated murder.

An important distinction concerning alternative methods that Vermont women used to control family size, beyond abortion, relates to economic status and evolving societal attitudes towards poor, pregnant mothers. Early in the state's history, in 1779 lawmakers noted the presence of many "lewd women, that have been delivered of bastard children," and that "to avoid their shame, and to escape punishment," they would "secretly bury, or conceal" their deaths. If later detected, the women sought to excuse themselves and explain that "the child was born dead" when it was suspected, instead, that they "were murdered by the said woman, their lewd mothers, or by their assent or procurement." If proven that the mother had "endeavored privately, either by drowning, or secret burying" of a child, or obtained the assistance of others to conceal the death, she could "be accounted guilty of murder, and shall suffer death."[652] An 1803 law removed the potential for a death penalty, but a mother found guilty of murdering her infant after birth faced a penalty of $500, a sentence of two years hard labor, or both. An 1818 law increased the potential sentence to three years hard labor and reduced the fine to $200 that remained in effect until a century later when it was repealed in 1941.[653] Ecclesiastically, in 1814 Rupert church fathers excommunicated a twenty-two-year-old old man for impregnating a sixteen-year-old girl and then abandoning her and their illegitimate child. They imposed that draconian penalty only after he refused to "make a public confession and marry [his] criminal associate" in order to provide an example to others to "guard against illicit intercourse, which is followed by such deplorable consequences."[654] Laws intended to lessen the burden on towns required to maintain illegitimate children allowed for intrusive measures that required reluctant mothers to swear under oath and identify their fathers to force them to bear the costs and responsibility instead of the town. Many accounts of bastardy proceedings in Vermont demonstrate the challenges humiliated women faced when their pregnancy became known and courts intervened to identify the father. To avoid those embarrassments, terminating a pregnancy by the use of drugs or employing a midwife or physician required access to money and the rural and dispossessed members of the state's town and city populations had little means.[655] Absent an ability to pay for abortions, ridding themselves of children that survived the birthing process by quietly smothering them became a viable option.[656]

As cities increased in size and more liberal lifestyles became the norm, prostitution and pregnancy inescapably went together. Vermont's newspapers between the 1850s and 1870s and court records describe the presence of many houses of ill fame around the state, prostitutes working the county fairs, and the occasional homicide that accompanied the practice. The state had no ability to place the unwanted children that resulted from these unions until 1865 when the Home for Destitute Children was established in Burlington.[657] Before then, "in every county in the State were to be found homeless waifs, whose only shelter was the poor-house or the jail."[658] Their mothers, members of the victimized working-class, immigrant servants and native farm girls who fled rural hardships in search of opportunities, found themselves alone and pressured to take extreme action to rid themselves of their burden. Their reasons for resorting to murder of infants involved "behavior ranging from deliberate to unconscious" that included "deliberate killing, placing [them] in a dangerous situation, abandonment where survival is possible, 'accidents,' excessive physical punishment, lowered biological support, and lowered emotional support."[659] The persuasive claims of young pregnant women that they experienced depression and insanity (puerperal mania) because of their condition led sympathetic officials to turn a blind eye to their indiscretions and allowed them to escape investigation and prosecution. As a result, instances of infanticide increased so substantially that one national estimate called it "larger by an order of magnitude than the number of adult homicides."[660] The situation in North America differed little from the experiences unfolding in Britain in the late 1850s. In 1859, George Eliot (the pen name of Mary Ann Evans) published her *Adam Bede,* a tale of child murder based upon an actual event from decades earlier. The book marked the beginning of a period of infanticide throughout England that the *Dublin Review* called "the great social evil of the day" leading commentators to indulge in providing "lurid descriptions of public places clogged with the corpses of newborn babies."[661]

Ohio State University history professor Randolph A. Roth's noteworthy and prodigious work on homicide in America, including infanticide in nineteenth-century Vermont and New Hampshire, constitutes perhaps the most ambitious projects of its kind. He recites many instances of child murder that occurred in both states and concludes that infanticide, together with abortion, increased five-fold between 1820 and 1870.[662] A number of factors explain this phenomena, but principally include the challenges that the class of poor, transient females experienced in entering into stable relationships, obtaining reliable employment and securing adequate housing.[663] Between the late 1840s and 1850s the region experienced a decline in opportunities for steady employment and a noticeable spike in the number of homicides occurred, reflected in increased instances of infanticide in the following decades. Roth explains that while it is impossible to definitively identify the cause, the "most common threads seem to have been desperation, depression, and nonfarm occupations, compounded by the fact that the child was illegitimate or its parents' marriage unstable."[664] Faced with the physical, emotional and economic burdens in raising a child, the young women viewed infanticide as a safer alternative to abortion and most frequently committed it on the day of a child's birth before bonding occurred that made it less likely thereafter. Roth further notes that the increasing mobility provided by modernity accelerated its pace as railroads allowed for pregnant women to arrive in a community, give birth, abandon infants and leave without detection.

Vermont women had many examples of the practice to follow, exemplified by the works of British authors. Walter Scott's *The Heart of Midlothian* (1818), Thomas Carlyle's *Past and Present* (1843), Charles Dicken's *The Chimes* (1844) and *The Haunted Man and the Ghost's Bargain* (1848), and Alfred Tennyson's *Maude* (1855) each recalled instances of infanticide in publications readily available to the Vermont public.[665] Additionally, the state's newspapers repeatedly described the practice in China and India, among the destitute in Ireland in the mid-1830s where it "extensively" replaced deserting children into the countryside, and the many instances when it occurred in surrounding states.[666] An early account in 1830 reported that a young woman working as a domestic servant in Rutland killed "her illegitimate child, under aggravating circumstances" and abandoned it in a "vault," or privy, designed to contain waste.[667] In Burlington in 1847, a year after abortion became illegal, "the body of a new-born child, wrapped in rags, was found" that bore "marks upon the body [indicating] that violence had been used."[668] In 1851, Samuel Lathe of Craftsbury was so panicked at the birth of his child that he "immediately" seized it, took it to his basement and, as a witness heard the commotion and its crying, cut its throat.[669] In 1854 two cases of infanticide occurred in Burlington that presented the possibility they occurred at the hands of respectable, "innocent" people. The first concerned the discovery of "newborn male infant... found in the door yard of a house on Cherry Street occupied by three Irish families." The body, "badly mutilated and had been frozen," was uncovered "by swine from under a pile of manure, where it had been hidden for some days." An arm and a foot had been "devoured" by the animals and "the head bruised as if by a violent blow." While not identifying the person responsible, after hearing testimony from two local doctors that the child had been born alive "and perished by violence of wanton neglect," a coroner's inquest agreed, but was unable, or chose not, to impose liability on anyone.[670] A second case occurred a short time later when "an infant was found under the Rail Road track at Pearl Street." The occurrence of these two events so close together led the *Vermont Tribune* to conclude that "These facts reveal a dreadful state of debauchery among us; and they may well raise the question as to the tendency of certain associations which are quite fashionable and deemed 'innocent.'"[671] Although the article did not identify the alleged "associations," only the ongoing medical disputes between the regulars and empiricists that continued to rage commanded the public's attention; men it tolerated and sought out for a variety of treatments, including abortion.

Beginning in 1857, the handwritten Vermont registration returns filed with the secretary of state by town clerks based on information gathered from school district clerks contain many raw, cryptic entries that indicate possible instances of infanticide. Importantly, none of them ever appeared in the published reports that officials consulted. Typical entries describe an array of infant deaths that took place under questionable circumstances. They attributed the cause of death for an unnamed, two-day old female who died in Burlington in 1858 to drugs: "Fits contracted from Mother's setative [sic]," the clerk recorded. Many other entries of "Fits" accompanied by "Convulsions," "Teething," "Sickly from birth," "Want of care, motherless," "Marasmus [severe under nourishment]," "Premature birth," "Heart disease," "Measles," "Croup," "Canker rash," "Unknown," or simply "Infancy" dot the records of deaths of newborns and infants only a few days old. Additional instances of death attributed to consuming harmful substances appear. An unnamed twelve-day old male from Brandon died from "too much paregoric," and one-day old Mary Ann Dority died in Rutland because she was "Fed on Spirits." The registry recorded the highly unlikely cause of death for a twenty-day-old infant as "Supposed consumption caused by a severe cold the mother had while pregnant." One-year-old Lilla Sanger died in Chelsea because she "Smothered in bed, accidental," while in Lowell one-month old George Fleming died due to "suffocation in bed." "Stillborn" accompanies the entries of many others without names, including a female who "Died at birth. . . Illegitimate" and another identified only as "female & of negro origin on the mother's side." Infant Herbert McAllister died "ten minutes" after arrival, the cause listed as "premature." In Brookfield, Mary Penny "Died about 1 hour after birth of her child seemingly of the nervous shock as she lost but little blood," while the registry listed the infant as "stillborn." Three male infants (two of them twins) died over the course of two days in October 1857 and had their deaths recorded simply as "Infantile." The records provide other telling aspects of Vermont life not recorded elsewhere. In Castleton, two infants were "Killed to save the mother" and in Chester twenty-two-year-old Achsah A. Brown died two days after giving birth to a stillborn daughter, "caused by grief in burying her."[672]

A physician testified before a Lamoille County grand jury and described his interactions with a woman who indicated she committed infanticide after a self-induced abortion. A "Mrs. Lowell came to my place," he related, "She said she was in trouble & wanted to know if I could do anything for her. I told her I could not – I was not in that business." "She claimed to me to be about 5 months along," he said in describing her condition, "but I thought by her looks that she was more." When he refused to assist the woman, she explained that he "kneed [sic] not be afraid of my pay for she had got $25 off one fellow & was going to have $25 more" from another. He said he later learned that she had "got rid of her child by taking Cedar Oil" and that it had apparently "breathed after it was born" before someone snuffed out its life.[673]

Until rates of infanticide declined in the early twentieth-century, Vermonters continued to read in newspapers about dead babies. In Bolton, "the dead body of a fully developed male child was discovered in a hog yard. . . with the appearance of having been recently disinterred by hogs."[674] Burlington officials arrested Susan McGinning after she left the house she worked in as a domestic servant leaving behind a "disagreeable odor" in the home. When a search was conducted of her room "a new-born child" was discovered.[675] On another occasion, "A dead infant has lately been found in the outbuildings connected with a school in South Shaftsbury."[676] "A male infant child was found under a bridge near Irasburgh village. . . by some boys who were fishing," another related.[677] In Windham County, Lydia Pratt, told to retrieve her child from the doorstep of house where she abandoned it, took it into the woods and left it where, five days later, a male friend returned to bury it.[678] She was later tried for neglect and found not guilty as an understanding community supported her with a petition "against any further proceedings."[679]

Many other instances of official disinterest in prosecuting these distressed females exist. "Kate Cummings of Brattleboro," another account related, "was arrested. . . for infanticide [and] was after two days hearing discharged."[680] In the town of Georgia, "the bodies of two infant female children were recently found. . . near the traveled highway, wrapped in a newspaper. No steps have been taken to ascertain the circumstances connected with their birth, or cause of death."[681] In Starksboro, an abandoned child was buried, dug up, wrapped in a paper sack, laid beside the road and, finally, "thrown into a hole dug for it." No official inquiry was conducted.[682] That lack of interest occurred elsewhere when children were clearly murdered. In Burlington, Julia Ihrens, an employee at the

Vermont Episcopal Institute, took her new born infant and "threw it into Lake Champlain" without facing repercussions.[683] Francis Rollins, so stressed with his newborn, drowned it in a pail, buried it in the cellar and told a family member that had "got the [damned] thing out of the way [so] he could sleep."[684] In Weston, Clifford Hessletine, described as "a coarse, brutal and shiftless fellow, and has often shamefully ill treated his wife," struck a newborn on its head and killed it. He bragged later that "he would kill the next child born to him."[685] In 1879, a Montpelier newspaper noted the dual presence of infanticide and drugs. "The body of a female infant was recently found by the roadside in Bennington Center," it related, "The child was evidently a day or two old, and there was a contusion on the head, with finger marks about the throat, pointing clearly to murder." While in an adjoining column it reported that "Lots of people now-a-days are making intemperate use of opium chloral, and other opiates, among those who are slaves to this habit being many who make loud talk about total abstinence from all intoxicating liquors, some of whom never make a speech except more or less under the influence of vile narcotics." "Now why," it asked, "not place these drugs under the same restrictions as alcoholic liquors?"[686]

Modernity's multi-faceted impact on Vermonters' family planning practices presented many moral and legal challenges. Not all of them were attractive and until alternative methods of contraception became available in the 1870s, abortion and infanticide remained the primary responses to unwanted pregnancies that threatened to upend the stability that women sought to maintain in their lives. However, the passage of laws that criminalized that behavior meant little because the resistant population did not fear that, even if charged with an offense, a jury of their sympathetic peers would actually convict. Practicality in the face of imposing modernity dictated otherwise and those prohibitions sat essentially as "dead letters" on the statute books, evidenced by the actions of a Vermont physician at the very moment that the state's first abortion law was passed.

STATE OF NEW HAMPSHIRE VS. DR. JOHN MCNAB OF BARNET, VT.

In December 1848, two years after Vermont outlawed abortion, lawmakers gathered in Concord, New Hampshire to do the same; Virginia also passed similar legislation that year, followed by California, New Jersey, and Wisconsin in 1849. The widespread dissemination of information describing the recent notorious actions of a Vermont physician responsible for killing a Manchester woman prompted the Granite State's legislative effort. In the process, their proceedings revealed the close connection between oversight of the medical profession and abortion policy. As in Vermont, the New Hampshire solons considered whether to infringe on a woman's common law right to have an abortion prior to quickening or to impose liability on anyone, including her, for attempting the act at any time during pregnancy. Unlike Vermont where the absence of medical licensing continued to define the separation between the regulars and quacks as the legislature dallied and refused to intervene, New Hampshire authorities addressed the problem directly. The prospect of whether or not to authorize incorporation of the New Hampshire Botanic Medical Society caused them to force the issue. Despite fierce opposition of the regulars to the effort, the alternative "steam system" proved too powerful and by a vote of 125 ayes to 107 nays they recognized the NHBMS. They also addressed abortion when they decided to criminalize any attempt to perform it and, as New York had done, held women accountable for their participation, imposing a punishment of up to a year in jail and a $1,000 fine. Yet again, abortion policy in mid-century "was still decided in the context of who should be allowed to do what to whom in the name of public health and safety" and not because of any concern over the wellbeing of the fetus.[687]

Six months before the New Hampshire legislature wrestled with abortion and medical infighting, the event that brought the two issues together took place on May 17, 1848 when twenty-two-year-old Sarah Furber walked into the Manchester office of a Vermont physician, Dr. John McNab. Their meeting quickly set off a chain of events unlike any ever witnessed before in the state and became so notorious that it ignited the public's disgust at the practice of abortion in its midst. Sometime between their meeting and legislature's convening, local journalist George Carroll published a tract entitled *The Manchester Tragedy* that described the salacious events surrounding Sarah's grisly death that convinced the lawmakers the time to act had arrived.[688]

Sarah arrived in Manchester in the spring of 1847 and found work at a local mill. She followed a path common to many other New England women her age who struck out from their parents' farms in search of what seemed a better life in the age of modernity that included millwork and domestic service. Before arriving in Manchester, Sarah lived in other New Hampshire towns and in one became intimately involved with an artist named Gardner Ingalls, a man already married and with a child. As the evidence demonstrated during court proceedings in June 1848, Ingalls became alarmed with Sarah's pregnancy and arranged for her to consult with a local doctor to take care of the problem. He apparently met with a friend, Horace McNab, a local clerk and the son of Dr. McNab, to meet with Sarah to arrange an appointment with his father. The meeting between Sarah and Horace occurred at her boardinghouse from where she soon departed to purportedly visit an uncle. Before she left, Sarah instructed her landlady's daughter that "she was going away, that if any one called for her, either man, woman or child, I must not tell them where she had gone – as she had told her overseer she was sick, and if he found out she was visiting her uncle's he would discharge her from the mill."[689] It was the last time that anyone saw her alive. After two weeks the community became alarmed because of her absence and newspapers speculated about her "mysterious disappearance."[690] "Where was she – and what could be her fate?," journalist Carroll asked and described their collective distress, "This was the only subject of conversation upon the streets or in the family circle."[691] Erroneous reports circulated that her body had been found in Goffstown "with her throat cut," but the true state of her condition proved much worse.[692]

Sarah Furber, The Manchester Tragedy (1848).

Vermont physician Dr. John McNab, sixty-four-years-old when he met Sarah, had first arrived in Barnet in 1785 at the age of one with his family when they migrated from their Scottish homeland. He graduated from the nearby Dartmouth Medical College in 1823 and began practice in the Newbury and Barnet area, followed by brief sojourns to Maine and Ontario, before he returned to Vermont and took up residence in the village of McIndoe Falls in Barnet, where the Barnet Maternal Association began to assemble in 1835. In his personal and medical lives, John McNab presented two radically different sides that only became apparent after Vermont passed its abortion law in 1846. As an educated regular doctor, his public pronouncements and private conduct diverged radically from that of his responsible peers and demonstrates the kind of internal conflict that the profession experienced. In 1845, Joseph Gallup lamented the splintering he witnessed among the regular's ranks and McNab's example clearly shows that even many educated regulars publicly espousing opposition to abortion often followed a different path in their actual practice.

In his personal life, McNab presented himself as "a man of remarkably vigorous physical and mental constitution and, in his theological views, "liberal to the extreme."[693] While characterized as a "prominent mason" from the Ancient Land Mark Lodge, he was expelled from its membership in 1827 "for unmasonic conduct."[694] In 1841 McNab was one of Orange County's authorized retailers who pedaled Dr. Phelp's Compound Tomato Pills for sale, a concoction purportedly able to cure a variety of ills.[695] He expressed his extreme religious views most prominently as a member of the short-lived Mental Liberty Society that formed around 1845 across the river in North Haverhill, New Hampshire. A history of that town dismissively described the Society as "not a church, nor did it profess to be a religion, but, organized in open and avowed opposition to churches and to all forms of supernatural religion."[696] Among the thirteen members who joined from communities on each side of the Connecticut River, McNab, identified as one of two doctors, became its vice president.[697] The Society's members forcefully rejected any notion of accepted religion and claimed their intention to pursue universally shared truths, but only as they chose to interpret them. "Shall we then honest and firm in our own convictions," their president exhorted, "conscious of the purity of our motives. . . hesitate to act up to the full measure of our convictions, and thus prove traitors to ourselves and recreants to our race?"[698] Article Nine of their Constitution went further and unequivocally stated their code of conduct requiring:

each and every member of this Society, by candid and careful examination, to render firm their own convictions, and the wavering or doubtful opinions of others; to meet with candor and frankness, but temperate firmness, the opposing prejudices of those swayed by different influences, and convince the world by the practical utility and careful observance of our own moral precepts, that while we eschew, and are Infidels to the modes, forms, ceremonies, and general influences of all supernatural religion, we are faithful to Science, Truth, Morality, and the great and universal Brotherhood of man. (The true Religion.)[699]

The impact of the Society was limited to just the attendees for a brief time as the town history relates with relief that it had no effect on the community and "soon passed out of sight, and it has been long lost to memory."[700] Nonetheless, McNab's membership in it and the high regard that his brethren had for him reveals the conflicted roles experienced by physicians in the prevailing laissez-faire atmosphere surrounding healthcare when they faced no real threat of official intervention in the event of their dereliction.

In his professional life, McNab earned glowing acclaim as "a skillful physician, accurate in diagnosis, somewhat brusque in manner and daring in operation." A witness thought "He was a canny Scot, whose quick wit and ready tongue enlivened every occasion of a visit, and left with his patient renewed courage and good cheer, effective adjuncts to his other remedies."[701] A cancerous infection he contracted while performing an operation caused the amputation of his left arm. Despite his disability and admirable qualities, Manchester journalist Carroll's description of McNabb's conduct at the time of Sarah Furber's death in 1848 provides important information that describes other aspects of his practice when he administered to communities alongside the upper Connecticut River. According to Carroll, McNab arrived alone in Manchester less than two years before Sarah's disappearance as "a total stranger." While Carroll acknowledged McNab's reputation as "a skillful physician [who] could number among his friends many of the most influential citizens" in his hometown of Barnet, he declared it "by no means enviable." He did not use the word "abortion," but Carroll clearly meant it and wrote that McNab had "a reputation gained by a course of practice that respectable physicians look upon with abhorrence."[702] The timing of McNab's appearance in Manchester, one hundred miles removed from his family still living in Barnet but easily connected by the railroad, coincides precisely with Vermont's passage of its abortion law. His relocation to a state with no similar prohibition at the time to interfere with its practice strongly suggests that McNab relied principally on performing abortions to sustain himself in both locations.

No evidence suggests that Sarah Furber had a pre-existing relationship with McNab and it appears that she met him for the first time when she entered his office on Wednesday, May 17, 1848. Witnesses later provided extensive information about McNab's movements thereafter beginning on May 22, but could relate nothing concerning what happened in the intervening five days. He was last seen in Manchester shortly afterwards on May 24 when he boarded a train after he urgently told a witness that "he had received a letter from his wife and must *go immediately* to Vermont."[703] The reason for the panicked McNab's departure became obvious as additional testimony demonstrated that Sarah died soon after their meeting because of a botched abortion. Before he fled, McNab had five days to dispose of her body, beginning on May 22 when he approached a witness looking for paint in order to "mark a box." A coachman who transported McNab and the box to the local train depot shortly afterwards described it as "2-1/2 feet long, 2 feet high, and about 20 inches wide; there were leather handles on each end, the box was marked 'glass' and 'handle with care,' in black paint; it was pretty heavy." Because of the cumbersome and heavy load (described by McNab to the witness as weighing around 150 pounds), the coachman had to summon help to wrestle it down the stairs and into his wagon. After he delivered McNab and the box to the depot to board the express train to Boston the witness did not see him again until two days later when he returned McNab to the station for his rushed departure back to Vermont.

Upon his arrival in the city, a medical student encountered McNab at the Boston Medical College when he inquired "if the medical school [wanted] subjects for dissection." McNab explained that he had one available, "a young girl, about 20 years old, and perfectly fresh, and had only been dead about 8 hours." The student referred him to Dr. Oliver Wendell Holmes (father of a future U. S. Supreme Court justice) who had the responsibility to obtain cadavers for students and McNab met him later that day. As Holmes testified, McNab explained to him that "he had a subject for me, a young and good subject, [who] died of peritonitis," but admitted she died because of an abortion. When he later met with Holmes at his boarding house to discuss the purchase and conversed near the box containing Sarah, the landlord overheard McNab admit to Holmes that "abortion was the primary cause of her death." After the two men agreed to a price of ten dollars and parted, the witness observed that "while the box set there, something ran from it upon the floor, a liquid matter I should judge a half-pint" oozing onto the carpet. Confronted about the mess, McNab became defensive and "excited, and said they could prove nothing." When a man arrived with cash to pick up the box, McNab inquired if he could remain quiet about what was happening. When the man said he could, McNab told him to pay only seven dollars rather than the ten he agreed upon with Holmes because he had only paid "a trifle" for it when he bought the corpse.

The next day when students opened the box in the college's dissecting room, several witnesses described what they saw. "Three or four students were present," one related, "and I took a hatchet and pried it open, the box contained a layer of fine straw, then some charcoal fell out, leaving the subject in view; it was so black with charcoal, we thought it was a colored person. I procured water and washed it when it was laid out on the table." When Holmes and another physician entered and examined Sarah, they became immediately suspicious because she appeared to have been both beautiful and "in full health" leading them to believe that McNab's explanation of her death did not seem plausible. When confronted by the doctors, McNab disingenuously explained that she had come to his house "sick" and had "died" before being "boxed up there and brought to Boston." Convinced that a crime had been committed, the doctors ordered McNab to remove the box and its contents immediately. He then met with the man that helped move it into the dissecting room who testified that McNab called out to him, "You are the very man I wanted to see" and admitted that "he had got into a bad mess and I must get out of it the best way he could." In a panic, McNab asked the man "to take the body out of the way, bury it, cut it up and throw into the vault," concerned that if word got out it would ruin him. The man agreed to help, but after McNab left the building he spoke with his frightened superiors who reported the matter to city officials. By that time McNab had already boarded a train for Manchester where he continued his hurried flight back to Vermont.

[Price 6 Cents.]
FULL REPORT OF THE TRIAL
OF
Dr. John McNab,
OF BARNET, VT.,
AND OTHERS IMPLICATED IN THE MISTERIOUS
ABDUCTION AND MURDER
OF
SARAH H. FURBER,
A BEAUTIFUL YOUNG FEMALE
Employed in the Mills, at Manchester, N. H., on the night of May 21st, 1848.

"It is said the excitement is greater here than it was at the time of Parker's Murder."
Daily Mail.

MANCHESTER, (N. H.) JUSTICES' COURT,
MONDAY, JUNE 13, 1848.
Present Justices Cochran and Riddle.

Cover page, *Full Report of the Trial of Dr. John McNab, of Barnet, VT., 1848.*
Courtesy of Glenn G. Bartle Library, State University of New York, Binghamton, NY.

On learning of Sarah's death, New Hampshire authorities moved quickly and arrested McNab's son Horace and Sarah's lover, Gardner Ingalls, charging each with murder. With McNab in Vermont, and after a short delay to obtain the necessary New Hampshire governor's warrant, a Manchester officer quickly traveled to the Green Mountain state, arrested McNab and brought him back to Manchester before alerting Vermont officials.[704] Charged with murder, witnesses observed McNab in court wearing "a glossy black wig" that made him appear years younger.[705] He was initially held in custody, but managed to post a $3,000 bond that allowed him to return to Vermont. Charges were dropped almost immediately against his son, while Ingalls was later acquitted following a jury trial. McNab, reportedly "sick" after his release and unable to return for his own trial, forfeited his bond and never faced prosecution. Public outrage followed as a Portsmouth, New Hampshire clergyman placed blame on the tolerant community and its lack of morals as the root of the problem. "Our wives and daughters and sisters in the shops and mills of their daily care and labor, by hundreds and thousands, are unavoidably exposed to the ravages of 'unclean devils,'" he wrote before reasonably asking "shall we coldly look on and see them waylaid, seduced, disgraced, ruined and murdered?"[706] At its core, he identified lewdness, the loss of virtue and "crimes committed in darkness" as the main problems and wondered when these "unclean devils" would receive "their just and proper due."

Dr. John McNab, the vice president of the Mental Liberty Society who professed a disdain for religion and admiration for science and a reportedly respected Vermont physician, wholly escaped any accountability for his actions. It also raises the question of what other deaths could be attributed to his activities before he left the state for Manchester. His botched abortion of Sarah, probably not his first, extensive efforts to conceal and preserve her corpse for sale, lies to protect his reputation, and flight to avoid prosecution across three states reveal the opposite of one who professed to occupy the moral high ground. While other New England newspapers repeatedly expressed revulsion at Sarah's fate ("packed in a box *two and a half feet square and was sold for $7*," they repeatedly exclaimed), no Vermont newspaper ever acknowledged McNab's involvement in the sordid affair beyond a single sentence that he and his son were "recently of Barnet."[707] Other papers in New England also avoided confronting the presence of abortionists among them that led the Portsmouth clergyman to ask, "What! Is the press afraid to speak? Or, is the subject too shocking, too revolting, and too forbidding to be given in detail to the whole world!"

Safe at home and away from Massachusetts and New Hampshire law enforcement authorities, whatever "sickness" McNab suffered from did not hinder his ability to continue in his role as a respected Vermont physician. In 1855 he proudly gave notice to the public that Dr. William H. Hurd was working under his tutelage and described him in a way that obscured his own past behavior, calling Hurd "a man of honor, strict integrity and entitled to the patronage of the public."[708] By 1859, McNab appears entirely forgiven when he became an elected member of the VMS and the following year came in third in a four-man contest in the House of Representatives to become Vermont's commissioner for the insane.[709] In 1868 "the venerable Doctor" was elected President of the White Mountain Medical Society when he regaled his audience with a description of the Society's existence in past decades.[710] He appears to have also regained masonic membership after his earlier expulsion and when he died in 1878, at the age of ninety-four and the oldest physician in the state, was accorded Masonic Orders at his funeral. McNab's generous obituary also related, in marked understatement, that while highly thought of, he was "somewhat venturesome in his profession."[711]

CONCLUSION

Barnet's John McNab's ability to avoid prosecution and maintain a position of respectability in Vermont society served as an example of invincibility, of one immune from official sanction that other doctors in communities near his hometown emulated. Within a short time after his escapades in Barnet, Manchester, and Boston, others interested in the easy money that abortion provided made themselves known and inflicted egregious harm on Vermont's female population, most notably in the state's eastern counties of Orange and Caledonia (where Barnet is situated). Those tragic events further demonstrate the unsavory aspects of modernity that became increasingly evident by 1857 when the legislature debated the relocation of their capital, ones it refused to acknowledge in the form of abortions, infanticide and increased drug usage, as it postured and maintained an indefensible position that the Vermont population enjoyed good health when it was actually under attack. The comfort the lawmakers found in the attractive physical aspects of modernity brought by the railroad were soon severely questioned as one of the most notorious moments in Vermont's medical history exploded into view that further questioned their ability to protect the inhabitants from harm.

CHAPTER VII

Prisoner 1641: The Scientific English Surgeon

"Women seldom die unless the abortion has been produced by criminal means in which case death may occur." [712]

DARTMOUTH MEDICAL COLLEGE STUDENT ALBION K. STROUT, 1872

GARY G. SHATTUCK

INFECTED BY AN INCUBUS

In 1893 the Supreme Court of Kansas decided a convoluted estate and trust case that involved the relatives of a deceased, former Vermont "doctor," William Henry Mansfield Howard. The complicated matter cast Howard's third wife in the role of a defendant concerning claims made against her by a child from his second marriage. The evidence so clearly demonstrated the many ways that he misled and took advantage of his relations and friends that the court called him "quite an operator" and "a very extravagant and reckless man, [who] seems to have had the ability to secure the confidence of those he came in contact with, without profit to them."[713] The court's insightful, and understated, characterizations of Howard emphasized the ample evidence from Vermont years earlier that demonstrate he was, it seems, the most notorious, lawless medical practitioner/abortionist in the state in the nineteenth century. By his actions he not only inflicted great harm on many Vermonters in the 1850s, but also presented several significant moral and legal issues concerning abortion and the interaction of the struggling medical profession with the state's legal process. While modernity in the form of the railroad and state-of-the-art medical practices from afar became more readily available to residents, the concurrent presence of an individual such as Howard demonstrates the complexity of the challenges they presented.

Howard's toxic effects also coincided with an observation made by the leading botanical empiricist at the time in the ongoing battle between that practice and the regular medical profession concerning the difficulties that Vermont women faced in giving birth. In the thirty years previously, Samuel Thomson recalled, "the practice of midwifery was in the hands of experienced women. . . and there was scarce an instance known in those days of a woman dying in childbirth and it was very uncommon for them to lose a child." However, he said, the situation recently changed and that "at the present time, these things are so common that it is hardly talked about."

The only reason he could offer to explain the phenomena was because of "the improper treatment they experience from doctors, who have now got most of the practice into their own hands."[714] Thomson may have been prejudiced against the regulars, but his accurate observations cannot be dismissed as they show that even with an education, trained physicians committed their share of harm on Vermont women.

As John McNab re-established himself in Barnet after killing Sarah Furber, William Howard, who likened himself as one of the educated regulars that Thomson derided, began his own infamous rise to prominence killing women and babies. Evidence of his devastating impact on the many people he encountered exists in period newspapers and court documents from the 1850s that includes the dispositive decision from the Vermont Supreme Court in 1859 that described his abortion-related activities, authored by railroad law expert Chief Justice Isaac Redfield, recently-appointed Professor of Medical Jurisprudence at Dartmouth in 1858.[715] They reveal that Howard possessed little of the knowledge and training he wanted the public to believe he had. Instead, he was the epitome of a lone, reckless quack, a braggadocio, grifter and conniving gigolo who took full advantage of the lack of any medical licensing requirement in the state and which allowed him to cause great harm to many naive Vermonters. Between 1857 and 1859, he inflicted injury and death to four women that included his first wife, was suspect in three additional deaths, extracted at least seven documented fetuses (one abused by his dogs), was a suspect in two rapes, and attempted to murder the sheriff who tried to arrest him. He was also the subject of multiple prosecutions brought by the Orange County state's attorney and a litigant in several lawsuits that unfolded in the supreme, county, chancery, and probate courts. As a newspaper succinctly described at the time of Howard's sentencing in November 1859 in an article captioned *Caged at Last,* "his capacity in rascality is only equaled by his unblushing impudence."[716] Recreating Howard's path to notoriety over the course of a dozen different disputes in such a short period of time requires evidence from each of these forums that overlapped and occurred simultaneously when he was either incarcerated in the Orange County Jail in Chelsea or allowed out on bail and which provided him with additional opportunities to commit further harm. Howard represented all that was wrong with the permissive laissez-faire environment that officials fostered because of their refusal to adopt the protections imposed in other states on the medical profession, and the persistent calls of its responsible members, to implement a licensing law that could have minimized, or avoided, the harm he and others like him caused.

The ability of a charismatic individual with questionable medical training such as William Howard to move about easily because of the railroad technology and actually flourish demonstrates the power of a quack when he lived among an ill-educated, permissive rural population. Removed from the growing centers of industry in Burlington, Rutland and Brattleboro where conservative, trained physicians concentrated, outlying towns and villages attracted the untrained pursuing their unrestrained inclinations to set up business. When women interested in limiting the size of their families sought abortions, they faced rejection by the regulars sworn to uphold the Hippocratic Oath that condemned the practice.[717] Recognizing their own deficient knowledge concerning women's health, the awakening, responsible regulars of the time did, however, understand that they had to address the issue. In 1856, the VMS began to study aspects of childbirth after a member presented "a paper on miscellaneous subjects connected with midwifery." "Considerable general discussion" ensued among the attendees, its minutes disclosed, and a committee established to report to the membership "upon the Chronic Diseases of the Female Generative Organs."[718] Their tentative work progressed slowly and the next year members heard a presentation on fetus malposition before delivery and saw demonstrations of "mechanical appliances" used to correct the problem.[719]

The Society also established a "Tariff of Fees" for various medical services, including obstetrics, that allowed attending physicians $5 for "Regular Natural Labor terminating in 24 hours," $2 for "each additional 18 hours," and $10 for "Eviserotomy [sic] of Child." Their attention and concern to implement modern treatments to alleviate the hardship women experienced in childbirth were of little importance to quacks such as William Howard as there is no evidence he ever studied medicine, sought to affiliate himself with medical professionals or to practice in a responsible manner. Where and how he learned to perform abortions is unknown, but publications that explicitly explained the process remained available for general consumption. Their great detail, accompanied by illustrations of instruments used in the procedure, allowed for anyone with general knowledge of female anatomy to attempt to perform it. If the necessary instruments were unavailable, they could always improvise and learned that one device in particular could "readily be constructed from a piece of iron or steel wire" to pierce the embryonic sac. If that was not available, then "A large sized knitting-needle answers for this quite well."[720]

At the same time that Howard inflicted his harm in rural Vermont, in the metropolitan cities in Massachusetts and New Hampshire that easily connected all three states by railroads and allowed the flow of information between them, the unsavory practice of criminal abortions was under attack. "The frequency of Criminal Abortion in this Commonwealth," the Suffolk District Medical Society wrote in 1857, "though already notorious, is much greater than generally supposed; and it is probably steadily increasing." It also claimed that, while statistics of its taking place were unknown, "the instances of its occurrence, even when accidental, in advanced pregnancy, are but seldom reported to the proper authorities, who acknowledge that many of the so-called still-births are in consequence of induced abortion."[721] The Society's startling observation further insinuates the widespread practice of criminal abortions in Vermont as revealed by the huge number of stillborn births reported in the next couple of years following establishment of the state's registration system. The New Hampshire Medical Society also recognized the problem and admitted that in Manchester, the scene of McNab's crime and only 100 miles away from Howard in Bradford, "we have personal knowledge that the evil is no less prevalent in our own community." There was "a woman engaged in this nefarious occupation," it related, "with whom our authorities are unwilling to meddle, on account of her personal popularity as a *devoutly pious person, and we have daily evidences that to procure abortion is one of the first desires of a large proportion of pregnant women.*"[722] Practitioners clothed with an air of respectability living among a population that demanded access to abortions in these places so close to Vermont are phenomena that have never been acknowledged in the state's historiography. They also explain why Howard and other Vermont abortionists were able to practice in the ways they did and wreak their havoc on the female population without fear.

With a reported thick Irish brogue, William Howard captivated an Orange County community that welcomed his unconventional ways with open arms. So self-confident of himself, he openly displayed aborted fetuses in glass jars in his office to convince patients of his abilities. When later called to account for his actions by the prosecuting state's attorney, Howard went on the offensive and unhesitatingly, and incessantly, harangued to his large number of followers that he was a victim of persecution. His aggressive manner drew both friend and foe to the county courthouse in Chelsea in January 1859 where he was finally tried in what was described as "the most important criminal case ever. . . in this County."[723] It was remarkable spectacle to see such a character, one who many believed untouchable, summoned to answer for his conduct in a single death when entries 4, 5 and 6 in Bradford's 1858 registration report indicates that other women also died by his hand.

Prisoner 1641: The Scientific English Surgeon

Initially, the public never knew with confidence William Howard's specific origin, or actual name, as newspapers that described his many misdeeds reported he was an Irishman and others that he was an Englishman who held himself out as "a Surgeon in the British Army, and Surgeon extraordinary to Her Majesty the Queen."[724] Before Howard arrived in

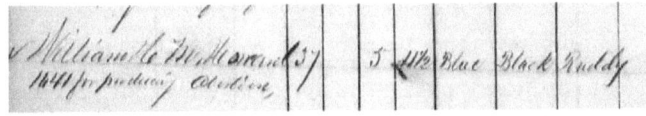

Detail. Windsor Prison entry for William Howard, prisoner number "1641 for producing abortion," November 19, 1859. Vermont State Archives.

Vermont he reportedly "lived in Canada and the West, doing business of various kinds at each place, under an assumed name." One publication stated that he was born around 1827, while newspaper reports of his arrival in Burlington by 1850 make any claim of a medical education, military service and being a royal confidant by the twenty-three-old questionable.[725] However, when he was finally jailed at Windsor Prison in November 1859, his admission records reveal he was thirty-seven-years-old making him five years older than was generally understood. He measured five-feet, eleven-and-one-half inches in height, had blue eyes, black hair, a ruddy complexion and reported that he was born in Dover, England.[726] Whether or not Howard served in the British Army, and if so in what capacity, is unknown, but contested probate court records from the months before he entered prison indicate he possessed an unidentified set of epaulets. If he actually had medical training, his practice in Vermont demonstrated his lack of competence when he encountered the female anatomy.

Howard was initially known by a series of last names, Drew, Houghton and Haughton, before pursuing Burlington creditors located him in Bradford (a short distance south of McNab in Barnet) around 1856 calling himself Howard.[727] Before he left Burlington he cut a noticeable figure representing himself as "an Englishman of rank and great fortune" and was seen driving about with "tandem teams followed by a handsome greyhound" where he "lived fast."[728] The discerning in the community were not fooled and the regular medical men recognized such ostentatious conduct as a common, cheap practice engaged in by the quacks calculated to draw the public's attention to themselves.[729] Despite the general understanding that "a very large proportion of his patients died" from his treatments, Howard did gain a popular following within the community, but only, as one newspaper described, among those "of a character that honest men would shun."[730] Before his sudden departure from their company, Howard swindled a local Burlington bank out of $1,000 and left behind "a number of unliquidated obligations to his landlord [and] several merchants."

A CONNECTICUT RIVER QUACK

In 1853 Howard relocated to the east side of the state and worked in towns near the Connecticut River that included Vershire, Thetford, and Bradford where he claimed during later probate proceedings he established himself as "a physician and. . . that his services were very much sought after by the people of Bradford and the surrounding towns in [Vermont] and New Hampshire." On November 17, 1854, Vershire farmer William Liddicoat suffered a severe fracture of his right femur and consulted with Howard for treatment. Liddicoat later sued him for malpractice and reported that he only agreed to submit to Howard's care because he held "himself out to the Public as a scientific English Surgeon having service as such in the English Army" and that he relied specifically on his representations of being "a scientist & a Surgeon of great experience & skill." Howard examined the leg and told Liddicoat that it had "broken into four or five fragments & some of the fragments split & again broken and [that] were it not for his superior skill, the leg would have to be amputated." Liddicoat agreed to proceed with treatment and Howard set the fracture, but by the following March it became clear it was not healing properly because the leg had become shorter than the other. Liddicoat instituted his lawsuit the following January in the Orange County court through local attorney Robert McKinley Ormsby and sought $6,000 in damages.[731] In his suit, Ormsby alleged that Howard had "ignorantly, unskillfully, carelessly & negligently" set his client's leg and accused him of being "wholly incompetent so to do" because he "was unacquainted with the art of surgery & was & is in his said pretensions an imposter." Ormsby's familiarity with Howard's derelict ways later afforded him the opportunity to assist the county state's attorney in prosecuting him in 1859 for killing a woman he performed an abortion on.

While Liddicoat's lawsuit was pending, and despite increasing suspicion of his being an imposter, Howard sought to ingratiate himself further into the Bradford community dispensing his unique form of "scientific" medicine. Before encountering Liddicoat, in 1853 he treated local farmer forty-three-year-old William Waterman for an unspecified ailment. Waterman died the following November and, because it preceded the 1857 registration requirement to record the causes of Vermonters' deaths, the reason is unknown. However, it does mark the first recorded instance, beyond the allegations of his involvement with deaths in Burlington, of a series of people dying under his care. Waterman left behind a wife, thirty-five-year-old Jane, three children, Jane, William and Emma, and a modest estate. Jane subsequently filed her husband's will with the probate court to obtain authority to disburse his assets in a process that became increasingly complicated when that case intermingled with her own following her suspicious death in 1858 while under the care of her second husband, William Howard.[732]

Howard maintained contact with Jane following her husband's death and, only a month after he terminated his strained relationship with farmer Liddicoat, was the recipient of a large windfall. He and Jane had become close in the interim and, in contemplation of marriage at a future date, on April 2, 1855 she bestowed on Howard all of her children's interests in her deceased husband's land in Bradford and Fairlee that included a farm with 102 acres of land, a sixty-acre wood lot with a sawmill, and various implements, valued at over $5,000. The terms allowed Howard to maintain possession and control of the property only until her son, five-year-old William, attained his majority when it would revert to him. Jane conditioned the transaction upon Howard providing for the family in "a good, handsome, prudent and comfortable manner" that included clothing and board "in sickness and in health" and to "give a good and complete academical education" to the children. When he was later confronted with allegations that he had taken advantage of Jane in her distressed situation, Howard vehemently denied the insinuation and argued that she had given him the property because she loved him. That may have been true at the time, but there is much reason to question his own motives because on January 28, 1856, an Orange County court ordered him to pay $559.97 to Edward Sprague, Jr. for a promissory note he defaulted on.[733]

On March 13, 1856, the financially-pressed Howard married Jane in a ceremony performed in Boston.[734] Two days later, home in Fairlee, he sold fourteen head of beef cattle to John Patterson for $1,400.[735] As with many events involving Howard, Patterson also had to institute a lawsuit in 1858 against him to resolve issues surrounding the sale.[736] Attorney Robert McKinley Ormsby appeared once again in those proceedings on Patterson's behalf to oppose Howard while Chelsea attorneys Asa M. Dickey and Calvin W. Clark represented him. Dickey was later forced to sue Howard in June 1858 for $150 for failing to pay him for his services while Clark represented him at the time of his January 1859 trial for an abortion-related death.[737]

A month after the sale of cattle to Patterson, Ormsby was back in court representing Vershire farmer Liddicoat for the first of two trials against Howard for his incompetent treatment of his client's leg. The proceedings did not go well for Howard who was found liable by a jury that awarded

Liddicoat $1,000 in damages. His attorneys filed an appeal that resulted in a second trial in January 1857 that was also a disaster for Howard. During the proceedings it was revealed his medical knowledge was so destitute he could not convey even "the first principles of anatomy and surgery" that convinced his attorney to refuse to allow him to testify. Even Liddicoat's attorneys joined in the derision and offered "to abandon the suit if Howard would take the stand and give a scientific description of the thigh bone." The offer was refused and Howard relied instead on Dartmouth Medical College's Dr. Dixie Crosby, the first surgeon in the United States sued for malpractice, to testify on his behalf. That effort proved unsuccessful once again when the jury awarded Liddicoat damages and increased them to $1,400.[738] Following the trial, one newspaper spoke for many in the community in their recognition of Howard's lack of medical knowledge, "Such is the ignorance of the man to whom many entrusted their health and lives."[739] In June 1857, Howard moved to set aside the verdict and, apparently tired of the litigation, Liddicoat agreed to reduce his claim to $1,000. Probate proceedings reveal that Howard prevailed on Jane to co-sign a mortgage of their property for $900 that appears to have been to pay the judgment. However, it was not the end of their legal entanglement as the unrepentant Howard refused to fulfill his obligation and Liddicoat was forced to hound him over the next years in court proceedings that enveloped the interests of Jane's children following her death.

The circumstances of Howard's association with the Dartmouth Medical School is unknown, but was probably because of his consultation with Crosby about Liddicoat's suit. Only months after his marriage to Jane and between the two malpractice trials, a local paper reported in October 1856 that Howard was "brought before Justice Prichard upon a charge of assault and attempt to commit rape upon the person of Mrs. D. T. Corbin, of Norwich, wife of D. T. Corbin, a member of the senior class of Dartmouth College."[740] After a two-day hearing, the court ordered Howard to face charges in the next term and released him on $500 bond. His victim, and patient, twenty-two-year-old Eunice Fowler, had married David Corbin in Norwich just weeks before the assault and the two of them quickly instituted their own suit against Howard.[741] However, both the prosecution and suit were later abandoned after Eunice died in March 1858, reportedly of consumption.[742] While the timing of her convenient death allowed Howard to escape those allegations, others gathered and a newspaper related that Eunice's "dying declaration still hangs over him."[743]

After Howard took up residency with Jane at her deceased husband's farm in Bradford, he constructed outbuildings separated from his family that played a role in his abortion-related activities where he could meet and consult privately with patients. He later described his work on the property in probate papers and reported that he "removed and repaired and built an addition to the house and erected two small buildings occupied by him as offices in his business as a surgeon and physician." Together with a separate privy, Howard estimated that he spent $1,800 in the construction, but was later awarded only $375 by the probate court when Jane's estate was settled.[744] In March 1857, Howard was back in court charged with selling "a quantity of salt pork which it was alleged was unfit for food on account of disease in the pig." A lengthy hearing ensued and despite evidence that the last days of the poor beast (named Chucky) were "anything but pleasant or peaceful," several witnesses who consumed it testified on his behalf they were unaffected. Howard won the case after he, "being a physic [doctor]," disputed the allegations of an unnatural end and rendered "his professional opinion [that] Chucky died of a natural knife."[745] Extant court records also relate that Howard was involved with at least three additional lawsuits during this time for unspecified reasons or outcomes that continued into 1858 when he was charged with abortion-related manslaughter; two named him as a defendant and one he instituted against a husband and wife.[746]

Prisoner 1641: The Scientific English Surgeon

Howard required privacy apart from his family in 1857 as his activities became increasingly suspicious. His agreement with Jane to turn over all of the property to her young son upon his majority seems to have played a role in his conduct during this time. His obsession with maintaining his status in the community, evident fear of eventually losing possession of the property to the boy and his access to harmful substances able to induce death all provide sufficient evidence of premeditation, motive and opportunity to further advance his personal interests and explain why seven-year-old William died suddenly on May 3, 1857. Whether it was connected to the allegations of Chucky's tainted meat weeks earlier is not known, but the resourceful and creative Howard could well have concealed his involvement in the death when he simply explained to Bradford's respected town clerk Preston Adams, who recorded it in the town's registry, that the child died because of "Disease of the head."[747] Of note, such a meaningless entry, similar to many others in the state's registration reports ascribing a death to "brain fever," served as a convenient way to mask the presence of cerebral hemorrhages attributable to forceful blows to a decedent's head.[748] The description of a death in this manner did not fulfill the specificity expected on the state's registration reports. However, it was consistent with the many other entries that offer little information to accurately identify causes of death and which allowed those involved in them to avoid detection.

Jane became pregnant that spring around the time of her son's passing, and rape charges pended against her husband, and delivered another son in February 1858. Howard did not treat her well during her pregnancy and there is evidence he sought to terminate it by administering harmful medicines to her in order to induce an abortion just as evidence of his other criminal conduct exploded into public view. Tellingly, when Jane died in August 1858 the cause of her death, also recorded in Bradford's registry by Adams, attributed it to "Improper treatment at Child Birth (injurious Medicines, harsh treatment & continued family trouble causing disease of the womb, general debility & death)."[749]

As the summer of 1857 progressed and authorities in Boston and Manchester rallied to address the increased instances of criminal abortion in their communities, Howard gained, in the coded words used to describe the practice, "an unenviable notoriety, in his assumed profession."[750] This is evident because of another brief, explosive entry made by Adams in the town's registration reports unlike any of the many thousands of others contained in the hundreds of pages of the state's registry and which did not appear in the secretary of state's official published report. Howard clearly had much to hide when, on October 6, 1857, an individual, identified by Adams only as "Jones," died "at WHM Howards." When inquiries were made into the circumstances of her death, Adams could only write that "Information positively refused respecting death at Dr. Howards."[751] Howard's refusal to cooperate and provide information proved sufficient enough to frustrate any further investigation by authorities. While the registration reports for Bradford and surrounding towns do not specifically identify his involvement with other abortions that year, entries attributing the deaths of young females in the all-inclusive "consumption" category continue to suggest such a possibility. Additionally, an 1859 newspaper account of Howard's abortion-related activities added to the community's growing alarm when it reported that in the past summer "there died. . . three young women in the course of a few weeks who sought his aid to hide their shame."[752] A further review of the registration records does not provide sufficient information to identify these women, but does not mean that they are not actually named and wrongfully classified as victims of consumption. Two women, ages fifteen and thirty-eight, are listed in Brookfield's returns for 1859 whose cause of death is described as "Not known (6 days)" indicating they declined over that period of time following a traumatic event of some kind. As events unfolded in Howard's life in the next months, six days was the amount of time that elapsed between one of his abortions and the death of a woman that finally marked his downfall. Before that happened, as stymied officials found it difficult to conduct meaningful investigations and he refused to cooperate or participate in accurately reporting the cause of his patients' deaths, Howard's reputation continued to grow. It reached beyond Bradford eighty miles to the north into Canada where, from Stanstead, Quebec on the Vermont border and in Sutton, fifty miles away in Vermont, two women in desperate situations decided they wanted abortions.

INNOCENCE DESTROYED

In November 1857, after the Vermont legislature decided to rebuild the destroyed statehouse, it authorized "the design of a suitable figure" to place atop the building.[753] Ceres, the Roman goddess of agriculture, was chosen and later installed. The depiction of a tall female standing in an elevated position holding sheaves of grain representing fruitfulness, plenty and promise stood in stark contrast to what was about to happen in Howard's recently constructed office. There, on January 27 and 29, 1858, two young women identified only as "Miss Young" of Stanstead and Olive Ashe of Sutton died. The circumstances of Young's appearance at Howard's office or how her body was surreptitiously returned home to Canada immediately after her death are unknown. However, it is certain that when a Stanstead physician examined it, he attributed her death to, as Bradford clerk Adams dutifully entered into the registry, "in consequence of an abortion having been produced."[754] Local officials might have never known that Young died in their midst had not evidence of a second one burst into public view at the same time.

Nineteen-year-old twins Olive and Olivia Ashe came from a farming family in Sutton where they lived with their mother and two siblings; their father was deceased. The twins' situation differed little from the earlier experiences of Sarah Furber, also a farmer's daughter, who sought an abortion. During the summer of 1857 Olive lived and worked as a domestic servant in a local home where she became intimate with her employer's son,

Daniel Beckwith. After she returned home, sister Olivia later testified that "had it not been for the condition of her mind," she appeared normal.[755] As time passed, Olive became more concerned when her six-month pregnancy made her condition so obvious that the two women discussed an abortion. They devised a plan to go to Bradford to speak with Beckwith, where he was living, to see if he could arrange it. At first, they did not intend to go to Howard, but, as Olivia explained, they had heard of him. After they spent two weeks visiting a relative in Bradford, they made contact with Beckwith and he agreed to arrange the procedure with Howard.

After Beckwith advised the women that Howard agreed to meet with them, they took the trip to his office by a short train ride on January 15, 1858. When they got off, the depot master recalled their asking him how to get to his office. Well aware of the type of work that Howard did, he related that "The place they inquired for caused me to take notice of them." He also noted that neither of the women "look[ed] as though they needed doctoring, they looked rugged, did not see any difference in them."[756] The sisters finally found their way to Howard's office, separated in another building away from the family residence, where Olivia testified they "saw some infants there, one-half dozen perhaps of all sizes, preserved in spirits." They explained to Howard that Olive was six-months pregnant and she wanted an abortion. Cautious, before agreeing to do it Howard said he wanted to meet with Beckwith. While they awaited his answer, the women stayed at Howard's business for the next several days in a second-floor room during the time when Miss Young from Stanstead must have been present. After they received a letter from Beckwith and showed it to Howard, he agreed to perform the abortion for $100 and explained it would take three to four weeks to complete. The process began immediately and Olivia recalled that Howard gave Olive a drink of "medicine in the form of bitters, about a goblet full at a dose, two or three times," but she could not tell what it did to her sister.

A week after Olive consumed the last dose, Howard performed the abortion. It took place in the room the women occupied and required three separate invasions of her body over two days to accomplish. Olivia was the only witness and she described in detail what she saw. As Olive lay on her bed, Howard used, according the Supreme Court's recitation of Olivia's testimony, "three or four instruments. . . internally upon the private parts of Olive." She complained that she was experiencing pain and Olivia witnessed "that discharges of water came from her, which continued for two or three hours and more." Howard returned the following day and repeated the process as Olivia related that "the result of this operation was flowing," accompanied by "considerable blood." After several hours passed, Howard performed a third procedure using the same instruments, but this time he "introduced his hand" and extracted "a child about two-thirds as large as full grown." Olivia told the jury that she observed the fetus in Howard's hands and the last time she saw it was when he "carried it out of the room."

Over the next six days, Olive experienced an excruciating time as she descended into what other witnesses (possibly friends of Miss Young also dying nearby) characterized as insanity. In a lucid moment, Olive told a visiting friend that "she could not live and did not expect to, that she had been taking powerful poison medicines before she came to Dr. Howard's and she thought she had destroyed her life. . . and she hoped they would not blame the doctor, and she thought he had done everything he could to restore her health, that she had been out of health a long while." At other times she was irrational and could barely be restrained as she violently kicked and thrashed on the bed. Somebody telegraphed Olive's mother that her daughter was very sick and she immediately traveled to Howard's office. There, he told her that Olive had typhoid fever and that when she first arrived she "had a humor; then she had the dropsy; her blood was near water as could be; and her liver was twice as large as a common one."[757] After days of suffering, Olive died on "Friday about six o'clock in the evening, January 29th."

Unaware that her daughter had undergone an abortion, Olive's mother brought the body home to Sutton where it was immediately interred. However, after others quickly learned of the event and "representations and solicitations of the leading citizens of Bradford" were made to authorities, State's Attorney Charles C. Dewey ordered Howard's confinement while additional evidence was gathered. As one newspaper reported, Howard remained at his house, purportedly because of "sickness," and where "keepers are watching him." Perhaps confused by what took place, it also related that "two corpses were taken from his house on the 29th and 30th," but did accurately describe that "the village is in a state of great excitement."[758] This latest death occurring so soon after Howard's refusal to answer questions about Jones's death in October convinced officials of the need to take aggressive action to ascertain what happened to Olive. Dewey then traveled to Sutton to arrange for a post mortem examination of her body, interred for the past two days. After she was exhumed, three doctors, including St. Johnsbury's Dr. Carleton Pennington Frost, attended the inquiry on February 4. All of them concluded that her death was because of "violence in the use of instruments applied to the neck of the womb in the attempts to induce abortion."[759] Town clerk Adams duly noted the cause and recorded: "Died in consequence at Dr. Howard's of an abortion having been produced."[760] Frost then secured evidence of the crime by removing Olive's uterus and ovaries and placed them into a preserving jar with alcohol for use as an exhibit in court proceedings. Authorities soon learned of the death of Stanstead's Miss Young at Howard's business and the opinion of local doctors that abortion was also the cause. The following week, on February 11, 1858, Jane Howard survived her husband's ill treatment of her and gave birth to a son, William.[761]

Days after Olive's autopsy, the discovery of Miss Young's passing and the birth of a son he tried to abort, Howard appeared in court on February 16 to face charges of "illegal operations resulting in the death of two young females."[762] The salacious allegations caused an uproar and hordes of people flocked to the Bradford court house as rooms filled up at the nearby Trotter House, "crammed from basement to roof with visitors from all the country round," to witness the spectacle.[763] It attracted a variety of people to witness Howard's predicament, an individual who, the press wrote, was "enjoying a great but by no means enviable reputation throughout all this region." Many of his supporters from neighboring towns, those described as "of an equivocal character, to say the least," arrived and set up "a cry of persecution" against him as seventy-five of them pooled their money to bail him out of custody. A bewildered Boston reporter succinctly described the scene where presumably upright, decent Vermonters clamored to assist the killer of two women. "To say the least," he wrote, "the affair and the developments connected with it are anything but credible to a quiet and moral community. It shows too plainly that moral depravity is to be found not alone in large cities, but may invade even pastoral communities." Others shared his disbelief when the court allowed Howard free and set bail at a minimal $600 for each of the two cases, paid for by his "rag-a-muffin crew of admirers." "We were greatly surprised," a newspaper reported, "that a Justice could be found in a State considered as law-abiding as is Vermont, who should have so low an estimate of a crime of man-slaughter as to consider $600 sufficient bail. . . . Such decisions seem to us to offer a premium to crime, and to make our laws like a dead letter upon the Statute Book."[764]

Howard continued to pose a huge challenge to anyone in his way after his release in February. The following month he ran afoul of the law once again and was arrested and charged with raping an "Irish woman who had been in his employ."[765] The arrest did not go well when county Sheriff Charles C. P. Baldwin appeared at his business and Howard confronted him with a pointed revolver and threatened to "make a hole through him." A struggle ensued and Howard "immediately found himself upon the floor underneath the Sheriff, who held him down." The rape charge was later dismissed because of inconsistencies with the victim's testimony, but a charge of assault to commit murder on Baldwin was lodged and Howard ordered held on $3,000 bond. "Some of his warmest friends," a newspaper reported in reference to those who provided money for his prior release "say that a man who will go bail for him now... ought to be hung."[766]

Howard's next attempt to obstruct the judicial process and delay his trial for killing Olive Ashe involved his contacting Olivia. Locked up and unable to do the job himself, he relied on the assistance of Fairlee friend Charles Knapp to persuade her to leave her home in Sutton and go to Montreal to avoid testifying against him, promising to pay her expenses. Olivia agreed, but was later tracked down in the city and returned to Vermont to provide testimony before a grand jury. Even that did not stop Howard as he again sought to delay his trial and filed a sworn affidavit with the court stating that a woman named "Mrs. Green" could prove his innocence, but that "she could not be procured as a witness on account of indisposition."[767] Green appears to have been present at Howard's house at the time of the deaths of the two women, but also reportedly lived in Canada that made it difficult to require her presence. An officer was dispatched northward, but found the woman living in Vermont with her husband on the border in Derby. Surprised at being dragged into the controversy, she provided her own affidavit and refuted Howard's allegations as "entirely false and destitute of the least particle of truth."[768] Green later appeared at his trial and testified that she visited his home as a friend of Jane's (then in the throes of her own difficult pregnancy) and had witnessed Olive's last hours when she thrashed on her bed before dying. When Howard's latest falsehoods were revealed the court had no alternative but to delay the trial because his attorney was not ready to proceed. However, the judge made his anger known in such fashion that, according to witnesses, it would "probably be long remembered by Howard, and the great drops of sweat which beaded his brow while he was being castigated by the court will long be remembered by the spectators." Howard and Knapp were both charged with obstructing justice in their attempt to keep Olivia from testifying and Howard's bail increased to $12,000; he remained in custody between late May and early August.[769]

When Howard was first arrested in February, Jane's mother, Agnes Wilson, came to their house to attend her child birth. She also testified at his trial and described some of the things she saw in May while he was locked up, briefly recounted by the Supreme Court:

> As she was passing from the office to the house, she saw one of [Howard's] dogs come out from under the office privy, with the form of a child in its mouth; that he dropped it on being ordered by her, and the witness examined it and found it to be a child; in the judgment of the witness, four or five months grown; that it was putrid and decayed; that she had noticed the dogs digging about the privy vault for some time previous till they had worked a hole in the dirt under the plank, out of which hole the dog came with the child in its mouth; that while she was looking at it a large dog belonging to [Howard] came up and snatched it away and ran off with it.

Wilson also described the child's size and "pointed out its length and size on her arm, indicating it to be. . . similar to the child which Olivia Ashe testified she saw taken from her sister." That spring, Jane made a will that appears to have allowed Howard some portion of her estate, but as the evidence of his depravity mounted, she feared what he could do with it and her children's interests she conveyed to him in 1855 if he was released from custody. After her mother's experience with the fetus and Howard's dogs, on June 7 she wrote out a second will that excluded him entirely and bequeathed her property to her children by William Waterman and to recently-born infant William.[770] Jane knew she was not well, no doubt because of the medicines her husband was feeding her, and prefaced her wishes with words that acknowledged her condition: "being in a very infirm state of health and sensible too of my liableness to sudden death." She took further precaution and filed papers in the Supreme Court seeking a divorce from Howard because of his adultery and the way he treated her with "intolerable severity." Lastly, she obtained an injunction in the Chancery Court to prohibit him from doing anything to harm the two estates' assets and had both sets of papers served on him at the Chelsea jail on July 23.

Chelsea is Orange County's shiretown, located in what was considered in the mid-nineteenth century as "a typical middle-sized rural Vermont township." With a population of 1,958 in 1850 (that decreased to 1,757 by 1860) engaged primarily in agriculture, the village was occupied by a bank, post office, general stores, workshops, hotel, livery stable, academy, two churches, a jail and a courthouse.[771] At the time of Howard's escapades, Chelsea and the surrounding area was in a state of transition moving from a period fraught with raucous political differences in the 1840s to a more ameliorating time. Whigs and Democrats alike shared and pursued the ideals of capitalism, but it brought the latter's ire because of the inequitable way that towns experienced its dividends.[772] Whigs also assumed the high moral ground and sought to impose blanket alcohol prohibition on the town's inhabitants that its democrat members resented. To increase their influence, some within the democratic party drew unwanted attention from their peers because of the way they confronted the Whigs, including women whom they disparaged as "agents of respected society" attracted by the area's "unsuccessful and unregenerate" members of the community into their ranks.[773] While the two factions shared opposition to slavery that drew the two sides closer together by the mid-1850s, their differences remained when issues concerning the degree of enforcement that prohibition should receive. Throughout the decade, those opposed to stringent prohibition in the community prevailed to such an extent that in 1862 a town meeting concerned about its deteriorating reputation described it as "a low place filled with rum shops [where] drunkards staggered through the streets" and scared away those that could help the town to develop.[774]

Despite the abhorrence that many in Chelsea and Orange County had for Howard in this divisive time, his influence did not diminish. Upon its birth in Vermont in 1855, the Republican Party became the predominate political force that attracted between seventy-five to eighty-five percent of the town's voters for the rest of the century.[775] Orange County's Republican State's Attorney Dewey served his constituents well following his first election to the post in 1856 and was again the party's choice in 1857 when Howard, and his fellow democrats, decided to replace him.[776] Dewey was busily engaged in a number of other cases at the time that included, among others, prosecutions for illegally selling liquor, assault with intent to kill, assault and battery, larceny and perjury.[777] Respected local attorney and side-judge Philander Perrin was the democrats' first choice to oppose Dewey, but agreed to step aside and let Howard's attorney, Calvin W. Clark of Chelsea, replace him.

Chelsea, Vermont 1860. Vermont Historical Society.

As these developments unfolded, the incarcerated Howard unashamedly "sought and had an interview" with the state's attorney. When the two men met, he told Dewey that "if he would use his influence with the court and get him released... he would 'range the whole county' in favor of his re-election," but if he did not, he would "use his influence [and] endeavor to defeat him."[778] Unfinished with his threats, after their meeting two of Howard's friends spoke with Dewey and warned him that Howard "had a number of friends amongst the Republicans" and promised to make "a personal question with them" in an effort to split the ticket. A vicious war of words ensued between area newspapers that revealed the untowardness of Howard's association with the editor of Bradford's *National Telegraph*. While the paper existed for a short time (published by Methodist minister Rev. William M. Mann between 1856 and 1858), it earned sufficient disdain from the established *Vermont Journal* calling it *"the organ of Howard,"* used to discredit Dewey. The *Telegraph* continued to advocate on Howard's behalf and the next year another newspaper, Newbury's *Aurora of the Valley*, in an article entitled "The Dr. Howard Influence," dismissed the paper's infatuation with him and suggested that it save its support "unless they intend to make him Governor."[779] The courts were not the place for politics the *Journal* pleaded: "We make an earnest appeal to the sober second thought of *all* the citizens of Orange County, whatever other foolish thing they may do, to let the criminal jurisprudence of the county run in its accustomed and legal channel, uninterrupted and unimpeded by popular clamor or any such thing." The division that Howard caused in the community was so bad that the paper equated his followers' efforts with the "multitude who cried out 'Crucify him!' and had 'Barnabus released unto them.'" "We hope never to witness similar scenes in our State," it concluded, "and we shall not if the people do but stop to reflect upon the sad consequences of such a course." The continuing attacks on the earnest Dewey alleging he exploited his position for the sake of "emolument and malicious prosecution" proved unsuccessful when, despite Howard's ranging through the county giving speeches vilifying him following his release, he won reelection.

In early August before the election, Howard, now called by one paper "the notorious scoundrel," obtained his freedom with the help of several individuals from Bradford, Fairlee and Corinth who paid his bond.[780] The efforts on his behalf did not sit well with many. "We do not know how it may appear to others," the paper wrote,

> but it seems to us a great wrong that this man was let his liberty; but, after all, the greater the rascal the more likely is he to have sympathy, and friends to go his bail, and thereby defraud justice of her dues. We doubt if the poor fellows put into our jail last

week for stealing old clothes, will find friends to bail them. . . . Outraged justice demands a reform.

As soon as Howard left the jail carrying Jane's bills of divorce and injunction with him, he went straight to Bradford, accompanied by one of the men who bailed him out. By then, Jane's condition had deteriorated so badly that only three days before she had local attorney Charles M. McDuffie appointed guardian of her children. When Howard arrived at the home, McDuffie refused him entry into Jane's bedroom (stopped "with a strong hand to keep him out" according to Howard), but was eventually allowed in. McDuffie later explained what occurred: "Jane lay feeble & sick which so worried her in her feeble condition & born down by the misconduct, crimes & wickedness. . . & shocked by his presence. . . she deceased." In his defense, Howard protested otherwise and alleged that "Jane at her own request received and embraced him with great apparent cordiality and. . . assured him that she desired no separation from him till separated by death," which she did two days later on August 7. Howard later alleged that McDuffie tried to prevent him from attending her funeral, but was once again allowed entry. He also sought to avert blame for her alienation from him and said that he was not the cause of Jane's displeasure, but, rather, it was because of the actions of others. Her "attachment & confidence" in him only wavered, he alleged, after he "had been torn from the bosom of his family and committed to jail upon charges which are entirely false and groundless." The problems between the two arose, he said, only because of "the guile & misrepresentations of his enemies for the purpose of breaking up his peace & happiness & working [his] ruin."

Howard's blatant lies were only a part of his mean character and the challenges he posed to poor Jane, dying at age forty because of the "improper treatment" she received from him during her pregnancy. His administration of "injurious Medicines" to her was only one contributing factor listed in the town's registration report, accompanied by "harsh treatment & continued family trouble" that led to her "general debility & death."[781] As Jane steadily declined, she sought relief from Doctor William H. Carter of Newbury in an effort that resulted in even more litigation. Carter was already well-known for the quack concoction he created in the 1840s called "Carter's Pulmonary Balsam," purportedly "prepared from vegetables only" to treat a variety of ailments. He marketed it widely and obtained some success, but ran afoul of the medical profession when it was found to contain morphine.[782] Unwilling to permit such a person to obtain a medical degree, the Dartmouth Medical College where he attended refused to allow him to graduate unless he disavowed the concoction named after him. He agreed to do so and received his medical diploma in 1848.[783] Carter was present at Jane's home when Howard arrived after his release from the Chelsea jail and advised him that he was attending to her, which Howard did not object to. He later sued Howard in 1866 for unpaid money owed for his services to Jane, but was unsuccessful when the Supreme Court ruled that Howard had not agreed to assume responsibility for paying them.[784]

Court-appointed guardian Charles McDuffie proved a zealous protector of the departed Jane's interests and those of her surviving children. As soon as Howard left her death chamber, he obtained an arrest warrant for him and his companion later the same day alleging they had trespassed by coming to the residence.[785] It does not appear that the charge was pursued in the following days and on August 12 Howard did what Jane and McDuffie sought to avoid when the injunction was issued prohibiting him from harming her and William Waterman's estates. On that day, he conveyed the rights to livestock and portions of the property to John Sanborn, one of the men who bailed him out of jail. His actions in violation of the court's order only exacerbated an already difficult situation and for the rest of the year he and McDuffie fought out their respective positions in the chancery and probate courts. Howard filed numerous objections in opposition to McDuffie's efforts that included contesting Jane's June 7 will and argued that she was "not of sufficient mental capacity... of least and feeble intellect [and] under influence induced to execute" it. He further alleged that Jane's relatives, Willard Waterman and his wife Mary Ann, "have secreted in their possession [Jane's] last will & testament" and obtained a court order for their appearance at a hearing. He also sought $500 in damages from McDuffie "for his cruel inhumane & unchristian refusal of the meeting of husband & wife in the last stages of the wife's sickness & still worse making it a crime in the husband to weep over the ashes of the wife he loved."

In response, McDuffie listed Howard's egregious conduct: "deceitful wiles & practices having won the confidence of Jane"; his "extravagant and reckless" lifestyle after he obtained the Waterman estate; that he "gives out in speeches" he had a right to the property; how he "became involved in & committed many enormous & high crimes & misdemeanors under color of his professional practice"; and that "Howard does pretend that he is wealthy" but "is wholly bankrupt." Fearful that Howard would not abide by court orders and "forcibly possess himself" of the property, McDuffie made additional allegations that "others of Howard's sympathies & confederates" would aid him to evade "the just penalties of the law for his crimes & enable [him] to escape from & avoid the same." Court-appointed referee Asahel Peck received evidence on their claims and counterclaims during five days of contentious hearings in Bradford between December 7-11, 1858. Another month passed and only days before Howard's trial for killing Olive Ashe, Peck issued his decision ruling that Jane's June 7 will that excluded him from any of her assets was proper, denied his allegations of her insufficient mental capacity and undue influence exerted in its execution, that McDuffie had not acted "maliciously" in his allegations against Howard, and that whatever assets were allowed to Howard now became the property of John Sanborn to whom he transferred his rights for bail.

While Howard remained free and contested with McDuffie, in the fall his mother-in-law made a startling discovery in the building where Miss

Young and Olive Ashe died. Holding a decomposed fetus pulled out from under the privy and having it snatched from her hands by one of his dogs was only a prelude for Agnes Wilson who found yet additional evidence of Howard's responsibility for their deaths. While cleaning the premises she discovered "two female chemises, a small quilt or pad some two feet wide and three or four feet long. . . very much besmeared with blood." The items were deliberately hidden, she reported, concealed in the rafters and behind a board that held them in place. "When she took them out," the Supreme Court decision recounted, "a black stuff like dry clots of blood sifted off from them," and one of them "had the appearance of having been removed from the person by cutting."

The Law Confronts Medical Modernity

Howard's trial began on Tuesday, January 25, 1859 to determine his guilt or innocence on six counts: three for each of the attempts to procure an abortion on Olive Ashe by means of instruments that caused her death; two for attempting to cause an abortion by means of "poisons and noxious things;" and, manslaughter by wounding Olive with instruments in her womb. The charges for manslaughter involving Miss Young and the attempt to murder Sheriff Baldwin were not before the jury at the time. Fourth Associate Supreme Court Justice James Barrett (elected in 1857) presided, described as a man who was "temperamentally unfitted for the agreeable discharge of judicial duties" and who unnecessarily alienated members of the bar.[786] The contest unfolding before him lasted ten days in a courtroom so crowded that "at no time during the whole trial was such a thing heard of as a *spare seat*, but generally the house was crowded to suffocation."[787] An estimated 500 people ("perhaps more") witnessed the proceedings, so many crammed into any available space that officials thought "the floor might give way." All of the rooms at the local public house and private homes were filled and temperance meetings experienced less than usual attendance as crowds flocked to the courthouse. Dewey and Howard's nemesis who hounded him in civil lawsuits, Robert McKinley Ormsby, represented the state, while former Vermont Supreme Court justice William Hebard (1842-1844) and future Civil War general Peter T. Washburn appeared on his behalf.

Twenty-seven area residents appeared as potential jurors and the process to pick twelve of them to decide the case took up the first morning. Testimony followed and the courtroom heard of Olive's travails in chronological order. It began with her mother, unaware of the true reason for her daughters' trip, who told the jury about Olive and Olivia leaving their home in Sutton to visit a relative in Bradford. Other witnesses testified they had seen the women in town, about their train trip to Fairlee, and inquiry made at the depot for directions to Howard's business. Then Olivia told them what she had done to assist Olivia, about their trip, meeting with Howard and seeing the six fetuses in jars, staying at his business, Olive's consumption of the medicine he gave her, the abortion process, and his removal of the fetus from the room. Evidence of Howard's attempts to keep Olivia quiet and out of the investigation by sending her to Montreal was also introduced. Others present at his house testified what they saw as Olive suffered over the course of six days before she finally died.

Evidence that Howard performed an abortion necessarily required the testimony of medical experts to interpret the injuries inflicted on Olive's uterus and presented an important moment in Vermont jurisprudence concerning their involvement in the legal process. Dr. Frost attended her autopsy a year earlier and removed the organ from her as evidence, preserved in a jar of alcohol. It was produced and became the center of attention as doctors for both the state and defense testified about the information that could be gained from it. This battle between the experts followed a similar dual that unfolded in the Windsor County Court in Woodstock in 1854 where the nation's first lawsuit for medical malpractice unfolded. It involved Dartmouth's Dr. Dixie Crosby, accused of failing to properly set a broken thigh bone and who testified on Howard's behalf that year in the similar claim made against him by William Liddicoat. While Howard lost his case, Crosby won and was found not liable.[788]

Since that time, a recent legal twist presented itself to a British jurist in 1858 that involved the use of medical experts at trial. The issue concerned the obligation of a physician to provide testimony based on either firsthand, factual knowledge he might have about an event, such as Frost's personal examination of Olive, or his professional opinion about what certain evidence might mean. The judge opined that while a doctor with knowledge about the facts of a case could be compelled by subpoena to testify, one with only an opinion could not. "If he knew any question of fact," he wrote, "he might be compelled to attend, but Her Majesty's subjects were not compellable to give their attendance to speak on matters of opinion." The practical problem that doctors faced ("certainly a very important little item to medical men" a Philadelphia journal recorded at the time) concerned their actual physical removal from the street by a sheriff, without warning, and being brought unwillingly into a courtroom to provide an opinion about a case they had no familiarity with, and without any compensation for their troubles. "If scientific men are necessary in courts of justice," the Philadelphia correspondent wrote, "then they are as much entitled to pay for their services as are the lawyers who question them."[789]

While Frost willingly attended Howard's trial as both a fact witness and to provide an opinion, the defense retained the services of Dr. Edward E. Phelps, of Windsor, who also appeared the entire time, but without being subpoenaed.[790] His role was to render an opinion based upon his examination of Olive's preserved uterus and the testimony he heard from the other medical experts. Phelps's willingness to participate without being compelled by a subpoena caused concern among members of the state's medical profession who believed that he "ought not to have volunteered to testify in behalf of Howard as it is assumed Howard is an imposter."[791]

Ignoring the opposition, he did so, but then experienced further disapproval months later when he sought to become a member of the VMS. When his name came up for a vote during its June meeting, "owing to some complaints having been made by some of the members" the minutes record, "Dr. Phelps preferred to postpone the vote... in order that he might make some explanations." He did so later in the day when he "made further remarks on the character of the complaints made against him" after which he became an "admitted a member of this Society by a unanimous vote." The circumstances presented by Phelps's participation in Howard's case posed many important questions among the membership and a three-man committee, including Phelps, was appointed to guide them and to report "at some future meeting on the duties & privileges of Physicians as medical witnesses & witnesses as experts."[792]

Phelps later returned and presented the committee's views. Doctors still sought a licensing requirement for the profession and identifying an appropriate balance that satisfied both the needs of the legal process for their input and advanced their independence and integrity required sensitivity in negotiating those concerns. Phelps engaged his audience on several levels as he sought to alleviate the prickly issues that Howard's case presented and told them that:

> The difference between a medical witness & expert consists in the first instance being called upon to give testimony as to facts, and the other to give his opinion on a medical question which may be raised.
>
> Of the duty & privilege of witnesses & experts, first the duty of witnesses is to make clear the facts of the case while that of experts is to give an opinion involving the principles at issue.
>
> As a witness, the medical man should understand what he is in court for. He should never be a partisan. He is there for the benefit of the jury, to enable them to understand, by his explanations, the true merits of the case & give a just verdict. His explanations should ever be intelligible; never technical.

> He should be aware of giving too positive opinions. His opinions should be guarded. He will be called upon to hear the testimony, and give a professional opinion deduced from all the facts & circumstances of the case. He may say, it seems to be so & so, from what I can learn.
>
> The lawyer will propose or suppose cases, if things were so & so, what would be your opinion? In this manner a shrewd lawyer will be likely to entrap the unwary. Of the medical witness be not slow to answer & exceedingly cautious, he will be pretty sure to bring confusion on himself & reflect discredit on the profession.
>
> With regard to the privilege & compensation of the medical witness, it is the same as with any other witness.
>
> With regard to the medical expert, [the] expert need not answer the subpoena or summon of the court unless he please [followed by a reference to the British jurist's opinion].
>
> Of the adequate remuneration of a medical expert, we need only say that if he is not compellable to appear in court, he has it in his power to make such arrangements with respect to his fee with the party who wishes his opinion, as he pleases.

Following Phelps's presentation, the VMS minutes record that "further discussion of the subject by different members of the society" took place and his report was accepted. But not everyone was satisfied and the secretary's last entry indicating that "Dr. Phelps was then requested to give a written report to the society" was crossed out.[793]

The contest between the medical experts during Howard's trial focused on the narrow opening at the cervix, or neck, where the uterus met at the top of Olive's vagina. Frost provided extensive testimony and told the jury that there was indeed a fetus present at the time and attributed the clear harm this part of her anatomy suffered to "violence in the use of instruments applied to the neck of the womb in the attempts to induce abortion." Dr. Selim Newell, of St. Johnsbury, followed Frost and agreed with his assessment that Olive's injuries were "due to mechanical violence" and that "he knew of no other satisfactory way of accounting for those appearances."

Newell also testified that while the use of instruments was acceptable to induce abortion in appropriate cases, it was "the uniform practice of physicians. . . to call in counsel [witnesses], that they may be shielded against the charge of criminal abortion."[794]

Howard's attorneys sought to counter the two doctors' testimony by introducing the opinions of three of their own. Phelps, who sat through all of the prosecution's case, testified first and described several other factors that could explain the appearance of injury. He listed disease, the use of mechanical devices to reach and remove "some unnatural growth" and manifestations of depression as alternative causes. He also related that he was not satisfied that Olive was even pregnant, or that a fetus had been removed, and that the appearance of those conditions could be attributed to other causes. Dr. Samuel Johnson Allen of White River Junction followed and provided the same opinion.[795] The third physician, Dr. Asa George of Calais, contributed little of importance other than levity when he struggled to explain Olive's condition. When asked by the prosecutor during cross-examination "what causes inflammation?," George became confused. "Inflammation sometimes results from mechanical injuries, and sometimes from chemical causes," he answered. When asked to explain what he meant by "chemical causes," he stated "by taking cold" and then assumed what a witness described as a "puzzled" look, "evidently anxious to have counsel help him out." The solicitous prosecutor recognized his embarrassment and suggested an answer for him. "You mean by this, Doctor, that the chemical properties of the air (yes, yes eagerly interposed the witness, evidently gratified with the proffered assistance) unites with the chemical properties of the lungs (yes, yes, again interposed the witness) and *form a chemical compound called cold* ?" "Yes, that is what I mean," George answered, earning a response from the prosecutor, "I am perfectly satisfied, Doctor. I think I now understand you." While neither the witness or attorney displayed other than a serious demeanor during the exchange, a newspaper recorded that "the court, jury and the crowded audience were convulsed with laughter."[796] When the evidence ended, Howard declined to testify on his own behalf.

Closing arguments lasted between three and five hours for each side as Ormsby led off for the prosecution followed by Hebard and Washburn for the defense. Washburn's performance was described as so "brilliant and powerful" that he was overcome and "attacked by spasms, which continued for several hours." State's Attorney Dewey provided the last word and made the government's rebuttal case speaking for four and one-half hours. A newspaper glowingly described his presentation and wrote that it was "one of exceeding rare ability" that "abounded in happy and adroit illustrations; invective which occasionally mounted to the sublimely terrific; and in pathetic passages which drew tears from the eyes of the jury and the whole vast audience." Judge Barrett's instructions to the jury describing the six counts for them to consider lasted for two and one-quarter hours to accomplish, "pronounced by nearly everyone who heard it as impartial, able, and comprehensive." After a long day, the jury received the case at 5:00 p.m. and returned its verdict the next morning. The vagaries of what happens during jury deliberations presented itself in its determination of Howard's guilt or innocence and turned on the decision of a single juror. Unwilling to convict him of the most serious charge of manslaughter as the other eleven wanted, the sole juryman brought the stalemate to an end when he agreed to convict on the lesser misdemeanor offense of attempting to procure an abortion and the others agreed. Following the verdict, Howard's attorneys said they would appeal and Judge Barrett reduced his bail from $5,000 to $1,500 that allowed his release. The next set of proceedings scheduled to take place in the Supreme Court in Montpelier would determine whether or not Howard served a possible sentence of not less than one or more than three years imprisonment in the state prison. Frustrated at the outcome, one newspaper simply hoped for "Something better next time." [797]

Howard's name stayed out of both the newspapers and court proceedings for the next several months as his appeal to the Supreme Court was delayed and Jane's estate lingered in the probate court. During that time, he continued to engage in his dapper ways and during the Orange County Agricultural Society Fair in late September he received a $4 award for "Best Pair Matched Horses."[798] Howard's day of reckoning finally came on November 19, 1859, when, despite his history of falsehoods and efforts to take advantage of others, he faced sentencing. The proceedings before the Supreme Court were succinctly described in the press:

> At the hearing of his case at Montpelier. . . Howard was not to be found at first, he having fled the state. The court would not go on with the hearing however, unless he should be present at the decision. Howard's counsel gave a pledge that he should be forthcoming. . . . On Saturday morning Howard drove into Montpelier with a team of great splendor (his usual style of equipage) and gave the hostler orders not to put up his horses, as he had a little business at the court house and should return in a few minutes. Upon arriving at the court house, he took a seat near the door; the presiding judge inquired of his counsel if [Howard] was present, and when answered in the affirmative, he ordered the sheriff to arrest him. Howard 'smelt a mice,' and started for the door, but the officers were too quick for him. The court then ordered the sheriff to bring him within the dock, where he received his sentence. It is said that he was very much overcome by his sentence, as was also his counsel. Howard had relied upon the assurance of his lawyer that he would be acquitted and had thus come right into the clutches of the law. The wicked are taken in their own craftiness.[799]

Another paper reported that the objections to the trial that Howard's attorneys filed were "overruled," as Chief Justice Redfield "sentenced him to two years hard labor in the State's Prison, and to pay a fine of one dollar and costs of prosecution." "Our hero," the account continued, "did not go back to the hotel for his team, but remained in the care of the jailer until Wednesday, when he was put in care of the sheriff and removed to the boarding house of Col. Harlow, the excellent superintendent of the State's

Prison, where we hope he will learn better manners."[800] The prison records from the time of his arrival reveal further that Howard, identified with a number and his crime as "1641 for producing abortion," entered into an inmate population absent of any others convicted for a similar offense.[801] A St. Albans newspaper took the opportunity to ridicule Bradford's *Telegraph* that had supported Howard so strongly before his trial and reported that it was publishing "The Life and Exploits" of the man who was reportedly "late surgeon in the British Army, and later physician and accoucheur to Queen Victoria, and now resident physician and surgeon at the Vermont State Prison."[802] In Orange County, people breathed a sigh of relief at Howard's removal from their midst, demonstrated by one correspondent who tired at the lack of enforcement present in an environment where so "many culprits go 'unwhipt of justice' every year, simply by a forfeiture of bonds." "Never within my recollection," he wrote,

> (and that extends over a period of nearly half a century) has it been so difficult to bring an offender to justice as in this case. Surrounded as he was by troops of friends who supported him with their money and their influence, and aided by ingenious counsel, who *almost* succeeded in "making the *worse* appear the *better* reason," it has been a task of no little magnitude for the young and able prosecuting officer [Charles Dewey] to bring him to the bar. . . . We of Orange County owe him our thanks for his independent and unbiased exertions to rid us of the incubus we have borne so long and which was making our region an offence to the nostrils of the people.[803]

Howard remained in custody for precisely two years and was released on November 19, 1861. On September 18, 1865, identified as a resident of West Fairlee, Vermont, he married Catherine Sumner.[804] In January 1869, he reported to police in New Haven, Connecticut that he was the victim of a bizarre theft of $22,500 in bonds and greenbacks from his person when he was jostled in the city's crowded railroad depot and it was cut from his clothing where it was sewed in and concealed. Despite such a significant loss, and in duplicating the flight of Dr. John McNab who fled New Hampshire authorities after killing Sarah Furber, Howard quickly departed for Vermont after telling police that his "family required his immediate attention."[805] His conduct seemed strange and a newspaper concluded that "the fact that he has offered no reward, and manifested no disposition to follow up his alleged loss, looks a little queer."[806] While newspapers throughout New England reported the spectacular circumstances, a jaundiced Vermont press, tired of his shenanigans, dismissed it as a hoax. "It was probably arranged by the Dr.," one wrote, "in order to get considerable advertising free. He enjoys notoriety, and he has had his full share of it, in one way or another."[807]

By 1870 Howard experienced such financial trouble that he executed mortgages in favor of other individuals to secure loans of many thousands of dollars. In June 1875, Catherine divorced him and resumed her maiden name, received custody of their daughter, Katherine, and was awarded alimony of $500 every six months. Predictably, Howard absconded and moved to Chicago where Vermont creditors, and Catherine, unsuccessfully pursued him in the courts.[808] In the next years, Howard engaged in a dizzying amount of yet more fraudulent conduct and continued to tell outrageous lies that he owned estates in England and Ireland that allowed him to duplicate the same kind of scheme he committed on unwitting Jane Waterman in 1855. Before marrying his third wife, Salome, in Geneva, Illinois in 1877, he promised to take care of her in exchange for her signing over her interests to property she owned in Chicago only to experience the same heartache that Jane did. The frauds continued as Howard convinced her to accompany him to Europe to track down his assets, only to be delayed in Washington, D. C. where he said he was ill and unable to continue but still pilfer yet more money from another unwary couple with sizeable assets. The trip overseas never took place and Howard appears to have died in Illinois sometime before 1884, where he was entangled in more litigation involving pursuing creditors, leaving Salome to face a tangled lawsuit brought against her by daughter Katherine that concerned land in Kansas.[809]

CONCLUSION

The example set by quacks such as William Howard did not abate with his departure from Vermont. In 1870 a disgusted VMS president lamented the continued presence of competing empiricists and their effects on the profession: "chicanery and quackery still exist and exert a benumbing influence in the pathway of every regular physician," and repeated the call for a united effort to oppose them.[810] "Strange as it may appear," he said, "still it is a notorious fact that there are medical men in our ranks who stand in direct antagonism to this desired reformation, men who advertise to cure almost every grade of incurable disease, who travel through the country with éclat and power, victimizing communities by wholesale; professing to cure cancer, tubercle, scrofula; set bones, cure impotence, cause the blind to see, the deaf to hear, the lame to walk." As a result, he ridiculed the state of affairs that pitted the public against those in the profession whose "mode of proceeding in the treatment of diseases is sometimes not only repulsive and vulgar, but so absolutely ridiculous that even the patients themselves who have submitted to it are ashamed to divulge the facts of the case; and regular physicians hesitate to criticize or expose their impositions knowing that the public would consider them actuated by selfish motives." The public relations nightmare the regulars faced to convince the public of their professionalism while the quacks offered their outrageous treatments at the same time only got worse as the Vermont legislature continued to ignore the clear harm taking place, to rein in the empiricists, or allow the educated ones to obtain licenses that would validate their scientific approaches in treating the inhabitants' health. As evidenced in the next decades, while modernity provided welcomed technological advances at first, it could not overcome the parochial views of many in positions of authority unwilling to upset tradition.

CHAPTER VIII

Consequences

"Where, then, is the most eligible and desirable place to locate our State House? Where will it best accommodate the farm we are all occupying?" [811]

REPRESENTATIVE RODNEY V. MARSH OF BRANDON, FEBRUARY 25, 1857

Phoenix Rising

Following the adjournment of the Vermont legislature in 1859, the editor of Montpelier's *Vermont Watchman and State Journal* looked back with relief on its latest session and characterized it as "an exceedingly agreeable one."[812] The solons accomplished an admirable amount of work that year, he wrote, conducted in an atmosphere absent of the "deeply exciting questions of public interest" that consumed its attention in the recent the past, specifically "the railroad and state-house question." The 1850s in Vermont posed difficult challenges and, while two years had passed since the legislature's memorable debates in 1857, they continued to resonate throughout the state and were not easily forgotten. While the relocation and rebuilding of the capital were the stated reasons for their assembling and talking for nine days, it could not disguise the ill-feeling and distrust among them that dated back a decade. The principle reasons for this most recent discord concerned not just the impact of the railroad technology, but the ongoing national debate over slavery, the rise of alternative political parties (Liberty and Free-Soil) and local efforts to institute prohibition that emboldened the temperance movement to the consternation of the drinkers. By 1850, nine of the past twelve gubernatorial elections could not muster sufficient votes to declare a winner that required the legislature to ultimately decide. Vermont historian Sam Hand recounts that "By 1853 political fragmentation paralyzed Vermont government" to such an extent dozens of ballots were required by legislators to fill various state offices and chose representatives to the national government.[813] Whigs gathered in Montpelier in July 1854 to resolve their differences and recast themselves so successfully as the Republican Party that it remained the dominate political influence for over a century. By the time of the Capitol fire in 1857, democrats unable to overcome internal strife accounted for only twenty to thirty percent of the vote, characterized by Hand as "a hopeless minority."[814]

Consequences

Much of the continued division and distrust in 1857 can be attributed to the persistent effects of Vermont's geography. Repeatedly, the legislators' debates to relocate and rebuild their capital referenced the interests of those that came from the east and west sides of the Green Mountains that fostered the historical divides among them. To minimize that possibility, they adhered to a practice that dated back to the state's founding as holders of high office rotated from each side of the spiny north-south divide every two years; a phenomenon Hand termed "The Mountain Rule," that bore no formal name in 1857.[815] Their political differences, real and imagined, had the prospect of improving their lot if they could join together in the common interest to resolve the problems caused by the fire in this "predominately agricultural economy."[816] From among the 258 representatives and senators that came from both sides of the mountains and attended the debates, forty-seven of them stood up to debate and assert a variety of issues, many of them repeatedly. Their arguments were grounded on the comfort that tradition and symbolism provided to them, impacted practically by modern technology delivered by the railroad and telegraph. Committees met outside of the formal proceedings to consider these issues and report back their findings, but none of their discussions were recorded. The public watched closely for any indication of how they would resolve the challenges, but without luck. As one newspaper reported, "The outside pressure on the Legislature is the strongest ever put forth and it renders all attempt at a prophecy as to their final decision utterly nugatory."[817]

When in the presence of large audiences, lawmakers argued over the prospect of breaking with tradition because their repeated meetings in Montpelier for half a century marked it as an "ancient landmark," one set in a central mountain location they cherished and that formed their collective identity. What "moral obligation" did they owe to Montpelier, some asked, to remain in that town because of prior concessions it made to accommodate past Capitols and the meetings of representatives for so long? One representative argued that other states facing the prospect of moving their capitals to a central location had considered "the rights of all – of the inhabitants of the humble agricultural towns as well as the proud 'centers of wealth and civilization'" and they must do likewise.[818] Scenery and beauty also played important roles as some looked admiringly at the rugged landscape to support their positions and others towards the views offered from Burlington's high bluff overlooking Lake Champlain into the Adirondack Mountains. Did it make sense to relocate their capital to that community when it already possessed an embarrassment of riches with the state university, customs house, and marine hospital, as well as a higher cost of living? How healthy was the environment in Burlington and Montpelier where the fog made some uncomfortable and others wanted to punish it for tolerating intemperate behavior? Was Burlington too "Yorkish" because its economic interests looked westward into that state or its location militarily indefensible because it might be subject to invasion from the north, others asked? Were those living on the east side of the mountains too harsh against those on the west side that they believed possessed "less of the New England feeling" and too much of the New York? Should they start anew elsewhere, such as Rutland, and not rebuild in Montpelier where the destroyed Capitol building was set in a such a damp environment it made legislators physically uncomfortable, derided as "not a house on a mountain, but a house under a hill"?

The railroad and its technology presented the legislators with a new set of considerations that had to be included in their debates. They recognized that past inconveniences of time and distance in getting from one place to another no longer existed because of the "lightning speed" it could travel at thirty to forty miles an hour. Arguments in favor of a central location made little sense because railroad construction was happening so quickly that anyone could travel almost anywhere in the state with ease. Rutland's explosive growth because of the railroad, availability of rich mineral resources in worldwide demand, and prospects for further development, now called the "Young America of Vermont," marked it as an attractive alternative to either Montpelier or Burlington.[819] Rutland also afforded stronger ties to the past than any other town because of its connections to those who led and fought in the Revolutionary War. "Shame!," a legislator from nearby Hubbardton exclaimed, "Shame! on those who would forget that the men, who made the New Hampshire Grants a State, were men of western Vermont." How could anyone forget their sacrifices, he demanded, still evident by "the bones of those who fell there, fighting for their country's liberties. . . occasionally found in the soil which they wet with their own life blood." To slander those from the west side and allege they were "New Yorkers in interest and feelings," he said, was anathema ("palsied be the tongue") and only stirred up "strife and sectional jealousy!"[820]

Allegations of "corrupt motive" among the representatives and of their bribery prompted repeated references to the abhorred presence of "*sectional prejudice*" that alarmingly issued from their lips.[821] One member observed that "every one knows that there were influences about a legislative body which no discreet father would wish to have his sons exposed to" that included those individuals who did not act "manfully."[822] The "junto at Burlington," where the "aristocracy that elevates itself head and shoulders above the common people" resided, was unhesitatingly disparaged.[823] They also raised the existence of a lobbyist "third house" as one representative called for an investigation into efforts to buy votes with gold in favor of Burlington.[824] The strong economic interests presented by Burlington's close proximity to New York and the benefits offered by the railroad continued to pose a problem. One newspaper alleged that "near connections and personal interests" allowed an "untold amount of gold" to flow into the state provided "by New York State and City capitalists who are anxious that the Capitol of Vermont. . . be in more direct communications with them." If permitted, whatever "influence Vermont has in wealth or population [will] go to New York, instead of to the commercial mart, and success of our own flourishing and intelligent New England."[825] Arguments that the federal customs house in Burlington meant that the capital should relocate there were met with dismay. "The customs house!!," one representative exclaimed, "the avenue through which for forty years the dominant national parties have made all their dirty approaches to the legislature of Vermont. We do not wish or need to be near it."[826] Calling the customs officers "spiders," he equated the legislators as flies sitting in Montpelier in a better position there to see their coming than if they moved into their nest in Burlington. "Keep the operations of the two governments separate," he said, "and do not invite the dispensers of patronage of one to become the chronic and perpetual and established lobbyers of the other."

Patronage and the specter of sectionalism infused other concerns of legislators when raw allegations of "Dastard Treachery" appeared in the press, launched against attorney David Allen Smalley of Brattleboro, described as the leader of "the small squad of slave democrats."[827] Smalley was only recently appointed on February 3, 1857 as the state's sole federal district court judge to replace deceased Whig-Republican Samuel Prentiss who passed away only days after the statehouse fire. Other legislators feared that removing the capital from Montpelier would upset the overall peace that that location allowed and result in "such a war as the State never witnessed before" when one of them invoked the words of a Napoleonic War veteran in an extremist manner promising "a 'war to the knife, and the knife to the hilt.'"[828] The debates veered far from the accord that the attendees hoped to achieve in the early days of their meeting and ranged from hopes of their collectively pulling together for "the farm we are all occupying" to outright division of east versus west, the corrupt interests of aristocrats, and allegations of gold exchanged for votes.

The debates ended on February 26, 1857 with voting in both houses, preceded by one representative reminding others of their traditions and to "remember the wise decision of our fathers, who, in the spirit of compromise and of peace, located our capital in the center of the State, and in a County bearing the sacred name of WASHINGTON."[829] Their balloting in the House recorded that Montpelier (116 in favor) should remain the capital, followed by Burlington (67), Rutland (35), Bellows Falls (8), Middlebury (1), and Northfield (1).[830] In the Senate, a different result occurred when Burlington received the most votes (15), followed by Montpelier (13) and Rutland (1), but with the House numbers so heavily in favor of Montpelier it agreed to concede to its decision.[831] Throughout the debates the legislators entertained proposals from several towns agreeing to fund the Capitol building construction without cost to the state if they were chosen. Montpelier did so on prior occasions and, while an attractive way to avoid taxing the state's entire population, this most recent demand required officials to reconsider that process. Allegations that the ultimate decision was being degraded and compared to an auction where the highest bidder won or that towns sought to curry favor for their promises frequently arose in the debates forcing some to consider that this obligation was owed by the population at large. However, it became more difficult when a Senate committee reported on the availability of funds that "the State have no means in the Treasury [to rebuild] and a tax must therefore be levied or the State must borrow money."[832] As they sought to resolve the problem, one member, who was also a judge, offered his opinion concerning a requirement that the winning community post a bond to assure their performance. His suggestion ignited a fierce response from another representative who disparaged him directly with the notion that a member of the judiciary "had condescended. . . to come down from the bench and mix with us on this troublesome question." Dismissing any notion that the judiciary could interfere with the legislative process, he angrily, and facetiously, stated that "'Old fogies' may complain that it is dangerous and corrupting. . . and an infringement upon the spirit of the Constitution, but who of us care a fig for their antiquated notions."[833]

As their differences continued to degrade the atmosphere, the legislators understood the need to make a rapid decision on the construction of their iconic structure that differed significantly from the way past Capitols had been financed. Fearful that it would not be rebuilt and harm their economic interests, Montpelier residents pledged over $94,000 in individual amounts of between ten to four thousand dollars.[834] It was not enough to cover the entire cost and the state agreed to assume the balance of over $61,000; an obligation that continued into 1860 when it was required it to take out additional loans.[835] The new financing arrangement was not entered into without regret as Governor Hiland Hall recalled that, until this recent crisis, frugal state policy from the time of its "first organization [was] against the creation of a permanent state debt."[836] More than two years passed before the solons could meet once again in their new statehouse on October 13, 1859 (just weeks before abortion-murderer William Howard was sentenced in a nearby courtroom) and heard words of greeting from their newly elected speaker, George F. Edmunds, a strong proponent of Burlington during the debates. After proudly exclaiming that the "our Capitol has been restored to us in more than its former magnificence," he graciously called on the members to put aside their differences and to work in "the noble spirit of the [state's] motto. . . 'Freedom' of opinion, while we cultivate 'Unity' in action."[837]

Third Capitol building, 1876. Vermont Historical Society.

CONSEQUENCES

CONTINUED VICTIMIZATION OF THE VULNERABLE

Expressing happiness at the reconstruction and a wish to set aside their differences to purse the future in "Freedom and Unity" does not mean that the impact of the decisions they made, and their dereliction on those not made, can escape further inquiry. Among the several points that separated the solons' differences during the debates, the juxtaposition of their consensus to locate and rebuild the Capitol in Montpelier as they simultaneously dismissed any notion that Vermonter's health was threatened is most notable. It is not the spurious complaint of the presence of that town's fog, or the dampness of the building's location, affecting their health that is questionable. Instead, it is the repeated, emphasized assertions by government officials, legislators and newspapers of the period that no reason prompted deep inquiry into the issue because, in their myopic view, there was no state in the Union healthier than Vermont and that claims by physicians to the contrary were ridiculous, that presents such a remarkable, untrue representation. Beyond any bias or specific intention to misrepresent the situation as part of a public relations ploy to spur investments from afar, their misplaced, subjective impressions were, in fact, markedly contrary to the objective facts that medical professionals provided, and their own experiences. Whereas other states saw the harm that warring members of the medical profession, drugs and abortions posed to their populations and took action, Vermont legislators withheld official recognition of those unsavory aspects of their society and failed/refused to institute vigorous enforcement measures, or needed intervention, that allowed the problem to escalate and inflict continued harm on the population. The initial, favorable effects of modernity on the transportation of people and goods via the new railroad technology have been well told, but those of an unfavorable nature that adapted and continued into the future after its arrival and adversely affected the health of the state's vulnerable females inflicted by abortions have not. At a time when women continued to face the prospect of embarrassing bastardy proceedings that exposed their private lives to a curious public, the situation in Vermont in mid-century asks further, if the men suffered in the same mental and physical fashion as they did, would reforms have been so delayed?

If any members of the legislature walked the short distance from where they met in 1857 to Col. Fred E. Smith's drug store at the corner of State and Main streets they could find a variety of concoctions purportedly able to treat consumption and allow women to obtain abortions. Smith recently purchased the business in 1853 from Dr. Charles Clark, a respected, conscientious physician who served the community well, but who chose to abandon it because of "his constant uneasiness lest some fatal mistake might be made in compounding prescriptions."[838] Smith had no such fears and soon became the "General Agent for the State of Vermont" until the war broke out supplying all other drug stores with strong medications able to cause abortions that were becoming increasing available. He advertised them for sale in many newspapers that included the local *Vermont Watchman and State Journal* with their outlandish claims, ones located near columns that described the legislators' proclamations of the state's great health. Most notably, they concerned the persistently present Sir James Clarke's Celebrated Female Pills, Dr. Duponco's French Periodical Golden Pills and Bach's American Compound.[839] The efficacy of these drugs to cause abortions was uncertain as conflicted physicians related on various occasions that they thought them both able to produce the desired result and ineffective. Regardless of the actual result, women voraciously consumed them in the belief that they did and, when they did not deliver on their promises, continued to submit their bodies to the quacks and professionals willing to break the law in pursuit of gain.

Evolving modernity permitted people such as William H. M. Howard to inflict his egregious harm on Vermont's young women and unborn at a time when many naive people simply acceded to his outlandish claims and law enforcement was unprepared to fully respond. While officials already knew that abortions were a widespread practice that other New England states vigorously tried to halt, it was only after the explosive, embarrassing news of Howard's arrest for killing two women that authorities in Washington, Caledonia and Orleans counties sprang into action. Their responses repeated past experiences when public safety was in issue, conducted in a reactive manner when realistic assessments of the times called for proactive measures. Local abortionists plying their barbarous trade suddenly became of such interest that those counties' state's attorneys and sheriffs began their own investigations. While records of their efforts are not as complete as those that concerned Howard, the ones that exist reveal the presence of other trained, and untrained, individuals preying on young women in remote locations where they also had little fear of being caught. Geography played a role that allowed them to exploit their situation and they did it fully. Reports of similar offenses taking place outside of these four northeastern counties elsewhere in Vermont appear absent. However, with the examples of those that were caught, together with the many taking place in New Hampshire, Massachusetts and in nearby Troy, New York (where a professional female abortionist killed her latest victim and was discovered with "several other girls" she had performed the procedure on), the practice was undeniably just as prevalent throughout the rest of the state.[840]

Two days after Howard's release following his first arrest in Bradford, on February 18, 1858 another abortionist was arrested thirty-five miles away in Montpelier. "Moses Bass, of Marshfield, a colored man," a newspaper reported, appeared before a judge charged with "procuring an abortion" and "committing adultery with Betsey Ann Young, a white woman."[841] During his arraignment, twenty-eight year old Washington County State's Attorney Charles H. Joyce presented the court with "a very novel and yet conclusive piece of evidence" that demonstrated Bass's complicity, "the result of the abortion." As Howard had done in his own practice, Bass maintained possession of his handiwork, described by the attending press as "nicely preserved in a large glass jar in alcohol" that made it clear to all, "at a single glance," the child encased within was in "every feature and lineament plainly *African*." Unlike Howard facing two counts of manslaughter and released with the assistance of friends, Bass remained in jail, ordered held on a $500 bail. Thankful of Bass's arrest and in apparent reference to what just occurred with Howard in Orange County, the newspaper wrote further that "We are glad to see that the State's Attorney and Deputy Sheriffs are making themselves useful by bringing offenders like these to justice. They certainly evince a commendable zeal, and prove conclusively the old adage that we want old men for counsel, but young men for war."

In neighboring Caledonia County, there was "considerable excitement" when State's Attorney Oliver T. Brown began his own investigation into the circumstances surrounding an abortion performed a year earlier on twenty-year-old Abigail H. Davidson of Peacham.[842] Her story provides a telling example of the kinds of challenges that poor, rural women experienced when faced with ending a pregnancy despite the advantages that modernity allowed. Evidence that she underwent the procedure was presented to a grand jury in St. Johnsbury over several days in early June 1858.[843] It included information that involved a Cabot physician identified only as "Dr. Prevost" who conducted the abortion, but whose full name was never firmly established. Additional evidence indicated that a "Dr. George" was also involved which may have been a reference to Dr. Asa George, the befuddled witness from Calais whose testimony about inflammation during Howard's trial invoked much mirth in the courtroom audience. Extant notes that Brown appears to have prepared further reveals that Abigail's mother, bearing the same name, had discussed with her daughter "getting the Doctor X from Barnet" for assistance, but that "I declined." Whether or not the two women referred to Sarah Furber's killer, the notorious Dr. John McNab from that town, is not known, but the repeated references to abortion practitioners living there and in Cabot, Calais, and Marshfield in the Bass case, all communities close to one another and immediately north of Howard in Bradford, reveals the ready presence of individuals in the northeast part of the state willing to assist women in trouble.

The investigation into young Abigail's difficult abortion and the travails she experienced appears to have caused such great concern to those involved that she abruptly left the area. She was last seen on Saturday, April 10, 1858 when, Brown recorded, George W. Martin "carried her off... to Barnet Depot" to board a train thereby making her unavailable as a witness. Despite her absence, in addition to her mother, the grand jury also heard from her brother Oliver H. Davidson, her unnamed father and his employer, Henry Walker, to whom he confided that the procedure was performed at his house. Brown's notes describe Abigail's predicament after she became pregnant by John B. Hand around the time that the Vermont legislature met to debate rebuilding the destroyed Capitol in early 1857. Hand had much to lose if his involvement with her became known because he was Peacham's elected justice of the peace and a repeatedly appearing judge of horses presented at the Annual Fair of the People's Agricultural Society of Caledonia County. Did his respected public role cause the delay in investigating Abigail's abortion, suddenly peeled away by the revelations of William Howard's barbarity? Abigail lived apart from her parents and, on April 4, 1857, a concerned friend of Hand's, George Martin, brought Abigail to her parent's home. Martin admitted to them that "he had taken the job to get Hand out of [the problem]" and, together with another friend, Willard F. Brown, the two came to the Davidson house on many occasions during the next month to attend to Abigail's needs. They were clearly panicked about her pregnancy and went to great trouble to keep others from knowing about her growing condition. Martin told Abigail's father when they first arrived that "she was in trouble... she was in a family way & he wanted I should take her." Martin explained that it was necessary for him to agree to do so because "he could not get a place for her, said he had been to several places & could not get her in & if we would take her he would pay the bills." Despite their reluctance, Abigail's parents relented and allowed her to remain until the abortion took place.

In the interim, Martin and Brown sought a physician to perform the procedure. Hand arrived at one point and admitted to Abigail's mother that he was responsible for her condition, but cautioned her to "not betray anybody this side of Heaven or Hell," to hold on to the secret and that she "must carry my head as high as ever." At first, her parents did not want the procedure to take place in their home and suggested that Abigail be taken to a cedar swamp in Cabot to meet with the doctor. Brown was able to find one willing to work under these conditions, identified as the mysterious Dr. Prevost, who made two trips to the swamp to meet Abigail. That effort seems to have been unsuccessful, but they finally met at her parents' home on May 10 when she was between four and five months pregnant.

Members of the Davidson family provided detailed information about what took place sometime around ten or eleven o'clock on a moonless night. Despite their close proximity to Prevost during his one-half hour stay at the home, the most anyone could recall to identify him was his last name, that he came from Cabot Branch, and arrived riding a large bay horse while carrying a short switch. Much secrecy surrounded his entry into the house as he sought to keep his identity hidden. A single lamp burned in the kitchen and, when Abigail's mother escorted him to her daughter's second-floor room, she extinguished the one she carried. Abigail's father, her brother and Brown remained in the kitchen while her mother stood outside the room to hear what was happening. When her daughter "made some ado" and called out, she entered the darkened room to find her lying on the bed with her legs parted and hanging over the foot board with Prevost sitting in a chair preparing to do his work. Abigail's mother mentioned to Prevost about how dark it was, but, unworried, he told her that "it would do no hurt" in allowing him to accomplish his work.

State's Attorney Brown's notes relate further that after her mother entered the room, she positioned herself on the bed to support Abigail's upper body with her "head & shoulders. . . on my stomach." She knew that Prevost had used "an instrument" of some kind during the procedure, but said she "was not aware how the Doct[or] was operating [because] it was so dark. I could not see him." "Nothing was administered to Abigail," she recalled and it took only five minutes for Prevost to perform his work that caused "no twitch or shudder" to his patient who reported that "it did not hurt." Any comparison between his deft and skillful performance with the hacking that William Howard inflicted on his victims just thirty miles away cannot be demonstrated any more clearly. After Prevost left, her mother lit a lamp and observed that "there was water on the floor." Abigail remained on the bed for a time and eventually went into labor at two o'clock the next afternoon that lasted until four a.m. the following morning, when "she was delivered of a dead child." Her brother testified that he took it "out back of the barn" and buried it.

After hearing the testimony from various witnesses, on June 7, 1858, the grand jury returned a twelve-count indictment that charged Hand, Brown and Martin with misdemeanor offenses in procuring Abigail's abortion. It also charged them with engaging in a conspiracy with "a certain evil disposed person whose name. . . is unknown" and who used "a certain instrument made of silver or other metal, the name of which instrument. . . is unknown" by "forcing, thrusting and inserting the said instrument into the private parts" of Abigail causing her "to miscarry and abort." As a result, "said child was killed and its life destroyed and taken away in its mother's womb" to "the great evil example of all others." After the indictment was filed there no other documentation that describes what followed and it appears that all of the defendants, and the evasive Dr. Prevost, avoided accounting for their actions in either the public press or court proceedings.

Months later, Orleans County officials began to investigate the suspicious circumstances surrounding the death of Miss Leafy Drown of Brownington. She died in November 1858 after arriving at her parent's home in September in a "sick" condition. When authorities learned that "some person or persons" had conducted an abortion on her, that reportedly "served the double purpose of killing mother and child," they had her body exhumed. An examination conclusively established that while "an abortion was proven" and "who the guilty ones were," insufficient evidence existed "to warrant a State prosecution." Leafy's parents apparently had information able to "throw light upon the authors of this great crime," a newspaper reported, but were prevented ("hermetically sealed") by the legal process from revealing anything outside of the proceedings.[844]

As physicians were summoned to examine and harvest evidence of crimes from the disinterred bodies of women who suffered their silent deaths and the consequences of abortion on the unborn became more obvious, there was perceptible movement within Vermont's medical community to study more closely their wellbeing during pregnancy. Minutes of the Addison County Medical Society in 1856 reveal a robust discussion among doctors concerning the challenges they faced with several of their "enceinte" patients. They included treating one woman "who did not dream" she was pregnant, another who experienced a spontaneous abortion while sitting in a chair, and others who received the potent labor-inducing ergot to rapidly abort their fetuses ("in an hour was delivered of a dead child") they administered to protect their lives. Although not pregnant, Sophronia Croix suffered from such dire urinary problems that over "a period of 21 years she had consumed morphine at the rate of $22 per annum;" the equivalent of four pounds of the drug each year.[845] Minutes of the VMS relate that its members first considered women's reproductive needs in 1856 when they engaged in a discussion on midwifery. Four years passed before they returned to the subject in 1860 when "Dr. Perkins made some remarks on the subject of female diseases" and displayed "a variety of pessaries [to treat vaginal prolapses] & explained their use & method of adaption."[846] Women's needs were addressed again later that year concerning the "Relation of diseases of the sexual organs in females to Insanity."[847]

Perhaps delayed because of the demands of the Civil War, in 1864 the Society revisited women's complaints when they engaged in a lengthy discussion that revealed their deep division concerning the existence of uterine disease. While some believed it was a common complaint that required injecting treatments into the uterus, another disagreed and said he thought those problems were psychological. As the minutes describe, the speaker was "incredulous about this complaint being so very common." He did "not believe that physicians really inject substances into the body of the uterus; and furthermore, if they should succeed in accomplishing that purpose that it would be – to say the least – exceedingly hazardous." He believed their conduct was in response to "a sort of morbid sentiment among women at this day which enables the [doctor] to get the whole catalogue of symptoms which point in the direction of this form of disease [because] they can't find anything else to account for their troubles and therefore it must necessarily be uterine trouble of some form." When presented with their complaints, he said "I always back out when they begin to talk uterine disease to me."[848] In opposition, another doctor related his own opinion, "that this is not an uncommon disease and, instead of avoiding it, the true physician should examine patiently and candidly and treat it with conscientious common sense." Another attempted to bridge the various viewpoints and offered that he thought "many physicians have not had the necessary training and experience to form correct opinions" because "the opportunities for the study of this specialty are limited in a country practice." He also noted with concern the aggressiveness of some doctors who treated hernias because "some of the younger members of the Society were growing most too ambitious for operating" and blamed the increasing use of opium that allowed them to do so. Their efforts to resolve the differences had little effect on others among them who professed to be regular doctors, but also preyed upon the vulnerabilities of unsuspecting women. "It is a notorious fact," the VMS president stated in 1870, "that Physicians, claiming to be and passing for intelligent men, make a practice of daily [repositioning] a retroverted uterus and assuring the patient that this is her only hope of recovery from her tiresome complaint, and encouraging all his female patients in the belief that nine-tenths of all the diseases to which their flesh is heir, are caused by that little, innocent, essential but much abused organ, the uterus."[849]

Despite their differences, the concerns of the educated members of the medical community reveals the effects of modernity forcing them to rethink and adapt to changing theories that advanced the wellbeing of women with whom they had such intense relationships. Their familiarity was particularly noted by one University of Vermont professor in 1856 who told graduating medical students that "The attachment of a woman to her physician – I speak of woman because it is with her we have most frequent dealing in the sickroom – her attachment to her physician is one of the strongest she knows."[850] That connection grew even stronger in the next decade as women assumed positions away from the household that otherwise required their presence for childrearing responsibilities. Vermont physician Dr. Lucius Butler noted the challenges that women faced in negotiating these conflicting demands made on them in an address before the VMS in 1867. "She must occupy the pulpit, the forum, the rostrum, the stump," he listed, as well "She must answer the demands of sociability, by visiting, travel, social parties, the dancing hall, the street, the places of public amusement, the whirl of fashion." However, he warned, these demands "are inconsistent with the condition of pregnancy" and that, as a result, "One or the other must give place."[851] And when their health suffered in consequence, Vermont women turned to their trusted physicians.

CONSEQUENCES

By 1865, the widespread practice of criminal abortion was unquestionably present in Vermont. Whereas Massachusetts, New Hampshire and New York acknowledged the phenomenon in their own jurisdictions years earlier, it was finally made unequivocally clear to the public that year when Woodstock's Dr. William McCollom provided a telling exposé before the VMS.[852] Vermont's registration report for 1862 briefly acknowledged its practice in the state when it referred to the experiences of Massachusetts doctors who utilized it and condemned it as harmful to the health of both fetus and mother, but said little more. However, McCollom went further and confronted the Society's members with the fact that "There is every reason to believe that the crime is frequent" and that "applications are continually made to apothecaries as well as physicians, for drugs for this purpose." "We can hardly realize the great and alarming prevalence" of it, he emphasized, and specifically identified the kinds of women involved: "It is practiced to a great extent by the married, and the married of all classes, who look upon the rearing of children as a heavy burden, full of trouble and care, and to be avoided." He also decried that "accidental conception is assaulted with a frequency and moral indifference to the crime that is perfectly astounding." McCollom then noted the marked difference in birth rates between native Vermonters and immigrants and concluded that "Our own population seem to have a greater aversion to the rearing of families than those of a foreign origin – and every physician must notice how much more prolific are the French, the Irish and the Germans." The effects that the large numbers of criminal abortions had in Vermont, also called "modern improvements," was so noticeable that even if emigrants leaving the state were factored in, it was clear that the practice contributed to the stagnant population level.[853] In 1867, the VMS revisited McCollom's statements and again acknowledged "the alarming prevalence of the crime" and "its dangerous consequences and effect on population."[854] Each of their conclusions are consistent with the findings of modern-day investigators who have determined that between 1840 and the 1870s the United States experienced a significant increase in instances of abortion.[855]

McCollom's jarring statements constituted a remarkable revelation to many and the editor of Brandon's *Vermont Record* challenged his readers to seriously consider them because they came from someone with direct knowledge of what was taking place. McCollom "disclosed facts which none but a physician could know," he wrote, "in regard to the prevalence of that crime, and placed in a clear light its exceeding wickedness." He then posed a challenge that confronted the shocking family planning practices that snuffed out the lives of newborns and presented what appears to be the only direct admission in the state's mid-century historiography that murder was a part of it. "A thoughtful hearer," he alleged, "could hardly refrain from asking the question, is not infanticide, as practiced by the people of India and China, ignorant as they are of the divine law, a less atrocious sin and punishable less severely by a just God, than infanticide as practiced in a great many of the intelligent, enlightened, and even professedly Christian families of Vermont?"[856] Years later, McCollom returned to the persistent practice of criminal abortions and recalled an earlier time. "I attended a woman," he wrote, "the wife of an attorney-at-law, seven months or more advanced in pregnancy, the child stillborn; the brain had been punctured through the eye from some instrument. . . I bluntly charged the mother with murder in the presence of her husband and friends, pointing out the evidence of it, and there was no denial." He reasonably observed in the same way he did in 1865 that "It is very easy to speak upon this shocking criminality practiced by professed Protestant Christian men and women, as well as by the ungodly, and to moralize upon the destructive influence, especially upon woman, but it is difficult to solve the question when we ask, What is the remedy? How can it be checked?"[857]

McCollom's warnings and the protestations of newspaper editors notwithstanding, in 1867 Butler reported again to the VMS that women continued to seek out abortions. "These applications are not only numerous," he said, "but fearfully increasing in number. Almost every physician is importuned to engage in the nefarious business," called upon "in many cases [by] intelligent, high-minded women." "They come in such form and with such imploring importunity," he lamented, "that it is difficult to resist. The fees are large, and no credit is given or required. If the physician has moral or religious or legal scruples in regard to the matter, and attempts to reason or argue with the applicant, to dissuade her from the act, she will reply. . . 'I don't want to hear any preaching, I am determined to have no more children. I want this operation performed, and if you will not do it, I will try someone else; and if I can't get it done in this town I'll travel west till I find some one that will do it.'" Regardless of their patients' clamoring demands, Butler admonished Vermont's doctors to resist them because of the harm that abortion inflicted, "We know that a large number of cases prove fatal, and that the lives of the remainder are sooner or later rendered miserable."[858]

Butler also looked beyond the physical impact that abortion had on women's bodies and argued that it was "detrimental to society, to the peace and happiness of domestic life, and to the moral well-being of all concerned in it."[859] The challenge to the medical profession was great as Butler acknowledged just how strongly Vermonters depended on abortion: "The current of public opinion among the middle and lower classes has been so strongly setting in its favor for years past, that it has become fashionable for married people to have no children, or to have but one or two; fashionable to escape the joys and duties of maternity; fashionable to use means, internal and local, to avoid the cares of an increasing family. Like other fashions, this has become strong and general." Abortion was so prevalent that physicians referred to it as a "habit" that many women engaged in. Members of the clergy also took up the refrain as the widely read author and respected Pittsfield, Massachusetts congregational minister

Rev. John Todd, originally from Rutland, published an important article in 1867 on abortion, captioned "Fashionable Murder."[860] Todd appreciated how unusual his public statements were and their potential impact on female readers, but asked them to remember three things: "first, that the practice is fearfully common; second, that probably they are every week associating with those who are guilty of the practice; and third, that seventy-five per cent of all the abortions produced are caused and effected by females." He blamed women's failure to appreciate the immorality of their actions when they terminated the life of a living fetus in pursuit of a "fashionable" practice that occurred more frequently among members of the Protestant religion than the Catholic. They could not refute how widespread it was, he said, because "women in all classes of society, married and unmarried, rich and poor, otherwise good, bad or indifferent" sought out physicians to perform the operation and condemned their "boasting and vanity, to tell the number of times they and their friends have been guilty of the deed." Meanwhile, the Vermont public learned that "Mrs. Polly Pendolph, of Sandgate. . . died very suddenly the other day, from the effect of drugs, taken to produce abortion; so the doctors say" and that in a contested bastardy case, Ella Sterling's attorneys fought the introduction of evidence concerning her promiscuity and use of drugs to abort.[861]

Physician Butler and Minister Todd also lamented the lack of oversight of newspapers, dependent on revenue from the outlandish advertising they published and advanced unconvincing arguments that they bore no responsibility to monitor the content their customers chose to include. "The press is an engine of great power," Butler wrote, "for good or evil in the land, and those who control it ought to be held to a strict accountability for the influence they exert in [the] community through its columns." The time was ripe for further action and the VMS created a three-man committee to lobby the legislature to strengthen the existing 1846 abortion law and to criminalize the advertising, as Massachusetts had done decades earlier, of bogus products and services that allowed it to take place. The Connecticut River Medical Society also submitted its own resolutions to the state senate that condemned criminal abortions.[862] Their efforts succeeded and in November 1867 the law was changed to penalize attempts by others to abort not only any woman actually pregnant, but also those "supposed by such a person to be pregnant;" women remained immune to prosecution for their involvement. The law also made it illegal to advertise any product or service "for the purpose of causing or procuring the miscarriage of any pregnant woman," punishable by a sentence of between three and ten years imprisonment.[863] The VMS remained vigilant thereafter and appointed physicians from every county to monitor the state's newspapers "for the purpose of bringing offenses against the law, so far as advertisements in the local papers are concerned, to the notice of the proper authorities (unless the advertisements are voluntarily suppressed)."[864] Their efforts gained attention and in 1869 one paper distinguished itself from others claiming it was THE BEST ADVERTISING MEDIUM IN THE STATE because it refused to publish ads pertaining to, among several concerns, "Female Pills [and] Professional Abortionists."[865] Despite the VMS's good intentions, it was forced to admit that some of its members continued to engage in the practice of criminal abortions relating it was "well known" that it "is being carried on to an alarming extent, and we fear that some members of the *regular* profession are quite too familiar" with it.[866]

Undissuaded, the Society turned to address the pressing problem that increased substance abuse posed and in 1868 proposed changes to the liquor prohibition law to diminish Vermonter's huge consumption of alcohol that totaled $786,065 the preceding year, a sum described by Butler as "larger than our State debt." The law failed so badly, he related, that "There is scarcely a hotel in the state in which liquors are not sold either secretly or openly. They are sold in every drug stop. They are sold and drank in the highways and byways; at home and abroad; in the public place and behind the door; by the rich and by the poor; by men in high stations and low stations; in public life and private live; in office and out of office."[867] The Society also examined the effects that opium imposed on the population and appointed the intrepid Dr. Carleton Pennington Frost to examine the situation, one he alarmingly described in 1870 in the state's first account of substance abuse entitled "Opium: Its Uses and Abuses."[868] Despite his warnings, the problem quietly flourished in the next decades before it exploded into public view as an epidemic at the turn of the century.[869]

The VMS received timely assistance in its efforts when the Vermont Pharmaceutical Association (VPA) formed in 1870 "for the benefit and improvement of the profession and protection to the public."[870] The pharmacy trade experienced a radical change when the railroad arrived that provided it with immediate access to markets and practices outside of the state. Business transitioned overnight from rough country stores that provided raw materials from filthy back rooms to the public and doctors who processed them to sell to their patients into more sophisticated, pleasing surroundings. The most notable changes included the installation of marble floors and counters that displayed glistening glass jars containing a variety of colored substances. Druggists also sought to duplicate the successes of those businesses in metropolitan centers by imposing on themselves educational requirements to keep abreast of the most modern practices. They necessarily became closely associated with the medical profession as the two trades wrestled with their respective responsibilities to each other and to the public. As the physicians sought to improve themselves as a body, the pharmacists did likewise and sought to assure the public of the quality of the drugs they sold. Vermont experienced a rapid change at the time, acknowledged by VPA President Frederick Dutcher, of St. Albans, in 1871. Speaking before his membership, he recalled how "the remedies which our fathers thought to be good" and "the work of a good housewife to gather and keep [them] ready for emergency" were "superseded by the modern theory of concentrated medicines." "The age is progressive," he said, "Root doctors have had their day. People are through with large doses, and prefer to take the 'bitter pill' sugar-coated; or the nauseous draught in concentrated form."[871]

As progressive as the processing of drugs was by those in the trade, official oversight lagged far behind. In 1872 Dutcher again addressed the VPA to decry the absence of laws to regulate the sale of medicines and attributed the situation to "the fact that, in this land of freedom, any one has a right to enter upon any of the trades or professions. Indeed, they seem to succeed better in medicine than in almost any other." As a result, the deficiencies that the medical men experienced was repeated in the pharmacy trade and Dutcher laid the blame squarely on *"ostensibly respectable* men." He did not identify these individuals, but the context of the times indicates he was concerned about the most recent entrant to the drug trade, Wells, Richardson & Co., established in Burlington the same year. Over the next two decades, Wells, Richardson assumed such a huge presence in the formulation and distribution of drugs worldwide that it dwarfed the efforts of any other pharmacies in Vermont and throughout New England.[872] Its ability to work in an unregulated field was critical to its success as it sold large amounts of both credible and questionable substances, particularly the wildly popular Paine's Celery Compound infused with a high concentration of alcohol. Stowe's Dr. C. E. Gates further described the huge problem coming to light caused not by the small nostrums emanating from the state's kitchens and farms, but those spewing out from the expanding "manufacturing swindle" then underway.[873] Emphasizing specifically the "uncertainty" and "inferior" quality of these larger producers' products failing to deliver promised relief to a sufferer, he related that they "not only bring distrust and discredit upon the practice of medicine…but also tend to foster and uphold the 'Quackeries' and Nostrums of the day, such nostrums receiving *more* care and attention in manufacture than the products that are now flooding our markets." None of this could have been accomplished if Vermont had laws that assured the quality of the substances offered to the public were in place. It is ironic that the state legislature imposed stringent prohibition on the manufacture and sale of alcohol when, at the same time, it ignored the actions of Wells, Richardson as it peddled so much of it in the name of medicine. Powerful drug capitalists with easy access to lawmakers could account for much of the problem.

MEDICAL LICENSING INSTITUTED

During the next years, and despite its continuing displeasure with the presence of wayward regulars and empiricists still among them, the VMS largely abandoned its efforts to convince the legislature to require licensing of the medical profession. However, with a new generation of doctors, in 1874 their minutes relate that after the membership received a copy of New York's law regulating the practice they revived the effort and a committee was formed "to enlist the influence of the physicians and people in favor of the passage of a similar law in Vermont."[874] There is no information that describes what happened immediately afterwards, but in 1876 events moved quickly that revealed the deep divisions that continued between the two schools of medicine compelling a legislature witnessing the harm they posed to finally take action. The disdain that some of the legislators had for physicians who were also elected representatives was apparent when they refused to allow them the opportunity to consider the proposed legislation independently.[875] The law that was finally passed in November required that practitioners of medicine, surgery and midwifery obtain a certificate from chartered medical societies before being allowed to offer their services to the public. Violations constituted a misdemeanor offense, punishable by a fine of between fifty and two hundred dollars for a first conviction and up to five hundred dollars for a subsequent violation.[876]

Consequences

The empiricists instantly recognized the threat the new law posed to them and strongly argued that licensing a particular class of men (the educated) afforded them unwarranted recognition and an impermissible extension of power. "The State may enlighten and protect her citizens," a member of the Homeopathic Medical Society wrote, "but she cannot arbitrarily interfere with their right of choice among physicians" that included those without a formal education. "As citizens, it is plainly our duty to oppose," he continued, "by every possible means, the erection of any standard of orthodoxy in matters regarding which each individual has a right to form his own opinion and to exercise his own choice."[877] The existence of national and domestic institutions devoted to ensuring public health, such as the American Medical Association, the American Public Health Association, the Vermont Medical Society and the proposed state board of health had no place in society, he argued, and were strongly condemned by the irregulars who felt threatened at what they could do to their profession. "A State Medicine has no more place in the Republic," the member said, "than has a State religion. If there is to be a Minister of Medicine... why not also a Minister of Religion. If there is to be a National Medical Council as a branch of the Government, why not also a National Religious Council?... Again, as citizens, it is our duty to oppose the imposition of any useless burdens by the State upon any class of its people in the prosecution of their business affairs." This persistent opposition to state interference with Vermonters uninhibited access to medical practitioners of their own choosing, regardless of the extent of their education or the harm they inflicted from their treatments, dated back decades and formed the basis for repeal in 1839 of the state's first licensing requirement.[878] While this new law sought to change that and impose much needed order, the regulars were, one paper reported, unprepared for it because it came as "an utter surprise to them." And while "The law is now on the statute books," it continued, "its enforcement is quite another matter."[879]

The oversight of the medical profession that the licensing law sought to impose remained, as with the many unenforced ones the Vermont legislature passed, a "dead letter upon the statute books." The lawmakers' good intentions provided little safety for the state's inhabitants because they did not enact a critically needed enforcement component to assure its implementation that waited until the beginning of the twentieth-century. Their immediate failure can be attributed to the abiding strength of the Jacksonian philosophy. While the effectiveness of the law remained an open question, when some sought to repeal it in 1878, only two years after its passage, one concerned citizen raised his voice in opposition to express the opinion of many others in favor of it. The challenge in bringing professionalism to the medical trade, he said, was the presence of the persistent *"medical tramp,"* the charlatan who continued to operate in the recesses of the law and took advantage of others. He described this imposter as "a well-known character who travels from town to town exhibiting great pretensions to wonderful skill, sending circulars to every house with bogus certificates of remarkable cures, etc. Thus, he reaches the attention of those afflicted with diseases long since pronounced incurable by competent authority, and by strongly asserted promises of cure extorts from the poor and credulous large sums of money always paid in advance." He described in detail the great devastation that these medical tramps caused across Vermont:

> I have known more than one instance where a poor man has sold his only cow to procure from one of these tramps the medicine which was surely to cure his wife of consumption or cancer. Of course, no cure is effected in any case. The poor victim is robbed of his money – worse than that – he is robbed of the remnant of health by ill-advised drugs and often of life itself; and the irresponsible tramp is away seeking for new victims elsewhere. Hundreds of such instances have heretofore been known in all our large villages. Hundreds and sometimes thousands of dollars have been taken annually from each village, with no equivalent left. Loss of money, ruin of health and sometimes destruction of life follow in their course. Still, as each new imposter comes in new guise, some fresh invalids are found to risk money and

health upon the false promise of a medical tramp who has neither responsibility, position nor character.

He concluded by noting that while "Common tramps are great nuisances; the medical tramp is worse."[880]

Despite the legislature's late efforts to rein in the wayward doctors, Vermonters continued to tolerate the actions of abortionists, even when the mother died as a result of their actions. As they had in the years following passage of the 1846 abortion law, they rarely singled them out for punishment because they believed that those results were an unavoidable aspect of a practice that vulnerable women demanded access to. Just months before the licensing law was passed, on May 22 and 31, 1876, Barnet physician, Dr. H. J. Hazelton, performed an abortion on thirty-seven-year-old Achsah Holmes that resulted in her death. The grand jury charged him with using a mechanical means (a device called a "Uterine Sound") by "forcing and thrusting the instrument. . . into [her] body and womb," accompanied by his administration to her of "three ounces of a certain noxious thing called spurred rye [ergot], and certain other noxious things."[881] Despite strong evidence of his guilt, following a trial in June 1877, Hazelton was "unanimously acquitted by the jury."[882]

Similarly, contemporary newspapers describe the notorious Dr. Alvin R. Stokes of St. Johnsbury who wreaked havoc on several females and treated the fetuses he extracted in ways that disgusted many in the community.[883] The allegations against him were so notorious that, in the same manner experienced in the William Howard matters twenty years before, many observers attended proceedings where the courtroom was "packed to its utmost capacity with men and boys hungry for the details of a dirty court trial." Charged with committing multiple counts of abortion, Stokes escaped conviction when surprised observers thought the evidence so strong it was impossible for a jury to determine otherwise. On another occasion in 1879, a particularly egregious offense involved testimony that

Stokes had taken a young woman and her father "to an out-of-the-way and lonely logging-camp in one of the back towns" where he performed the procedure that left her, years later, unable to enter the courtroom without assistance. As the public struggled to understand why a jury could allow him to escape punishment for his conduct, one newspaper concluded that "The only reason suggested for this strange verdict is the general impression. . . that the medical profession generally, even in good standing otherwise, commit this same crime."[884] Stokes was finally convicted in 1882 for abortion-related offenses, fled, unsuccessfully attempted to enter Canada, went to Maine and was later arrested in Boston before returning to Vermont to begin serving a seven year sentence. In 1886, Governor Samuel Pingree commuted his sentence because "most of the jury who tried him, the officers of the law who prosecuted him, and [the] Judge," together with a petition signed by "more than a hundred of the good citizens of St. Johnsbury," sought his release.[885]

The public continued to read many other accounts of abortionists working in other parts of the state. In December 1877, Rutland doctor B. H. Haynes, and a female "doctress," performed an abortion on twenty-three-year-old Irishwoman Harriett Gaudette, who had already performed three self-induced abortions on herself using drugs and knitting needles. On this occasion, the procedure resulted in her death and afterwards "the remains of [her] slaughtered babe were put into a stove and burned."[886] While many newspapers reported the salacious details, as well as additional accounts of abortion taking place in other places around the state, one of them chose to ridicule the Rutland community on this particular occasion. "Though St. Johnsbury, St. Albans and Vergennes are wicked places," it wrote, "yes, very wicked, Rutland is the wickedest of them all. Hardly a week passes but that mighty town of marble, of many railroads, of big scale works and a state work house, trots out a scandal in high life [including] the disgusting details of abortion cases. Naughty, naughty Rutland !"[887]

Rutland County did have its share of wayward practitioners and in nearby Middletown Springs, Dr. Oscar F. Thomas, described as "a notorious abortionist," and another man were arrested for causing the death of twenty-five-year-old Eliza McMahon, a West Rutland housekeeper, whose funeral was interrupted to allow officials to conduct an inquest.[888] In January 1878, a newspaper reported that Brandon resident "Mrs. Julia F. Moore, alias Donah, is under arrest, charged with being a regular abortionist and having committed abortion on six women, the last of whom lies in a critical condition."[889] In September, Juliette Darrah was "indicted for procuring abortion" in Rutland.[890] North of Burlington in Milton, Dr. William Johnson was charged with killing a French girl, Charlotte Bettis, because of an abortion.[891] A thirty-four year old mystery was solved in November 1879 when the body of a missing eighteen-year-old girl was found buried in a Connecticut River sandbank opposite Wells River that had been "doubled up and the head twisted under," also the victim of an abortionist.[892] In June 1880, Dr. F. M. Smith, identified as "Smith the Abortionist," of Johnson was charged with the death of a young girl and when he appeared in court it was also "crowded with spectators"[893] Reports of the woes experienced by young women that implicated the medical profession drew the public's rapt attention and one newspaper deemed it appropriate to call out those that allowed it to continue. "Vermont seems to abound in nasty doctors, and they appear to have plenty of work to do, too. We should hardly want to generalize from local experience, and say that this is the case throughout the profession everywhere. But it is fair to say that the medical practitioners are slow to rid their associations of unworthy members, if indeed, it is a possible thing for a medical society to free itself from the rascals it may chance to cover."[894] A hands-off legislature that abrogated its responsibilities for decades, beginning with its awarding of generous charters to railroads in 1843, continued to inflict the most dire of consequences on the public.

Gary G. Shattuck

Free Pass Abuse

The railroads' promises of the 1840s and 1850s to allow Vermonters to engage more fully in the stream of commerce with the outside world were largely fulfilled, but also, at times frustrated by its rapidly aging physical infrastructure and the devolving financial problems its managers faced. While their products found far off markets and new forms of other goods returned into the Green Mountains, people took full advantage of opportunities to travel long distances for business, pleasure, and to seek out places able to advance their health. For members of the clergy, a tradition began early on when railroad officials extended a courtesy to various denominations allowing them to travel without cost. Clergymen both within the state and priests traveling under orders from Boston superiors to answer the call of recently-arrived large numbers of Irish and French immigrants made frequent use of the privilege. It allowed them to identify and purchase abandoned buildings and convert them into churches and to establish new parishes throughout the state to further advance the interests of the Catholic Church.

The issuing of free passes served as an uncomfortable consequence of modernity that soon drew the attention of many others clamoring for the same privilege that the clergy received. No laws prevented the practice and in the absence of any other regulatory control in this lax environment the numbers of passes issued accelerated and became such a nuisance by 1874 that concerned members of the legislature tried to intervene. Respected Civil War colonel and Franklin County senator Albert Clarke served as the principal gadfly who forced official recognition of a practice that few wanted exposed.[895] He deemed it such a pervasive problem, one of "gigantic proportions" he said, that Vermont's experience showed it had "crept into our body politic" to such an extent it had "no parallel in this country." He called the practice "unrepublican in its very nature" because it "established "a hateful system of caste. . . that makes the rich richer and the poor poorer," and deemed it "the handiest instrument of corruption, and the ready lash of petty despotism. It is the fatal ooze that is undermining the foundation stones of liberty and equality upon which our government is built."

It was indeed a large problem and one judge explained to Clarke that many of the passes, a reported "three thousand" issued annually, were being distributed in order to promote the railroad's interests before the legislature. Another individual estimated that as many as "one fourth to one half of all the passengers" rode free and the volume of passes issued so great that it posed a hardship on its managers and interfered with its operations. An investigative report prepared by a legislative committee in 1872, suppressed from public view, further revealed the extent of the problem. Its findings concluded that "railway management grants passes to all the state officers and their families, to each judge of the supreme court and his family, to United States officials within the state, to one or more representatives of nearly every newspaper in the state, to many members of the legislature, and to almost every prominent lawyer and politician." Even purveyors of liquor to authorized town agents during prohibition took advantage of the practice and bragged that they could "ride from one end of the state to the other without paying any fare." News of the abuse was so concerning and explosive that Clarke believed had it occurred in England "it would have caused an appeal to arms."

Clarke embraced the findings of a legislative committee calling to abolish the free pass system and reiterated the need to do so because of its insidious ability to "create a privileged class" that, in turn, gave the railroads "an undue political influence" that was "opposed to a sound policy." The cozy relationship that developed between legislators and railroad men was apparent to all and Clarke abhorred "the too widely prevalent spirit of solicitude for the wishes of the few who govern the corporations, instead of the interests of the many who govern, or ought to govern, the state." Clarke further identified the effects of all this on public perceptions swayed by impressions they were the victims of "favoritism, bias, injustice, demoralization, and servitude." The need for immediate reform was further magnified because of the railroads' importance in Vermont where, he said, "there is no business in the state, from the quarrying in the west to the mining and manufacturing in the east, from the immense lumbering on [Lake Champlain] to the smallest farming on the hills" that it did not touch. As honorable as Clarke's and his fellow legislators' intentions were, opponents arguing in the same tired manner that others had decades earlier when they sought to institute legislative oversight of such an important corporate enterprise constituted "hostility to the roads," defeated it by a vote of three in favor and twenty-seven opposed.

Conclusion

After Vermont passed its abortion law in 1846 and the railroad arrived two years later, the next three decades presented ample evidence of change and its profound influence on the health of the state's inhabitants contemporaneous with the ability of newly created corporate railroads and drug companies to insulate themselves from official oversight. While the law that prohibited the manufacture and sale of alcohol in 1852 experienced varying degrees of success, ineffective enforcement of violations relating to abortion and infanticide became more common. With the invention of the hypodermic syringe in 1853, the state's indulgent residents found a convenient alternative allowing them to continue to consume mood-altering substances. This included their increased use of opium, and its condensed derivative morphine, from modest amounts taken in prior decades to such an extent it became of great concern to the medical community in the 1860s and blossomed into an epidemic in the next decades. In other aspects, the regular members of the medical profession, still clamoring for the privilege of licensing, were summoned by a legal system that depended on their expertise to resolve the increasingly common medically-related disputes. Instances of abortion, and the barbarity of its practice so clearly demonstrated by William Howard and those that followed in his footsteps, presented legislators and the responsible members of the medical profession with the difficult challenge of determining what restrictions a population resistant to governmental intrusion would tolerate. By 1880, methods of contraception had advanced to such a degree that, while not extinguished, the need for abortions may have occurred less frequently and, for those that took place, reports of doctors performing them drew less attention.[896] The moral and legal questions presented by intrusive modernity that surround the practice continue to current times and their proposed answers will certainly never satisfy everyone affected by the consequences that attend the act of procreation.

Epilogue

"What's the railroad to me?"

Henry David Thoreau's reserved dismissal of the bell-clanging, screeching engines and rumbling railroad cars he heard when they passed near Walden Pond in 1854 meant little to the many others in Vermont eagerly awaiting their arrival. No one, including Thoreau, could escape either its imposing physical infrastructure or the undeniably favorable results it allowed so many to increase their economic, physical and psychological wellbeing by the introduction of modern conveniences enjoyed in metropolitan cities and brought into the distant regions of the Green Mountains. Such significant, improving change meant large-scale accommodation throughout all of Vermont society, even among the recluses.

Bridging those varied interests, and widening differences, among the state's inhabitants in mid-century exploded into view when legislators debated their respective points in favor of a particular location for their destroyed statehouse. Evidence of percolating discord among them was evident as their arguments descended from respectful observations based upon objective reality to instances of invective derision that stemmed from subjective prejudices. Divisions, and the prospect of regional sectionalism, existed among those who clung to tradition and others looking into the future upon the sudden loss of their symbolic cultural center that brought it all into view. Their deep-felt emotions differed little from the raw distress that exposed racial and class tensions most recently demonstrated when the rebuilding of communities were fiercely debated following the destruction wrought by Hurricane Irma after it crossed Saint-Martin, French West Indies in September 2017.[897] Similarly, the worldwide disruptions caused by the novel coronavirus (COVID-19) in 2019 and 2020 present evidence of similar challenges forced upon different societies called upon to alter their past ways of life. Natural disasters severely test the ability of victims to maintain a sense of decorum when their personal health and livelihoods are threatened at the same time they are challenged to part from their traditional practices.

Mid-nineteenth century Vermont, accentuated by the diverse opportunities that modernity provided because of the railroad, also presented an important moment for officials to consider their stewardship responsibilities in protecting the state's heritage for future generations. The destruction of the statehouse forcibly revealed that their existing, deficient practices seriously threatened the vulnerable books and documents in their care, housed in the building's library. When librarian Harvey Webster rushed to the room as the fire advanced, he assisted other members of the Montpelier community in carrying, and throwing from the windows, as many volumes as they could retrieve. Some were carried to a local judge's home, while others were recovered from the snow the next morning, cleaned, and stored that allowed more than 5,400 volumes to survive, while 1,629 were destroyed.[898] Even before the fire the collection's overall condition was questionable because it was housed in a room described by one of the debating legislators as being "as bad as it could be." It was "a mere lounging room," he said, open to the public where "instead of being the pride of the State [it was] but a shame and a disgrace" that revealed "how unfaithful the State has been in preserving the valuable State property intrusted to its care."⁸⁹⁹ A Burlington newspaper agreed and called the library "altogether unworthy of a sovereign state."⁹⁰⁰

As the new Capitol building rose up, a legislative committee imposed strict rules requiring library employees to closely supervise anyone using the volumes and limited their removal to select members of government. Their condition notwithstanding, a detailed inventory at the time revealed the eclectic extent of the library's holdings that included many books relating to the legal and cultural aspects of other states and countries. Notably, among the hundreds of titles only three of them pertained to Vermont history: Nathan Hoskin's *A History of the State of Vermont* (1831); Zadock Thompson's *The History of Vermont, Natural, Civil, and Statistical* (1842); and Benjamin Hall's recently published *History of Eastern Vermont* (1858).⁹⁰¹ Had a member of the legislature or a government official any desire to learn about the current state of medicine, including consumption and abortion, their library also held copies of New York physician Martyn Payne's *Medical and Physiological Commentaries* in three volumes (1840), *Institutes of Medicine* (1853) and *Materia Medica* (1854). Whether they engaged in the kinds of deep research that these and the many other volumes offered is unlikely. When they considered relocating the capital to Burlington, one legislator argued that access to the University of Vermont's "very excellent library" in that town for information made it an attractive reason to relocate there. However another disagreed and derisively ridiculed the idea exclaiming "Dear me!, what time, I ask, have legislators for reading extraordinary books?"⁹⁰² It made no sense, he said, to think that any of them had either the time or inclination to "pursue a brief legislative Collegiate course of study at the Vermont University during their session." His dismissive comments directed at gaining information on subjects that could impact their legislative work provides important insight into the amount of considered, reflective effort. and thought that some believed their responsibilities required.

The limited involvement that solons exhibited towards their work was further demonstrated by their persistent unwillingness to intrude into the lives of Vermonters insistent on maintaining their Jacksonian common man lives. The three aspects of their lives described herein that address the direct effects of the railroad on the Rutland community, the Grass Interest and their inhabitants' health, followed by their consequences, represent the diverse kinds of challenges they faced in mid-century. The prevailing emphasis on caveat emptor that made their constituents responsible for their own well-being permeated Vermont life at a time when enforcing the dictates of the very few laws directed at harmful substances, other than prohibition, remained woefully absent. Suffering caused by the burgeoning drug trade, increasing addiction to opium and untrained, unlicensed individuals allowed to call themselves "doctor" administering them or wreaking their havoc on vulnerable, frightened females subject to embarrassing bastardy proceedings and the stresses of unwanted children that drove them to consume drugs of questionable efficacy to abort them or, when not successful, call on medical practitioners to remove them from their bodies when not also experiencing the ravages of consumption was readily apparent to all. Quacks, exemplified by Bradford's notorious William Howard, took their dire toll on the population as the responsible medical men saw and repeatedly reported these problems and their adverse impact to legislators unwilling to acknowledge the true situation. Similarly, the accounts of mayhem, deaths and injuries directly attributable to the unregulated railroads was a daily occurrence that filled the state's newspapers, similarly ignored by the lawmakers.

Negligence, drunkenness, mangled bodies and destroyed lives reflected in the official records provide unassailable evidence of the presence of official irresponsibility and malfeasance that tolerated a degree of lawlessness. At the same time, the true causes of many Vermonters' deaths were either suppressed or misrepresented because there was no consequence for doing so. While the state's registration system begun in 1857 provided some information of value, its practical effect seems more, as the one observer described, a "tally of the evil done" than it was an effort "with a view of preventing the evil itself." Many other deaths also escaped official recognition that included the weak and vulnerable, the fetuses abandoned alongside railroad tracks and roadways, or in forests and piles of trash to be eaten by hogs. Instances of infanticide increased noticeably when infants received potent drugs or alcohol to quiet their crying or were "accidently" smothered in their beds, while the infirm, elderly or insane who posed heavy burdens on financially stressed households, and the disconnected transients who had nobody to watch out for them feared a similar ending. Officials were undeniably aware of these deficiencies, but the most they seemed willing to do was invoke individual moral responsibility and exhort the population to exercise personal control over their lives and to watch out for their neighbors.

"*A train of the Black Valley Railroad leaving Drunkard's Curve,*" Black Valley Railroad Guide, c. 1863. Vermont Historical Society.

The modernity of the railroad that arrived in mid-century in a mountainous state reaching out beyond its borders to take advantage of beckoning markets to allow it to participate in the larger economic stream of commerce proved an overwhelmingly attractive prospect. Other states with access to seaboard transportation already experienced those advantages, unhindered by the geographical seclusion of those living in the Green Mountains. The Rutland region, adjacent to beckoning New York and western markets, recognized its particular advantage over other parts of the state and aggressively embraced the prospect by exploiting its rich mineral deposits. Immigrant Irish flocked to the area and, together with native Vermonters, dug in and pulled it from the ground and built the railroad to carry it out to foreign markets. They created their own ethnic neighborhoods and furthered the presence of the Catholic Church in ways duplicated elsewhere in the country that also experienced rapid growth because of the railroad. The future was so bright that its brilliance overwhelmed official acknowledgment of the presence of the more untoward aspects of life that also existed. The time was simply not right to try and address those features of modernity and waited decades to evolve before hesitant officials finally acknowledged them and sought to ameliorate its unfortunate aspects.

Until then, the capitalists funding the new technology in the regulatory-free environment the solons permitted found ripe opportunities to advance their interests. Exercising the newfound power that corporate charters conferred on them, the railroad managers coursed over the landscape and seized whatever land they wanted from Vermonters and paid them only the sums they believed appropriate. Their actions demonstrated the accuracy of Senator Albert Clarke's reflective observation in 1874 that October 23, 1843 was the moment when "Vermont ceased to be a free and independent state" because the legislature surrendered its oversight responsibilities to the new corporations. The legal system struggled to respond to the economic aspects of the new technology and provided those unhappy victims of the condemnation process with limited rights that blocked them from appealing those awards to the state's highest court. Farmers who lost wandering livestock run down by engines also sought compensation with inconsistent results, while those injured by the new technology, or their families if they died, received little compensation for their losses. Other challenges in the legal and medical fields presented themselves because of abortionist William Howard's actions that caused consternation among the responsible doctors when called upon to render expert opinions in a court of law and how they should be compensated for their efforts.

Vermont's grab laws in mid-century that favored creditors to the disadvantage of entrepreneurs posed another legal challenge that made it easy for them to protect their interests and seize debtors' property. It also fostered a forlorn resentment among the young convincing many to leave the state in search of more favorable economic conditions. Advocating on the behalf of local capitalists and out-of-state investors presented a more favorable prospect to state officials at the time, fearful that any intrusion into their financial workings would deter their interest and cause them to take their money elsewhere leaving them stranded in their efforts to increase manufactures and connect to the outside world. Vermont's isolation also required imaginative thinking to portray its advantages in attractive ways while minimizing the presence of troublesome health-related problems such as the killing consumption that swept so many women away. It was a public relations conundrum that helps explain why legislators refused to acknowledge, and actually misrepresent, its heavy presence during their debates and argue instead that the state's inhabitants experienced excellent health. That was not true.

In bustling Rutland, the Rutland Land Company was formed and presented a vibrant example of industry where respected matriarch Harriet Strong worked alongside male business and political leaders selling undeveloped land to speculators. She represented an iconic image to a rapidly changing community as a woman who had lived in the past, but could bridge the demands that modernity presented and provided an example of steadfastness to her many admirers. Strong's passing in 1870 served as a moment for pause and reflection on the most recent past as her friends looked forlornly back to a simpler time when the challenges were not so complex. The huge Rutland railyard in Strong's backyard exploded into view in only a couple of years and became the pivotal location where huge numbers of railroad engines and cars from around New England, New York, and Canada crossed daily. The growth and sophistication of the yard's infrastructure utilized state-of-the-art design for specialized buildings and new styles of architecture exemplified by its grand depot, engine roundhouse, and machine shop that housed the most modern equipment to service the demands of behemoth engines. Businesses suddenly appeared on adjacent streets and the decades-long presence of the town's operations on the elevated terrace above moved downhill towards the yard to take advantage of all that modernity had to offer. Federal officials acknowledged the sudden changes and the new kinds of lawsuits that arose, convincing them to construct a new courthouse and post office away from the bustling downtown, equipped with a separate room for women to conduct their business away from loitering, leering males. Meanwhile, the hardworking Irish moved out of their shanties and into rough homes that sprang up in the Nebraska district, separated by the yard that hindered their full assimilation into the native population on the other side for decades. Notwithstanding, George Perkins Marsh's prescient call in 1847 for the cooperation of the herdsman and ploughman to join with the mechanic in their shared, common interest to take full advantage of modernity was readily apparent.

As the old man lamented in 1848 upon modernity's sudden appearance in Vermont, likening it to the sweeping "wand of some magician," it proved

Across the Continent engraving showing the railroad's march westward across the frontier. Currier and Ives, 1868.

a double-edged sword as demonstrated by the state's experiences in mid-century. Early optimistic enthusiasm fully embraced the prospect of change the railroad promised when there was no reason to believe that it could lead to a deterioration of a familiar lifestyle that existed in prior decades. Vermont was certainly not immune to the kinds of adverse effects that other states also experienced because of similar radical changes, but its population seems to have only slowly awakened from its complacency to acknowledge them in ways not evident elsewhere. Individual independence residing in a challenging geographical area proved a strong ameliorating influence to the intrusive aspects of technology, but it also exhibited an unusual degree of tolerance for practices that had clear adverse effects on the population. Modernity introduced the prospect of change, but was only incorporated into Vermonters' lives in ways and at times of their own choosing. Reacting to harm, rather than employing proactive measures to counter its threat that worked to advantage in other states seems to have been an important aspect of Vermont life in the mid-nineteenth century. Difficult lessons had to be learned in the next decades, many the hard way, but was how those in the Green Mountains, cautious at the prospect of fully embracing change, chose to react to the suddenness that modernity thrust into their lives.

APPENDIX

(1) JOSEPH GALLUP

Joseph Gallup to Jonathan Allen, June 16, 1845, Allen Family of Middlebury and Rutland, Vermont papers, 1804-1910, MSC 187:15, VHS.

To J. A. Allen, M. D. Rec Sec. of the Vermont M. Soc,
My Dear Sir,

Your kind letter reached me in due time, and on the day I had returned from a journey to Northampton May 31st and on traveling in bad weather had received some severe impressions which caused my confinement for several days, and from which I am not yet fully recovered. Were it not for this, as also my numerous cases, I might probably have attempted to comply with your courteous request to visit Castleton at the close of Lecture term and the meeting of the Vermont Medical Society. But as circumstances are I cannot avail myself of the pleasure of meeting some of my former friends and extending an acquaintance with gentlemen of the faculty.

Indeed, it would have been only a melancholy pleasure to revisit the place where I first went from the rounds of obscure practice to attempt to instruct students of medicine, and almost without the necessary preparations and arrangements. All territorial circumstances are liable to change and actually do change. Teno Sheki, the Indian Chief, said this made him melancholy; and so it becomes a melancholy circumstance to visit places where we do not find our former associates and collaborators. But this is the destiny of Providence, and it becomes us to submit without a murmur. They are resting from their labors, and we may hope in the bosom of their Father. My infirmities, with faltering voice and cautious step admonish me that I also soon must leave these [illegible] scenes; and if I should cast a lingering thought behind it would be directed to that profession to which I have been so ardently attached through life.

You desire me to communicate some views I have obtained by observation and experience in relation to disease and the means of its alleviation. This I would have more cheerfully done under more favorable circumstances. As it is I may attempt to offer some free thoughts without being technically confined to any one subject.

But, who shall we consider as <u>of</u> <u>the</u> <u>profession</u>, or what constitutes the profession? The votaries of medicine are divided into as many sects as religion or politics. Many of regular standing, as was supposed, have fallen off and become what are called homeopathics, hydropathics, &c. Besides these a new sect has arisen independent of the profession and becoming indeed very formidable; the steamers, or Thomsonians, one division of which are called <u>botanical</u> physicians.

With regard to the homeopathics, they find that having practiced on wrong principles in what they considered the regular system, they had bad senses and on observing that a greater number of the sick recovered when nothing, or next to nothing was done, they embraced the system which is tantamount to letting nature cure the disease if it can. Indeed, nature has been the most successful in a given number of cases, and as they find it an easy method of getting along, not requiring much thought, and charging very high for their services, they land the theory. This is nothing but refined quackery, in no point excelling the <u>rain</u>-<u>water</u> system. Yet very many are joining it and speak boldly of its merits. True, they had better follow an inert practice than pursue a pernicious kind which hastened the destruction of the sick. But this is not curing the sick, it is not the application of remedies to remove the morbid changes in the system, and give the vital actions opportunity to restore the morbid lesions. Notwithstanding the barefaced imposition of this new fangled system it is rapidly gaining advocates, especially in our larger towns and cities.

The hydropathics are less inimical in their proceedings, but equally erroneous. We ought not to doubt but that some morbid states of the system are alleviated, and indeed diseased action opposed by a free use of water internally and externally; but surely many states of disease will be aggravated by it. I believe they make little or no distinction between the varied habits of disease afflicting the human family. There are varied grades and conditions of the morbid habit, modified by intensity, by age, by modified susceptibility, by fixed local affections, by idiosyncrasy &c. One mode of application cannot suit them all. As man cannot do well on bread alone, so various and modified measures become necessary in the removal of the primary causes of disease.

With regard to the Thomsonian, or some modified Botanical System, it had its origins from a man in the state of nature, destitute of all science, but of a daring and preserving character. He alleges that his attention was mainly directed to the subject upon observing the bad means of some physicians belonging to the regular profession. As he originated in the vicinity of Woodstock and was occasionally here in the years 1801 – 2 and 3 when the typhoid fever first became epidemic and distressing in this place, he had an opportunity to observe the effects of the mercurial and opium treatment, with exposure to cold externally, and the moderately sweating method experienced without salivation or opium. No doubt he took some hints from observing the effects of the different methods of treatment pursued.

However, the system adopted by him and his followers was bold and energetic, but carried to that point as made it rash and dangerous, together with the severe method of vomiting by the use of an active article of the materia medica. This is a partial system when well conducted for they omit many means of great utility in the removal of the morbid habit, particularly bleeding and cathartics.

Although this sect by their active treatment have effected great revolutions in the system and made many cures of the less formidable orders of diseases, yet through their bad management of their own views, by profound ignorance, they have done considerable injury. The original Thompsonians are beyond all hope of improvement as they consider their system perfect; whilst the Botanical Thompsonians are far wiser and more discrete, for they are zealously striving at acquiring scientific information, and improvement in practical treatment. They seem to be an enterprising and determined sect, and leave no means untried to formulate their views and obtain business. They already have public lectures for the instruction of students at colleges in several of the states, they confer degrees &c. At some of these schools the collateral branches of science are quite well taught. When these partizans shall have acquired more general scientific information, and shall admit a few other remedies in their code of treatment, particularly bloodletting, by retaining their present perseverance, they may become powerful rivals to what they now style the regular physicians. They fail not to take advantage of the prejudices of the community and strive at radicalism.

In this hasty sketch I need make no remarks on what are called the herb doctors, neither on the great injury [illegible] to the so general use of patent medicines so liberally bestowed or suppyled by selfish and interested individuals.

Let us stop for a minute, and retire into the most secret recesses of our own consciousness, whilst we ruminate on the probable causes of the schisms that distract the profession, and produce the present chaotic state. We know that public opinion is fickle, that from slight causes it is liable to be misled and from erroneous conclusions, and the more so with regard to a profession like ours which deals in some mystery, and with operations, as it were, behind the curtains. Still, let us inquire whether all is right, and whether, peradventure, "there is not a rottenness in Denmark."

It is a fact not to be concealed that amongst what has been called the <u>regular</u> <u>faculty</u> there has been great discordance of opinion on the most cardinal points in relation to the character of disease, and the remedies best calculated for its removal. There seems to have been no general system of agreement in the details, but an almost constant clashing of opinion; even so much so that it is a common opinion that doctors seldom agree, and the question is then asked, <u>who</u> <u>shall</u> <u>decide</u> <u>when</u> <u>doctors</u> disagree. It is notorious that the most ignorant gossip will undertake to decide for them.

I will not undertake to say that the present faculty are unpardonably culpable for these discordant opinions. Every thing seems to have conspired to produce them. They depend mainly on early impression gained from preceptors during pupilage, from reading of authors of opposite opinions, some insisting that theory or certain well established principles are necessary as general landmarks to guide the mind through the intricacies of the protean appearance of diseases often presented for his treatment, whilst others disclaim all theory as is even now taught in some of our oldest medical schools, and say that experience of the good effects of certain empirical remedies should take the place of all theory. It is not a matter of surprise that students should become confounded and doubt every thing, and in this condition liable to be led into some Quixotic scheme to their utter ruin as successful practitioners. Going to practice in the sick room without a well grounded theory is like going to sea without chart or compass; whilst a wrong theory resembles a false compass and an erroneous chart.

It is hoped the gentlemen of the Faculty will excuse me whilst I may make a short and imperfect review of some of the most prevalent theories now influencing the treatment of diseases in this latitude & longitude. Or, perhaps, by advancing some pathological views of my own, developing a character of disease, you can discover the discrepancies, and the subjects may more easily be understood.

In the first place, do diseases of excitement or of the frynetic character arise from general impressions made upon the whole system and thence concentrating at focal points giving origin to local affections; or do such local affections first form from the causes of disease, and then radiate over the entire system producing general disease, or fever?

The advocates of this last position, therefore, say, that all fevers are symptomatic. But all my observations serve to convince me that fevers are idiopathic affections. I shall therefore maintain the first position, and feel near granted in this by considering that the causes of disease act by a general impulse on the whole system such as cold, contagions, fatigue, all general excitations &c. These are all such as make an universal impression on extended tissues both externally and internally. They all impress the vital susceptibility in a manner incompatible with health action. How can we suppose that such wide extended impressions shall only affect primarily some single tissue point? I can only offer opinions of the most permanent kind, such as external warmth by mild steaming with water or even alcohol, by sweating, by mild internal stimulations as the diluted essential oils &c. and even at the onset by mild doses of alcohol in some cases. You will readily appreciate my meaning when I say that to the more diffusible stimuli should be used such as readily pass off without permanent impressions. But opium and other narcotics are not of this sort, they make the most lasting impressions. The great absorbent and exhalant system, constituting the great centripetal and centrifugal actions of the capillary systems should be effectively excited without too much disturbing the sanguiferous system which is soon liable to assume enraged action destroying the organism unless timely restrained.

All the above circumstances should be kept in view in the treatment of the chronic morbid habit as well as the acute, for the former is often mainly a sequel of the latter. There is no physicalogical process more effectual in exciting the impeded action of the exhalants and absorbents than that of vomiting. Nature indicates it in numerous instances. The whole circulatory system is excited by it, and very often sweating cannot be effected without it in acute and chronic cases. I will here casually remark that no preparation of mercury is necessary for the removal of the morbid habit, for many other articles of Mat. Med. are preferable to this, and much mischief has been done by it.

I esteem it that we should be careful not to be guided by the names of diseases in our treatment, but by the state of the general morbid habit, having particular regard to the prevailing diathesis in every individual case. The local affection is liable to a metastasis, or to change from tissue or organ to another, and thereby giving a new name to the same disease; whilst the morbid habit remains the same; or peradventure, by moving to a different tissue the same diathesis may be varied. Thus, an inflammation of the venous tissue of the abdomen metastatizing to the fibrous membranes of the [illegible] will probably produce a more sthenic form of diathesis. All these circumstances require continual vigilance by the attendant, and he should always be adroit enough in his treatment to prevent a spoliation of organs.

I have no confidence in specifics; If not greatly mistaken, I meet with no more difficulty in treating a new form of disease without a name, as the most familiar; yet, I may have to bestow more attention whilst investigating its character. It may easily be conceived how the empirical advisor must be confounded to meet a disease he cannot readily give a name to. Everything must be done at random and by guessing. Considering all these things, in connection with the present state of medical science, how can it be expected that advisors should always agree? If they do not the profession is so far dissatisfied!

Although the local phenomena of diseases are greatly diversified from being seated in different tissues and organs, yet they have many things in common. There is a great affinity prevailing throughout the whole nomenclature. Take for example the whole order of what have been called the <u>malignant</u> fevers. In what do they differ except in their peculiar local affectations. The plague, yellow fever, cholera, severe dysentery, spotted fever, black tongue, puerperal fever, severe erysipelas, &c. with all the malignant fevers taking their names from the places where they first seem to originate. Setting aside their local affectations they have one intrinsic character, and require, with a few modifications, a similar treatment.

So, also, in chronic affections. All diseases have one intrinsic character, yet subject to modifications; all show a state of what is called reaction, producing a state of excitation just so soon as the embarrassed state of tissues admit of it. This seems to be an instinctive exertion to remove the derangements of disordered and injured tissues. It has been called the <u>vis medicatrix natura</u>. It is a real effort to restore the lesions of the [illegible] system, and it is the province of the physician to kindly aid these efforts, whilst he guards with [illegible] care, that the enraged efforts do not overact, and destroy the organism.

I am weary and must stop. Perhaps your patience may also be exhausted. If I were to say more it would be to lament the depressed, and even distracted state of the medical world taken on the broadest scale. I have no power to correct the evil, even if I were wise enough to know how to do it. I can meditate in silent sorrow that a profession which professes to relieve the maladies of human beings, and prolong the dubious duration of life should become so disorganized and degraded. Harmony of sentiment is, indeed, more needed in this profession than even in religion or politics. But these things are incidental to the depravity and ignorance of mankind. I see many conspicuous and worthy characters attached to the profession, but the voice of wisdom is stifled amid the clamor of demagogues. I can only say, persevere in the way of right doings, and perhaps the adage may become true, with the blessing of God, that <u>great is the truth and it will prevail</u>.

Yours very kindly, J. S. Gallup

Woodstock, Vt.
June 16, 1845
Note. I have no time nor strength to transcribe and correct this hasty sketch. I can scarcely offer it to anybody. If, however, you should think best to offer it in public, I wish it might be given to a good reader, and that he would first carefully look it over. I hope you will write me many particulars within a few weeks.

In the margin: The time is so short I thought best to send this directly to Castleton.

On reverse: Read before the Vermont Medical Society on June 19, 1845.

(2) THEODORE WOODWARD

Dr. Theodore Woodward Lecture at Castleton, "Lecture Book, Vermont Academy of Medicine, Augt. 1836," Special Collections, Castleton University, Castleton, Vermont

Vermont Academy of Medicine, 1 o'clock PM, Thursday, 9th Aug 1836

Pro. Woodward delivered the introductory lecture, before the medical class assembled, for the commencement of a regular and scientific course of lectures in the Vermont Academy of Medicine, and proceeded nearly as follows:

Gentlemen we need not attempt to lay before you, at this time the great importance of a thorough scientific and regular medical professional knowledge of all that is requisite to the successful surgeon, and practitioner of medicine; for it is self-evident that he ought to be profoundly learned in his profession in order to practice successfully. But as indispensably requisite as all this useful and necessary knowledge is, we find in almost every part of our enlightened land, those attempting to intrude themselves upon the notice and patronage of the Public almost destitute of the first rudiments of the science of medicine.

Yes, Gentlemen, the lives of the incredulous and unsuspecting are put in jeopardy by the empirical intrusion of men, or beings in the shape of human creatures who attempt to assume the responsibility of practitioners of Medicine and it is probable that those above named who will continue a pest, menace and curse to community [sic] will continue to be scattered over our country as they have been heretofore, trifling with the lives of those who are so unwise as to place themselves under the care and guidance of those insignificant quacks in the medication of this disorder.

But probably the best and sincerest course to pursue to rid ourselves of those prowling ostentatious braggadocios is to pursue a straight onward

APPENDIX

course disregardless [sic] of their existence, being indifferent to their presence and through all their folly will, we humbly hope are long be [sic] buried in the tomb of oblivion, and only remembered for their sin and inequity by those who may be living monuments to their malpractice and those who are called upon to mourn the loss of their friends who found a premature grave by being the unfortunate subjects of rash and empirical ignorance to practice upon.

As one, Gentlemen, who has been appointed prof[essor] to impart knowledge to you, in this institution you will please permit a comparison to be drawn between the Vt. Academy of Medicine and those more favoring in the Atlantic cities.

This institution, Gentlemen, has been in successful operation since the year 1818. It has had not a few difficulties to surmount in her onward career as all other Institutions have; her course has not been paved with gold from her infancy to the present flourishing condition. No, Gentlemen, she has been obliged to push her way through every impediment placed in her path to obstruct the successful course that enemies have witnessed her taking in become more and more popular.

While other institutions of a similar character have not been confined to patronage of private individuals but have received pecuniary aid from their respective states, we have been obliged to toil and maintain our existence unaided from any, save those who have been sufficiently kind to place themselves under our instruction. No, Gentlemen, while other institutions have been favored with both public & private donations, we have been left unaided from any such source, and permit me to inform you that the State of Vermont has lent us no aid; save one donation which being so liberal in its nature & character as well as interesting and churning to the physician I will take the liberty to repeat it which is the following:

"Be it enacted by the Legislature of Vermont here assembled, if any person or persons shall be engaged in digging up or aiding in the removal of any person or persons interred, and found guilty of the same shall be fined not exceeding one thousand dollars or confined not exceeding one year in the State Prison in the state where the case may be tried at the discretion of the Court."

This, Gentlemen, is all the aid our State has seen fit to give us and with this liberal and patriotic donation we have been enabled to maintain our standing and character and by a regular & gradual increase of public patronage have not, as we trusted, failed to extend our reputation.

Gentlemen, it is probably considered by you as by many others that all old institutions are superior to new ones in imparting knowledge and of valifying [sic] the student to take the responsibilities of a physician and be adequately qualified for every emergency he may be called to see and lend professional aid. But, Gentlemen, I cannot see any superior advantage an old institution can have in very particular area over that had not been in operation as long.

An argument used in establishing the superiority of old medical schools over new ones is this, Professors in new ones are not as experienced as those who hold professorships in others of more celebrated reputation. But Gentlemen I think that this objection against new medical colleges and favor in longer established schools can be removed in many schools that have not been established but a short time, that is in regard to the age, standing and supposed knowledge and experience of [professors].

It is the case in [institutions] that are in their state of infancy when we speak comparatively [and] favored in having as able and in every way as well qualified professors as can be obtained for any [institution] and upon that is the fact we think that this objection must be removed.

It is the case that the institutions of our Atlantic cities have perhaps an advantage over us, and that may be in the advantage the student has in witnessing hospital practice; and beholding more capital operations than in our Institution. But, gentlemen, it is a fact in my opinion that this is not of as much advantage to the student as it aftertimes appears to him. Professors have not time to demonstrate as minutely to the student as is necessary, that is they have not time to make the operations appear as plain and clear to 2, or 3 hundred students as what they wish. And as the lecture term is quite short we think it would be about as beneficial to the student to devote some other time besides that devoted to a term of lectures for seeing such practice as may be connected with some of the medical colleges in our country.

We then take the liberty to say, gentlemen, that we think your opportunity will not be in this Institn. much inferior to that of any other in our Country. And shall on our part endeavor to convince you of the fact that your progress will be full as rapid here as you could reasonably expect or anticipate.

Gentlemen, the medical profession is not in all its relations attended with pleasure. The Physician as you all doubtless know has many embarrassing difficulties to surmount in his professional career through life. It is his lot to enter the habitations of misery and distress and must become familiar with suffering in every form and shape, but I am happy, gentlemen, that I can assure you that our profession has its pleasures as well as its evils.

How delightful it must be to the spirited physician to rise in honor and skill in his profession. He can ascend the hill of science and inhale the salubrious breezes of that enchanting clime and bask in the bright sun shine of intellectual glory surrounded with many pleasures & joys in his exalted elevation.

Gentlemen, how pleasing it must be to find yourselves successful in combatting disease and restoring your friend from sickness to health. And what a pleasing sensation of pleasure you must experience when by your profound skill you see disease give way of the most alarming nature & kind when some near and bosom friend lies at the point of death you successfully medicate so as to remove the disease and continue the valuable life of an affectionate friend to a be a blessing and ornament to society and honor and comfort to his relations. These with many other congratulatory and happy circumstances & results in life from something of the pleasure of our sign[ificant] profession.

BIBLIOGRAPHY

MANUSCRIPTS

Addison County Medical Society Papers, Henry Sheldon Museum of Vermont History, Middlebury, Vermont.

Diary of Ambrose Lincoln Brown and Rutland Railroad records, Rutland Historical Society, Rutland, Vermont; Ambrose Lincoln Brown Day Book, Vermont Historical Society.

Land Records, Clerk's Office, City of Rutland, Vermont.

Land Records, Clerk's Office, Town of Clarendon, Vermont.

Land Records, Clerk's Office, Town of Mt. Holly, Vermont.

Land Records, Clerk's Office, Town of Shrewsbury, Vermont.

Manuscript Vermont State Papers; Rutland Railroad Company records, 1845–1951; Court records, Vermont State Archives and Records Administration, Middlesex, Vermont.

Medical Manuscripts, Vermont Historical Society, Barre, Vermont.

Medical School Theses, Rauner Library Special Collections, Dartmouth College, Hanover, New Hampshire.

Records of the U. S. District and Other Courts in Vermont, 1791–1983, National Archives and Records Administration, Waltham, Massachusetts.

Vermont Collection, Rutland Railroad Archives, Middlebury College.

Vermont Medical Society minutes of meetings and Burlington town records, Silver Special Collections Library, University of Vermont, Burlington, Vermont.

Newspapers

Argus and Patriot (Montpelier)
Aurora of the Valley (Newbury)
Bellows Falls Gazette
Bennington Banner
Boston Daily Bee
Boston Herald
Bradford Inquirer
Brattleboro Eagle
Burlington Daily Times
Burlington Free Press
Burlington Weekly Free Press
Burlington Weekly Sentinel
Caledonian (St. Johnsbury)
Christian Herald (Newburyport, MA)
Christian Repository (Montpelier)
Connecticut Journal
Essex County Herald (Island Pond)
Farmer's Herald (St. Johnsbury)
Granite State Farmer (Manchester, NH)
Green Mountain Freeman (Montpelier)
Lamoille Newsletter
Middlebury Free Press
Middlebury Galaxy
Middlebury Register
National Police Gazette (New York City)
New England Farmer (Boston)
New Hampshire Patriot and State Gazette
New York Times
North Star (Danville)
Norwich Aurora
Orange County Telegraph (Bradford)
Orleans County Monitor
Orleans Independent Standard (Irasburgh)
Rutland County Herald

Bibliography

Rutland Daily Globe
Rutland Daily Herald
Rutland Herald
Rutland Independent
Rutland News
Rutland Weekly Herald
St. Albans Advertiser
St. Alban's Weekly Messenger
St. Johnsbury Caledonian
St. Johnsbury Times
Sentinel and Democrat (Burlington)
Spirit of the Age (Woodstock)
Swanton Courier
The Brandon Post
The Democrat (St. Albans)
The Enterprise and Vermonter (Vergennes)
The Horn of the Green Mountains (Manchester0
The Repertory (St. Albans)
The Reporter (Brattleboro)
The Rutland News
The United Opinion (Bradford)
The Universal Watchman (Montpelier)
The Vermont Record and Farmer (Brattleboro)
The Vermont Union (Lyndon)
The Vermont Union Whig (Rutland)
The Voice of Freedom (Montpelier)
Vermont Aurora (Vergennes)
Vermont Chronicle (Bellows Falls)
Vermont Journal
Vermont Patriot and State Gazette (Montpelier)
Vermont Phoenix
Vermont Standard
Vermont Telegraph (Brandon)
Vermont Watchman and State Journal (Montpelier)
Watchman, Impartialist, and Christian Repository (Lebanon, NH)

Books and Periodicals

Abbott, Jacob. *Marco Paul's Voyages & Travels: Vermont*. New York: Harper & Brothers, 1852.

Acts and Resolves passed by the General Court of Massachusetts, in the year 1845. Boston: Dutton and Wentworth, 1845.

Acts and Resolves Passed by the Legislature of the State of Vermont, at the October Session, 1838. (Montpelier: E. P. Walton and Son, 1838.

Acts and Resolves passed by the Legislature of the State of Vermont at the October Session, 1843. Montpelier: E. P. Walton & Sons, 1843.

Acts and Resolves Passed by the Legislature of the State of Vermont at the October Session, 1845. Burlington: Chauncey Goodrich, 1845.

Acts and Resolves Passed by the Legislature of the State of Vermont, at the October Session, 1846. Burlington: Chauncey Goodrich, 1846.

Acts and Resolves Passed by the Legislature of the State of Vermont, at the October Session, 1849. Montpelier: E. P. Walton & Son, 1849.

Acts and Resolves Passed by the General Assembly of the State of Vermont, at the October Session, 1852. Montpelier: E. P. Walton & Son, 1852.

Acts and Resolves passed by the General Assembly of the State of Vermont at the October Session, 1856. Montpelier: E. P. Walton, 1856.

Acts and Resolved passed by the General Assembly of the State of Vermont, at the October Session, 1858. Bradford: Joseph D. Clark, 1858.

Acts and Resolves Passed by the General Assembly of the State of Vermont at the Annual Session, 1865. Montpelier: Freeman Steam Printing, 1865.

Acts and Resolves Passed by the General Assembly of the State of Vermont, at the Annual Session, 1867. Montpelier: Freeman Steam Printing, 1867.

Acts and Resolves Passed by the General Assembly of the State of Vermont, at the First Biennial Session, 1870. Montpelier: J. & J. M. Poland Steam Printing, 1870.

Acts and Resolves Passed by the General Assembly of the State of Vermont at the Fourth Biennial Session, 1876. Rutland: Tuttle & Company, 1876.

Acts and Resolves Passed by the General Assembly of the State of Vermont at the Ninth Biennial Session, 1886. Springfield, MA: Published by Authority, Springfield Printing Company, 1887.

Acts Passed by the Legislature of the State of Vermont, at their October Session, 1826. Bennington: D. Clark, 1826.

Adams, Charles Francis. "The Era of Change." In Charles Francis Adams and Henry Adams, *Chapters of Erie and Other Essays*. Boston: James Osgood, 1871; reprint, New York: Augustus M. Kelley, 1967.

Albers, Jan. *Hands on the Land: A History of the Vermont Landscape*. Cambridge, MA: MIT Press, 2000.

BIBLIOGRAPHY

Alcott, William A. *Dosing and Drugging, or Destroying by Inches.* Boston: George W. Light, 1839.

Allen, Ira. *The Natural and Political History of the State of Vermont.* London: J. W. Myers, 1798.

American Railroad Journal and Advocate of Internal Improvements. New York: D. K. Minor and George C. Schaeffer, 1836.

American Railroad Journal and General Advertiser for railroads, canals, steamboats, machinery and mines. Philadelphia: D. K. Minor, 1846.

An American Matron. *The Maternal Physician; A Treatise on the Nurture and Management of Infants.* New York: Isaac Riley, 1811.

Andres, Glenn M. and Curtis B. Johnson. *Buildings of Vermont.* Charlottesville: University of Virginia Press, 2014.

Annual Report of the Secretary of the Treasury on the State of the Finances for the Year 1876. Washington: Government Printing Office, 1876.

Appleton, William Sumner. *Record of the Descendants of William Sumner.* Boston: David Clapp & Son, 1879.

Appletons' Illustrated Hand-Book of American Travel. New York: Appleton & Co., 1857.

Bailey, Harold L. "Vermont's State Houses: Being a Narration of the Battles over the Location of the Capitol and Its Construction." *Vermont Quarterly* 12 (1944): 135–156.

Barnes, Albert. *Notes, Critical, Explanatory, and Practical, on the Book of Psalms.* Vol. 3. New York: Harper & Brothers, 1869.

Barron, Hal S. *Those Who Stayed Behind: Rural Society in Nineteenth-Century New England.* Cambridge: Cambridge University Press, 1987.

Bassett, Thomas Day Seymour. "Urban Penetration of Rural Vermont, 1840–1880." Unpublished Ph.D. dissertation, Harvard University, 1952.

_____. "500 Miles of Trouble and Excitement: Vermont Railroads, 1848–1861." *Vermont History* 49, no. 3 (Summer 1981): 141.

_____. *The Growing Edge: Vermont Villages 1840–1880.* Montpelier: Vermont Historical Society, 1992.

Baxter, J. H. *Statistics, Medical and Anthropological, of the Provost-Marshal-General's Bureau derived from Records of the Examination for Military Service in the Armies of the United States During the Late War of the Rebellion of Over a Million Recruits, Drafted Men, Substitutes, and Enrolled Men.* Washington: Government Printing Office, 1875.

Beardsley, William H. "The Changing Landscape and the Role of State Government." Vermont Arch Arts & Science Occasional Paper 5 (1970).

Beaudry, Mary C. "The Lowell Boott Mills Complex and Its Housing: Material Expressions of Corporate Ideology." *Historical Archaeology* 23, no. 1 (1989): 19–32.

Beck, John B. *An Inaugural Dissertation on Infanticide.* New-York: J. Seymour, 1817.

Beck, Theodric Romeyn and John B. Beck. Eds. *Elements of Medical Jurisprudence*. Vol. 1. Albany: H. H. Van Dyck, 1850.

Biographical Sketches of the Leading Men of Chicago. Chicago: Wilson & St. Clair, 1868.

Bluestone, Daniel. "Civic and Aesthetic Reserve: Ammi Burnham Young's 1850s Federal Customhouse Designs." *Winterthur Portfolio* 25, no. 2/3. (Summer-Autumn 1990): 132.

Brighton, Stephen A. "Degrees of Alienation: The Material Evidence of the Irish and Irish American Experience, 1850–1910." *Historical Archaeology* 42, no. 4 (2008): 132–153.

Bryan, Frank M. "Vermont: The Politics of Ruralism." Unpublished PhD dissertation, University of Connecticut.

Burns, John. *Observations on Abortion*. Troy: Wright, Goodenow, and Stockwell, 1808.

Burroughs, John. *The Writings of John Burroughs, Signs and Seasons*. Vol. 1. Boston: Houghton Mifflin Company, 1886.

Bushman, Richard Lyman. *The American Farmer in the Eighteenth Century: A Social and Cultural History*. New Haven: Yale University Press, 2018.

Butler, James Davie. *Deficiencies in our History: An Address Delivered before the Vermont Historical and Antiquarian Society, October 16, 1846*. Montpelier: Eastman & Danforth, 1846.

Bynum, Helen. *Spitting Blood: The History of Tuberculosis*. Oxford: Oxford University Press, 2012.

Carey, H. Gatch. "Abortion: A New Method of Treatment." In E. H. Parker and J. H. Douglas, *American Medical Monthly*, vol. 7, no. 1 (January 1857), 4.

Carroll, George. *The Manchester Tragedy. A Sketch of the Life and Death of Miss Sarah H. Furber, and the Trial of her Seducer and Murderer*. Manchester: Fisk & Moore, 1848.

Chapman, George T. *Sketches of the Alumni of Dartmouth College*. Cambridge: Riverside Press, 1867.

Charles, Sheila. *The Return of the Rutland Railroad: An Archaeological Phase 1A literature review and sensitivity assessment for the proposed Rutland railroad pedestrian crossing and path, City of Rutland, Rutland County, Vermont*. Prepared for City of Rutland, March 1999.

Charters and Ordinances of the City of Rutland. Rutland: Carruthers & Thomas, 1894.

Child, Hamilton. *Gazetteer of Orange County, Vt. 1762–1888*. Syracuse: Syracuse Journal Company, 1888.

Childs, Mark C. "The incarnations of Central Avenue." *Journal of Urban Design* 1, no. 3 (1996): 281–298.

Clark, Kenneth. *Civilisation: A Personal View*. London: British Broadcasting Corporation, 1969.

Bibliography

Coleman, Peter J. *Debtors and Creditors in America: Insolvency, Imprisonment for Debt, and Bankruptcy, 1607–1900*. Madison: The State Historical Society of Wisconsin, 1974.

Collier, Peter. *First Annual Report of the Vermont State Board of Agriculture, Manufactures and Mining for the Year 1872*. Montpelier: J. & J. M. Poland, 1872.

Cormier, William A. *Coming of Age: The Diary of Young Man Thaddeus H. Walker, 1851–1854*. Salem, NY: New Perth Publishing 2010.

Crosby, Dixi. *Report of a Trial for Alleged Mal-Practice against Dixi Crosby, M.D.* Woodstock: Lewis Pratt, 1854.

Cross, Paul J., Jr., "A History of Rutland High School, Rutland, Vermont (1855–2008)." *Rutland Historical Society Quarterly* 39, no. 1 (2009): 3.

D'Agostino, Lorenzo. *The History of Public Welfare in Vermont*. Winooski: St. Michael's College Press, 1948.

Davenport, Horace W. *University of Michigan Surgeons 1850–1970, Who They Were and What They Did*. Ann Arbor: Historical Center for the Health Sciences, 1993.

Davison, F. E. *Historical Rutland: An Illustrated History of Rutland, Vermont, from the granting of the charter in 1761 to 1911*. Rutland: Phil. H. Brehmer, 1911.

Dean, Benjamin W. Ed. *First Report to the Legislature of Vermont, relating to the Registry and Returns of Births Marriages and Deaths in this State for the Year ending December 31, 1857*. Burlington: Daily Times Book and Job Printing, 1859.

_____. *Instructions Relative to the Registry and Return of Births, Marriages and Deaths, in Vermont*. Middlebury: Register Book and Job Office, 1859.

Debow, J. D. *Statistical View of the United States*. Washington: A. O. P. Nicholson, 1854.

De Chadarevian, Soraya. "Microstudies versus big picture accounts?." *Studies in History and Philosophy of Biological and Biomedical Sciences* 40 (2009): 13–19.

Dellapenna, Joseph W. *Dispelling the Myths of Abortion History*. Durham, NC: Carolina Academic Press, 2006.

Demeritt, David. "Climate, Cropping, and Society in Vermont, 1820–1850." *Vermont History* 59, no. 3 (Summer 1991): 156.

Doten, Dana. *Vermont: A Guide to the Green Mountain State*. Boston: Houghton Mifflin Company, 1937.

Douglas, George H. *All Aboard: The Railroad in American Life*. New York: Paragon House, 1992.

Douglas, J. H. Ed. *American Medical Monthly and New York Review*. Vol. 14. (July–December 1860).

Draper, Alexander C. *Observations on Abortion. With an account of the means both medicinal and mechanical, employed to produce that effect, together with advice to females*. Philadelphia: 1839.

Duffy, John J., Samuel B. Hand and Ralph H. Orth. *The Vermont Encyclopedia*. Hanover: University Press of New England, 2003.

Eighth Annual Report of the Directors of the Rutland & Burlington R. R. Co., and the Report of the Trustees of the Second Mortgage 1855. Rutland: George A. Tuttle & Co., 1855.

Eighth Report to the Legislature of Vermont relating to the Registry and Returns of Births, Marriages and Deaths, in this State, for the year ending December 31, 1864. Montpelier: Freeman Steam Printing, 1866.

Eighty Years' Progress of the United States. Hartford: L. Stebbins, 1869.

Encouragement and Promotion of Agriculture, Domestic Manufactures and the Mechanic Arts, The Compiled Statutes of the State of Vermont. Burlington: Chauncey Goodrich, 1851.

Epstein, Julia. "The Pregnant Imagination, Fetal Rights, and Women's Bodies: A Historical Inquiry." *Yale Journal of Law and the Humanities* 7 (1) (1995): 155.

Feeney, Vincent E. *Finnigans, Slaters and Stonepeggers: A History of the Irish in Vermont.* Bennington: Images from the Past, 2009.

Fifth Annual Report of the Directors of the Rutland and Burlington Railroad Company, submitted to the stockholders July 31, 1852. Boston: Eastburn's Press, 1852.

Figes, Orlando. *The Europeans: Three Lives and the Making of a Cosmopolitan Culture.* New York: Metropolitan Books, 2019.

Fink, Leon. *Workingmen's Democracy: The Knights of Labor and American Politics.* Urbana: University of Illinois Press, 1985.

Fifth Annual Report of the Railroad Commissioner of the State of Vermont, to the General Assembly, 1860. Rutland: Geo. A. Tuttle & Co., 1860.

Fifth Annual Report of the Vermont Board of Education, September, 1861. Burlington: Times Book and Job Printing, 1861.

Fifth Report to the Legislature of Vermont, relating to the Registry and Returns of Births, Marriages and Deaths, in this State, for the Year Ending December 31, 1861. Montpelier: Freeman Printing, 1863.

First Annual Report of the Railroad Commissioner of the State of Vermont to the General Assembly, 1856. Rutland: Geo. A. Tuttle & Co., 1856.

First Annual Report of the State Superintendent of Common Schools made to the Legislature October, 1846. Montpelier: Eastman & Danforth, 1846.

First Report to the Legislature of Vermont, relating to the Registry and Returns of Births, Marriages and Deaths. Burlington: Daily Times Book and Job Printing Establishment, 1859.

Fitch, Calvin M. *The Invalid's Guide, and Consumptive's Manual.* New York: Taylor and Hoyt, 1856.

Fitch, Samuel Sheldon. *Diseases of the Chest. A Treatise on the Uses of the Lungs and on the Causes and Cure of Pulmonary Consumption.* Philadelphia: Hooker and Agnew, 1841.

_____. *Six Lectures on the Uses of the Lungs; and causes, prevention, and cure of Pulmonary Consumption, Asthma, and Diseases of the Heart; on the Laws of Longevity; and on the mode of preserving male and female health to a hundred years.* New York: H. Carlisle, 1847.

Bibliography

_____. *The Family Almanac, and Guide to Health*. New York: S. S. Fitch & Co., 1857.

_____. *A Popular Treatise on the Diseases of the Heart*. New York: S. S. Fitch & Co., 1860.

Flaherty, Jeremy. "A Multivariate Look at Migration from Vermont." *Vermont History* 74 (Summer/Fall 2006): 127–155.

Fornication binds the criminal parties to marry. The Decision of the Congregational Church in Rupert, Vt. Relative to a case of discipline, August 31, 1814. Bennington: Darius Clark, 1815.

Fourth Biennial Report of the Board of Railroad Commissioners, 1894. Vol. 4. Burlington: The Free Press Association, 1894.

Fourth Report to the Legislature of Vermont relating to the Registry and Returns of Births, Marriages and Deaths, in this state, for the Year ending December 31, 1860. Middlebury: The Register Office, 1861.

Fox, Gerald B. and Jean Ballantyne. "William Hale, Railroad Surveyor: His Life, His Work." *Vermont History* 86, no. 1 (Winter/Spring 2018): 20–30.

Frank Leslie's New York Journal of Romance, General Literature, Science and Art. New York: Frank Leslie, 1856.

French, Nahum W. *Equality Mental and Political Liberty and The Progress of Nature*. 1913.

Geber, Jonny and Barra O'Donnabhain. "'Against Shameless and Systematic Calumny': Strategies of Domination and Resistance and Their Impact on the Bodies of the Poor in Nineteenth-Century Ireland." *Historical Archaeology* 54, no. 1 (2020): 160–183.

Giddens, Anthony and Christopher Pierson. *Conversations with Anthony Giddens: Making Sense of Modernity*. Stanford: Stanford University Press, 1998.

Gillen, Paul and Devleena Ghosh. *Colonialism and Modernity*. New South Wales, Australia: UNSW Press, 2007.

Gillies, Paul S. *The Law of the Hills: A Judicial History of Vermont*. Barre and Montpelier: Vermont Historical Society, 2019.

Gilman, M. D. Ed. *Bibliography of Vermont*. Montpelier: Free Press Association, 1897.

Gold, David M. "Redfield, Railroads, and the Roots of 'Laissez-Faire Constitutionalism.'" *The American Journal of Legal History* 27, no. 3 (July 1983): 257.

González-Ruibal, Alfredo. "Archaeology and the Time of Modernity." *Historical Archaeology* 50, no. 3 (2016): 144–164.

Gordon, Robert J. "Is U.S. Economic Growth Over? Faltering Innovation Confronts the Six Headwinds." Working Paper 18315, National Bureau of Economic Research, Cambridge, MA, August 2012.

Gould, Benjamin Apthorp. *Investigations in the Military and Anthropological Statistics of American Soldiers*. New York: Hurd and Houghton, 1869.

Graf, Nancy Price. Ed. *Celebrating Vermont: Myths and Realities*. Middlebury: The Christian A. Johnson Memorial Gallery, 1991.

Graffagnino, Kevin J. *The Shaping of Vermont: From the Wilderness to the Centennial 1749–1877.* Rutland and Bennington: Vermont Heritage Press and the Bennington Museum, 1983.

_____. *Vermont in the Victorian Age: Continuity and Change in the Green Mountain State 1850–1900.* Bennington and Shelburne: Vermont Heritage Press and Shelburne Museum, 1985.

Guthrie, C. B. "Report on the Control of Poisons." *Proceedings and Debates of the Fourth National Quarantine and Sanitary Convention.* Boston: George C. Rand & Avery, 1860.

Haddock, Charles B. *Addresses and Miscellaneous Writings.* Cambridge: Metcalf and Company, 1846.

Hager, Albert D. *Report of the Geology of Vermont: Descriptive, Theoretical, Economical and Scenographical.* Claremont: Claremont Manufacturing Company, 1861.

Haig, Maham H. and B. W. Benedict. Eds., *Railway Shop Up to Date: Reference Book of Up to Date American Railway Shop Practice.* Chicago: Crandall Publishing Company, 1907.

Haines, Michael R. "The Population of the United States, 1790–1920." *Historical Paper No. 56.* Cambridge, MA: National Bureau of Economic Research, 1994.

Hall, Samuel Carter and Anna Marie Hall. *Ireland: It's Scenery, Character, &c.* Third edition. London: Jeremiah How, 1843.

Hamilton, John B. *The Journal of the American Medical Association.* Vol. 22. Chicago: The Journal of the Association, 1894.

_____. *The Journal of the American Medical Association.* Vol. 26. Chicago: American Medical Association Press, 1896.

Hance, Dawn D. *Early Families of Rutland, Vermont.* Rutland: Rutland Historical Society, 1990.

_____. *The History of Rutland, Vermont 1761–1861.* Rutland: Academy Books 1991.

Hand, Samuel B. *The Star that Set: The Vermont Republican Party, 1854–1974.* Latham, MD: Lexington Books, 2002.

_____. "Mountain Rule Revisited." *Vermont History* 71 (Summer/Fall 2003): 139

_____. "Thomas Day Seymour Bassett (1913–2001)." *Vermont History* 69 (Winter/Spring 2001): 142.

_____. Jeffrey D. Marshall, and D. Gregory Sanford. "'Little Republics': The Structure of State Politics in Vermont, 1854–1920." *Vermont History* 53, no. 3 (Summer 1985): 141–166.

Hannon, Patrick T. *"home": A History of St. Peter's Parish, Rutland, Vermont.* Rutland: St. Peter Church, 2000.

Harris, Christopher. "The Road Less Traveled By: Rural Northern New England in Global Perspective, 1815–1960." Ph. D. dissertation, Northeastern University, 2007.

Bibliography

Hausfater, Glenn and Sarah Blaffer Hrdy. Eds., *Infanticide: Comparative and Evolutionary Perspectives*. New York: Aldine Publishing Company, 1984.

Hemenway, Abby Maria. *The History of Washington County in the Historical Gazetteer*. Montpelier: Vermont Watchman and State Journal, 1882.

_____. *The Vermont Gazetteer: A Magazine embracing a History of Each Town*. Claremont: The Claremont Manufacturing Company, 1877.

Henderson, Thomas. *Hints on the Medical Examination of Recruits for the Army*. New Orleans: John J. Haswell, 1840.

Herwig, Wesley. "A Patient Boiled Alive (Or: Why Jehiel Smith, a Thomsonian Physician, Left East Randolph, Vermont, in a Hurry")." *Vermont History* 44, no. 4 (Fall 1976): 227.

Heslin, Thomas E. "The Irish in Vermont: Their Contrary Nature Helped Shape the State." *Rutland Historical Society Quarterly*. Vol. 13, no. 1 (Winter 1983), 13.

Hoffbeck, Steven R. "'Remember the Poor' (Galatians 2:10): Poor Farms in Vermont." *Vermont History* 57, no. 4 (Fall 1989): 226

Holbrook, Jay Mack. *Vermont 1771 Census*. Oxford, MA: Holbrook Research Institute, 1982.

Hosack, David. "Observations on Ergot." *Essays on Various Subjects of Medical Science*. New-York: J. Seymour, 1824.

Hoskins, William George, ed. *The Making of the English Landscape*. London: Hodder and Stoughton, 1955.

Hubbard, George H. Ed. *The New-Hampshire Journal of Medicine*. Manchester: Fisk & Gage, 1857.

Hudson, John W. and Suzanne C. *The Rutland Railroad: Rutland to Bellows Falls*. Loveland, OH: Depot Square Publishing, 2010.

Hungerford, Edward. *The Modern Railroad*. Chicago: A. C. McClurg & Co., 1911.

Hunt, Freeman. Ed. *The Merchants' Magazine and Commercial Review*. New York: 1857.

Hunt, James. "On the Acclimatisation of Europeans in the United States of America." *The Anthropological Review* 8, no. 29 (April 1870): 119.

Ingersoll, George G. *An Address delivered before the Literary Societies of the University of Vermont, August 2, 1837*. Burlington: Hiram Johnson & Co.)

Jacobs, Eldridge C. Jacobs. *Report of the State Geologist on the Geology and Mineral Industries of Vermont 1945–1946*. Burlington: Free Press Printing, 1946.

John, Richard R. *Spreading the News: The American Postal System from Franklin to Morse*. Cambridge: Harvard University Press, 1995.

Johnson, Curtis B. and Elsa Gilbertson. *The Historic Architecture of Rutland County including a listing of the Vermont State Register of Historic Places*. Montpelier: The Vermont Division for Historic Preservation 1988.

Johnson, Paul. *The Birth of the Modern: World Society 1815–1830*. New York: HarperCollins, 1991.

Jones, Robert C. *The Central Vermont Railway: A Yankee Tradition*. Vol. 1. Silverton, CO: Sundance Publications, 1981.

Journal of the House of Representatives of the State of Vermont, October Session 1844. Montpelier: E. P. Walton & Sons, 1845.

Journal of the House of Representatives of the State of Vermont, October Session 1845. Windsor: Bishop & Tracy, 1846.

Journal of the House of Representatives of the State of Vermont, October Session, 1850. Burlington: Chauncey Goodrich, 1851.

Journal of the House of Representatives, of the State of Vermont, October Session, 1853. Burlington: Chauncey Goodrich, 1854.

Journal of the House of Representatives of the State of Vermont, October Session 1855. Montpelier: E. P. Walton: 1855.

Journal of the House of Representatives of the State of Vermont, October Session, 1856. Middlebury: The Register Book and Job Office, 1856.

Journal of the House of Representatives of the State of Vermont, Annual Session, 1865. Montpelier: Freeman Steam Printing Company, 1866.

Journal of the House of Representatives of the State of Vermont. Biennial Session, 1870. Montpelier: Freeman Steam Printing House and Bindery, 1871.

Journal of the Senate and House of Representatives of the State of Vermont, Special Session, 1857. Montpelier: E. P. Walton, 1857.

Journal of the Senate of the State of Vermont, October Session 1836. Montpelier: E. P. Walton & Son, 1836.

Journal of the Senate of the State of Vermont, October Session, 1837. Montpelier: E. P. Walton, 1837.

Journal of the Senate of the State of Vermont. October Session, 1846. Windsor: Bishop & Tracy, 1846.

Journal of the Senate of the State of Vermont. October Session, 1848. Burlington: Free Press Office, 1849.

Journal of the Senate of the State of Vermont. October Session, 1854. Middlebury: The Register Book and Job Office, 1854.

Journal of the Senate of the State of Vermont. October Session, 1855. Middlebury: Register Book and Job Office, 1855.

Journal of the Senate of the State of Vermont, October Session, 1859. Montpelier: E. P. Walton, 1859.

Journal of the Senate of the State of Vermont, October Session 1860. Montpelier: E. P. Walton, 1860.

Journal of the Senate of the State of Vermont, Biennial Session, 1912. Montpelier: By Authority, 1912.

Kendall, John S. "The Connecticut and Passumpsic Rivers R.R." *The Railway and Locomotive Historical Society Bulletin* 49 (May 1939): 23–32.

Bibliography

King, William S. *Addresses Before the Vermont State Agricultural Society at its Exhibition held at Rutland, September 1852*. Middlebury: Justus Cobb, 1853.

Kingsbury, Henry D. and Simeon L. Deyo. *Illustrated History of Kennebec County, Maine.* New York: H. W. Blake & Company, 1892.

Kneeland, Stillman F. *The Commercial Law Register, A Manual of the International Merchants' Protective Law Association.* Albany: Law Book and Law Blank, 1873.

Kozub, Andrea Zlotucha. "'To Married Ladies It is Peculiarly Suited': Nineteenth-Century Abortion in an Archaeological Context." *Historical Archaeology* 52, no. 2 (2018): 264–280.

Larson, Erik. *The Devil in the White City: Murder, Magic, and Madness at the Fair that Changed America.* New York: Vintage Books, 2003.

Larson, John Lauritz. *Internal Improvement: National Public Works and the Promise of Popular Government in the Early United States.* Chapel Hill: University of North Carolina Press, 2001.

Lathrop, George Parsons. Ed., *The Complete Works of Nathaniel Hawthorne.* Vol. 12. Boston: Houghton Mifflin Company, 1878.

Laws of the State of New-York, passed at the Sixty-Eighth Session of the Legislature, begun and held in the City of Albany, the seventh day of January 1845. Albany: C. Van Benthuysen and Co., 1845.

Lees, F. R. *Text-Book of Temperance.* New York: J. N. Stearns, 1869.

Lepore, Jill. "Historians Who Love Too Much: Reflections on Microhistory and Biography." *The Journal of American History* 88, no. 1 (2001): 129–144.

Lindsey, John. *A Discourse Delivered Before the Honorable Legislature of Vermont, on the Anniversary Election, October 10, 1822.* Montpelier: E. P. Walton, 1822.

Lord, Robert H., John E. Sexton and Edward T. Harrington. *History of the Archdiocese of Boston in the Various Stages of Its Development 1604 to 1943.* New York: Sheed & Ward, 1944.

Ludlum, David M. *Social Ferment in Vermont 1791–1850.* New York: Columbia University Press, 1939.

Magnússon, Sigurour Gylfi. "Views into the Fragments: An Approach from a Microhistorical Perspective." *International Journal of Historical Archaeology* 20 (2016):182–206.

Map and Description of the Western Vermont Railroad, and the District through which it runs. New York: George F. Nesbitt, 1852.

Mapes, James F. *The Working Farmer: Devoted to Agriculture, Horticulture, Floriculture, Kitchen Gardening, Management of Hot Houses, Green Houses, &c. &c.* Vol. 5. New York: Frederick McCready, 1853.

Marsh, Caroline Crane, Ed., *Life and Letters of George Perkins Marsh,* Two Volumes. New York: Charles Scribner's Sons, 1888.

Marsh, George P. *Address delivered before the Agricultural Society of Rutland County, Sept. 30, 1847.* Rutland: Herald Office, 1848.

_____. *Man and Nature; or, Physical Geography as Modified by Human Action.* New York: Charles Scribner, 1864.

McDonagh, Josephine. "Child-Murder Narratives in George Eliot's *Adam Bede:* Embedded Histories and Fictional Representation." *Nineteenth-Century Literature* 56, no. 2 (September 2001): 228–259.

Meeks, Harold A. *Time and Change in Vermont: A Human Geography.* Chester, Conn.: The Globe Pequot Press, 1986.

Mills, Katherine B. "The Remedies of Grandmother's Day." *The Vermonter* 34 (1929):27–28.

Mohr, James C. *Abortion in America: The Origins and Evolution of National Policy, 1800–1900.* Oxford: Oxford University Press, 1978.

Monkkonen, Eric H. "A Disorderly People? Urban Order in the Nineteenth and Twentieth Centuries." *Journal of American History* 68, no. 3 (December 1981): 539–559.

Moses, Lyria Bennett. "Recurring Dilemmas: The Law's Race to Keep up with Technological Change." *Journal of Law, Technology & Policy.* Vol 2007, no. 2:253.

Obituary Record, Report of the Commissioner of Education, Report of the Secretary of the Interior. Vol. 2 Washington: GPO, 1877.

Perkins, Joseph. *An Address delivered before the Medical Society of the State of Vermont, October 22, 1856.* Rutland: George A. Tuttle & Co., 1857.

Phelps's Travelers' Guide through the United States. New York: Ensign & Thayer, 1850.

Poor, Henry V. Ed. *American Railroad Journal.* Vol. 22. New York: J. H. Schultz & Co., 1849.

Powers, Amos H. *The Powers Family: A Genealogical and Historical Record.* Chicago: Fergus Printing Company, 1884.

Proceedings at the Annual Meeting of the Vermont State Temperance Society, held at Windsor, Jan. 16, and 17, 1850. Windsor: The Chronical Press, 1850.

Proceedings of the Convention, holden at Windsor, VT., January 20, 1836: for the purpose of taking preliminary measures for a rail road through the valleys of the Connecticut and Passumpsic Rivers to the St. Lawrence. Windsor: Chronicle Press, 1836.

Proceedings of the Free Convention held at Rutland, Vt., July [sic] *25th, 26, and 27th, 1858.* Boston: J. B. Yerrinton and Son, 1858.

Proceedings of the Vermont Pharmaceutical Association, 1871. Rutland: Tuttle & Co., 1871.

Proceedings of the Vermont Pharmaceutical Association, September 24–25, 1873. Rutland: Globe Paper, 1874.

Procter, Jr., William. Ed. *The American Journal of Pharmacy.* Vol. 30. Philadelphia: Merrihew & Thompson, 1858.

Putnam, Constance. *The Science We Have Loved and Taught: Dartmouth Medical School's First Two Centuries.* Lebanon: University Press of New England, 2004.

Bibliography

Randall, Gurdon P. *Book of Designs for School Houses, and Suggestions as to Obtaining Plans, and How to Heat and Ventilate School Buildings.* Chicago: Knight & Leonard, 1884.

——————. *A Hand Book of Designs, containing Plans in Perspective, of Court Houses, Universities, Academies, School Houses, Churches, Dwellings, Etc., Etc., Etc., and Suggestions Relative to their Construction, Heating and Ventilation.* Chicago: Church, Goodman and Donnelly, 1868.

Reagan, Leslie J. *When Abortion was a Crime: Women, Medicine, and Law in the United States, 1867–1973.* Berkeley: University of California Press, 1997.

Redfield, Isaac F. *A Practical Treatise upon the Law of Railways.* Boston: Little, Brown and Company, 1857.

Reese, David Meredith. *Medicines, Their Uses and Mode of Administration.* New-York: Harper & Brothers, 1844.

Renehan, Edward J. Jr. *Dark Genius of Wall Street: The Misunderstood Life of Jay Gould, King of the Robber Barons.* New York: Basic Books, 2006.

Report of the Board of Commissioners, for Common Schools, October 25, 1828. Woodstock: Rufus Colton, 1828.

Report of the Directors of the Rutland and Burlington Railroad Company, at their Annual Meeting, at Rutland, Held 12th January, 1848. Burlington: Free Press Office, 1848.

Revised Statutes of the State of Vermont, passed November 19, 1839. Burlington: Chauncey Goodrich, 1840.

Robbins, Daniel. *The Vermont State House: A History & Guide.* Montpelier: Vermont Council on the Arts, 1980.

Roberts, Gwilym R. "The Struggle for Decent Transportation in Western Rutland County, 1820–1850." *Vermont History* 69, Symposium Supplement, 2001.

Rosenberg, Charles E. *The Cholera Years: The United States in 1832, 1849, and 1866.* Chicago: University of Chicago Press, 1962.

Roster of the Graduates and Past Cadets of Norwich University 1819–1907. Bradford, Vt.: Opinion Press, 1907.

Rubertone, Patricia E. "Landscape as artifact: Comments on 'the archaeological use of landscape treatment in social, economic and ideological analysis.'" *Historical Archaeology* 23, no. 1 (1989): 50–54.

Roth, Randolph A. *The Democratic Dilemma: Religion, Reform, and the Social Order in the Connecticut River Valley of Vermont, 1791–1850.* Cambridge: Cambridge University Press, 1987.

——————. "Child Murder in New England." *Social Science History* 25, no. 1 (Spring 2001): 119–120.

——————. *American Homicide.* Cambridge: Harvard University Press, 2009.

Rotman, Deborah L. "The Fighting Irish: Historical Archaeology of Nineteenth-Century Catholic Immigrant Experiences in South Bend, Indiana." *Historical Archaeology* 44, no. 2 (2010): 113–131.

Rozwenc, Edwin C. *Agricultural Policies in Vermont 1860–1945.* Montpelier: Vermont Historical Society, 1981.

Rutland Newsliner: The Rutland Railway Magazine. Vol. 4, no. 4 (October – November 1955).

Rutland Railroad Company. *Historical Sketch of Rutland Railroad Company 1849–1949.* Rutland: Rutland Railroad Company, 1949.

Ryle, Gilbert. *The Concept of the Mind.* New York: University of Chicago Press, 1949.

Sanford, D. Gregory. "Vermont Corporations: An Index to Private Corporations Formed by the Legislature." *State Papers of Vermont,* vol. 20. Montpelier: Secretary of State, 1987.

Schwartz, Lita Linzer and Natalie K. Isser. *Endangered Children: Neonaticide, Infanticide, and Filicide.* Boca Raton: CRC Press, 2000.

Searls, Paul M. *Two Vermonts: Geography and Identity, 1865–1910.* Hanover: University Press of New England, 2006.

Second Annual Report to the Legislature: Under the Act of March, 1842, relating to the Registry and Returns of Birth, Marriages and Deaths in Massachusetts. For the year ending May 1st, 1843. Boston: Dutton and Wentworth, 1843.

Second Annual Report of the Secretary of the State Board of Health of the State of Vermont for the Year Ending Sept. 1st, 1888. Rutland: Tuttle Company, 1888.

Second Report to the Legislature of Vermont, relating to the Registry and Returns of Births, Marriages, and Deaths, in this state, for the year ending December 31, 1858. Middlebury: Register Book and Job Office, 1859.

Selectmen's Report to the Town of Rutland, March 3, 1857. Rutland: George A. Tuttle & Company, 1857.

Selectmen's Report. Town of Rutland, March 1, 1859. Rutland: Tuttle & Co's Steam Printing, 1859.

Sessions, Gene, "Vermont's Nineteenth Century Railroad Workers." In Michael Sherman and Jennie Versteeg, eds. *We Vermonters: Perspectives on the Past.* Montpelier: Vermont Historical Society, 1992.

Seventh Biennial Report of the Board of Railroad Commissioners of the State of Vermont, June 30th, 1898 to June 30th, 1900. St. Albans: The Messenger Company Print, 1900.

Shattuck, Gary G. *Green Mountain Opium Eaters: A History of Early Addiction in Vermont.* Charleston: History Press, 2017.

Shaughnessy, Jim. *The Rutland Road.* Syracuse: Syracuse University Press, 1997.

Sherman, Michael, Gene Sessions and P. Jeffrey Potash. *Freedom and Unity: A History of Vermont.* Barre: Vermont Historical Society, 2004.

Siegel, Reva. "Reasoning from the Body: A Historical Perspective on Abortion Regulation and Questions of Equal Protection." *Stanford Law Review* 40 (2) (1992): 301.

Bibliography

Silgoe, John. "Plugging Past Reform: Small Scale Farming Innovation and Big-Scale Farming Research." In Ronald G. Walthers, ed., *Scientific Authority and Twentieth-Century America*. Baltimore: Johns Hopkins University Press, 1997.

Silliman, Stephen W. "A View from the East: Reflections on Historical Archaeology in Western Massachusetts." *Historical Archaeology* 53, no. 2 (2019): 367–371.

Sinclair, John. *Sketch of an Introduction to the Proposed Analysis of the Statistical Account of Scotland*. London: W. Bulmer and Company, 1802.

Slade, Jr., William. *Vermont State Papers*. Middlebury: J. W. Copeland, 1823.

Smith, John David. "The Health of Vermont's Civil War Recruits." *Vermont History* 43, no. 3 (Summer 1975): 185.

Smith, H. P. and W. S. Rann. *History of Rutland County, Vermont*. Syracuse: D. Mason & Co., 1886.

Smith, J. V. C. Ed. *The Boston Medical and Surgical Journal*. Boston: David Clapp, 1849.

Smith, William Prescott. *The Book of the Great Railway Celebrations of 1857*. New York: D. Appleton & Co., 1858.

Speech of Hon. Albert Clarke, November 13, 1874. The Free Pass Abuse. The Constitutional Power of the State to Regulate Railroads. Boston, 1907.

Stilwell, Lewis D. *Migration from Vermont*. Montpelier: Vermont Historical Society, 1948.

Storer, Horatio R. *On Criminal Abortion in America*. Philadelphia: J. B. Lippincott & Co., 1860.

Taksa, Lucy. "The Material Culture of an Industrial Artifact: Interpreting Control, Defiance, and Everyday Resistance at the New South Wales Eveleigh Railway Workshops." *Historical Archaeology* 39, no. 3 (2005): 11.

Tarlow, Sarah. *The Archaeology of Improvement in Britain, 1750–1850*. Cambridge: Cambridge University Press, 2007.

Thayer, William Henry. *Address to the Graduates of the Vermont Medical College, of the Class of 1856*. Keene: 1856.

The School Journal, and Vermont Agriculturist, vol. 1, no. 2 (Windsor: Bishop and Tracy, 1847).

Taylor, George Rogers. *The Transportation Revolution 1815–1860*. New York: Rinehart & Company, 1951.

The College Journal of Medical Science. Vol. 1. Cincinnati: Moore, Wilstach, Keys & Co., 1856.

The Eastern Tourist; being a Guide through the States of Connecticut, Rhode Island, Massachusetts, Vermont, New Hampshire, and Maine. New York: J. Disturnell, 1848.

The Executive Documents of the House of Representatives for the First Session of the Forty-Eighth Congress, 1883–'84. Washington: Government Printing Office, 1884.

The Journal of the American Pharmaceutical Association. Columbus: By the Association, 1913.

The Journal of Materia Medic, vol. 8, no. 1 (January 1869).

The New-England Mercantile Union Business Directory. New York: Pratt & Co., 1849.

The Seventh Census, Report of the Superintendent of the Census for December 1, 1852, to which is appended the Report for December 1, 1851, The Seventh Census of the United States: 1850. Washington: Robert Armstrong, 1853.

Third Annual Report of the Railroad Commissioner of the State of Vermont to the General Assembly, 1858. Burlington: Free Press Print, 1858.

Third Biennial Report of the Board of Railroad Commissioners of the State of Vermont. June 30th, 1890, to June 30th, 1892. Burlington: The Free Press Association, 1892.

Third Report to the Legislature of Vermont, relating to the Registry and Returns of Births, Marriages, and Deaths, in this State, for the year ending December 31, 1859. Middlebury: Register Book and Job Office, 1860.

Thirteenth Annual Report of the Boston and Maine Railroad Corporation, Annual Reports of the Railroad Corporations in the State of Massachusetts for 1847. Boston: Dutton and Wentworth, 1848.

Thirty-sixth Annual Report of the Vermont Domestic Missionary Society. Montpelier: E. P. Walton Jr., 1854.

Thomas, William G. *The Iron Way: Railroads, the Civil War, and the Making of Modern America*. New Haven: Yale University Press, 2011.

Thompson, Daniel P. *History of the Town of Montpelier, from the time it was first chartered in 1781 to the year 1860*. Montpelier: E. P. Walton, 1860.

Thompson, Zadock. *History of Vermont, Natural, Civil and Statistical in Three Parts*. Burlington: Stacy & Jameson, 1853.

Thomson, Samuel. *New Guide to Health; or Botanic Family Physician*. Montpelier: 1851.

Thoreau, Henry David. *Walden, or, Life in the Woods*. Boston: Houghton, Mifflin and Company, 1854.

Transactions of the Vermont Medical Society, at the Annual Session, Held at Montpelier, October 19th and 20th, 1864. Woodstock: Vermont Standard, 1864.

Transactions of the Vermont Medical Society for the Year 1865. Burlington: R. S. Styles, 1865.

Transactions of the Vermont Medical Society, for the years 1867 and 1868. Burlington: R. S. Styles, 1869.

Transactions of the Vermont Medical Society for the years 1869 and 1870. Burlington: R. S. Styles, 1870.

Transactions of the Vermont Medical Society for the Years 1871, 1872 and 1873. Montpelier: Argus and Patriot, 1874.

Triennial Catalogue of the University of Vermont 1854. Burlington: Free Press Print, 1854.

True, Marshall. "Middle-Class Women and Civic Improvement in Burlington 1865–1890." *Vermont History* 56, no. 2 (Spring 1988): 112.

Tucker, William Howard. *History of Hartford, Vermont, July 4, 1761–April 4, 1889*. Burlington: The Free Press Association, 1889.

Bibliography

Twenty-Third Report to the Legislature of Vermont, relating to the Registry and Returns of Births, Marriages and Deaths, in this State. For the year ending December 31st, 1879. Montpelier: Freeman Steam Printing House and Bindery, 1882.

Van de Warker, Ely. *The Detection of Criminal Abortion and a Study of Foeticidal Drugs.* Boston: James Campbell, 1872.

Vermont State Board of Health. Vol. 2. Brattleboro: 1901.

Walton, E. P. *Records of the Governor and Council of the State of Vermont.* Montpelier: J. & J. M. Poland, 1879.

⸻. *Vermont Family Visitor, A Monthly Paper, Devoted Exclusively to Agriculture and Miscellaneous Matter.* June 1845.

Waterman, Edgar F. *The Waterman Family.* Vol. 2 New Haven: Tuttle, Morehouse & Taylor, 1942.

Wells, Frederic Palmer. *History of Barnet, Vermont.* Burlington: Free Press Printing, 1923.

⸻. *History of Newbury, Vermont.* St. Johnsbury: The Caledonian Company, 1902.

West, Robert Edward, ed. *Rutland in Retrospect.* Rutland: Rutland Historical Society, 1978.

White, Richard. *Railroaded: The Transcontinentals and the Making of Modern America.* New York: W. W. Norton & Company, 2011.

Whitlaw, Charles. *A Treatise on the Causes and Effects of Inflammation Fever.* London: By the author, 1831.

Williams, Chauncey K. *Centennial Celebration of the Settlement of Rutland, VT.* Rutland: Tuttle & Company, 1870.

Williams, Samuel. *The Natural and Civil History of Vermont.* Walpole, NH: Isaiah Thomas and David Carlisle, 1794.

Wilson, Harold Fisher. *The Hill Country of Northern New England: Its Social and Economic History 1790–1930.* New York: Columbia University Press, 1936.

Willard, Emma. *Guide to the Temple of Time; and Universal History, for Schools.* New York: A. S. Barnes & Company, 1849.

Wing, Joseph A. "Burning of the State House." Abby Maria Hemenway, ed., *The History of the Town of Montpelier, including that of the town of East Montpelier, for the first one hundred and two years.* Montpelier: By Miss. A. M. Hemenway, 1882.

Whitcher, William F. *History of the Town of Haverhill, New Hampshire.* 1919.

Wolmar, Christian. *The Great Railroad Revolution: The History of Trains in America.* New York: Public Affairs, 2012.

Zeilenga, Jack. "George Peck and Mary Greene Nye: Correspondence on the State House Fire of 1857." *Vermont History* 82, no. 2 (Summer/Fall 2014): 143–148.

Ziegenbein, Linda. "The Sensory Landscape of the Mid-Nineteenth Century Connecticut River Valley." *Historical Archaeology* 53, no. 2 (2019): 354–366.

Notes

1 *St. Alban's Weekly Messenger*, 8 January 1857.

2 Jack Zeilenga, "George Peck and Mary Greene Nye: Correspondence on the State House Fire of 1857," *Vermont History* 82, no. 2 (Summer/Fall 2014): 143–148.

3 Joseph A. Wing, "Burning of the State House," Abby Maria Hemenway, *The History of the Town of Montpelier, including that of the town of East Montpelier, for the first one hundred and two years* (Montpelier: By Miss. A. M. Hemenway, 1882), 338. Ms. Hemenway's volume further records her impressions of Montpelier, the state capitol, on the title page: "Fair land of hill and dale, Sweet Freedom's chosen throne, Revered of all Vermont, Pre-eminent our own."

4 *Journal of the Senate and House of Representatives of the State of Vermont, Special Session, 1857* [hereafter *Special Session 1857*] (Montpelier: E. P. Walton, 1857), 26.

5 Freeman Hunt, ed., *The Merchants' Magazine and Commercial Review*, vol. 37 (New York: 1857), 363. Chicago stores and a Mobile, Alabama cotton press, each valued at $850,000, headed the list.

6 *Special Session 1857*, 200.

7 *The Enterprise and Vermonter* (Vergennes), 9 January 1857.

8 *Special Session*, 245–246.

9 William Prescott Smith, *The Book of the Great Railway Celebrations of 1857* (New York: D. Appleton & Co., 1858), 175.

10 Dawn D. Hance, *The History of Rutland, Vermont 1761–1861* (Rutland: Academy Books 1991), 43–44.

11 British philosopher Gilbert Ryle fashioned the Ghost in the Machine idiom to describe dual functions (i.e., mind-body) operating simultaneously but separately in the same body. *The Concept of the Mind* (New York: University of Chicago Press, 1949), 22.

12 Gary G. Shattuck, *Green Mountain Opium Eaters: A History of Early Addiction in Vermont* (Charleston: History Press, 2017), *passim*.

13 *Vermont Record*, 4 November 1865.

14 Erik Larson, *The Devil in the White City: Murder, Magic, and Madness at the Fair that Changed America* (New York: Vintage Books, 2003), 307.

15 Kenneth Clark, *Civilisation: A Personal View* (London: British Broadcasting Corporation, 1969), 160.

16 Orlando Figes, *The Europeans: Three Lives and the Making of a Cosmopolitan Culture* (New York: Metropolitan Books, 2019), 40.

17 Richard White, *Railroaded: The Transcontinentals and the Making of Modern America* (New York: W. W. Norton & Company, 2011), xii.

18 Charles Francis Adams, "The Era of Change," in Charles Francis Adams and Henry Adams, *Chapters of Erie and Other Essays* (Boston: James Osgood, 1871; reprint, New York: Augustus M. Kelley, 1967), 365.

19 Figes, *The Europeans*, 43–44.

20 Anthony Giddens and Christopher Pierson, *Conversations with Anthony Giddens: Making Sense of Modernity* (Stanford: Stanford University Press, 1998), 94. British historian Paul Johnson adopted a more pragmatic understanding of modernity when he described the great technological and societal changes unleashed in the fifteen years following Napoleon's defeat in 1815. Paul Johnson, *The Birth of the Modern: World Society 1815–1830* (New York: HarperCollins, 1991). Johnson explained his views in preparing the book: "I was anxious to show how ordinary people were affected by these changes. What I try to do is like the 'total history' of the French Annales School. But they tend to write static history, while I believe that one should convey the sense of history rumbling along like a railroad." "Why History is Like a Railroad," *New York Times*, June 23, 1991.

21 Paul Gillen and Devleena Ghosh, *Colonialism and Modernity* (New South Wales, Australia: UNSW Press, 2007), 54.

22 William G. Thomas, *The Iron Way: Railroads, the Civil War, and the Making of Modern America* (New Haven: Yale University Press, 2011), 8.

23 Stephen W. Silliman, "A View from the East: Reflections on Historical Archaeology in Western Massachusetts," *Historical Archaeology* 53, no. 2 (2019): 369.

24 Gillen, *Colonialism and Modernity*, 54.

25 *What's the railroad to me?*
I never go to see
Where it ends.
It fills a few hollows,
And makes banks for the swallows,
It sets the sand a-blowing,
And the blackberries a-growing.
Henry David Thoreau, *Walden, or, Life in the Woods* (Boston: Houghton, Mifflin and Company, 1854), 190–192.

26 Hal S. Barron, *Those Who Stayed Behind: Rural Society in Nineteenth-Century New England* (Cambridge: Cambridge University Press, 1987), 28–29

Notes

27 Jeremy Flaherty, "A Multivariate Look at Migration from Vermont," *Vermont History* 74 (Summer/Fall 2006): 150.

28 Hunt, *Merchants' Magazine 1850*, vol. 23:279.

29 Ibid., vol. 31:181.

30 Joseph Perkins, *An Address delivered before the Medical Society of the State of Vermont, October 22, 1856* (Rutland: George A. Tuttle & Co., 1857), 11.

31 *Fifth Annual Report of the Vermont Board of Education, September, 1861* (Burlington: Times Book and Job Printing, 1861), x [hereafter *Fifth Annual Report, 1861*].

32 Samuel W. Johnson, "Exhaustion of Soils, read before the Vermont Board of Agriculture, at Burlington, Jan. 24, 1872," Peter Collier, *First Annual Report of the Vermont State Board of Agriculture, Manufactures and Mining for the Year 1872* (Montpelier: J. & J. M. Poland, 1872), 369.

33 See, e.g., Graffagnino, *Vermont*, 11–13, for an overview of Vermonters' impressions of out migration.

34 *The Seventh Census, Report of the Superintendent of the Census for December 1, 1852, to which is appended the Report for December 1, 1851, The Seventh Census of the United States: 1850* (Washington: Robert Armstrong, 1853), 138.

35 *Fourth Report to the Legislature of Vermont relating to the Registry and Returns of Births, Marriages and Deaths, in this state, for the Year ending December 31, 1860* (Middlebury: The Register Office, 1861), 89.

36 "Remarks upon the Schedules of 1850, etc.," *The Seventh Census of the United States: 1850, Appendix*, iv.

37 Michael R. Haines, "The Population of the United States, 1790–1920," Historical Paper No. 56, (Cambridge: National Bureau of Economic Research, 1994), 7.

38 July 1, 1858, Semi-Annual Meeting, Vermont Medical Society, Minutes of meetings, 1851–1867, Vol. 3, Howe Library, University of Vermont (hereafter UVM).

39 *Fifth Report to the Legislature of Vermont, relating to the Registry and Returns of Births, Marriages an Deaths, in this State, fro the Year Ending December 31, 1861* (Montpelier: Freeman Printing, 1863), 85. "Until the Census Bureau is removed from political influences and exactions, and the appointment of its subordinate clerical corps offers encouragement to scientific capacity and fidelity, rather than a reward to partisan favorites of questionable fitness for the important business entrusted to their charge, all the efforts of the able and accomplished Statist at the head of the Census Bureau, will only enable him to present reports of approximate certainty and value." *Sixth Report to the Legislature of Vermont. . . for the year ending December 31, 1862* (Montpelier: Freeman Steam Printing, 1865), 96.

40 J. Kevin Graffagnino, *The Shaping of Vermont: From the Wilderness to the Centennial 1749–1877* (Rutland and Bennington: Vermont Heritage Press and the Bennington Museum, 1983), 104.

41 *Connecticut Journal*, 7 June 1786.

42 Samuel B. Hand, "Thomas Day Seymour Bassett (1913–2001)," *Vermont History* 69 (Winter/Spring 2001):142.

43 T. D. Seymour Bassett, "Urban Penetration of Rural Vermont, 1840–1880," (unpublished Ph.D. dissertation, Harvard University, 1952), 111. In 1992, the Vermont Historical Society published a shortened version of Bassett's dissertation that omitted many of the helpful footnotes, re-titled *The Growing Edge: Vermont Villages 1840–1880*. While it is easier to handle and read than the two cumbersome typewritten volumes ("sap boiled down is sweeter," Bassett wrote), the latter version leaves one wanting to know exactly where the information he recited came from, leaving the more inquisitive to track down the dissertation.

44 J. Kevin Graffagnino, *Vermont in the Victorian Age: Continuity and Change in the Green Mountain State 1850–1900* (Bennington and Shelburne: Vermont Heritage Press and Shelburne Museum, 1985), ix.

45 Michael Sherman, Gene Sessions and P. Jeffrey Potash, *Freedom and Unity: A History of Vermont* (Barre: Vermont Historical Society, 2004), 210–211.

46 David M. Ludlum, *Social Ferment in Vermont 1791–1850* (New York: Columbia University Press, 1939), 272–273.

47 Randolph A. Roth, *The Democratic Dilemma: Religion, Reform, and the Social Order in the Connecticut River Valley of Vermont, 1791–1850* (New York: Cambridge University Press, 1987).

48 See, e.g., Lewis D. Stilwell, *Migration from Vermont* (Montpelier: Vermont Historical Society, 1948), 216.

49 Nancy Price Graff and William Hosley, "Celebrating Vermont: Myths and Realities of the First Sixty Years of Statehood," in Nancy Price Graff, ed., *Celebrating Vermont: Myths and Realities* (Middlebury: The Christian A. Johnson Memorial Gallery, 1991), 39.

50 Harold Fisher Wilson, *The Hill Country of Northern New England: Its Social and Economic History 1790–1930* (New York: Columbia University Press, 1936).

51 Dana Doten, State Director, *Vermont: A Guide to the Green Mountain State* (Boston: Houghton Mifflin Company, 1937), ix.

52 Paul M. Searls, *Two Vermonts: Geography and Identity, 1865–1910* (Hanover: University Press of New England, 2006), 17.

53 Alfredo González-Ruibal, "Archaeology and the Time of Modernity," *Historical Archaeology* 50, no. 3 (2016): 145.

54 Sigurour Gylfi Magnússon, "Views into the Fragments: An Approach from a Microhistorical Perspective," *International Journal of Historical Archaeology* 20 (2016):182–206; Soraya de Chadarevian, "Microstudies versus big picture accounts?," *Studies in History and Philosophy of Biological and Biomedical Sciences* 40 (2009): 13–19; Jill Lepore, "Historians Who Love Too Much: Reflections on Microhistory and Biography," *The Journal of American History* 88, no. 1 (2001): 129–144.

NOTES

55 James Davie Butler, *Deficiencies in our History: An Address Delivered before the Vermont Historical and Antiquarian Society, October 16, 1846* (Montpelier: Eastman & Danforth, 1846), 15.

56 Gary G. Shattuck, *Insurrection, Corruption and Murder in Early Vermont: Life on the Wild Northern Frontier* (Charleston: History Press, 2014) and *Green Mountain Opium Eaters*.

57 *Special Session 1857*, 221.

58 John Lauritz Larson, *Internal Improvement: National Public Works and the Promise of Popular Government in the Early United States* (Chapel Hill: University of North Carolina Press, 2001), 1–7.

59 William H. Beardsley, "The Changing Landscape and the Role of State Government," Vermont Arch. Arts & Science Occasional Paper 5 (1970).

60 The Banks of Vermont, Freeman Hunt, *Merchants' Magazine, 1848*, vol. 19:109.

61 D. Gregory Sanford, "Vermont Corporations: An Index to Private Corporations Formed by the Legislature," *State Papers of Vermont*, vol. 20 (Montpelier: Secretary of State, 1987); Victor R. Rolando, "Incorporation Data," unpublished analysis.

62 E. P. Walton, ed., *Records of the Governor and Council of the State of Vermont*, vol. 7 (Montpelier: J. & J. M. Poland, 1879), 479.

63 Christian Wolmar, *The Great Railroad Revolution: The History of Trains in America* (New York: Public Affairs, 2012), 18.

64 Gwilym R. Roberts, "The Struggle for Decent Transportation in Western Rutland County, 1820–1850," *Vermont History* 69 (Symposium Supplement, 2001): 127.

65 Walton, *Governor and Council*, vol. 7:484.

66 *Whitehall Palldaium*, quoted in *The Repertory* (St. Albans, Vermont), 1 September 1831.

67 Jim Shaughnessy, *The Rutland Road*, second edition (Syracuse: Syracuse University Press, 1997), 2.

68 "Petition of Reuben Washburn & others" praying for the incorporation of a Rail Road Company between Rutland and Connecticut River, October 12, 1835. Manuscript Vermont State Papers, Petitions to the General Assembly, 1832–1836, volume 64, SE118-00064, Vermont State Archives and Records Administration (hereafter VSARA).

69 *Proceedings of the Convention, holden at Windsor, VT., January 20, 1836: for the purpose of Taking preliminary measures for a rail road through the valleys of the Connecticut and Passumpsic Rivers to the St. Lawrence* (Windsor: Chronicle Press, 1836).

70 "Petition of Hosea Williams and others for a Rail Road," October 24, 1836, ibid.

71 "Petition of John Colbrook and others for an appropriation from the surplus revenue to aid in the construction of the Connecticut & Passumpsic River Rail Road," October 19, 1836, ibid.

72 *Bloodgood v. Mohawk & Hudson R. R. Co.*, 18 Wend. 9, 48 (N.Y. Ct. Err. 1837).

73   Wolmar, *The Great Railroad Revolution*, xxi.

74   George T. Chapman, *Sketches of the Alumni of Dartmouth College* (Cambridge: Riverside Press, 1867), 181.

75   Address delivered before the Railroad Convention, at Lebanon, N.H., October 10, 1843 and Address delivered before the Railroad Convention at Montpelier, Vermont, January 8, 1844, Charles B. Haddock, *Addresses and Miscellaneous Writings* (Cambridge: Metcalf and Company, 1846) 77, 105.

76   Preamble, Constitution of Vermont, July 8, 1777.

77   Samuel Williams, *The Natural and Civil History of Vermont* (Walpole, NH: Isaiah Thomas and David Carlisle, 1794), 376. In 1797 Williams continued in his push for better conditions and published *The Rural Magazine, or Vermont Repository,* devoted to "Literary, Moral, Historical and Political Improvement." M. D. Gilman, ed., *Bibliography of Vermont*, (Montpelier: Free Press Association, 1897), 335.

78   *Orleans Independent Standard*, 13 May 1859.

79   William Howard Tucker, *History of Hartford, Vermont, July 4, 1761–April 4, 1889* (Burlington: The Free Press Association, 1889), 354–355.

80   *Middlebury Free Press*, 15 November 1836; *American Railroad Journal and Advocate of Internal Improvements*, vol. 5 (New York: D. K. Minor and George C. Schaeffer, 1836), 725–726.

81   *Journal of the Senate of the State of Vermont, October Session 1836* (Montpelier: E. P. Walton & Son, 1836), 73.

82   Silas H. Jenison, Oct. 13, 1837, "Message," *Journal of the Senate of the State of Vermont, October Session, 1837* (Montpelier: E. P. Walton, 1837), 12.

83   Ibid., 102.

84   Albert D. Hager, *Report of the Geology of Vermont: Descriptive, Theoretical, Economical and Scenographical*, vol. 1 (Claremont: Claremont Manufacturing Company, 1861), 10.

85   Eldridge C. Jacobs, *Report of the State Geologist on the Geology and Mineral Industries of Vermont 1945–1946* (Burlington: Free Press Printing, 1946), 45.

86   E. P. Walton & Sons, *Vermont Family Visitor, A Monthly Paper, Devoted Exclusively to Agriculture and Miscellaneous Matter*, vol. 1 (June 1845), 202–203.

87   Address of William Slade, October 11, 1844, *Journal of the House of Representatives of the State of Vermont, October Session 1844* (Montpelier: E. P. Walton & Sons, 1845), 11.

88   *Report of the Board of Commissioners, for Common Schools, October 25, 1828* (Woodstock: Rufus Colton, 1828), *passim*.

89   "An Act Relating to Common Schools," *The Acts and Resolves Passed by the Legislature of the State of Vermont at their October Session, 1845* (Burlington: Chauncey Goodrich, 1845), 25.

NOTES

90 Horace Eaton, State Superintendent of Common Schools, October 19, 1846, *First Annual Report of the State Superintendent of Common Schools made to the Legislature October, 1846* (Montpelier: Eastman & Danforth, 1846), 3.

91 Emma Willard, *Guide to the Temple of Time; and Universal History, for Schools* (New York: A. S. Barnes & Company, 1849), 4.

92 The Vermont House of Representatives also took notice when seventeen petitions bearing hundreds of names were filed demanding improvements in the schools. Further debates took place and described the squandering of large amounts of money on education calling for change. *Journal of the House of Representatives of the State of Vermont, October Session 1845* (Windsor: Bishop & Tracy, 1846), 10.

93 *St. Johnsbury Caledonian*, 31 October 1837 and 10 July 1838; *Watchman, Impartialist, and Christian Repository* (Lebanon, NH), 12 March 1836.

94 George G. Ingersoll, *An Address delivered before the Literary Societies of the University of Vermont, August 2, 1837* (Burlington: Hiram Johnson & Co.), 18.

95 The Addison County Agricultural Society met for the first time on October 1, 1844 to hear their president discourse on the need for improvement on the state's farms, noting that up to then "improvement has mainly been the result of accident, rather than of any enlightened and scientific course of investigation and experiment." Walton, *Vermont Family Visitor*, 11–16.

96 "C. S. P.," 9 March 1846, ibid., 346. The editor of the publication noted further in 1846 that "a Farmer's Club has been formed in Bakersfield, having for its object the improvement of agricultural productions, useful domestic manufactures, and the mechanic arts." He also reported that the publication directed towards farmers was ending due to a lack of interest. Ibid., 353.

97 George P. Marsh, Address delivered before the Agricultural Society of Rutland County, Sept. 30, 1847" (Rutland: Herald Office, 1848). Just weeks earlier, farmers in Windsor County were also advised to pay attention to similar approaching changes. "The railroads are about to place [farmers]," one paper wrote, "in such a position that, to prosper, he must be able to direct his attention quickly and intelligently to new sources of profit, and facilities for making the most of his means." Education allowed that to happen because "success in farming among us is getting to depend more and more upon *mind;* upon habits of intelligent observation and inquiry; upon reading and study." *The School Journal, and Vermont Agriculturist*, vol. 1, no. 2 (June, 1847).

98 *The Vermont Union Whig* (Rutland), 14 October 1847.

99 Ira Allen, *The Natural and Political History of the State of Vermont* (London: J. W. Myers, 1798), 260. He continued later in his explanation, stating that "Notwithstanding I have said that every farmer is in some respect a mechanic, you should take it as I intended it, rather a general expression, for there are handicrafts who find encouragement enough to apply to particular trades, without so much as scarce ever putting the hand to the plough, such as smiths, taylors, carpenters, shoemakers, &c. they find employment enough, and in a few years I am persuaded that the manual arts will become more visible and distinct." Ibid., 277–278.

100 The times had changed radically from the picture that Ira Allen painted in 1798 when he noted the strong attachment the settlers had to tradition: "The little [diet] may be said to be hereditary, for there is scarce a family that has attempted to introduce any luxury in that line, which their ancestors would be ashamed to see on their table except tea, on which many now breakfast." Ibid., 261.

101 Sarah Tarlow, *The Archaeology of Improvement in Britain, 1750–1850* (Cambridge: Cambridge University Press, 2007), 11.

102 Ibid., 19.

103 Larson, *Internal Improvements*, 3.

104 *Special Session 1857*, 183.

105 Ibid., 136.

106 Ibid., 183.

107 Ibid., 188.

108 Ibid., 10. The record does not reveal why twenty-nine votes were cast by twenty-eight senators.

109 Ibid., 236.

110 Ibid., 40, 209.

111 Ibid., 234.

112 Hunt, *Merchants' Magazine 1852*, vol. 26:678

113 Linda Ziegenbein, "The Sensory Landscape of the Mid-Nineteenth Century Connecticut River Valley," *Historical Archaeology* 53, no. 2 (2019): 360–362.

114 Frank M. Bryan, "Vermont: The Politics of Ruralism," unpublished PhD dissertation, University of Connecticut, 1970, 46.

115 *Special Session 1857*, 133.

116 Ibid., 149.

117 Ibid., 22.

118 Ibid., 177.

119 Ibid., 179.

120 Ibid., 213; Albert Barnes, *Notes, Critical, Explanatory, and Practical, on the Book of Psalms*, vol. 3 (New York: Harper & Brothers, 1869), 65.

121 *Special Session 1857*, 205–206.

122 Ibid., 148.

123 Ibid., 24.

124 Ibid., 133.

125 Ibid., 185.

126 Ibid., 127.

127 Ibid., 169.

128 Ibid., 240.
129 Hance, *History of Rutland,* 145.
130 Glenn M. Andres and Curtis B. Johnson *Buildings of Vermont* (Charlottesville: University of Virginia Press, 2014), 60. That impact was so impressive and lasting that the Vermont Division for Historic Preservation (Agency of Development and Community Affairs) effusively deems Rutland's architectural legacy as "second to none." Curtis B. Johnson and Elsa Gilbertson, *The Historic Architecture of Rutland County including a listing of the Vermont State Register of Historic Places* (Montpelier: The Vermont Division for Historic Preservation 1988), 205.
131 U.S. Census for 1850 and 1860. Because Bellow Falls is not identified in either report, the population figures for nearby Rockingham are described.
132 *Special Session 1857,* 19.
133 Robert Edward West, ed., *Rutland in Retrospect* (Rutland: Rutland Historical Society, 1978), 19.
134 Chauncey K. Williams, compiler, *Centennial Celebration of the Settlement of Rutland, VT.* (Rutland: Tuttle & Company, 1870), 89.
135 Doten, *Vermont: A Guide,* 128–129.
136 *Map and Description of the Western Vermont Railroad, and the District through which it runs* (New York: George F. Nesbitt, 1852), 4.
137 *Special Session,* 27, 176.
138 Ibid.
139 William George Hoskins, ed., *The Making of the English Landscape* (London: Hodder and Stoughton, 1955), 14.
140 Patricia E. Rubertone, "Landscape as artifact: Comments on 'the archaeological use of landscape treatment in social, economic and ideological analysis,'" *Historical Archaeology* 23, no. 1 (1989): 50–54.
141 Lucy Taksa, "The Material Culture of an Industrial Artifact: Interpreting Control, Defiance, and Everyday Resistance at the New South Wales Eveleigh Railway Workshops," *Historical Archaeology* 39, no. 3 (2005): 11.
142 Mark C. Childs, "The incarnations of Central Avenue," *Journal of Urban Design* 1, no. 3 (1996): 281–298.
143 Mary C. Beaudry, "The Lowell Boott Mills Complex and Its Housing: Material Expressions of Corporate Ideology," *Historical Archaeology* 23, no. 1 (1989): *passim*.
144 *Special Session 1857,* 121–122.
145 Leon Fink, *Workingmen's Democracy: The Knights of Labor and American Politics* (Urbana: University of Illinois Press, 1985), 67.
146 Harold A. Meeks, *Time and Change in Vermont: A Human Geography* (Chester, Conn.: The Globe Pequot Press, 1986), 115.
147 Shaughnessy, *Rutland Road,* 2–4.
148 Hunt, *Merchants' Magazine, 1852,* vol. 26:678.

149 Ibid., vol. 21:642–643.

150 *The Eastern Tourist; being a Guide through the States of Connecticut, Rhode Island, Massachusetts, Vermont, New Hampshire, and Maine* (New York: J. Disturnell, 1848), 77.

151 *Appletons' Illustrated Hand-Book of American Travel* (New York: Appleton & Co., 1857), 104; *Appletons' Illustrated Hand-Book Advertiser, 1857,* 16.

152 Sherman, *Freedom and Unity,* 226, citing Bellows Falls, Randolph, Danby, Essex, St. Albans, Newport, Barton, Newbury, and Hartford as also similarly affected.

153 November 16, 1779, Land Records, Volume 1, Town of Rutland, Clerk's Office, City of Rutland, Vermont.

154 Johnson and Gilbertson, *Historic Architecture,* 268; John J. Duffy, Samuel B. Hand and Ralph H. Orth, *The Vermont Encyclopedia* (Hanover: University Press of New England, 2003), 323.

155 H. P. Smith and W. S. Rann, *History of Rutland County, Vermont* (Syracuse: D. Mason & Co., 1886), 180–188.

156 *Rutland Herald,* 1 May 1845.

157 Ibid., 15 May 1845.

158 *The Voice of Freedom* (Montpelier), 15 May 1845.

159 Larson, *Internal Improvement,* 224.

160 *Burlington Weekly Free Press,* 16 October 1846.

161 *Journal of the Senate of the State of Vermont. October Session, 1848* (Burlington: Free Press Office, 1849), 14.

162 *Fifth Annual Report of the Railroad Commissioner of the State of Vermont, to the General Assembly, 1860* (Rutland: Geo. A. Tuttle & Co., 1860), 14.

163 *Journal of the Senate of the State of Vermont, Biennial Session, 1912* (Montpelier: By Authority, 1912), 1051.

164 Speech of Hon. Albert Clarke, November 13, 1874, The Free Pass Abuse. The Constitutional Power of the State to Regulate Railroads (Boston: 1907), 7.

165 *Vermont Phoenix,* 27 October 1843.

166 Speech of Hon. Albert Clarke, 8–9.

167 Haddock, Addresses, 106.

168 Economist Robert Gordon posits that periods of economic growth in the United States can be traced to three distinguishable industrial revolutions: 1) 1750 to 1830; 2) 1870 to 1900; and, 3) 1996 to 2004. "The first," he writes, was the result of "the inventions of the steam engine and cotton gin through the early railroads and steamships, but much of the impact of railroads on the American economy came later between 1850 and 1890. At a minimum it took 150 years for [it] to have its full range of effects." Robert J. Gordon, "Is U.S. Economic Growth Over? Faltering Innovation Confronts the Six Headwinds," Working Paper 18315, National Bureau of Economic Research, Cambridge, MA, August 2012, 3.

Notes

169 The Vermont Central Rail Road Company received its charter on October 31, 1843 and the Champlain and Connecticut River Rail Road on November 1, 1843. *Acts and Resolves passed by the Legislature of the State of Vermont at their October Session, 1843* (Montpelier: E. P. Walton & Sons, 1843), 43–56.

170 *Sprit of the Age,* (Woodstock), January 13, 1843; Shaughnessy, *Rutland Road,* 2–4.

171 *Rutland Herald,* 1 May 1845.

172 *American Railroad Journal and General Advertiser for railroads, canals, steamboats, machinery and mines* (Philadelphia: D. K. Minor, 1846), 91–92.

173 "Proceedings of the Corporation, 14 January 1846," *Rutland Railroad Company records, 1845–1951,* Minute Books, PRA-00432, VSARA.

174 Ibid.

175 *American Railroad,* 92.

176 F. E. Davison, *Historical Rutland: An Illustrated History of Rutland, Vermont, from the granting of the charter in 1761 to 1911* (Rutland: Phil. H. Brehmer, 1911), 19.

177 *Acts and Resolves Passed by the Legislature of the State of Vermont at the October Session, 1849* (Montpelier: E. P. Walton & Son, 1849), 40.

178 *First Annual Report of the Railroad Commissioner of the State of Vermont to the General Assembly, 1856* (Rutland: Geo. A. Tuttle & Co., 1856), 3–11.

179 Caroline Crane Marsh, ed., *Life and Letters of George Perkins Marsh,* vol. 1 (New York: Charles Scribner's Sons, 1888), 400.

180 *Third Annual Report of the Railroad Commissioner of the State of Vermont to the General Assembly, 1858* (Burlington: Free Press Print, 1858), 3–7.

181 George Perkins Marsh, *Man and Nature; or, Physical Geography as Modified by Human Action* (New York: Charles Scribner, 1864), 53–56.

182 Proceedings of the Directors, February 3, 1848, *Rutland Railroad Company records,* VSARA.

183 Wolmar, *The Great Railroad Revolution,* 36.

184 Edward J. Renehan, Jr., *Dark Genius of Wall Street: The Misunderstood Life of Jay Gould, King of the Robber Barons* (New York: Basic Books, 2006).

185 Shaughnessy, *Rutland Road,* 4.

186 *Roster of the Graduates and Past Cadets of Norwich University 1819–1907* (Bradford, Vt.: Opinion Press, 1907), 13.

187 Henry V. Poor, ed., *American Railroad Journal,* vol. 22 (New York: J. H. Schultz & Co., 1849), 280.

188 Gerald B. Fox and Jean Ballantyne, "William Hale, Railroad Surveyor: His Life, His Work," *Vermont History* 86, no. 1 (Winter/Spring 2018): 20–30.

189 Gene Sessions, "Vermont's Nineteenth Century Railroad Workers," in Michael Sherman and Jennie Versteeg, eds. *We Vermonters: Perspectives on the Past* (Montpelier: Vermont Historical Society), 240–242.

190 Thos. P. Chappell, Chief Engineer, Explanation & Reference of the Rutland Railroad Re-location Plans 1893," Rutland Railroad records, 1845–1951, PRA-02247, VSARA.
191 Rutland resident engineer W. H. Lyon to Frost, Brown & Co., October 12, 1849, private collection.
192 *Fifth Annual Report of the Railroad Commissioner*, 17.
193 *The Boston Herald*, 24 February 1909.
194 *The Rutland News*, 20 September 1921.
195 George Rogers Taylor, *The Transportation Revolution 1815–1860*, (New York: Rinehart & Company, 1951), 89.
196 Vermont 1793 Constitution, Chapter 1: A Declaration of the Rights of the Inhabitants of the State of Vermont, Article 1st.
197 *William Gold, Jr. v. Vermont Central Rail Road Company*, 19 Vt. 478, 483 (1847).
198 Lyria Bennett Moses, "Recurring Dilemmas: The Law's Race to Keep up with Technological Change," *Journal of Law, Technology & Policy*, vol. 2007, no. 2:253.
199 Sec. 7–8, An Act, to incorporate the Champlain and Connecticut River Rail Road Company, *Acts and Resolves 1843*. In 1846 the legislature codified railroad condemnation proceedings. An Act in Relation to Rail-Roads, *Acts and Resolves Passed by the Legislature of the State of Vermont at the October Session 1846* (Burlington: Chauncey Goodrich, 1846), 14. Notably, the 1843 charters of the Vermont Central Rail Road and the Champlain and Connecticut River Rail Road differed significantly with the former restricted to rights of way not exceeding six rods in width and the latter without limitation. *Acts and Resolves, 1843*, 46, 52.
200 Land Records, Vol. 17, Town of Rutland, 234–236.
201 *Report of the Directors of the Rutland and Burlington Railroad Company, at their Annual Meeting, at Rutland, Held 12th January, 1848* (Burlington: Free Press Office, 1848), 10.
202 *Report of the Directors of the Rutland and Burlington Railroad Company, at their Annual Meeting, at Rutland, Held 20th June, 1849* (Burlington: Free Press Office, 1849), 8.
203 Directors Meeting, Boston, Sept. 16, 1851, *Rutland Railroad Records*, VSARA.
204 Proceedings of the Directors at Burlington, February 18, 1851, ibid. The minutes also identify what appears the first instance of injury of the public on its line when it cryptically directed Follett to settle "the claim of Mary Lynsky injured at Charlotte."
205 Rutland Land Records, vol. 17:237–283.
206 Mt. Holly Land Records, vol. 12, *passim*; Shrewsbury Land Records, vol. 8, *passim*; Clarendon Land Records, vol. 14. Notice of the railroad's centerline location was filed in the first two towns on the same day, March 22, 1848 and never entered into Clarendon's files. Mount Holly Land Records, vol. 12:45–47; Shrewsbury Land Records vol. 8:376–378.
207 Rutland Land Records, vol. 17:243; Smith and Rann, *History of Rutland County*, 269.

NOTES

208 Rutland Land Records, vol. 17:244.
209 Smith and Rann, *History of Rutland County*, 267.
210 Rutland Land Records, vol. 17:277; 260; 250; 246.
211 *Rutland Weekly Herald*, 17 March 1870.
212 The commissioners' awards for the many claims ranged from $14 for Sophia Gates to $1,300 for Ruggles who owned much of the land that the railroad yard was constructed on. Williams and Pierpoint received, respectively, $275 and $316, and Harriet Strong, one of several surviving relatives of land owned by her husband that was the subject of the proceedings, received $29 as her share.
213 Rutland County Court docket, record and case files, RUCC-00008, -00027, and -00089, VSARA.
214 *Special Session 1857*, 204.
215 Maham H. Haig and B. W. Benedict, eds., *Railway Shop Up to Date: Reference Book of Up to Date American Railway Shop Practice* (Chicago: Crandall Publishing Company, 1907), *passim*.
216 Johnson and Gilbertson, *The Historic Architecture of Rutland County*, 271.
217 Smith and Rann, *History of Rutland County*, 405.
218 In 1848, the Board of Directors advised that "the quantity of [land] taken varies at different localities, as in the judgment of the board the future wants of the corporation may require." *Report of the Directors. . . 1848*, 8.
219 Wolmar, *The Great Railroad Revolution*, 46.
220 Sheila Charles, *The Return of the Rutland Railroad: An Archaeological Phase 1A literature review and sensitivity assessment for the proposed Rutland railroad pedestrian crossing and path, City of Rutland, Rutland County, Vermont*, Prepared for City of Rutland, March 1999.
221 Proceedings of the Directors, February 3, 1848, *Rutland Railroad Records*, VSARA.
222 Smith and Rann, *History of Rutland County*, 273.
223 Diary of Ambrose Lincoln Brown inscribed in a commercial publication, *Stewart's Diary for 1848; or Daily Register, for the use of Private Families, and Persons of Business*, Rutland Historical Society, Rutland, Vermont.
224 *Rutland Newsliner: The Rutland Railway Magazine*, vol. 4, no. 4 (October – November 1955), 5.
225 James Chatterton, Sophia Gates and Jacob Reynolds are specifically identified by Brown, verified by their names on corresponding commissioners' decisions in the Rutland Land Records.
226 George Parsons Lathrop, ed., *The Complete Works of Nathaniel Hawthorne*, vol. 12 (Boston: Houghton Mifflin Company, 1878), 14–15.
227 Robert H. Lord, John E. Sexton and Edward T. Harrington, *History of the Archdiocese of Boston in the Various Stages of Its Development 1604 to 1943* (New York: Sheed & Ward, 1944), 570.

228 Thomas E. Heslin, "The Irish in Vermont: Their Contrary Nature Helped Shape the State," *Rutland Historical Society Quarterly* vol. 13, no. 1 (Winter 1983), 13.
229 Seventh Census, 1850; Vincent E. Feeney, *Finnigans, Slaters and Stonepeggers: A History of the Irish in Vermont* (Bennington: Images from the Past, 2009), 58.
230 Feeney, *Finnigans,* 70.
231 Heslin, "The Irish in Vermont," 14.
232 Rosenberg, *The Cholera Years,* 135.
233 Papers of Jonathan A. Allen (1787–1848), autopsy and medical notes (1840–1848), MSC 187:14, Vermont Historical Society (hereafter VHS), Barre, Vermont.
234 *Proceedings at the Annual Meeting of the Vermont State Temperance Society, held at Windsor, Jan. 16, and 17, 1850* (Windsor: The Chronical Press, 1850), 9–11.
235 *Vermont Chronicle* (Bellows Falls), 7 May 1850.
236 N. P. Bowman (Sheriff) account adjust Town of Burlington, Dec. 21, 1854, Burlington, Vermont Town/City Records, Howe Library, University of Vermont.
237 Record of Commitments, Rutland County Jail, AC 974.30 R936j, VHS.
238 *St. Albans Weekly Messenger,* 13 April 1854; Report of the Select Committee on the Petition of Matthew Halloran, praying that his punishment be commuted, *The Journal of the Senate of the State of Vermont. October Session, 1854* (Middlebury: The Register Book and Job Office, 1854), 304–306.
239 "Strong Chamberlain Co. Time Roll Sections 25&26 Rutland Div R&B RR Sutherland Falls 1st June 1848," PRA-2246, no. 0096470, VSARA.
240 William A. Cormier, *Coming of Age: The Diary of Young Man Thaddeus H. Walker, 1851–1854* (Salem, NY: New Perth Publishing 2010).
241 That incident involved Irish workers not being paid in a timely fashion and their seizing a contractor to assure payment. *Burlington Free Press,* 10 July 1846. In Wells River the following year a fight between Irishmen from different parts of the island resulted in the murder of a foreman and in 1850 frustrated gangs of Irish laborers rioted in Brattleboro ("All Irishdom in this quarter has been in a high state of excitement") angry over the lack of work. Sherman, *Freedom and Unity,* 216; 24; John S. Kendall, "The Connecticut and Passumpsic Rivers R.R,," *The Railway and Locomotive Historical Society Bulletin* 49 (May 1939): 23–32; *Aurora of the Valley* (Newbury), May 9, 1850.
242 *Burlington Free Press,* 25 August 1849.
243 Johnson and Gilbertson, *The Historic Architecture of Rutland County,* 272; *The Rutland News,* June 16, 1921.
244 Jonny Geber and Barra O'Donnabhain, "'Against Shameless and Systematic Calumny': Strategies of Domination and Resistance and Their Impact on the Bodies of the Poor in Nineteenth-Century Ireland," *Historical Archaeology* 54, no. 1 (2020): 164.
245 Samuel Carter Hall and Anna Marie Hall, *Ireland: It's Scenery, Character, &c.,* third edition (London: Jeremiah How, 1843), 290.
246 Davison, *Historical Rutland,* 20.

Notes

247 Smith and Rann, *History of Rutland County,* 404.

248 Ibid., 405.

249 Ibid., 223.

250 Ownership interests were not equally divided as Harrington, Cain and Perkins each held 2/10s interest and Strong, Pierpoint and Robbins each had a 1/10 interest. The remaining 1/10 interest was split evenly between Harrington, Pierpoint, Perkins and Robbins. Rutland Land Records, vol. 18:64.

251 Rutland Land Records, vol. 15:343.

252 *Spirit of the Age* (Woodstock), 6 March 1845; *Vermont Patriot and State Gazette* (Montpelier), 21 August 1845.

253 *Rutland Herald,* December 25, 1849. In 1857 Cain continued to combat the established order. He sought to have one of the railroad's engines named after himself and solicited a friend to advocate on his behalf by obtaining a number of signatures on a request made to the local superintendent. "If you do this," he wrote, "I do not want any body to see these letters of mine, in my handwriting, but you burn them up.... I do not wish the least hint thrown out that I have any hand in this." John Cain to C. C. Holden, Esq., Nov. 18th 1857, Rutland Historical Society.

254 *Vermont Chronicle,* 29 January 1850.

255 Rutland Land Records, vol. 17:250; 18:65.

256 Dawn D. Hance, ed., *Early Families of Rutland, Vermont* (Rutland: Rutland Historical Society, 1990), 324; Rutland Land Records, vol. 17:277, 642; vol. 22:107

257 Rutland Land Records, vol. 17:260, 264.

258 Ibid., vol. 17:242.

259 Ibid., vol. 17:364; 18:301. In 1848 Ruggles received $1,300 for a seven-acre parcel and in 1852 was paid $2,412 for five acres.

260 Ibid., vols. 16, 18, 19, and 20, *passim.*

261 Ibid., 18:578.

262 *Charters and Ordinances of the City of Rutland* (Rutland: Carruthers & Thomas, 1894), 309. Their names continued to intersect in other capacities (i.e., fire, school, library, fair and cemetery committees) and demonstrates how much they were involved in Rutland's development.

263 Petition, "May 9, 1893, signed by Thomas J. Gaffney and 115 others," *Records -1-, Board of Alderman, City of Rutland,* Clerk's Office, Rutland, Vermont.

264 Other theories attribute the name to a local store, McGinnis' Nebraska Store, and to a priest who compared the drinking and fighting members of his congregation to the outlaws in Nebraska. Patrick T. Hannon, *"home": A History of St. Peter's Parish, Rutland, Vermont* (Rutland: St. Peter Church, 2000), 18.

265 Deborah L. Rotman, "The Fighting Irish: Historical Archaeology of Nineteenth-Century Catholic Immigrant Experiences in South Bend, Indiana," *Historical Archaeology* 44, no. 2 (2010): 114.

266 Lord, *History of the Archdiocese of Boston*, 130.

267 Johnson and Gilbertson, *The Historic Architecture of Rutland County*, 272.

268 Hannon, *"home,"* 11.

269 "Irish woman on Grove st., 30 [cents] per week," *Selectmen's Report to the Town of Rutland, March 3, 1857* (Rutland: George A. Tuttle & Company, 1857), 11.

270 Stephen A. Brighton, "Degrees of Alienation: The Material Evidence of the Irish and Irish American Experience, 1850–1910," *Historical Archaeology* 42, no. 4 (2008): 133.

271 Hannon, *"home,"* 4–7.

272 Lord, *History of the Archdiocese of Boston*, 461.

273 Hannon, *"home,"* 8–9.

274 Smith and Rann, *History of Rutland County*, 405; Davison, *Historical Rutland*, 20.

275 *The Rutland News*, 22 December 1923.

276 *The Middlebury Galaxy*, 28 March 1848.

277 Poor, *American Railroad Journal, 1848*, vol. 22:549.

278 *Journal of the Senate, 1849*, 15.

279 *Rutland Daily Herald*, 31 January 1997.

280 *Phelps's Travelers' Guide through the United States* (New York: Ensign & Thayer, 1850), 10–11.

281 George H. Douglas, *All Aboard: The Railroad in American Life* (New York: Paragon House, 1992), 53.

282 "Proceedings of the Directors," dated June 1, 20 and 21, 1849, *Rutland Railroad Company records*, VSARA.

283 Ibid., June 21, 1849.

284 Zadock Thompson, *History of Vermont, Natural, Civil and Statistical in Three Parts*, Part 2 (Burlington: Stacy & Jameson, 1853), 130.

285 John W. and Suzanne C. Hudson, *The Rutland Railroad: Rutland to Bellows Falls* (Loveland, OH: Depot Square Publishing, 2010), vi.

286 Daniel Robbins, *The Vermont State House: A History & Guide* (Montpelier: Vermont Council on the Arts, 1980), 27–28.

287 *Burlington Free Press*, 2 March 1849.

288 G. P. Randall, *Book of Designs for School Houses, and Suggestions as to Obtaining Plans, and How to Heat and Ventilate School Buildings* (Chicago: Knight & Leonard, 1884), 6–7.

289 *Biographical Sketches of the Leading Men of Chicago* (Chicago: Wilson & St. Clair, 1868), 327.

290 Gurdon P. Randall, *A Hand Book of Designs, containing Plans in Perspective, of Court Houses, Universities, Academies, School Houses, Churches, Dwellings, Etc., Etc., Etc., and Suggestions Relative to their Construction, Heating and Ventilation*

(Chicago: Church, Goodman and Donnelly, 1868); *The Executive Documents of the House of Representatives for the First Session of the Forty-Eighth Congress, 1883–'84,* vol. 22, no. 73 (Washington: Government Printing Office, 1884), 263.

291 Thomas P. Chappell, "Explanation," *Rutland Railroad Company records,* VSARA.

292 Abby Maria Hemenway, *The Vermont Gazetteer: A Magazine embracing a History of Each Town,* vol. 3. Orleans and Rutland Counties (Claremont: The Claremont Manufacturing Company, 1877), 1115. The Lawrence engine-house was completed in 1847. Thirteenth Annual Report of the Boston and Maine Railroad Corporation, *Annual Reports of the Railroad Corporations in the State of Massachusetts for 1847* (Boston: Dutton and Wentworth, 1848), 14. In 1852, the board acknowledged to their shareholders the huge amounts of money being spent in "replacing temporary structures with Station Houses, Machine, Shops &c." as being "absolutely required by the increasing business of the Road." *Fifth Annual Report of the Directors of the Rutland and Burlington Railroad Company, submitted to the stockholders July 31, 1852* (Boston: Eastburn's Press, 1852), 4.

293 Amos H. Powers, *The Powers Family: A Genealogical and Historical Record* (Chicago: Fergus Printing Company, 1884), 77.

294 Andres and Johnson, *Buildings of Vermont,* 82; Paul J. Crossman, Jr., "A History of Rutland High School, Rutland, Vermont (1855–2008)," *Rutland Historical Society Quarterly* 39, no. 1 (2009), 3.

295 *The Rutland County Herald,* September 9, 1853.

296 "Directors Meeting at Bellows Falls, Aug. 19, 1851," *Rutland Railroad Records,* VSARA.

297 "Monthly meeting of the Directors, Boston, Feb. 18, 1852," *Rutland Railroad Records,* VSARA. Railroad facilities rapidly evolved to create a hierarchy among workers engaged in their various specialties. Edward Hungerford, *The Modern Railroad* (Chicago: A. C. McClurg & Co., 1911), *passim*

298 In 1851 a comprehensive inventory was conducted of the Rutland machine shop that demonstrates the wide range of tools in use: lathes, planes, drilling and boring machines, saws, files, a crane, jack screws, benches, blacksmithing equipment, pulleys, axles, wheels, hangers, bolts, screws, nuts, bar iron, castings, locomotive hose, large amounts of leather, paint (white, gold leaf and black vermillion), varnish, turpentine, brushes, glass, patterns, candles and lumber. In the next years, the inventory descriptions increased substantially. "R & B R Road Inventory of Machine Shop April 1st 1851," Vermont Collection, Rutland Railroad Archives, Middlebury College.

299 Emails, December 23, 25, 26, 2016, William C. Badger, Rutland Railroad Historical Society; Smith and Rann, *History of Rutland County,* 148. In 1852, the board of directors authorized the Engine House and Machine Shop at Rutland be "covered with slate, if it can be done on satisfactory terms." While that may have occurred with the machine shop, the engine house appears to have been covered with metal. Directors Meeting, Bellows Falls, March 17, 1852, *Rutland Railroad Records,* VSARA.

300 *Rutland Weekly Herald,* 14 January 1864.

301 *Rutland Daily Herald,* 25, 26, 27 July 1899.

302 Hemenway, *Vermont Gazetteer*, vol. 3:1117.
303 "Directors Meeting, Burlington, May 20th 1852," *Rutland Railroad Records*, VSARA.
304 Randall, *Book of Designs*, 9.
305 *Rutland R.R., V.S. 2 Building Inventory*, Rutland Railroad Archive, Middlebury College Special Collections & Archives, Middlebury, Vermont.
306 Ibid.
307 Email exchange with Rutland architect Alvin Figiel, January 13, 2017.
308 *Rutland Herald*, 26 February 1853.
309 Ambrose Lincoln Brown Day Book, 1853–1861, MSC 151:12, Vermont Historical Society.
310 *Fourth Biennial Report of the Board of Railroad Commissioners, 1894*, vol. 4 (Burlington: The Free Press Association, 1894), 39.
311 *Third Biennial Report of the Board of Railroad Commissioners of the State of Vermont. June 30th, 1890, to June 30th, 1892* (Burlington: The Free Press Association, 1892), 93.
312 *Seventh Biennial Report of the Board of Railroad Commissioners of the State of Vermont, June 30th, 1898 to June 30th, 1900* (St. Albans: The Messenger Company Print, 1900), 155; "Directors Meeting July 30, 1901," *Rutland Railroad Records*, VSARA.
313 *Rutland Daily Herald*, 17, 23, and 30 June 1902.
314 Ibid., September 26, 1902.
315 *Granite State Farmer* (Manchester), 8 September 1852.
316 William S. King, Address, in *Addresses Before the Vermont State Agricultural Society at its Exhibition held at Rutland, September 1852* (Middlebury: Justus Cobb, 1853), 18–19.
317 *Rutland Herald*, July 29, 1852.
318 *Rutland County Herald*, May 28, 1853.
319 Hemenway, *Historical Gazetteer*, vol. 3:1048.
320 Wolmar, *The Great Railroad Revolution*, 83.
321 *Rutland Weekly Herald*, October 9, 1913.
322 Smith and Rann, *History of Rutland County*, 912.
323 *The Rutland News*, April 12, 1919.
324 Andres and Johnson, *Buildings of Vermont*, 81; Smith and Rann, *History of Rutland County*, 149.
325 *Rutland Weekly Herald*, 6 February 1851.
326 Daniel Bluestone, "Civic and Aesthetic Reserve: Ammi Burnham Young's 1850s Federal Customhouse Designs," *Winterthur Portfolio* 25, no. 2/3 (Summer-Autumn 1990): 132.

Notes

327 "Directors Meeting. Boston June 14 & 15, 1853," *Rutland Railroad Records,* VSARA.

328 *The Burlington Weekly Sentinel,* 1 January 1852.

329 Bluestone, "Civic and Aesthetic Reserve," 150.

330 Ibid., 151.

331 *Cong. Globe,* 34th Cong., 1st Sess. 6 (1855). Other bills sought compensation for George Perkins Marsh, who had spoken so forcefully before the Rutland Agricultural Society in 1847, for his services as minister at Constantinople, a mission to Greece and in negotiating a treaty with Persia. In 1857, the highest earning post offices in Vermont were, in order, Burlington, Montpelier, Brattleboro, Rutland, and St. Johnsbury. *The St. Johnsbury Caledonian,* May 2, 1857.

332 Record Group 21, 21.48 Records of the U. S. District and Other Courts in Vermont, 1791–1983, National Archives and Records Administration, Waltham, Massachusetts.

333 Thirty-fourth Congress, 1st Sess., 1856, Chapter 129, 93.

334 Bluestone, "Civic and Aesthetic Reserve," 154.

335 The identity of Merchants Row was challenged around 1890 when residents authorized a name change to Broadway during an annual meeting. However, petitions of others who lived alongside the road in 1893 and 1894 resulted in a return to the original name. Petitions, April 3, 1893 and August 20, 1894, *Records -1-, Board of Alderman, City of Rutland,* Clerk's Office, Rutland, Vermont.

336 *Vermont Chronicle,* May 19, 1857.

337 *Burlington Weekly Free Press,* May 29, 1857.

338 *Bellows Falls Times,* 14 January 1850.

339 Davison, *Historical Rutland,* 20–21.

340 *Annual Report of the Secretary of the Treasury on the State of the Finances for the Year 1876* (Washington: Government Printing Office, 1876), 682; *Vermont Journal,* May 1, 1857.

341 National Register of Historical Places Inventory – Nomination Form, Rutland Courthouse Historic District, April 23, 1976, United States Department of the Interior No. 84285653, National Archives.

342 Andres and Johnson, *Buildings of Vermont,* 13.

343 Bluestone, "Civic and Aesthetic Reserve," 143.

344 Andres and Johnson, *Buildings of Vermont,* 81.

345 Hance, *The History of Rutland, Vermont,* 129.

346 Richard R. John, *Spreading the News: The American Postal System from Franklin to Morse* (Cambridge: Harvard University Press, 1995), 162.

347 "Oh dear," exclaimed Mary, throwing herself into the rocking chair. "I'll never go to the Post-Office again to be looked out of countenance by all those men standing around the halls and near the ladies delivery. It is so provoking! What can I do, Minerva, to stop those awful men from staring me in the face?" "Do as I do," replied Minerva,

with a sly look, "*show them your ankles!*" *Green-Mountain Freeman* (Montpelier), 26 January 1864.

348 *Rutland Daily Herald,* 2 April 1866.

349 Smith and Rann, *History of Rutland County,* 268-269.

350 Rutland Railroad Company, *Historical Sketch of Rutland Railroad Company 1849–1949* (Rutland: Rutland Railroad Company, 1949).

351 *Hunt's Merchants' Magazine 1854,* vol. 31, 318.

352 *Special Session, 1857,* 209.

353 *Rutland County Herald,* 23 December 1853.

354 Compare the inventory of Vermonters involved with various trades and professions in *The New-England Mercantile Union Business Directory* (New York: Pratt & Co., 1849), 227 with the 1850 Census returns, recited in *First Report to the Legislature of Vermont, relating to the Registry and Returns of Births, Marriages and Deaths* (Burlington: Daily Times Book and Job Printing Establishment, 1859), 78.

355 *Thirty-sixth Annual Report of the Vermont Domestic Missionary Society* (Montpelier: E. P. Walton Jr., 1854), 14.

356 *Journal of the House of Representatives of the State of Vermont, October Session, 1856* (Middlebury: The Register Book and Job Office, 1856), 460.

357 Wolmar, *The Great Railroad Revolution,* 219.

358 Daniel P. Thompson, *History of the Town of Montpelier, from the time it was first chartered in 1781 to the year 1860* (Montpelier: E. P. Walton, 1860), 143-145.

359 Jan Albers, *Hands on the Land: A History of the Vermont Landscape* (Cambridge, MA: MIT Press, 2000), 170-171.

360 Address of the Council of Censors, October 12, 1855, *The Journal of the Senate of the State of Vermont. October Session, 1855* (Middlebury: Register Book and Job Office, 1855), 249-251.

361 *Middlebury Register,* October 22, 1856; *Vermont Watchman and State Journal,* October 24, 1856; Vermont Colony in Kansas Report, Kansas Historical Society, https://www.kansasmemory.org/item/90374/page/1.

362 Josiah Hawkins to Charles Linsley, August 10, 1860, cited in T. D. Seymour Bassett, "500 Miles of Trouble and Excitement: Vermont Railroads, 1848-1861," *Vermont History* 49, no. 3 (Summer 1981): 141.

363 Z. E. Jameson, "Vermont As A Home," *First Annual Report of the Vermont State Board of Agriculture 1872,* 556.

364 In 1852 a list of twenty-five detailed requirements was created specifically describing railroad employees' duties, accompanied by many prohibitions. Robert C. Jones, *The Central Vermont Railway: A Yankee Tradition,* vol. 1 (Silverton, CO: Sundance Publications, 1981), 28.

365 Wolmar, *The Great Railroad Revolution,* 47.

Notes

366 *Eighth Annual Report of the Directors of the Rutland & Burlington R. R. Co., and the Report of the Trustees of the Second Mortgage 1855* (Rutland: George A. Tuttle & Co.)

367 Albers, *Hands on the Land,* 171.

368 *George W. Sabre, et. al. v. Rutland Railroad Company and Central Vermont Railway Company,* 86 Vt. 347, 357 (1913).

369 *Abijah Hurd v. The Rutland & Burlington Railroad Co.*, 25 Vt. 116 (1853); *John Jackson v. Rutland & Burlington Railroad Co.*, 25 Vt. 150 (1853); *James Morse & Brother v. The Rutland and Burlington Railroad Company*, 27 Vt. 49 (1854); *Fitch Holden v. The Rutland and Burlington Railroad Company*, 30 Vt. 297 (1858).

370 *John S. Thorpe v. The Rutland Railroad Company,* 27 Vt. 140 (1854).

371 David M. Gold, "Redfield, Railroads, and the Roots of 'Laissez-Faire Constitutionalism,'" *The American Journal of Legal History* 27, no. 3 (July 1983): 257. Isaac F. Redfield, *A Practical Treatise upon the Law of Railways* (Boston: Little, Brown and Company, 1857) was also widely accepted in England as a definitive contribution to railroad law. Redfield, also a past vice-president of the Vermont Historical Society (1848), was considered the nation's authority on wills for a half-century. Isaac F. Redfield, *The Law of Wills, Embracing Also, the Jurisprudence of Insanity; the Effect of Extrinsic Evidence; the Creation and Construction of Trusts So Far as Applicable to Wills* (Boston: Little, Brown and Company, 1864). For a list of Redfield's publications, see Gilman, *Bibliography of Vermont,* 230-231 and his obituary at *Argus and Patriot,* 30 March 1876.

372 In 1860 Redfield described his judicial philosophy: "I have always, and under all circumstances, felt it my duty to study to vindicate all laws, however odious, from that contumely and reproach which the well-disposed and truly patriotic will sometimes thoughtlessly heap upon the constitution or the laws of the state or the nation, without reflecting that, in so doing, they are doing all in their power to destroy that respect for law and order in society which is the only guaranty in free states, against outrage and abuse, from the reckless violence of the mob or assassin, on the one hand, or of overbearing and unscrupulous majorities on the other." J. T. M., "Isaac Redfield," *The American Law Register* 24, no. 5 (May 1876): 261.

373 Redfield, *A Practical Treatise,* 614.

374 *Sabre v. Rutland R. R.,* 86 Vt. 356.

375 Report of Commissioners on Laws Relating to Railroads, *Journal of the House of Representatives of the State of Vermont, October Session, 1855* (Montpelier: E. P. Walton: 1855), 642.

376 Ibid., 643.

377 *Burlington Weekly Sentinel,* 1 November 1855.

378 Report of the Committee on Roads on the Foregoing Bill Relating to Railroads, ibid, 650-651.

379 *The Brandon Post,* 16 May 1850.

380 Charles E. Rosenberg, *The Cholera Years: The United States in 1832, 1849, and 1866* (Chicago: University of Chicago Press, 1962), 19.

381 Ibid., 652-653.

382 *Journal of the House of Representatives, 1856*, 460.

383 An Act to Prevent Obstructions of the Public Highway by Freight Trains not in Motion on Railroads, *Acts and Resolves Passed by the General Assembly of the State of Vermont, 1856* (Montpelier: E. P. Walton, 1856), 35.

384 *St. Albans Weekly Messenger,* 18 December 1856.

385 *Sabre v. Rutland R. R.,* 86 Vt. 358.

386 See, *Biennial Report of the Board of Railroad Commissioners of the State of Vermont* for each year.

387 *Burlington Free Press,* 22 December 1849.

388 *Special Session, 1857,* 242.

389 Inaugural address, October 10, 1856, https://www.sec.state.vt.us/media/48665/FletcherR1856.pdf. "As a matter of fact, farmers have always constituted the largest occupational group by far in the history of Vermont's House of Representatives." Edwin C. Rozwenc, *Agricultural Policies in Vermont 1860–1945* (Montpelier: Vermont Historical Society, 1981), 8.

390 Inaugural Address, October 13, 1860, https://www.sec.state.vt.us/media/48647/FairbanksE1860.pdf

391 *Acts and Resolves Passed by the General Assembly of the State of Vermont, at the First Biennial Session, 1870* (Montpelier: J. & J. M. Poland Steam Printing, 1870), 127.

392 An Act, to incorporate the Vermont agricultural society, *The Laws of the State of Vermont,* vol. 2 (Randolph: Sereno Wright, 1808), 83.

393 Speech of Gov. Galusha, 1818, E. P. Walton, ed., *Records of the Governor and Council of the State of Vermont,* vol. 6 (Montpelier: Steam Press of J. & J. M. Poland, 1878), 436.

394 Speech of Gov. Galusha, 1809, E. P. Walton, ed., *Records of the Governor and Council,* vol. 5 (Montpelier: Steam Press of J. & J. M. Poland, 1877), 402.

395 Speech of Gov. Galusha, 1818, 436.

396 John Lindsey, *A Discourse Delivered Before the Honorable Legislature of Vermont, on the Anniversary Election, October 10, 1822* (Montpelier: E. P. Walton, 1822), 48.

397 An Act, to incorporate the Vermont Agricultural Society, *Acts Passed by the Legislature of the State of Vermont, at their October Session, 1826* (Bennington: D. Clark, 1826), 88-89.

398 Encouragement and Promotion of Agriculture, Domestic Manufactures and the Mechanic Arts, *The Compiled Statutes of the State of Vermont* (Burlington: Chauncey Goodrich, 1851), 533.

399 Rozwenc, *Agricultural Policies,* 13.

400 *Middlebury Register,* 27 December 1843.

401 Report, *Journal of the Senate of the State of Vermont. October Session, 1849* (Burlington: Free Press Office, 1849), 171-173.

Notes

402 Wilson, *The Hill Country,* 81-84.
403 Census 1850.
404 Inaugural Address, October 13, 1860.
405 D. B. Wheelock, "The Butter Dairy," *First Annual Report of the Vermont State Board of Agriculture,* 142-143.
406 *St. Albans Weekly Messenger,* 18 December 1856.
407 Report of the Committee on the Judiciary, *Fifth Annual Report of the Vermont Board of Education, September 1861* (Burlington: Times Book and Job Printing, 1861), 91.
408 Ibid., 90.
409 Christopher Harris, "The Road Less Traveled By: Rural Northern New England in Global Perspective, 1815-1960," (Ph. D. dissertation, Northeastern University, 2007), *passim.*
410 David Demeritt, "Climate, Cropping, and Society in Vermont, 1820-1850," *Vermont History* 59, no. 3 (Summer 1991): 156.
411 Harris, "The Road Less Traveled By," 15-58.
412 Ibid., 163-165.
413 Jacob Abbott, *Marco Paul's Voyages & Travels: Vermont* (New York: Harper & Brothers, 1852), 49
414 Report of the Committee on the Judiciary, 85.
415 John Burroughs, *The Writings of John Burroughs, Signs and Seasons,* vol. 7 (Boston: Houghton Mifflin Company, 1886), 251.
416 *First Annual Report of the Vermont State Board of Agriculture 1872,* 123-141.
417 *The Enterprise and Vermonter* (Vergennes), 8 September 1852.
418 *Bradford Inquirer,* 11 September 1852.
419 *The Vermont Patriot and State Gazette,* 14 October 1852.
420 Note, *Addresses before the Vermont State Agricultural Society, 1852,* 21-22.
421 Report of the Committee on Manufactured Goods, ibid., 4.
422 *Granite State Farmer* (Manchester), 8 September 1852.
423 Ibid., 15 September 1852.
424 King Address, *Address Before the Vermont State Agricultural Society*; James F. Mapes, *The Working Farmer: Devoted to Agriculture, Horticulture, Floriculture, Kitchen Gardening, Management of Hot Houses, Green Houses, &c. &c.* vol. 5 (New York: Frederick McCready, 1853), 109-111.
425 Gov. Seward's Speech, *Address Before the Vermont State Agricultural Society,* 5. In 1859 Lincoln similarly addressed the Wisconsin State Agricultural Society Fair and advocated for farmers to engage in "thorough agriculture," meaning intensive rather than extensive farming and to further their education. Richard Lyman Bushman, *The American Farmer in the Eighteenth Century: A Social and Cultural History* (New Haven: Yale University Press, 2018), 286-288.

426 *Eighty Years' Progress of the United States* (Hartford: L. Stebbins, 1869), 80.
427 Tarlow, *Archaeology of Improvement*, 62-63.
428 Harris, *Road Less Traveled*, 176-177.
429 Ibid., 186-187.
430 John Silgoe, "Plugging Past Reform: Small Scale Farming Innovation and Big-Scale Farming Research," Ronald G. Walthers, ed., *Scientific Authority and Twentieth-Century America* (Baltimore: Johns Hopkins University Press, 1997), 122.
431 Report on the Committee of the Judiciary, 76-104.
432 Obituary Record, Report of the Commissioner of Education, *Report of the Secretary of the Interior*, vol. 2 (Washington: GPO, 1877), 397.
433 Albers, *Hands on the Land*, 170.
434 Report on the Committee of the Judiciary, 101.
435 *Vermont Journal*, 15 June 1861.
436 *Journal of the House of Representatives of the State of Vermont, October Session, 1856* (Middlebury: The Register Book and Job Office, 1856), 460.
437 Address of the Council of Censors, October 12, 1855, *The Journal of the Senate of the State of Vermont. October Session, 1855* (Middlebury: Register Book and Job Office, 1855), 249-251.
438 Stillman F. Kneeland, *The Commercial Law Register, A Manual of the International Merchants' Protective Law Association* (Albany: Law Book and Law Blank, 1873), 548.
439 Peter J. Coleman, *Debtors and Creditors in America: Insolvency, Imprisonment for Debt, and Bankruptcy, 1607–1900* (Madison: The State Historical Society of Wisconsin, 1974), 70-71.
440 D'Agostino, *The History of Public Welfare in Vermont*, 64-65. The author notes the neglectful way that the state has continued to deal with creditor-debtor relations, writing that "A close scrutiny of the laws of Vermont regarding levying of execution, civil process and debts reveals that there has been very little change in legislation from 1839 to [1948]."
441 *The Middlebury Register*, 18 November 1857.
442 Thompson, *History of the Town of Montpelier*, 145.
443 Hunt, *Merchants' Magazine, 1857*, vol. 37:773.
444 Address of the Council of Censors, October 12, 1855; *Journal of the House of Representatives of the State of Vermont, October Session, 1856*, 460.
445 *Vermont Watchman and State Journal*, 25 November 1859.
446 Inaugural Address, October 6, 1870, *Journal of the House of Representatives of the State of Vermont. Biennial Session, 1870* (Montpelier: Freeman Steam Printing House and Bindery, 1871), 22-23.
447 *Rutland Daily Herald*, 25 January 1972.

NOTES

448 *Special Session, 1857,* 242. "For all flesh is as grass, and all the glory of man as the flower of grass. The grass withereth, and the flower thereof falleth away." 1 Peter 1:24-25.

449 *New York Times,* 1 October 1857.

450 *Special Session, 1857,* 40.

451 *Transactions of the Vermont Medical Society, at the Annual Session, Held at Montpelier, October 19th and 20th, 1864* (Woodstock: Vermont Standard, 1864), 27.

452 Helen Bynum, *Spitting Blood: The History of Tuberculosis* (Oxford: Oxford University Press, 2012), *passim.*

453 Solon O. Richardson, "Marasmus phthisis" (1831); Lewis Snow, "Marasmus Phthisis Consumption" (1832); David D. Hoyt, "Pulmonary Consumption" (1832); and, William B. Reynolds, "Etiology of Consumption" (1851), DA-3, file nos. 10929, 10930 and 10937, Rauner Library Special Collections, Dartmouth College, Hanover, NH (hereafter Dartmouth College).

454 Predisposition included the victim possessing "a clear white skin; large veins, bright, dark blue eyes; peculiar whiteness of the teeth; reddish hair; long neck; prominent shoulders; florid complexion; slender chest, and weak voice." Snow, "Marasmus." One student took strong exception to a style of dress: "The fashion of English dress is wrong when associated with the disease. I am [illegible] & those who import these fashions into this country are so G[od] D[amned] guilty of homicide than if they were directly 'speeding a bullet to the heads' of hundreds yearly of our finest & best." Hoyt, "Pulmonary Consumption."

455 Ibid.

456 Shattuck, *Green Mountain Opium Eaters, passim.*

457 Ludlum, *Social Ferment in Vermont,* 201-202.

458 *Acts and Resolves Passed by the Legislature of the State of Vermont, at the October Session, 1838* (Montpelier: E. P. Walton and Son, 1838), 12-13.

459 *The Vermont Statutes, 1894* (Rutland: Tuttle Company, 1895), 797-820; 905.

460 William A. Alcott, *Dosing and Drugging, or Destroying by Inches* (Boston: George W. Light, 1839), 47.

461 1850 and 1860 U. S. Census; *The New-England Mercantile Union Business Directory; Fourth Report to the Legislature of Vermont relating to the Registry and Returns of Births, Marriages and Deaths, in this state for the year ending December 31, 1860* (Middlebury: Register Office, 1861), 85.

462 June 17, 1857, Vermont Medical Society Minutes, UVM.

463 October 15, 1862, ibid.

464 *Special Session, 1857, Journal of the Senate,* 25; *Frank Leslie's New York Journal of Romance, General Literature, Science and Art,* vol. 3 (New York: Frank Leslie, 1856), 120; *Triennial Catalogue of the University of Vermont 1854* (Burlington: Free Press Print, 1854), 46.

465 Samuel Sheldon Fitch, *Diseases of the Chest. A Treatise on the Uses of the Lungs and on the Causes and Cure of Pulmonary Consumption* (Philadelphia: Hooker and Agnew, 1841); Samuel Sheldon Fitch, *Six Lectures on the Uses of the Lungs; and causes, prevention, and cure of Pulmonary Consumption, Asthma, and Diseases of the Heart; on the Laws of Longevity; and on the mode of preserving male and female health to an hundred years* (New York: H. Carlisle, 1847).

466 S. S. Fitch, *The Family Almanac, and Guide to Health* (New York: S. S. Fitch & Co., 1857), 1.

467 Fitch, *Six Lectures* (1850), 62.

468 Ibid., 97.

469 Bynum, *Spitting Blood*, 97.

470 S. S. Fitch, *A Popular Treatise on the Diseases of the Heart* (New York: S. S. Fitch & Co., 1860).

471 J. V. C. Smith, ed., *The Boston Medical and Surgical Journal*, vol. 39 (Boston: David Clapp, 1849), 321.

472 Fitch, *Six Lectures*, 131-132; 140.

473 *Special Session, Journal of the Senate, 1857*, 42.

474 Ibid., 85-86.

475 *Special Session, Journal of the House, 1857*, 162.

476 Ibid., *Journal of the Senate*, 16.

477 Affidavit, Samuel W. Thayer, Jr., SE118-00066, VSARA.

478 Ibid., *Journal of the House*, 171.

479 Ibid., 162.

480 Ibid., 197.

481 Act 24, *The Acts and Resolves Passed by the General Assembly of the State of Vermont, at the October Session, 1852* (Montpelier: E. P. Walton & Son, 1852, 19.

482 *Bellows Falls Gazette*, 10 January 1850.

483 *Vermont Watchman and State Journal*, 24 February 1853.

484 *Burlington Weekly Free Press*, 17 August 1905

485 F. R. Lees, *Text-Book of Temperance* (New York: J. N. Stearns, 1869), 257.

486 Burlington, Vermont Town/City records, cartons five and ten, UVM.

487 *St. Albans Weekly Messenger*, 9 June 1853.

488 Burlington, Vermont Town/City records, carton 7. A pint of brandy cost eight cents and a gallon of rum went for fifty cents.

489 Edward B. Sawyer, Liquor agent's account book, Hyde Park, VT, 1855-1856, small bound manuscript, UVM.

490 *Vermont Patriot and State Gazette*, 1 June 1855 and 14 May 1858.

491 *Vermont Watchman and State Journal*, 23 January 1857.

NOTES

492 *Vermont Chronicle,* 13 June 1854.
493 Joseph A. Davis, *Circular. To Whom It May Concern,* July 10, 1858, VHS.
494 Ambrose Lincoln Brown Day Book, ibid.
495 Report of the Grand Jury as to the situation of [sic] Jail, Caledonia county Court, June Term 1854, Judgments, Discontinuances and Miscellaneous, December term 1853-June term 1855, file 25, CACC-00039, folder 25, VSARA.
496 Lees, *Text-Book,* 257. An official at the University of Vermont also reported that "There is a very great diminution in the use of liquors by students. We have not had, for a year past, any rowdyism." Ibid.
497 *Aurora of the Valley,* 4 January 1855.
498 Burlington, Vermont records, carton ten, UVM.
499 Ibid., carton five.
500 Inaugural Address, October 13, 1860, https://www.sec.state.vt.us/media/48647/FairbanksE1860.pdf
501 Eric H. Monkkonen, "A Disorderly People? Urban Order in the Nineteenth and Twentieth Centuries," *Journal of American History* 68, no. 3 (December 1981): 542.
502 *Ellis Bliss v. Conn. & Pas. Rivers Railroad Company,* 24 Vt. 424 (1852), 426-427. In 1855 Bliss appears to have regained his senses and sold a partial interest in his hotel business to another individual that garnered yet more litigation reaching to the Supreme Court. *Harry B. Stevens v. David D. Pillsbury and Others,* 57 Vt. 204 (1884).
503 J. D. DeBow, *Statistical View of the United States* (Washington: A. O. P. Nicholson, 1854), 182.
504 *Journal of the House of Representatives, of the State of Vermont, October Session, 1853* (Burlington: Chauncey Goodrich, 1854), 77.
505 Petitions, SE118-00060, -00063, -00065, VSARA.
506 *Special Session, 1857,* 172-173.
507 *Special Session, 1857,* 218-219.
508 Ibid., 230-231.
509 Inaugural Address, October 13, 1855, https://www.sec.state.vt.us/media/48905/Royce1855.pdf
510 *Journal of the House of Representatives of the State of Vermont, October Session, 1856* (Middlebury: Register Book and Job Office, 1856), 709.
511 *Special Session, 1857,* 188.
512 Inaugural Address, October 9, 1857, https://www.sec.state.vt.us/media/48668/FletcherR1857.pdf
513 *Journal of the House of Representatives of the State of Vermont, October Session, 1851* (Burlington: Chauncy Goodrich, 1852), 375.
514 Report of Special Committee, *Journal of the Senate of the State of Vermont, October Session, 1859* (Montpelier: E. P. Walton, 1859), 345.

515 "England and Massachusetts are often referred to. . . because they are in so many respects similar to Vermont, rendering comparisons more trustworthy." *Second Report to the Legislature of Vermont, relating to the Registry and Returns of Births, Marriages, and Deaths, in this state, for the year ending December 31, 1858* (Middlebury: Register Book and Job Office, 1859), 90.

516 Reginald H. Fitz, "The Rise and Fall of the Licensed Physician in Massachusetts. 1781-1860," in John B. Hamilton, *The Journal of the American Medical Association*, vol. 22 (Chicago: The Journal of the Association, 1894), 877.

517 *Acts and Resolved passed by the General Assembly of the State of Vermont, at the October Session, 1858* (Bradford: Joseph D. Clark, 1858), 177; *Journal of the Senate of the State of Vermont, October Session, 1860* (Montpelier: E. P. Walton, 1860), 44.

518 Meeting of the Vermont Homeopathic Medical Society, *Vermont Watchman and State Journal*, 11 November 1859.

519 See, e. g., J. Emerson Kent, "Legitimate Medicine" in a "Transition State," in *The College Journal of Medical Science*, vol. 1 (Cincinnati: Moore, Wilstach, Keys & Co., 1856), 169.

520 *Vermont State Board of Health*, Bulletin No. 1, vol. 2 (Brattleboro: 1901), 42.

521 No. 93 – An Act to Prevent the Spreading of Contagious Diseases and to Establish a State Board of Health, *Acts and Resolves Passed by the General Assembly of the State of Vermont at the Ninth Biennial Session, 1886* (Springfield, MA: Published by Authority, Springfield Printing Company, 1887), 64.

522 *New York Times*, 16 June 1860; C. B. Guthrie, "Report on the Control of Poisons," *Proceedings and Debates of the Fourth National Quarantine and Sanitary Convention*, (Boston: George C. Rand & Avery, 1860), 271.

523 *Journal of the House of Representatives of the State of Vermont, Annual Session, 1865* (Montpelier: Freeman Steam Printing Company, 1866), 358.

524 S. Putnam, Sanitary Reform," Proceedings of the Sixty-Fourth Annual Meeting at Montpelier, October 11th and 12th, 1876, *Transactions of the Vermont Medical Society, 1864–1876*, 519.

525 John Sinclair, *Sketch of an Introduction to the Proposed Analysis of the Statistical Account of Scotland* (London: W. Bulmer and Company, 1802), 1.

526 *Second Annual Report to the Legislature: Under the Act of March, 1842, relating to the Registry and Returns of Birth, Marriages and Deaths in Massachusetts. For the year ending May 1st, 1843* (Boston: Dutton and Wentworth, 1843), 64.

527 *Fifth Annual Report, 1846*, ibid., 22.

528 *Journal of the House of Representatives of the State of Vermont, October Session, 1850* (Burlington: Chauncey Goodrich, 1851), 25.

529 Oct. 22, 1851, Vermont Medical Society, Minutes, UVM.

530 Oct. 24, 1855, ibid.

531 "The Massachusetts Registration reports are of inestimable value, as affording accurate statistics of life and death, and of the causes which produce death. When will the State

Notes

of Vermont by her Legislature make provision for enforcing registration laws? The law of this State which requires the registration of Births, Marriages and Deaths stands on our statute book a dead letter." *Burlington Free Press,* 5 April 1856.

532 Perkins, *An Address,* 14.

533 Ibid., 6.

534 Ibid., 12.

535 An Act Relating to the Registry and Returns of Births, Marriages and Deaths, *Acts and Resolves passed by the General Assembly of the State of Vermont at the October Session, 1856* (Montpelier: E. P. Walton, 1856), 65. 536 *St. Albans Weekly Messenger,* 18 February 1858.

537 "Instructions to be observed by School District Clerks," Registration Returns, 1858, PRA-00920, VSARA.

538 Benjamin W. Dean, ed., *First Report to the Legislature of Vermont, relating to the Registry and Returns of Births Marriages and Deaths in this State for the Year ending December 31, 1857* (Burlington: Daily Times Book and Job Printing, 1859), 81.

539 *Third Report to the Legislature of Vermont, relating to the Registry and Returns of Births, Marriages, and Deaths, in this State, for the year ending December 31, 1859* (Middlebury: Register Book and Job Office, 1860), 89–90. Notwithstanding the difficulty in obtaining physicians' cooperation, Rutland reported that in 1859 five individuals, including Gershom Cheney Ruggles who sold land for the local rail yard, were involved in "registering births and deaths." *Selectmen's Report. Town of Rutland, March 1, 1859* (Rutland: Tuttle & Co's Steam Printing, 1859), 10.

540 Address Before the Medical Society of Vermont, by Hiram F. Stevens, M. D., President, Delivered October 1858, *Transactions of the Vermont Medical Society at the Annual Session, Held at Montpelier, October 19th and 20th, 1864* (Woodstock: Vermont Standard, 1864), 20–22.

541 October 27, 1858, Vermont Medical Society Annual Session, Minutes, UVM.

542 October 26, 1859, ibid.

543 *Vermont Watchman and State Journal,* 23 November 1860.

544 *Eighth Report to the Legislature of Vermont relating to the Registry and Returns of Births, Marriages and Deaths, in this State, for the year ending December 31, 1864* (Montpelier: Freeman Steam Printing, 1866), 80.

545 *Transactions of the Vermont Medical Society, 1864,* 22.

546 *Second Annual Report of the Secretary of the State Board of Health of the State of Vermont for the Year Ending Sept. 1st, 1888* (Rutland: Tuttle Company, 1888), 12.

547 Ibid.

548 *Vermont Watchman and State Journal,* 15 March 1849.

549 *Vermont Phoenix,* 17 August 1849.

550 *Vermont Chronicle,* 24 January 1849.

551 Inaugural Address of Julius Converse, October 3, 1872, https://www.sec.state.vt.us/media/48554/Converse1872.pdf

552 *First Registration Report,* 94; *Fourteenth Registration Report,* 104.

553 Calvin M. Fitch, *The Invalid's Guide, and Consumptive's Manual* (New York: Taylor and Hoyt, 1856), 110.

554 S. Putnam, President's Address, *Transactions. . . 1864,* 266–267.

555 *Middlebury Register,* 2 February 1859.

556 *Eighth Report. . . 1864,* 80.

557 James Hunt, "On the Acclimatisation of Europeans in the United States of America," *The Anthropological Review,* vol. 8, no. 29 (April 1870): 119.

558 October 26, 1859, Vermont Medical Society Annual Session, Minutes, UVM.

559 In 1858 a VMS member cautioned the organization that while "figures cannot lie," it was equally true that "facts themselves are false when interpreted by false theories." July 1, 1858, ibid.

560 Benjamin W. Dean, *Instructions Relative to the Registry and Return of Births, Marriages and Deaths, in Vermont* (Middlebury: Register Book and Job Office, 1859), 4.

561 *Twenty-Third Report to the Legislature of Vermont, relating to the Registry and Returns of Births, Marriages and Deaths, in this State. For the year ending December 31st, 1879* (Montpelier: Freeman Steam Printing House and Bindery, 1882), 120–124.

562 Thomas Henderson, *Hints on the Medical Examination of Recruits for the Army* (New Orleans: John J. Haswell, 1840), 11.

563 Benjamin Apthorp Gould, *Investigations in the Military and Anthropological Statistics of American Soldiers* (New York: Hurd and Houghton, 1869), 132.

564 J. H. Baxter, *Statistics, Medical and Anthropological, of the Provost-Marshal-General's Bureau derived from Records of the Examination for Military Service in the Armies of the United States During the Late War of the Rebellion of Over a Million Recruits, Drafted Men, Substitutes, and Enrolled Men,* 2 vols. (Washington: Government Printing Office, 1875), i–ii; ; John David Smith, "The Health of Vermont's Civil War Recruits," *Vermont History* 43, no. 3 (Summer 1975): 185.

565 Obituary, *Burlington Weekly Free Press,* 28 May 1896.

566 VERMONT- SECOND DISTRICT, Extracts from report of C. P. Frost, June 14, 1865, Baxter, *Statistics, Medical and Anthropological,* vol. 1: 195–197.

567 Extracts from report of Dr. B. F. Morgan, June 9, 1865, ibid., 191–192.

568 Extracts from report of Dr. Daniel Perley, June 12, 1865, ibid., 207–208.

569 Albion K. Strout, *Abortion,* 1872, Medical School Theses, DA3, file no. 10949, Dartmouth College.

570 James C. Mohr, *Abortion in America: The Origins and Evolution of National Policy, 1800–1900* (Oxford: Oxford University Press, 1978), 130.

NOTES

571 William McCollom, "Criminal Abortion," *Transactions of the Vermont Medical Society for the Year 1865* (Burlington: R. S. Styles, 1865), 40.

572 J. S. Richmond, "President's Address," *Transactions of the Vermont Medical Society for the years 1869 and 1870* (Burlington: R. S. Styles, 1870), 107. A New York doctor agreed that the practice was so prevalent elsewhere that he believed members of the profession were engaged in the "the Science and Art of Abortion." Ely Van de Warker, *The Detection of Criminal Abortion and a Study of Foeticidal Drugs* (Boston: James Campbell, 1872), 7.

573 *Transactions of the Vermont Medical Society, 1865,* 20; *Green-Mountain Freeman* (Montpelier), 21 October 1868.

574 Strout went on to study medicine at Bellevue Hospital and the College of Physicians and Surgeons in New York City before establishing a private practice in Albion, Maine in 1873. Henry D. Kingsbury and Simeon L. Deyo, *Illustrated History of Kennebec County, Maine* (New York: H. W. Blake & Company, 1892), 370.

575 *Fourth National Quarantine and Sanitary Convention,* 34.

576 *Sixth Registration Report, 1862,* 96.

577 McCollom, *Criminal Abortion,* 41; Horatio R. Storer, *On Criminal Abortion in America* (Philadelphia: J. B. Lippincott & Co., 1860), 37.

578 Lita Linzer Schwartz and Natalie K. Isser, *Endangered Children: Neonaticide, Infanticide, and Filicide* (Boca Raton: CRC Press, 2000), 1.

579 An example of the widespread practice of Vermonters concocting their own medicines without the interference of trained professionals in the nineteenth century was recounted in 1929: "Grandmother had a dim room with rows of drying herbs looped from beam to beam: on the shelves are many boxes full of the dry herbs, while nearby are wooden scales for weighing, and the mortar and pestle. The gathering and compounding of herbs for medicinal purposes is almost a lost art. Grandmother took great care in the drying and storing of her herbs for unless properly done the flavor and keeping qualities were lost. Leaves were gathered on a fine dry day before the blooming as the sap was then up. Seeds were gathered just before they were ready to fall and must not be overripe. These were placed in a cool place away from the sun and when dry or crisp were often stored in corked bottles. There was often an especial room, usually near the attic, called a 'still-room where all the medicines were made." Katherine B. Mills, "The Remedies of Grandmother's Day," *The Vermonter* 34 (1929):27–28.

580 Mohr, *Abortion in America,* 31–35.

581 Joseph W. Dellapenna, *Dispelling the Myths of Abortion History* (Durham, NC: Carolina Academic Press, 2006), 302–303. Dellapenna's comprehensive study also describes the ongoing differences of those who contend that the regulars sought to suppress practitioners of alternative forms of medicine because of sexism as many midwives and herbalists were women. 288–293.

582 Schwartz and Isser, *Endangered Children,* 37.

583 Ibid., 28

584 Leslie J. Reagan, *When Abortion was a Crime: Women, Medicine, and Law in the United States, 1867–1973* (Berkeley: University of California Press, 1997), 9.

585 Dellapenna identifies these as injury, ingestion and intrusion techniques. *Dispelling the Myths*, 33–51.

586 Alexander C. Draper, *Observations on Abortion. With an account of the means both medicinal and mechanical, employed to produce that effect, together with advice to females* (Philadelphia: 1839), 31.

587 *Caledonian*, 13 February 1858.

588 *Burlington Weekly Free Press*, 24 January 1840.

589 *Rutland County Herald*, 25 February 1847.

590 *Vermont Watchman and State Journal*, 24 August 1848.

591 *Burlington Free Press*, 10 September 1855.

592 Ibid., 7 November, 1855; *Orange County Telegraph* (Bradford), 16 May 1862.

593 *Middlebury Register*, 4 June 1856.

594 *Brattleboro Eagle*, 29 April 1852.

595 Shattuck, *Green Mountain Opium Eaters, passim*.

596 Wesley Herwig, "A Patient Boiled Alive (Or: Why Jehiel Smith, a Thomsonian Physician, Left East Randolph, Vermont, in a Hurry)," *Vermont History*, vol. 44, no. 4 (Fall 1976): 227.

597 Draper, *Observations on Abortion*.

598 *The Reporter* (Brattleboro), 12 November 1808.

599 John Burns, *Observations on Abortion* (Troy: Wright, Goodenow, and Stockwell, 1808), 70–74.

600 Reynolds, "Etiology of Consumption," Dartmouth College.

601 John B. Beck, *An Inaugural Dissertation on Infanticide* (New-York: J. Seymour, 1817), 40.

602 *Albany Gazette*, 12 August 1813, 8 November 1813.

603 David Hosack, "Observations on Ergot," in *Essays on Various Subjects of Medical Science* (New-York: J. Seymour, 1824), 296.

604 Charles Whitlaw, *A Treatise on the Causes and Effects of Inflammation Fever* (London: By the author, 1831), 111–113; David Meredith Reese, *Medicines, Their Uses and Mode of Administration* (New-York: Harper & Brothers, 1844), 177.

605 Hosack, "Observations on Ergot," 296.

606 Beck, *Inaugural Dissertation*, 41.

607 *Revised Statutes of the State of Vermont, passed November 19, 1839* (Burlington: Chauncey Goodrich, 1840), 445.

608 *Sentinel and Democrat* (Burlington), 10 December 1819.

609 Ibid., 29 October 1819.

Notes

610 "Petition of Lewis Hutchins & 136 praying for the relief of Norman Cleaveland, October 20, 1830," Petitions, SE118-00065, VSARA; *Rutland County Herald*, 27 April 1830.

611 *Farmer's Herald* (St. Johnsbury), 28 April 1830 and 27 October 1830.

612 Ibid.; Theodric Romeyn Beck and John B. Beck, eds., *Elements of Medical Jurisprudence*, vol. 1 (Albany: H. H. Van Dyck, 1850), 440–441.

613 *Middlebury Free Press*, 10 November 1830.

614 *The Horn of the Green Mountains* (Manchester), 2 November 1830.

615 An American Matron, *The Maternal Physician; A Treatise on the Nurture and Management of Infants* (New York: Isaac Riley, 1811).

616 *Vermont Chronicle* (Bellows Falls), 12 July 1833.

617 *Vermont Telegraph* (Brandon), 21 December 1836.

618 *The Enterprise and Vermonter* (Vergennes), 8 February 1838.

619 *Vermont Telegraph*, 3 March 1841.

620 Mohr, *Abortion in America*, 46.

621 *Burlington Weekly Free Press*, 2 April 1841; Mohr, *Abortion in America*, 48–49.

622 Mohr, *Abortion in America*, 49; Shattuck, *Green Mountain Opium Eaters*, 71–73.

623 Julia Epstein, "The Pregnant Imagination, Fetal Rights, and Women's Bodies: A Historical Inquiry," *Yale Journal of Law and the Humanities* 7 (1) (1995): 155.

624 Reva Siegel, "Reasoning from the Body: A Historical Perspective on Abortion Regulation and Questions of Equal Protection," *Stanford Law Review* 40 (2) (1992): 301.

625 *Journal of the House of Representatives of the State of Vermont. October Session, 1846* (Windsor: Bishop & Tracy, 1846), 65, 157; *Acts and Resolves Passed by the Legislature of the State of Vermont, at their October Session, 1846* (Burlington: Chauncey Goodrich, 1846), 34.

626 *Journal of the Senate of the State of Vermont. October Session, 1846* (Windsor: Bishop & Tracy, 1846), 52; *Acts and Resolves, 1846*, 31.

627 Ibid., 30.

628 See, e.g. "Petition of E. H. Johnson & others, praying that the laws in relation to hawkers and pedlars may be altered," October 15, 1833, SE118-00063, VSARA.

629 Abby Maria Hemenway, *The History of Washington County in the Historical Gazetteer* (Montpelier: Vermont Watchman and State Journal, 1882), 86–104.

630 Mohr, *Abortion in America*, 121–130.

631 Ibid., 79.

632 *Acts and Resolves passed by the General Court of Massachusetts, in the year 1845* (Boston: Dutton and Wentworth, 1845), 406; *Laws of the State of New-York, passed at the Sixty-Eighth Session of the Legislature, begun and held in the City of Albany, the seventh day of January 1845* (Albany: C. Van Benthuysen and Co., 1845), 285–286.

633 Storer, *On Criminal Abortion*, 29.

634 Mohr, *Abortion in America*, 130–132.

635 *Acts and Resolves Passed by the General Assembly of the State of Vermont, at the Annual Session, 1867* (Montpelier: Freeman Steam Printing, 1867), 64–66.

636 *First Report, 1857*, 84.

637 L. C. Butler, "The Decadence of the American Race, as Exhibited in the Registration Reports of Massachusetts, Vermont [and Rhode Island]; The Cause and the Remedy," *Transactions of the Vermont Medical Society, for the years 1867 and 1868* (Burlington: R. S. Styles, 1869), 78. Stilwell recounts that in 1810, fifty-one percent of Vermont's population was composed of children under sixteen years of age. Stilwell, *Migration from Vermont*, 96. An 1870 account of the population of Lowell, Massachusetts related that, "in the first generation of settlers the families averaged from eight to ten children; in the next three generations seven to eight; the fifth about five; and in the sixth less than three. The present is less than this." Hunt, "On the Acclimatisation of Europeans," 123.

638 Jay Mack Holbrook, *Vermont 1771 Census* (Oxford, MA: Holbrook Research Institute, 1982), ii – iii.

639 Smith and Rann, *History of Rutland County*, 562.

640 *Fifth Report, 1861*, 85.

641 Ibid., 87–88.

642 Mohr, *Abortion in America*, 47.

643 Ibid., 17, 69.

644 *Burlington Daily Times*, 27 May 1858.

645 Mohr, *Abortion in America*, 50; 78–81.

646 *Sixth Report, 1862*, 87–89.

647 *Seventh Report, 1863*, 87–88.

648 *New York Times*, 29 June 1858.

649 *Proceedings of the Free Convention held at Rutland, Vt., July* [sic] *25th, 26, and 27th, 1858* (Boston: J. B. Yerrinton and Son, 1858), iii; *Burlington Free Press*, 30 June 1858.

650 *New York Times*, 30 June 1858.

651 Ibid., 29 June 1858.

652 An Act for the Punishment of Murder, Laws Passed, February 1779, William Slade, Jr. *Vermont State Papers* (Middlebury: J. W. Copeland, 1823), 375.

653 Lorenzo D'Agostino, *The History of Public Welfare in Vermont* (Winooski: St. Michael's College Press, 1948), 154.

654 *Fornication binds the criminal parties to marry. The Decision of the Congregational Church in Rupert, Vt. Relative to a case of discipline, August 31, 1814* (Bennington: Darius Clark, 1815), 7, 30.

Notes

655 Steven R. Hoffbeck, "'Remember the Poor' (*Galatians* 2:10): Poor Farms in Vermont," *Vermont History* 57, no. 4 (Fall 1989): 226; Marshall True, "Middle-Class Women and Civic Improvement in Burlington 1865–1890," *Vermont History* 56, no. 2 (Spring 1988): 112.

656 Andrea Zlotucha Kozub, "'To Married Ladies It is Peculiarly Suited': Nineteenth-Century Abortion in an Archaeological Context," *Historical Archaeology*, 52, no. 2 (2018): 267.

657 *Acts and Resolves Passed by the General Assembly of the State of Vermont at the Annual Session, 1865* (Montpelier: Freeman Steam Printing, 1865), 230.

658 *Burlington Free Press*, 30 September 1875.

659 Glenn Hausfater and Sarah Blaffer Hrdy, eds., *Infanticide: Comparative and Evolutionary Perspectives* (New York: Aldine Publishing Company, 1984), 442.

660 Thomas A. Crist, "Babies in the Privy: Prostitution, Infanticide, and Abortion in New York City's Five Points District," *Historical Archaeology* 39, no. 1 (2005): 26–27; Timothy J. Gilfoyle, "Archaeologists in the Brothel: 'Sin City,' Historical Archaeology and Prostitution," ibid., 133; Simone Caron, "'Killed by its Mother': Infanticide in Providence County, Rhode Island, 1870 to 1938," *Journal of Social History* 44, no. 1 (Fall 2010): 213–237.

661 Josephine McDonagh, "Child-Murder Narratives in George Eliot's *Adam Bede:* Embedded Histories and Fictional Representation," *Nineteenth-Century Literature* 56, no. 2 (September 2001): 232–233.

662 Randolph A. Roth, "Child Murder in New England," *Social Science History* 25, no. 1 (Spring 2001): 119–120.

663 Randolph Roth, *American Homicide* (Cambridge: Harvard University Press, 2009), 187.

664 Roth, *Child Murder,* 123.

665 McDonagh, "Child-Murder," 229–231.

666 See, e.g., *North Star* (Danville), 16 May 1836.

667 *Vermont Aurora* (Vergennes), 16 September 1830.

668 *Burlington Weekly Free Press*, 23 April 1847.

669 *Vermont Watchman and State Journal*, 1 January 1852.

670 *Burlington Free Press*, 4 March 1854; *Burlington Weekly Sentinel*, 9 March 1854.

671 Quoted in *Burlington Weekly Sentinel*, 23 March 1854.

672 Vermont Registration Returns, 1857, 1858, 1859, PRA-00920, -00921, -00922, VSARA.

673 Grand jury records, 1843–1893, LACC-00070, VSARA.

674 *Lamoille Newsletter,* 31 May 1861.

675 *Burlington Daily Times,* 1 June 1866.

676 *Burlington Weekly Free Press,* 26 October 1866.

677 *Burlington Times*, 20 April 1867.

678 *Burlington Free Press*, 30 April 1869.

679 Ibid., 5 May 1869.

680 *Rutland Independent*, 18 September 1869.

681 *Argus and Patriot*, 29 April 1869.

682 *Argus and Patriot*, 24 June 1875.

683 *St. Albans Advertiser*, 14 May 1875.

684 *St. Johnsbury Times*, 4 February 1870.

685 *Rutland Daily Globe*, 20 March 1875.

686 *Argus and Patriot*, 23 April 1879.

687 Mohr, *Abortion in America*, 133–135.

688 George Carroll, *The Manchester Tragedy. A Sketch of the Life and Death of Miss Sarah H. Furber, and the Trial of her Seducer and Murderer* (Manchester: Fisk & Moore, 1848).

689 *National Police Gazette* (New York City), 24 June 1848.

690 *New Hampshire Patriot and State Gazette* (Concord), 8 June 1848.

691 Carroll, *The Manchester Tragedy*, 10.

692 *Boston Daily Bee*, 10 June 1848.   693   William F. Whitcher, *History of the Town of Haverhill, New Hampshire (*1919), 132; Frederic P. Wells, *History of Newbury, Vermont* (St. Johnsbury: The Caledonian Company, 1902), 632.

694 *North Star*, 30 January 1827.

695 *The Universal Watchman* (Montpelier), 6 March 1841.

696 Whitcher, *History*, 132.

697 *Address of Dr. M. F. Morrison, before the Friends of Mental Liberty, at North Haverhill, N.H.* (Boston: J. P. Mendum 1846), in Nahum W. French, *Equality Mental and Political Liberty and The Progress of Nature* (1913), 74.

698 Ibid., 68.

699 Ibid., 72–73.

700 Whitcher, *History*, 133.

701 Frederic Palmer Wells, *History of Barnet, Vermont* (Burlington: Free Press Printing, 1923), 546.

702 Carroll, *The Manchester Tragedy*, 10.

703 *National Police Gazette*, 24 June 1848.

704 Ibid., 17 June 1848.

705 *Bennington Banner*, 24 June 1848.

706 *Christian Herald* (Newburyport, MA), 3 August 1848.

NOTES

707 *Caledonian* (St. Johnsbury), 17 June 1848; *Vermont Watchman and State Journal,* 29 June 1848.

708 *Aurora of the Valley,* 22 February 1855.

709 October 26, 1859, VMS Minutes, UVM; *St. Albans Weekly Messenger,* 25 October 1860.

710 *The Journal of Materia Medica,* vol. 8, no. 1 (January 1869), 63.

711 *North Star,* 2 August 1878.

712 Strout, Abortion, Dartmouth College.

713 *Howard v. Howard,* 32 Kan.469, *Pacific Reporter,* vol. 34 (1893), 1114, 1116.

714 Samuel Thomson, *New Guide to Health; or Botanic Family Physician* (Montpelier: 1851), 188.

715 *The New Hampshire Journal of Medicine,* vol. 8, no. 1 (January 1858): 224; *Dartmouth Medical College Centennial Exercises Tuesday, June 29, 1897,* 72–73. Unless otherwise noted, aspects of Howard's story are located in the following places: probate proceedings of the William Waterman (died November 18, 1853) and Jane Wilson Howard (died August 7, 1858) estates. Box 74114, Orange County Probate Court, Chelsea, Vermont; Orange County supreme, county and chancery courts, VSARA; and sworn trial testimony recited by the Vermont Supreme Court in *State of Vermont v. William H. M. Howard,* 32 Vt. 380 (1859).

716 *Vermont Phoenix,* 26 November 1859.

717 Mohr, *Abortion in America,* 35.

718 Vermont Medical Society Minutes, June 26 and October 22, 1856. UVM.

719 Ibid., June 17, 1857.

720 H. Gatch Carey, "Abortion: A New Method of Treatment," in E. H. Parker and J. H. Douglas, *American Medical Monthly,* vol. 7, no. 1 (January 1857), 4.

721 Suffolk District Medical Society, Report of the Committee on Criminal Abortion, 2, https://collections.nlm.nih.gov/catalog/nlm:nlmuid-101218760-bk; Storer, *On Criminal Abortions,* 22–25.

722 George H. Hubbard, ed., *The New-Hampshire Journal of Medicine* (Manchester: Fisk & Gage, 1857), 216.

723 *Vermont Journal,* 22 January 1859; *North Star,* 5 February 1859.

724 *Vermont Watchman and State Journal,* 2 December 1859; *Bellows Falls Times,* 11 February 1859.

725 Edgar F. Waterman, *The Waterman Family,* vol. 2 (New Haven: Tuttle, Morehouse & Taylor, 1942), 484; *Burlington Daily Times,* 29 November 1859.

726 Vermont State Prison, Registers 1809–1916, F-04551, VSARA.

727 *Orleans Independent Standard,* 9 December 1859.

728 *St. Johnsbury Caledonian,* 27 February 1858.

729 T. S. Brooks, "Relation of the Medical Profession to Quackery," *Transactions of the Vermont Medical Society for the Years 1871, 1872 and 1873* (Montpelier: Argus and Patriot, 1874), 312.

730 *Vermont Watchman*, 2 December 1859.

731 *William Liddicoat v. Wm. H. M. Howard*, County Court record book, vol. 19, June term 1854–1859, OECC-00021, VSARA.

732 *Vermont Journal*, 2 December 1853.

733 Ibid., 8 February 1856.

734 *New England Farmer* (Boston), 22 March 1856.

735 Howard claimed in probate proceedings that when he married Jane he brought eight wagon loads of furniture, fifty horses and cattle and 300 sheep to their Bradford home.

736 *John Patterson v. Wm. H. M. Howard*, Orange County Court, June Term 1858, County Court record book, vol. 19, June term 1854–June term 1859, OECC-00021, VSARA.

737 *Asa M. Dickey v. W. H. M. Howard*, Orange County June term 1858, OECC-00021, VSARA.

738 *St. Albans Messenger*, 19 March 1857; *Vermont Phoenix*, 14 March 1857; Horace W. Davenport, *University of Michigan Surgeons 1850–1970, Who They Were and What They Did* (Ann Arbor: Historical Center for the Health Sciences, 1993), 24.

739 *St. Johnsbury Caledonian*, 3 December 1859.

740 *Aurora of the Valley*, 25 October 1856.

741 *D. T. Corbin & wife v. W. H. M. Howard*, Charles Barrett Docket, June term 1858, County, Supreme and Chancery court dockets, 1849–1931, OECC-00029, VSARA.

742 "Vermont Vital Records, 1760–1954," FamilySearch (https://familysearch.org/ark:/61903/1:1:XFVM-V56: 6 November 2017, David T Corbin and Eunice L Fowler, 28 Sep 1856, Marriage; State Capitol Building, Montpelier; FHL microfilm 27,551.

743 *Orleans Independent Standard*, 9 December 1859. Corbin later served honorably with Union forces, was seriously wounded, captured, imprisoned and became United States Attorney and then U. S. Senator for South Carolina.

744 Those proceedings included a March 4, 1859 request to the court by the administrator of the estates for permission to sell the two buildings to an interested New Hampshire purchaser. They had fallen into such a state of disrepair and determined to be a hindrance to selling the property that they needed to be removed immediately before Connecticut River ice broke up and prevented their being sledded across. Otherwise, the request related, they were "so high that they will not go through the bridges."

745 *St. Johnsbury Caledonian*, 14 March 1857.

746 *Daniel Houghton v. W. H. M. Howard; Willard Waterman v. W. H. M. Howard;* and, *W. H. M. Howard v. A. W. Nourse & wife*, Charles Barrett Docket. VSARA.

747 State of Vermont. Vermont Vital Records through 1870. New England Historic Genealogical Society, Boston, Massachusetts. State of Vermont. Vermont Vital Records, 1871–1908. New England Historic Genealogical Society, Boston, Massachusetts.

Notes

748 Roth, "Child Murder," 103.

749 Vermont Registration returns, 1858, Town of Bradford, VSARA.

750 *Burlington Weekly Free Press,* 19 February 1858.

751 Vermont Registration record 1857, PRA-00922, VSARA.

752 *Orleans Independent Standard* (Irasburgh), 9 December 1859.

753 "Joint Resolution authorizing State House Commission to purchase suitable figure to put on dome of State House," Joint Assembly Papers, 1838–1858, A124-00002, VSARA.

754 *Vermont Journal,* 20 February 1858; Vermont Registration returns, 1857, Town of Bradford deaths, PRA-00920, VSARA.

755 *The State of Vermont v. William H. M. Howard,* 32 Vt. 380 (1859), *passim.*

756 *Vermont Journal,* 29 January 1859.

757 Ibid.

758 *Vermont Patriot and State Gazette,* 19 February 1858.

759 C. P. Frost, "Report of a Trial for Criminal Abortion," in J. H. Douglas, ed., *American Medical Monthly and New York Review,* vol. 14 (July–December 1860), 197.

760 Vermont Registration returns, 1858, Town of Bradford deaths, VSARA.

761 Ibid. William died young in Chelsea in 1878, reportedly from consumption. The record describes him as being a printer and erroneously identifies Jane's mother, Agnes Wilson, in her place. In Jane's will, dated June 7, 1858, she bequeathed one-eighth of her estate to "my infant son, Howard (who has no Christian name)," indicating that the infant bore no formal name for some time before being known as William.

762 *Vermont Phoenix,* 20 February 1858.

763 Ibid.

764 *Vermont Journal,* 20 February 1858.

765 *St. Johnsbury Caledonian,* 27 March 1858.

766 Ibid., 5 June 1858.

767 *Christian Repository* (Montpelier), 6 August 1858.

768 *Vermont Journal,* 11 September 1858.

769 State's Attorney Dewey's record book identifies three successive prosecutions against Howard: numbers 99, 100 and 101 that appear to correspond with offenses relating to the deaths of Young and Ashe and assault to commit murder with bails of $5,000, $2,000 and $5,000. Entry 96 describes a joint prosecution brought against Howard and Knapp, with $500 as the bail amount for the former. VSARA.

770 The will lists son William Frederick Waterman, who died in 1857, as a beneficiary that was probably intended to go to his estate.

771 Barron, *Those Who Stayed Behind,* 27, 52–53.

772 Roth, *The Democratic Dilemma,* 251.

773　Ibid., 255–256.

774　Barron, *Those Who Stayed Behind*, 119.

775　Ibid., 121.

776　Hamilton Child, *Gazetteer of Orange County, Vt. 1762–1888* (Syracuse: Syracuse Journal Company, 1888), 119.

777　State's Attorney Book, Orange County, OECC-00032, VSARA; *Vermont Chronicle*, 6 April 1858.

778　*Vermont Journal*, 11 September 1858.

779　*Aurora of the Valley*, 10 September 1859; *Vermont Journal*, 10 September 1859.

780　*St. Johnsbury Caledonian*, 14 August 1858. State's Attorney Dewey's record book identifies, in addition to Howard, John Sanborn, Henry Humphrey, Jesse Worthy, B. L. Worthy and Joseph Worthy as providing bonds in the amount of $1,000 each in three separate cases. OECC-00032, VSARA.

781　Vermont Registration returns 1858, Town of Bradford, VSARA.

782　Shattuck, *Green Mountain Opium Eaters*, 65.

783　Constance E. Putnam, *The Science We Have Loved and Taught: Dartmouth Medical School's First Two Centuries* (Lebanon: University Press of New England, 2004), 106.

784　*William H. Carter v. William H. M. Howard*, 39 Vt. 107 (1866). The court faulted Carter for choosing the wrong defendant and indicated that Jane's estate was the proper debtor. The probate proceedings from February 1859 reveal that Carter did make a claim of $9 against it, but was denied, along with others, because it "should come vs. D. Howard, but not against the estate." Carter did not appeal that decision and the Supreme Court ruled as a matter of law that when a creditor chose a debtor, as Carter had done with Jane, his claims were against that person and not others who had not obligated themselves to pay it.

785　*St. Johnsbury Caledonian*, 14 August 1858.

786　Paul S. Gillies, *The Law of the Hills: A Judicial History of Vermont* (Barre and Montpelier: Vermont Historical Society, 2019), 211–212.

787　*Vermont Standard*, 11 February 1859.

788　Dixi Crosby, *Report of a Trial for Alleged Mal-Practice against Dixi Crosby, M.D.* (Woodstock: Lewis Pratt, 1854).

789　William Procter Jr., ed., *The American Journal of Pharmacy*, vol. 30 (Philadelphia: Merrihew & Thompson, 1858), 461–462.

790　*Vermont Standard*, 11 February 1859.

791　*Vermont Journal*, 26 February 1859.

792　Vermont Medical Society Minutes, June 29, 1859, UVM.

793　Ibid., June 26, 1860.

794　Frost, "Report of a Trial," 198–202.

795　Ibid.

NOTES

796 *Vermont Standard,* 11 February 1859.
797 Ibid.; *Vermont Journal,* 12 February 1859; *Vermont Chronicle,* 8 February 1859.
798 *Aurora of the Valley,* 8 October 1859.
799 *St. Johnsbury Caledonian,* 3 December 1859
800 *Vermont Phoenix,* 26 November 1859.
801 Vermont State Prison, Registers 1809–1916, F-04551, VSARA.
802 *The Democrat* (St. Albans), 27 December 1859.
803 *Vermont Journal,* 26 November 1859.
804 William Sumner Appleton, *Record of the Descendants of William Sumner* (Boston: David Clapp & Son, 1879), 90.
805 *Norwich Aurora,* 20 January 1869.
806 Ibid.
807 *St. Johnsbury Caledonian,* 22 January 1869.
808 *Catherine A. Sumner vs. Wm. H. M. Howard,* Orange County Court, June Term, A. D. 1876 and *David E. Colby and Preston S. Smith vs. William H. M. Howard, Sarah C. Cleavland and Katherine A. Howard,* Orange County Chancery Court, December Term 1875, *Vermont Watchman and State Journal,* 22 September 1875, *The United Opinion* (Bradford), 6 May 1876.
809 *Howard v. Howard,* 32 Kan.469, *Pacific Reporter,* vol. 34 (1893), 1114.
810 President's Address, "Proceedings of the Annual Session, October 19 and 20, 1870," *Transactions of the Vermont Medical Society, for the Years 1869 and 1870* (Burlington: R. S. Styles, 1870), 106–107.
811 *Special Session 1857,* 211.
812 *Vermont Watchman and State Journal,* 25 November 1859.
813 Samuel B. Hand, *The Star that Set: The Vermont Republican Party, 1854–1974* (Latham, MD: Lexington Books, 2002), 3.
814 Ibid., 16.
815 Ibid., 36; Samuel B. Hand, "Mountain Rule Revisited," *Vermont History* 71 (Summer/Fall 2003): 139–151.
816 Samuel B. Hand, Jeffrey D. Marshall, and D. Gregory Sanford, "'Little Republics': The Structure of State Politics in Vermont, 1854–1920," *Vermont History* 53, no. 3 (Summer 1985): 142.
817 *The Enterprise and Vermonters* (Vergennes), 27 February 1857.
818 *Special Session, 1857,* 165.
819 Ibid., 27.
820 Ibid., 236–237.
821 Ibid., 178.
822 Ibid. 42–43.

823 Ibid., 30.
824 Ibid., 210; *St. Albans Weekly Messenger,* 12 February 1857.
825 *Burlington Weekly Free Press,* 27 February 1857.
826 *Special Session, 1857,* 177–178.
827 *North Star,* 28 February 1857.
828 Ibid., 249.
829 Ibid., 253.
830 Ibid.
831 Ibid., 48; 69.
832 Ibid., 41.
833 Ibid., 268.
834 Harold L. Bailey, "Vermont's State Houses: Being a Narration of the Battles over the Location of the Capitol and Its Construction," *Vermont Quarterly* 12 (1944): 148.
835 Ibid.; *Journal of the Senate of the State of Vermont, October Session 1860* (Montpelier: E. P. Walton, 1860), 16.
836 Inaugural address, *Journal of the House of Representatives, October Session 1858,* https://www.sec.state.vt.us/media/48728/Hall1858.pdf.
837 *Daily Journal,* 14 October 1859.
838 *The Journal of the American Pharmaceutical* Association (Columbus: By the Association, 1913), 468.
839 *Vermont Watchman and State Journal,* 27 February 1857.
840 *Bennington Banner,* 1 April 1859.
841 *Green-Mountain Freeman,* 25 February 1858.
842 *Orleans Independent Standard,* 19 February 1858.
843 *State of Vermont v. John B. Hand, Willard F. Brown, George We. Martin,* Case files, 1798–1945, CACC-00042, VSARA.
844 *Orleans Independent Standard,* 10 December 1858.
845 Minutes, January 23, 1856, Records of the Addison County Medical Society, vol. 1, 1835–1920, Henry Sheldon Museum of Vermont History, Middlebury, Vermont.
846 VMS Minutes, June 26, 1860, UVM.
847 Ibid., October 16, 1860. In 1867, the VMS continued to associate "uterine derangement" with "the perverted imagination of the patient" and suggested that boards of consulting examiners be established at hospitals, including the Vermont State Asylum, to consider these types of complaints. *Proceedings of the Vermont Medical Society, 1867 and 1868,* 4.
848 Ibid., June 16, 1864.
849 President's Address, *Transactions, 1869 and 1870,* 107.

Notes

850 William Henry Thayer, *Address to the Graduates of the Vermont Medical College, of the Class of 1856* (Keene: 1856), 9.

851 Butler, "The Decadence of the American Race," 81.

852 McCollom, "Criminal Abortion," *Transactions, 1865,* 40.

853 Ibid., 42–43; Storer, *On Criminal Abortion,* 26; contra, Hunt, "On the Acclimatisation of Europeans," 121–122.

854 *Proceedings 1867,* 4.

855 Mohr, *Abortion in America,* 82.

856 *Vermont Record,* 4 November 1865.

857 William McCollom, "Criminal Abortion," in John B. Hamilton, ed., *The Journal of the American Medical Association,* vol. 26 (Chicago: American Medical Association Press, 1896), 257–259.

858 Butler, "The Decadence of the American Race," 82.

859 Ibid., 86.

860 *St. Johnsbury Caledonian,* 19 April 1867; *Vermont Journal,* 4 May 1867.

861 *Green-Mountain Freeman,* 10 July 1867; *Sterling v. Sterling,* 41 Vt. 80 (1868).

862 *Journal of the Senate of the State of Vermont, Annual Session, 1867* (Montpelier: Freeman Steam Printing, 1868), 112.

863 *Acts and Resolves Passed by the General Assembly of the State of Vermont at the Annual Session, 1867* (Montpelier: Freeman Steam Printing, 1867), 64–66; Mohr, *Abortion in America,* 210–211.

864 *Transactions, 1867,* 10–12.

865 *The Vermont Record and Farmer* (Brattleboro), 16 July 1869.

866 *Transactions, 1870,* 107.

867 *Transactions, 1868,* 186.

868 *Transactions, 1870.*131.

869 Shattuck, *Green Mountain Opium Eaters, passim.*

870 *Proceedings, Constitution and By-Laws of the Vermont Pharmaceutical Association* (Rutland: Tuttle & Co., 1871), 3.

871 *Proceedings of the Vermont Pharmaceutical Association, 1871* (Rutland: Tuttle & Co., 1871), 23–25.

872 Shattuck, *Green Mountain Opium Eaters,* 97–101.

873 *Proceedings of the Vermont Pharmaceutical Association, September 24–25, 1873* (Rutland: Globe Paper, 1874), 41.

874 *Transactions, 1874, 1875 and 1876,* 399.

875 *Burlington Weekly Free Press,* 27 October 1876.

876 *Acts and Resolves Passed by the General Assembly of the State of Vermont at the Fourth Biennial Session, 1876* (Rutland: Tuttle & Company, 1876), 194–197.

877 *Burlington Free Press*, 21 November 1876. A member of the regular medical profession responded to homeopaths in a reasoned manner that dismissed his allegations. Ibid., 23 November 1876.
878 By 1851, fifteen states had repealed similar legislation and eight others had never passed any. Rosenberg, *The Cholera Years*, 155.
879 *Argus and Patriot*, 20 December 1876.
880 *St. Albans Daily Messenger*, 22 October, 1878.
881 *State v. H. J. Hazelton*, Procuring Abortion, Caledonia County Case files and miscellaneous, June term 1876–June term 1877, CACC-00053, VSARA.
882 *The Vermont Union* (Lyndon), 22 June 1877.
883 Ibid., 20 December 1878.
884 *Essex County Herald* (Island Pond), 18 July 1879.
885 *The United Opinion*, 29 October 1886.
886 *Middlebury Register*, 14 December 1877.
887 *Swanton Courier*, 22 December 1877.
888 *Argus and Patriot*, 19 December 1877.
889 *Orleans County Monitor*, 21 January 1878.
890 *Rutland Daily Herald*, 25 September 1878.
891 *Rutland Daily Herald*, 10 June 1878.
892 *St. Johnsbury Caledonian*, 21 November 1879.
893 *Vermont Watchman and State Journal*, 2 June 1880.
894 *The Lamoille News*, 26 December 1877, quoting the Springfield *Republican*.
895 Speech of Hon. Albert C. Clark, *passim*.
896 Mohr, *Abortion in America*, 242–245.
897 After a Caribbean Hurricane, the Battle Is Where, or Even Whether, to Rebuild, *New York Times*, October 7, 2019.
898 Ibid., 62–63.
899 *Special Session 1857*, 31–32.
900 *Burlington Weekly Sentinel*, 22 January 1857.
901 *Journal of the Senate of the State of Vermont, October Session 1858* (Ludlow: Warner's Book and Job Printing, 1858), 372. Other books concerning the state's past and its leaders also existed at the time, but were not a part of the library's holdings that included Hosea Beckley's *The History of Vermont with Descriptions, Physical and Topographical* (1846); Daniel Chipman's *Memoir of Colonel Seth Warner* (1848); and, Henry W. DePuy's *Ethan Allen and the Green Mountain Heroes of 1776* (1853).
902 *Special Session 1857*, 192–193.

Index

A

Abortion, *161, 177, 231, 260, 274, 285, 300, 322, 339*
Adams, John Sullivan, *169*
Adams, Preston, *285*
Addison County Medical Society, *326*
Aesthetics, *61, 67*
Agricultural societies, *55, 56, 87, 98, 129, 157, 164, 307, 323*
Agricultural Society of Rutland, *56, 87, 98*
Ainsworth, Lucy (Sleeping Lucy), *245*
Albers, Jan, *144*
Allen, Charles L., *213*
Allen, Ira, *59*
Allen, Jonathan A., *237, 357*
American Medical Association, *211, 337*
Anthropological Society of Paris, *220*
Ardent Spirits, *182, 192, 198*
Ashe, Olive, *287, 292, 300*

B

Barrett, James Jr., *97, 114, 131, 300*
Bass, Moses, *32*
Boston Medical College, *267*
Bowman, Alexander H., *133*
Bowman, Nathan B., *193*
Bradley, J. Dorr, *175, 201*
Branch, Julia, *252*
Brandon Railroad Association, *78*
Brown, Ambrose Lincoln, *37, 91, 94, 105, 110, 128, 140, 195*
Butler, Lucius Castle, *249, 328, 330*

C

Cain, John, *112, 116, 132, 137*
Camp, David M., *52*
Canals, *42, 45, 51, 61, 64, 70, 97*
Carroll, George, *262, 265*
Carter, William H., *298*
Catholic Church, *116, 332, 342, 352*
Champlain and Connecticut River Rail Road Company, *82, 88*
Chappell, Thomas, *91, 127, 132*

Chittenden County Medical Society, *241*
Cholera, *13, 108, 149, 207, 217, 362*
Clark, Calvin W., *282, 295*
Clark, Charles *320*
Clark, Kenneth *23*
Clarke, Albert, *81, 342, 352*
Clarke, James *236, 320*
Cleveland, Norman, *241*
Collamer, Jacob, *147*
Condemnations, *44, 92, 104, 113, 114, 122, 201, 243, 352*
Connecticut and Passumpsic Rivers Railroad Company, *197*
Connecticut River, *45, 48, 76, 82, 264, 280, 341*
Connecticut River Medical Society, *333*
Consumption, *22, 108, 137, 170, 180, 207, 212, 225, 239, 258, 284, 286, 320, 338, 349*
Coolidge, Carlos, *80, 117, 217*
Corbin, David S., *283*
Corbin, Eunice, *284*
Corporations, *37, 44, 81, 87, 93, 133, 145, 153, 197, 208, 343, 352*
Council of Censors, *96, 112, 142, 172, 174, 222*
Crosby, Dixie, *283, 301*
Cummings, Kate, *259*

D

Dartmouth College, *48, 56, 283, 301*
Dartmouth Medical College, *181, 188, 224, 229, 231, 239, 263, 273, 275, 283, 298, 301*
Davidson, Abigail H., *322*
Davidson, Oliver H., *323*

Dean, Benjamin W., *223*
Dellapenna, Joseph W., *234*
Derby Line Mutual Improvement Society, *55*
Dewey, A. S., *194*
Dewey, Charles C., *290, 295, 301, 306, 308*
Dickey, Asa M., *282*
Drown, Leafy, *326*
Dutcher, Frederick, *334*

E

Eaton, Horace, *80, 247*
Ellis Bliss v. Connecticut & Passumpsic Rivers Railroad Company, *198*
Ergot, *240, 247, 327, 340*
Exposition Universelle des Beaux-Arts, *25*

F

Fairbanks, Erastus, *51, 53, 156, 196*
Farmers and Mechanics Mutual Improvement Society, *55*
Fitch, Samuel Sheldon, *187*
Fitchburg Railroad Company, *25, 83*
Fletcher, Ryland, *17, 141, 150, 151, 156, 174, 204*
Follett, Timothy, *80, 82, 88, 94, 119*
Foot, Solomon, *134, 139*
Franklin Hotel, *75, 95, 118, 136*
Free Convention of the Friends of Human Progress, *251*
Free Passes, *342*
Frost, Carleton Pennington, *223, 231, 290, 301, 334*
Furber, Sarah, *262, 265, 275, 287, 309, 322*

INDEX

G

Gallup, Joseph A., *237, 246, 264, 357*
Galusha, Jonas, *157*
George, Asa, 305, 322
Gilbert, William Bradford, *84, 88, 106, 111*
Governance, *205*
Grab laws, *27, 169, 353*
Grass farms, *162*
Great Exhibition of the Works of Industry of All Nations, *25*
Great Lake, *74, 102*

H

Haddock, Charles B., *48, 82*
Hall, Hiland, *51, 147, 174, 318*
Hand, John B., *323*
Harrington, Caleb B., *112*
Harris, Christopher, *160*
Hawthorne, Nathaniel, *108*
Hebard, William, *301, 306*
Hessletine, Clifford, *260*
Holmes, Oliver Wendell, *267*
Holmes, Achsah, *339*
Home for Destitute Children, *254*
Howard, William Henry Mansfield, *13, 23, 274*

I

Infanticide, *13, 22, 36, 161, 177, 219, 231, 255, 271, 330, 344, 351*
Irish, *29, 90, 107, 122, 136, 143, 152, 196, 204, 217, 251, 257, 291, 329, 340, 342, 352, 354*
Irish Brogue, *64, 278*

J

Jackson, Andrew, *42, 112, 184, 202, 228, 338, 350*
Jenison, Silas, *52*
John S. Thorpe v. The Rutland Railroad, *146*

K

Kellogg, Daniel, *147*
King, William S., *166*
Koch, Robert, *181*

L

Ladies delivery windows, *139*
Laennec, Rene, *181*
Landscapes, *61, 70, 80, 87, 90, 94, 103, 122, 144, 153, 158, 180, 195, 352*
Liddicoat, William, *280, 302*
Linsley, Charles, *85, 151*
Lohman, Ann (Madam Restell), *244*
Lyman, John, *240, 246*

M

Marsh, George Perkins, *56, 72, 86, 105, 151, 166*
Maternal associations, *243, 246, 263*
McCollom, William, *230, 329*
McDuffie, Charles M., *297*
McGinning, Susan, *259*
McNab, John, *261, 275, 279, 308, 322*
Medical Licensing, *261, 275, 336*
Mental Liberty Society, *264, 269*
Mohr, James, *233*

Moral obligation, *62, 202, 211, 227, 313*
Mount Holly, *83, 96, 113, 118*
Mudgett, Herman Webster, *23*

N

Nebraska, *115, 122, 125, 130, 131, 136, 143, 153, 354*
New Hampshire Botanic Medical Society, *261*
New Hampshire Medical Society, *278*

O

Ormsby, Robert McKinley, *281, 301, 306*

P

Paine, Charles, *80, 82*
Perkins, Henry Olin, *113*
Perry, Allen, *246*
Petitions, *46, 70, 134, 183, 198, 242, 243, 246, 259, 340*
Phelps, Edward E., *302*
Pierpoint, Evelyn, *112, 115*
Pierpoint, Robert, *73, 96, 112, 115*
Population growth, *31, 38, 70, 74, 250*
Powers, Nicholas, *122, 152*
Powers, Thomas E, *66, 200*
Prevost, Dr., *322, 324*
Prohibition, *18, 22, 35, 145, 164, 176, 185, 192, 197, 227, 240, 260, 266, 294, 312, 333, 336, 343*

Q

Quarries, *11, 69, 77, 108, 139, 344*

R

Randall, Gurdon P., *121, 126, 133, 152*
Redfield, Isaac F., *146, 275, 307*
Registration, *38, 208, 257, 278, 285, 297, 329, 351*
Robbins, Orrick L., *113, 115*
Rose, Hannah, *241*
Roth, Randolph A., *31, 39, 255*
Ruggles, Gershom Cheney, *97, 115, 122, 135*
Rutland and Burlington Rail Road, *83, 96, 110, 124, 128, 131, 133, 140*
Rutland and Washington Rail Road, *89*
Rutland Land Company, *97, 112, 353*
Rutland Railroad, *37, 74, 85, 89, 94, 97, 104, 118, 144, 146, 149, 151*
Rutland Yard, *105, 117, 124, 129, 136, 144*

S

Sectionalism, *13, 16, 24, 32, 47, 50, 65, 68, 315, 316, 347*
Seward, William H., *129, 167*
Slade, William Jr., *51*
Stewart, John W., *174*
Strong & Chamberlain, *110*
Strong, Harriet, *97, 99, 112, 114, 131, 139, 353*
Strout, Albion K., *229, 231, 273*
Suffolk District Medical Society, *277*

INDEX

Supreme Court of Kansas, *274*

Surveying, *37, 52, 60, 67, 79, 83, 87, 105, 135, 197*

T

Taunton Locomotive Manufacturing Company, *104, 123*

Telegraph, *19, 64, 76, 118, 140, 227, 289, 295, 308, 313*

Thayer, Samuel W., *191, 207*

The Manchester Tragedy, *262*

Thompson, Daniel P., *141*

Thoreau, Henry David, *19, 24, 35, 347*

Thrall, Jonathan C., *97, 115*

Todd, John, *332*

U

Underwood, Joseph, *155, 175, 203*

Underwood, Levi, *193, 201*

V

Vermont Central Railway, *82, 93*

Vermont Homeopathic Medical Society, *206*

Vermont Internal Improvement Society, *51*

Vermont Medical Society, 28, 38, 215, 337, 357

Vermont Pharmaceutical Association, *334*

Vermont Society of the Improvement of Common Schools, *54*

Vermont State Fair, *163, 196*

Vermont Temperance Society, *109, 198*

W

Washburn, Peter T., *301, 30*

Waterman, Jane, *281, 293, 299, 309*

Waterman, Mary Ann, *299*

Waterman, Willard, *299*

Waterman, William, *281, 293, 298*

Webster, Harvey, *348*

Wells, Richardson & Co., *335*

Wells River, *67, 341*

Western Vermont, *84, 89, 117, 315*

Western Vermont Railroad, *88*

Willard, Charles W., *21,*

Willard, Emma, *55*

William Gold, Jr. v. Vermont Central Rail Road Company (1847), *93*

Williams, Charles K., *96, 210*

Williams, Samuel, *77, 96*

Wilson, Agnes, *293, 300*

Woman's Temperance Union, *199*

Woodward, John A., *66, 200*

Woodward, Theodore, *237, 364*

Y

Young, Ammi Burnham, *119, 133, 138, 152*

About the Author

Gary G. Shattuck is a New Hampshire native who served in the Vermont law enforcement community for over three decades. He received his B. A. degree from the University of Colorado, a Juris Doctor degree from the Vermont Law School, a Master's degree in Military History concentrating on the Revolutionary War and attended post-graduate courses in Archaeology and Heritage at the University of Leicester (UK). He served for many years as a patrol commander with the Vermont State Police and assistant Attorney General for the State of Vermont prosecuting Vermont Drug Task Force cases. Gary went on to become an assistant United States attorney with the U.S. Department of Justice where, in addition to prosecuting criminal offenses and acting as the District of Vermont's anti-terrorism coordinator and arguing cases before the U.S. Court of Appeals in the Second Circuit, he also worked as a legal advisor in Kosovo and Iraq. Since leaving government service, he has written six books and many articles on early Vermont history. Gary is also on the Board of Trustees of the Vermont Historical Society and the Vermont Historical Records Advisory Board (Vermont State Archives and Records Administration), is a member of the University of Vermont's Center for Research on Vermont and serves on the Fort Ticonderoga National Council.

www.ingramcontent.com/pod-product-compliance
Lightning Source LLC
Chambersburg PA
CBHW032122160426
43197CB00008B/485